IRELAND 1977

Area Editor:	EDWARD F. MACSWEENEY
Editorial Contributors:	KEVIN DANAHER, GARRY REDMOND, TERENCE DE VERE WHITE
Photographs:	PETER BAKER, C.I.E., IRISH TOURIST BOARD
Production:	EILEEN ROLPH

IRELAND 1977
EXCLUDING NORTHERN IRELAND

EUGENE FODOR
ROBERT C. FISHER
Editors

RICHARD MOORE
European Editor

DAVID McKAY COMPANY INC.—NEW YORK

© 1977 FODOR'S MODERN GUIDES INC.

ISBN 0 679 00211 1   *David McKay, New York*
      0 340 21414 7   *Hodder & Stoughton, London*

No part of this book may be reproduced in any form without permission in writing from the publisher

The following travel books edited by Eugene Fodor are current in 1977:

AREA GUIDES:
- CARIBBEAN, BAHAMAS AND BERMUDA
- EUROPE
- INDIA
- JAPAN AND KOREA
- MEXICO
- SCANDINAVIA
- SOUTH AMERICA
- SOUTH-EAST ASIA
- SOVIET UNION
- USA

COUNTRY GUIDES:
- AUSTRIA
- BELGIUM AND LUXEMBOURG
- CZECHOSLOVAKIA
- FRANCE
- GERMANY
- GREAT BRITAIN
- GREECE
- HOLLAND
- HUNGARY*
- IRELAND
- ISRAEL
- ITALY
- MOROCCO
- PORTUGAL
- SPAIN
- SWITZERLAND
- TUNISIA*
- TURKEY
- YUGOSLAVIA

U.S.A. REGIONAL GUIDES:
- NEW ENGLAND*
- NEW YORK AND NEW JERSEY*
- MID-ATLANTIC*
- THE SOUTH*
- INDIAN AMERICA
- THE MID-WEST*
- THE SOUTH-WEST*
- ROCKIES AND PLAINS*
- THE FAR WEST*
- HAWAII
- THE OLD WEST

CITY GUIDES:
LONDON – PARIS – PEKING – VENICE* – VIENNA

LANGUAGE GUIDE:
EUROPE TALKING*

FORTHCOMING GUIDES:
- CRUISES EVERYWHERE
- RAILWAYS OF THE WORLD
- CANADA
- IRAN

* *Not available in Hodder & Stoughton edition*

FOREWORD

This 1977 edition is a new-look *Fodor's Guide*. With travel getting more complicated every day, we decided it was time to start simplifying things a little. The result is this up-to-the minute, easy-to-use Guide which contains all the factual and background coverage that have made our books best-sellers over forty years, but in a different format.

♣ We open with a series of chapters—**The Irish Scene**—which outlines the quality of life in the Emerald Isle today. We hope that they will give you some idea of the kind of country you will find on your arrival.

♣ We then cover the whole of the Republic of Ireland, geographically and historically, in **The Face of Ireland,** nine chapters designed to act as your *vade mecum* while touring the country.

♣ Next comes the down-to-earth information of **Facts at Your Fingertips,** rigorously brought up to the minute and carefully tailored to help you while planning your trip and to smooth your path while on it.

♣ This is followed by a section, new to our Guides—**Ireland, Town by Town**—in which we give you a clear alphabetical listing of all the cities, towns and villages where we recommend hotels or restaurants, together with many other useful facts. Some places, Cork and Dublin for example, have much longer entries devoted to them, but all in the same listing.

♣ Lastly comes a **Vocabulary of English-Irish,** which we hope will help you to understand a little of the lilting music that is Gaelic.

We cannot pretend that Ireland is free from problems these days. Indeed, we have very reluctantly decided to omit Northern Ireland from this Guide for the time being. We simply feel that we cannot

FOREWORD

recommend anyone to go there. The Irish Republic, however, though not free from the dilemmas that affict its neighbor to the north has still a great deal to offer the visitor. Opportunities for exciting and memorable holidays are legion.

Over the last few years, many millions of pounds have been poured into developing tourist projects, with the result that the range of accommodations and the general quality of facilities have improved enormously. In every way Southern Ireland is an easier, nicer place to travel around in than it used to be. There are better hotels, the countryside has been opened up by road systems and scenic drives, beaches have been cared for and monuments restored. In sum, a great deal of thought, imagination and hard cash has been lavished on showing to the best advantage the beauties that were always there, though not always accessible.

The amenities which are now available for sports or for quiet relaxation ensure that Ireland has something to offer everyone, whatever his tastes. Golf and fishing head the list, of course, with all those lovely lakes and streams, how could it be otherwise? But close behind come the beaches, with surfing or scuba-diving readily available. Then there is the chance of wandering down those gently winding lanes in a horse-drawn caravan, or cruising along the peaceful rivers (the Shannon alone has 140 navigable miles of enjoyment). High on the list of popular attractions are the stately homes and gardens which form so rich a part of Ireland's heritage.

It is also an attractive fact (or at least it is as we go to press in mid-1976) that the dollar exchange rate gives visitors to Ireland almost a 20% increase in value in relation to the pound. This makes shopping for such essentially Irish items as Aran sweaters, linen and glass a more alluring prospect than ever.

In short, from busy Dublin, with its lovely Georgian architecture to the peaceful hills of Kerry, Ireland awaits. We hope that this new *Fodor's Guide* will prove a useful and informative companion for your trip.

Among the many people, Irish and non-Irish, who have helped us to produce this book, we owe a special debt to the following: the members of Bord Fáilte Éireann, the Irish Tourist Board, in particular its former Director General, Dr. T. J. O'Driscoll and his successors

FOREWORD

Mr. Aidan O'Hanlon, Publicity Manager; Mr. Stanley O. Wilson, Advertising & Publishing Controller, Mr. John O'Brien of the Dublin office and Miss May Boyd of the Photographic Section.

We would also like to thank Mr. T. J. Sheehy, Director of the London office of the Irish Tourist Board and his staff for their unfailing courtesy and interest.

Errors are bound to creep into any guide. When a hotel closes or a restaurant's chef produces an inferior meal, you may question our recommendation. Let us know, and we will investigate the establishment and the complaint. Your letters will help us to pinpoint trouble spots.

Our addresses are:

in the U.S.A., Fodor's Modern Guides, 750 Third Ave., New York, N.Y. 10017;

in Europe, Fodor's Modern Guides, 27b Old Gloucester St., London WCIN 3AF.

As faithful readers of the Fodor series know, merely listing an establishment in one of our books is sufficient recommendation, but in Ireland some towns have no licensed hotel, while in others licensed accommodation is deplorably inadequate, so that we have been obliged to include some very basic hotels whose principal merit is availability and cheapness. We have made a special effort to list only those which maintain a minimum standard of cleanliness.

We accept advertising in some books, but this does not affect the editor's recommendations. We include advertising because the revenue helps defray the high cost of our annual republishing, and the advertisements themselves provide information for our readers.

WORDS TO THE WISE
A Few Useful Travel Hints

Whether you are on holiday or have important business to do, after a flight through several time zones give your body's clock a chance to catch up. It is easy to underestimate the effects of jet-lag.

Don't carry all your cash, travellers' checks, passport etc. in the same place, spread them around a bit – and never carry your wallet in your hip pocket.

Experienced travellers travel light. Don't forget that the hand luggage you carry with you onto the plane is a vital part of your travel equipment. Make sure you have your essentials in it, not in your other baggage.

With strikes and the cost of excess baggage always in the background, you would be sensible when flying not to take more than you could comfortably carry yourself – in a pinch.

Don't leave already exposed film in your pockets or in any hand luggage while passing through airport X-ray machines. The process can sometimes fog the film and you may find a whole trip's photographs ruined. Put the film on one side while passing through.

Never make long-distance phone calls from your hotel room without checking first on the likely price. Some hotels have been known to mark up the cost of a call as much as 200%.

Several airlines will provide a cardboard carrying box for any loose items you might arrive clutching at the checking-in desk. It saves leaving a trail of last-minute purchases all the way to the plane.

You would be amazed the amount of free information that you can get from National Tourist Offices to help you plan your trip – all the way from brochures to movies.

Put a tag with your name and address on it *inside* your suitcase as well as outside. It will greatly help identification if the case goes astray.

Never leave valuables in your hotel room – put them in the hotel safe.

CONTENTS

	Page
FOREWORD	5

THE IRISH SCENE

THIS IS IRELAND	*Edward F. MacSweeney*	17
IRISH HISTORY—A Fabric of Disharmony *Kevin Danaher*		35
A WAY WITH WORDS—Music—and Blarney in Irish Literature *Terence de Vere White*		49
EATING AND DRINKING—Which is Mostly the Latter, and Why Not?		60
THE SPORTSMAN'S PARADISE—A Formula of Horses, Fish, Fowl and Water *Garry Redmond*		65
SHOPPING IN IRELAND—Where "Home-Made" Means "Best"		81

THE FACE OF IRELAND

DUBLIN—A Capital with Character	91

CONTENTS

THE ENVIRONS OF DUBLIN—Trips Not Beyond the Pale ... 112

THE SUNNY SOUTHEAST—Wexford, Waterford, Kilkenny and Carlow ... 127

TIPPERARY—The Heart of Ireland's Dairyland ... 141

THE CHARM OF THE SOUTH—Cork and Kinsale, Bantry and Blarney ... 154

THE SOUTHWEST—Ring of Kerry, Rose of Tralee ... 171

SHANNON—Ireland's Atlantic Gateway ... 186

THE WONDERFUL WEST—Where the Next Parish is America ... 197

SLIGO AND THE NORTHWEST—Yeats Country and the Donegal Highlands ... 212

FACTS AT YOUR FINGERTIPS

Planning Your Trip, How to Reach Ireland, Arriving in Ireland, Staying in Ireland, Traveling in Ireland, Leaving Ireland ... 223

IRELAND—TOWN BY TOWN

A Guide to Hotels and Restaurants ... 265

VOCABULARY ... 299

INDEX ... 307

CONTENTS
MAPS

FISHING IN IRELAND	70–71
DUBLIN	96–97
CORK	157
KILLARNEY	173
LIMERICK-SHANNON AREA	188
LIMERICK	191
GALWAY	201
IRELAND—COUNTRY MAP	318–319

INCLUDE MORE AND GO...

Maupintour!

MORE FOR YOUR MONEY! If you want to see all you should see and have everything included, then select a conducted Maupintour. Packed with sightseeing, most meals, entertainments, fun events, tips, expertly managed, limited size, the right hotels.

COMPARE! Ask for Maupintour's regional escorted tours such as Scandinavia, the Alps, Britain, Bavaria/Austria, Italy, Sicily, Rhine River cruise, France, USSR/Eastern Europe, the Balkans, Dalmatia, Greece, Spain, Portugal, Morocco, North Africa, Egypt, Turkey, Iran, Middle East, South Pacific, Orient, Latin America, India, and Hawaii.

ASK YOUR TRAVEL AGENT for *Maupintour's* folders or write:

quality touring since 1951

Maupintour, 900 Massachusetts Street, Lawrence, Kansas 66044

THE
IRISH
SCENE

THIS IS IRELAND

by

EDWARD F. MACSWEENEY

(Edward MacSweeney is a well-known Irish journalist and broadcaster whose interests take him to all parts of Ireland and among all sections of the community. Known to Irish radio audiences as "Maxwell Sweeney", he has earned a high reputation for his commentaries and production of public service, current affairs and arts programs.)

The Irish folk memory is long; and it is longer still among the descendants of emigrants. Second and third generation Irish—in America rather more than in Canada or Britain—view the homeland through the glazed eyes of their elders, through the mists of time to see a country far removed from the reality of today.

The Ireland of today is forward-looking, more so than at any time in its history, but its pace is more measured than most—hence its people still have time to talk and to enjoy life. It is less inward-looking than the Ireland of the past and more concerned with its role in the world of tomorrow. The Irish—like so many other peoples—are a mixture of races. They will talk of the

THE IRISH SCENE

ancient Milesians, the Celts, the Danes and the Normans, the English and the Scots . . . an agglomeration of peoples which created the Irish, a distinctive race but invariably warm-hearted. There are lilting voices in the South, harsher accents—almost akin to those of the Scots—in the North. Villages in the North are more formal in appearance than those in the South, perhaps a reflection of the Scottish Presbyterian tradition which came with the Planters centuries ago.

In the Hungry Forties—the 1840s of the last century, the years of the Great Famine—Ireland had a population of more than 8 million. Today the population, North and South, totals around 5 million, of whom just over 3 million live in the South—the Irish Republic.

Many Irish-Americans harbor an over-sentimental attitude towards the land of their forebears, an attitude deplored by many of the Irish at home although they appreciate the interest and value of the ethnic tie. Ireland today prefers to see itself not so much as the homeland of an emigrant race—with the emigrants preferring to regard themselves, more romantically, as exiles—as a participating partner in the UN and the European Economic Community. Its people can point, with some pride, to the service of Irish army personnel with the UN peace-keeping forces overseas, a service which has cost lives; to the distinction of its one-time representative, Frederick H. Boland, as President of the UN —he gavelled an obdurate Russian into conformity with the "rules of the house"—and, more recently, to the successful presidency of the EEC by its lively Foreign Minister, Dr. Garrett FitzGerald, who entered politics through the roundabout route of a University don with a particularly realistic approach to economics and international problems.

There is pride in the contribution of Ireland to American history, from the soldiers who fought in its wars to Presidents who have been of Irish blood—from Chester Alan Arthur and Andrew Jackson to John F. Kennedy who touched a particularly sentimental streak in the Irish and caused them to name streets, squares and parks for him; an enthusiasm which has since waned.

Strangely there is less pride in the impact of the Irish emigrants to Britain on political life in that country, although the "Irish vote" is still of particular value in a number of Parliamentary constituencies.

Political Development

There is no deep philosophical difference between the major

THIS IS IRELAND

political parties in the Republic, Fine Gael, Fianna Fáil and Labour. The first named are the successors of the men who accepted the Treaty signed with the British by Michael Collins and his colleagues in 1921; Fianna Fáil is the party that was led by Éamon de Valera, only surviving field officer of the Easter Rising of 1916. He was saved from execution at that time by his American citizenship, having been born in New York of a Spanish-American father and an Irish mother. After the Treaty de Valera led a breakaway party, first in civil war and then in parliament, dominating the Dáil (Lower House/Congress) for many years, achieving international status as a statesman during a stint as president of the ill-fated League of Nations, emphasizing neutrality during World War II (the only really practical course, according to many Irishmen) and ultimately retired respectability as President—something of a non-political figurehead role—of the Irish Republic. Strangely, for the republicanism of de Valera's party, it was the Fine Gael party (then led by John Costello) that declared the latter-day Irish Republic in 1948.

De Valera's elevation to "The Park" (the Presidential Mansion is the establishment in Phoenix Park which used to house the English Lord Lieutenant in the days of British rule) brought a new man to the forefront of his party, Sean Lemass. He may have shared the idealism of "Dev"—a term of endearment used by friend and foe—but he was more of a pragmatist. He started Ireland on its industrial development campaign and initiated the first talks with Northern Ireland leaders which, if allowed to continue, might well have brought a rapprochement and cooperation of benefit to both North and South. Before the meetings between Lemass and his Northern counterpart, Terence O'Neill, there was a tendency to ignore the North. Lip service was paid to the ideal of a united Ireland but there was undoubtedly an undercurrent of fear among the South's embryo industrialists that an end to the protective barrier of the Border between Northern Ireland and the Republic would mean a submerging of their projects by the more astute and more energetic fellow countrymen from the north-east corner of the island.

Mismanagement by influences outside the relationships established by O'Neill and Lemass, some of them with vested interests in the division of the island, brought the conflict of 1969 and afterwards in the six counties of Northern Ireland—still popularly referred to as Ulster although this is a misnomer since the six counties are only two-thirds of the historic province of Ulster —the others are in the Republic. That the conflict will eventually be resolved is undoubted, but the cost in lives and property in the North has been great without result: it has appeared, at times, as a fight against injustice—it was a root cause—but also as a sectarian war.

Catholics and Protestants lived long in amity in Northern Ireland, with vested interests controlling the Protestant working-class majority as an instrument of policy. The situation reached flashpoint at times—roughly at intervals of a decade—until the late 1960s when the visual media gave an added impact to any demonstration whether parade or bombing. The escalation of violence, which the Republic (and therefore the greater part of Ireland) has escaped, has been fostered by lawless elements—independently of "Republican" or "Loyalist" interests—and aggravated by a disproportionately high level of unemployment; the emphatic segregation of "Prods" (Protestants) and "Taigues" (Catholics) at schoolgoing age, and the growing out of childhood (in the last six years) of too many boys and girls who have never known a truly lawful community. There is a story told in the North of a boy rushing home from school and into the house, past his mother then engaged in talk with a neighbor woman. His schoolbag flung down, he made to dash out to the street again. "Where are you going?" demanded his mother. "To throw stones at the soldiers," answered the son. "Then go back and change your boots first," was the stern reproof.

In the Republic the Labour Party, wedded to traditional national-ownership policies, remains the smallest party despite the growth of the urban population. It has twice served in Coalition governments with the Fine Gael party, and achieved some effect in both social services and industrial legislation.

Education and Integration

Sectarianism is not a problem in the South—the Irish Republic—but fears have been expressed that the Catholic Hierarchy (and the older members of their flock) could, by their entrenched attitudes to multi-denominational schools, harden sectarian lines in the North. There is a belief, among a substantial section of the community—north and south—that integrated education in Northern Ireland would be a basic and major contribution towards future community relations: in the Republic many people seek denominational integration in primary schools but their campaign meets frequent opposition.

No such division affects third-level education. Technical colleges and universities embrace students of all faiths. Attitudes are changing: a decade ago parents were publicly warned by the

Catholic Hierarchy against allowing their children to attend Trinity College, Dublin, now nearing the 500th anniversary of its foundation. Today 60 per cent of the university's undergraduate population of 5,000 are Catholics; the faculties of University College, Dublin—successor of the Catholic University of Ireland founded by Cardinal John Henry Newman (1801-1890)—now absorb adherents of all faiths among its 10,000 students. Clearly religious denominations no longer have any relevance in third-level education, and it is a sign of progressive times that a lecturer in Modern History at UCD—recognized as an outstanding historian—is a Dominican nun, while the Professor of English Literature at the one-time English-oriented Protestant Dublin University is a poet from County Kerry, the most Irish of Ireland's counties.

Education is greatly prized among the Irish; it has been the break-out from the back-breaking life of the rural community, and it has never been assessed how many mothers' ambitions for a "priest in the family" or a daughter "in religion" was the reflection of piety or anxiety for her young "to better themselves". Financial aid was frequently available, and still is, for the young man with a vocation for the priesthood, but the "calls" are fewer, though still insistent when they come.

Materialistic attitudes undoubtedly influence many career choices today and are increasing pressures on university places. Trinity College, Dublin, claims it cannot expand beyond a maximum of 6,000 and University College, Dublin, does not wish to extend beyond its current 10,000; similar physical restraints are noted by University College, Cork, and University College, Galway (like UCD and St. Patrick's, Maynooth, constituent colleges of the National University of Ireland). There is—as yet—no such constraint on the recently established National Institute of Higher Education at Limerick which, in time, will become another university: incidentally, students at the National Institute of Higher Education are the most expensive for the State on a per capita basis—£1,634 per student annually, against £788 in universities and £820 in regional technical colleges.

Constantly raised standards are having an impact on the student body: in 1975 25 per cent of students at UCD taking "First Arts"—a preliminary stage of a degree essential for second-level teaching—failed their first year examinations; 28 per cent of law students failed at a similar stage. Entry requirements are likely to be raised, and the Incorporated Law Society of Ireland—the body controlling solicitors (a branch of the attorney's profession instructing trial lawyers and conducting other legal business)—now requires that all potential entrants to the profession must hold an Arts degree before starting their studies.

Wealth from the Land

While the far-off hills seemed greener to the emigrants of the past, the hills of home seem somber to the descendants of the people who left them. Their secondhand folk memories compress history and the oppressive laws and landlords into a package which has no relevance to the Irish Republic of today. The country has taken longer to accept modern ways than most of the western countries; it is still a developing country, and the slow pace with which it has been moving enables it to escape most—but not all—of the ills of the industrial revolution.

Raw materials seemed few, mostly the natural products of the farms, and only today are natural mineral resources being exploited effectively. The resources were always there—copper and some gold in Wicklow, copper in County Cork, the lead mines of County Dublin—but these workings and others were exploited by manual labor and became uneconomic when the customers (mostly in Britain) found cheaper sources. So the workings died and the workers moved away. In recent years vast zinc resources have been located in County Meath—Royal Meath, cattle and hunting country—and in Tipperary where the limestone in the land puts bone into the great Irish racehorses; barytes in County Sligo; natural gas has been located off the coast of County Cork, with indications that oil is also present in the off-shore areas around the coast, a fact which has attracted international consortia to seek concessions.

The Irish welcome these developments and the new industries which have been established by foreign interests—among them British, American, Japanese, Dutch and German companies. The newcomers have been encouraged by the State with grants and tax concessions. International ties were first formed through the imaginative development of the Shannon Free Airport Industrial Estate, a Customs-free zone on the perimeter of Shannon Airport which has now developed a new town, Shannon, to house the families of workers who have moved into the area. The industrial development, fostered by Government aid, has moved out into other areas where labor has become increasingly available with the drift from the land following mechanization of agriculture. But not all developments have been welcomed: strong environmentalist lobbies have blocked several projects and even in industrialized Dublin 400 objections were lodged by conservationists and others when a project for an oil refinery in Dublin Bay was proposed.

The Irish are conscious that mineral resources—no matter how substantial—must become exhausted in time, and planning for the future is cautiously taking cognisance of this drain. Agriculture remains the country's biggest industry (valued at over £642 million in 1975), while tourism ranks second (£162 million in 1975). Both these are basic assets: agriculture a natural and renewable asset, while the tourist appeal of the land which is still unspoiled by development is another asset to be carefully conserved.

The conservationists do not always act negatively. They have been responsible for the reconstruction of a number of historic buildings and sometimes their conservationism has a very practical character. The Industrial Training Authority organized its first month-long course for thatchers not far from Shannon Airport last year. The value of thatched cottages as a tourist attraction both for viewing and as summer homes has not passed unnoticed.

Church and Family

The Catholic Church, to which over 90% of the population belong, continues to exercise a role in Irish life, but its authoritarian character is declining and there is an increasing willingness on the part of clerics to enter into discussion with critics of what has been accepted as Church teaching. This has brought about a situation, undreamed of a decade ago, in which a Cabinet Minister—a professed humanist—was publicly in conflict with a Catholic Bishop. The Minister, Dr. Conor Cruise-O'Brien (a former UN official and—at the time—Minister for Posts and Telegraphs and therefore responsible for broadcasting) had said that defeat of a Bill in the Oireachtas (Parliament) to permit the sale of contraceptives was a set-back to non-sectarian thought, a view vociferously refuted by the distinguished academic Bishop Jeremiah Newman (former President of the main center of training for the priesthood—Maynooth College). The debate resolved nothing but indicated the wider freedom for the discussion of religious issues and stimulated an acrimonious correspondence in the columns of the *Irish Times,* a familiar forum for progressive viewpoints.

Twenty-five years earlier a medical doctor (like Dr. Cruise-O'Brien, a Labour Party member and Cabinet Minister) clashed with a Bishop of Galway on a matter of government policy concerning a mother and child scheme: the atmosphere of the time supported the bishop and defeated the scheme and the politician.

Divorce is not permitted under Irish Law, ostensibly respecting the sanctity of marriage emphasized by the Catholic Church. Yet the granting of decrees of annulment by the Church has been eased and an increasing number of Catholics have been loosed from their matrimonial bonds by their Church; but they are not, under the law of the country, permitted to remarry. A situation which is puzzling; whether—as might be expected—some of the parties separated by the Church have sought the comforts of matrimony anew is officially unknown, certainly there have been no publicized charges of bigamy since the Church's attitude became more attuned to the problems of married life.

Family planning clinics have been established in some cities, and while they may not be welcomed by the Catholic Church there is evidence that they are being used by women of that faith. In a country where the birth rate is around 22 per 1,000, and where women are beginning to assert themselves effectively this is not surprising.

Fading of the Middle Ages

There has been a considerable liberalization of expression of opinion and an easing of censorship which, through different channels, covers books and periodicals, and films but not the stage. Once a four-letter expletive was sufficient to get a book banned and sex was almost a dirty word. Today pornography is still frowned upon but the attitude to modern situations is far more realistic. A decade ago sexual morality was discussed as if it was the sole morality; violence, theft, dishonesty and drunkenness were virtually minor events in the morality calendar.

A leading Irish publisher, Sean Feehan, of the Mercier Press, has been quoted as saying: "There are only two sins in Ireland—sex and success. The first is the pleasanter, but the second is more vicious; the failure is everybody's friend." Maybe it is just jealousy, but denigration in conversation—particularly bar talk—seems as popular as it was back in the time of the English eighteenth-century litterateur, Dr. Samuel Johnson, who remarked: "The Irish are a very fair people, they never speak well of one another." But maybe it is all part of the great Irish talkfest because it was an Irishman, Oscar Wilde, who claimed: "We are the greatest talkers since the Greeks."

Nobody in the public eye is ever permitted to get a swelled head. The country is too small for that—the "big man" is just a neighbor's child, and if he is wise, he will not forget his origins or his neighbors. This close contact is very much part of the Irish way. While it is untrue to say that everybody knows everybody else, there is almost a small town atmosphere of intimacy. When a man in the city asks another where he's from, he is inquiring about the man's home area in the country, and the inquiry is not out of curiosity but neighborliness.

In remoter country areas of the south and west, where neighbors may live a considerable distance apart, the time for the men to meet and talk is after church on Sundays, and there is a provision in the licensing laws which enables bars to be opened shortly after the end of Mass in these centers. This is the time for political meetings. Latter-day political leaders say that one radio or television appearance means more votes to them than five or six of the "after-Mass" meetings, but no politician at local level would dare to forgo the personal contact which such get-togethers can offer.

The gregariousness of the Irish is reflected in bar-life, at one time almost solely restricted to men. The bars were frequently gloomy places, male in décor and outlook; and even if the woman of the house or her daughter did serve behind the bar women were seldom among the customers. All that has changed and there is a relaxed mixing of the sexes, particularly in the towns, despite the views of the more traditional males.

Television has done a great deal to spoil the art of conversation in bars, but where there is no dominating flickering box in the corner the talk—"the crack" if you are in the North—will be of the crops and their prices (invariably poor, in the view of all concerned), the prospects of a greyhound or a horse, and a play-by-play review of the most recent football or hurling game. In the city bars the talk will be little different—horses and dogs are always important, and so are the iniquities of whatever government may be in power—plus some comment on golf or fishing. In the more literary bars in Dublin the talk may be more barbed, a bit more self-conscious. It's been said that there's an actor in every Irishman; this is when it comes out!

On the subject of talking: officially the Irish Republic is bilingual—Irish (Gaelic) and English are the two languages; in Northern Ireland, the official language is English. Irish is preserved as a cultural heritage, although there are people who would like its status raised to that of the sole official language. This is unlikely. The English-speaking visitor will have no problems. He will hear Irish spoken in the west and south and see destinations on buses in Irish, but the general conversation is in

English. Some homes preserve the language closely by speaking Irish within the family group, and there is argument by the protagonists for the language that unless it is maintained—almost compulsorily (it is the second language in primary education)—the heritage of Irish nationalism and culture may be lost.

There is a tendency to self-dramatization among the Irish which sometimes manifests itself in "stagey" talk about nationalism and culture, possibly to impress the guest with the "difference" between the Irish and other English-speaking peoples. To have preconceived ideas about the Irish, and to show them, is to tempt the Irish to be their most "Irish"; and any suggestion of condescension will be resented and immediately raise a barrier. To a condescending visitor who expressed some words of surprise about a development I heard this reply given: "And were you surprised to find we wear shoes, too?"

Relaxations

The biggest single social recreation of the younger generation is dancing; this is common to both rural and urban teenagers. In the country areas, there are many ballrooms in places which apparently do not have the population to justify them—but the rural youngsters will travel considerable distances for a dance. Interest in the recreation is divided between modern dancing and the old-time Irish dances which are the special features of *ceilidhe* (pronounce it "kaylee"); solo Irish dances are also a competitive constituent of *feiseanna* (pron. "feshanna") music festivals throughout the country. Both the set dances and the solo items are particularly characteristic of the country, and their popularity is undiminished.

Similarly the Irish have a great affection for ballads, many of which are old narrative songs telling of brave or sad events of the past. There are others of more recent vintage which maintain the narrative tradition—Dominic Behan's *McAlpine's Fusiliers* is an example arising out of the life of the Irish laborers on construction sites in Britain and *The Men Behind The Wire*, a ballad focussing attention on men interned in Northern Ireland in 1971.

Pop groups and singers attract considerable followings, but outside of Dublin there are few auditoria big enough to take the money which attracts the big name stars.

Ireland once had the reputation of being a country with one of the largest percentages of cinema-goers per head of the population, but the impact of TV has caused a sharp decline in recent years. Many cinemas have become Bingo halls and others are now divided into smaller units.

Despite the impact of mass media communications, the people remain largely unsophisticated and even in Dublin or Belfast their taste in entertainment does not run to the high life and night clubs. Dancing may go on until four in the morning, but the nightclub life of other capitals is absent. This is not because of legal or religious influence, but because there has been no local demand for it. Moreover, the transient population which the development of tourism has brought apparently prefers the entertainment developed by the people in their own way—an "Irish Night", whether in a thatched cottage in Bunratty Folk Village (a short distance from Shannon Airport), or in a topgrade Dublin hotel, has a character which is essentially Irish and not pseudo-anything.

Living Standards

Incomes are lower in Ireland than in the United States or Britain, but the standard of living, so far as necessities are concerned, is high. The Irish are hearty meat eaters, and oddly (for a country with about 2,000 miles of coastline), eat little fish despite a wide variety. Possibly the fact that the very substantial Catholic population was, until 1970, bound to abstain from meat on Fridays gave fish a penitential characteristic and it is therefore not looked upon with much favor but the fresh fish from around Ireland's shores is really succulent; well worth enjoying, particularly if mussels or other shellfish like lobsters are on the menu. Potatoes, historically one of the main dishes of the Irish, have declined in importance as living standards have risen, and although the older generation in the country still regards them as a major constituent of a meal, the younger people are rather more diet- and weight-conscious. But no Irishman despises the value of a potato, and a good potato baked in its "jacket" (skin) in the traditional farmhouse way is one of the pleasures of a dinner in Ireland. Top-grade hotels offer this as a "special". The Irish eat well because they enjoy it, but there are few traditional dishes —Irish Stew, for example, is probably eaten more frequently in other countries than in the land of its origin. Bacon-and-cabbage is one truly national dish that few will reject, and it appears with regularity on the menus of most homes. It is, of course, a meal basic to the land where pig-raising has been a tradition on most farms for generations.

Possibly the greatest problem of today is the population over-

THE IRISH SCENE

flow from the farming hinterland. Modern farming absorbs less labor than in the old days and there is a constant drift to the major centers of population and particularly Dublin where the Government departments provide a great deal of employment. Much of this is for young women who live in "flats"—often single room homes in converted houses of a bygone generation. They live lonely lives five nights a week, eating canteen meals and take-away foods; many hitch lifts to their homes in the country at week-ends if they can't afford the rail or bus fares. Others seek the solace in what they see as the "bright lights"— lounge bars, which are expensive in relation to their pay levels, discotheques or "night clubs"—in quotes because they have no relation to sophisticated jet-set night clubs of other capitals.

Successive governments have announced their intention of decentralizing civil service departments to provincial cities—a highly desirable economic operation since office space is becoming increasingly expensive in Dublin (around £3 per square foot) and equally desirable from the social viewpoint but so far the intentions have not become a reality and it is felt that senior male civil servants have been a frustrating force: they have homes in Dublin, families, children at school—would it be just to move them? What would be the compensatory factors—socially, economically? Until these points are resolved the problems of young people from the rural areas adrift in a big city may well remain.

Alcoholism is another of Ireland's problems, despite the efforts of a long-campaigning total abstinence organization. The latest informed estimate is that there are 50,000 to 60,000 alcoholics in the country. Ireland has 11,000 pubs, ranging from the back premises of a grocery shop in a village to vast "lounges" in and around Dublin which feature entertainment from cabaret to serious plays in an effort to hold the customers. None of the publicans has yet staged the Victorian temperance melodrama *The Drunkard*, but no doubt somebody will—and pack in the audience because the Irish don't mind laughing at themselves although they don't like other people doing it. The latest comment among lighthearted drinkers is that what Father Matthew— the founder of the temperance movement—failed to achieve, Richie Ryan—the latest Minister for Finance to impose new and heavy taxes on drink—will!

Alcohol is certainly a more serious problem than drugs among the younger generation but the government has made it clear that it has no intention of easing laws against soft drugs—a concession which has been sought in the past two years.

Of course, the Irish are also very great tea drinkers too; they rank second only to the English in their consumption—and there's always "a cup on the pot" when you call to a house in the country. It seems that the brew of the tea leaf is as good a conversation-starter as the distilled brew of the barley in the bar.

Rural Life

Within the Irish rural community there are still tribal instincts, the desire to protect one another, to close ranks against the invader, the outsider. It is a situation which can sometimes frustrate the police investigating a crime. Yet these same people will make the stranger most welcome, greet him with the traditional Céad Míle Fáilte—"A hundred thousand welcomes"—and mean that welcome. Only when they feel threatened, or land ownership is at stake—even a modest amount of poorish land—does the tribal instinct assert itself. It is a characteristic of a peasant economy, an economy from which the country is not entirely free although the farming community—largely through its international relationships in the EEC and a thrusting Irish Farmers' Association—is emerging from its shadows.

Late marriage has always been one of the problems of the rural community in Ireland, frequently caused by the strong matriarchal influence of farm mothers and farmers who saw in their sons a source of cheap labor. This situation has been changing with the rising standards of education, the impact of the young farmers' clubs (Macra na Feirme) and the drift to the cities which is inducing a gradual reduction in the age at marriage. Efforts to persuade the older farmers to retire on pensions have met with some success, but the Irish farmer is the most conservative of men and the process of inducing him to relinquish his hold on the land is slow.

The way of life in rural Ireland has been hard until recently. The creation of a rural electrification network has brought light and power to all but the most remote farm holdings, and this has been followed by the development of a piped water supply to many places which formerly relied on a hand pump or well, sometimes a great distance from the house. The picturesque thatched cottage still exists, but the majority of farm homes are fairly modern. In the towns, preference is for the suburban pattern of living, mostly in semi-detached houses; apartment life is becoming increasingly familiar to Irish people and in the past few years a number of apartment blocks have been built in Dublin. The average housewife uses fewer domestic appliances than her counterpart in America, and she learned to do without domestic help a long time ago. A growing number have central heating; the principal source of heat in rural areas is peat (generally called turf) and in the cities, coal, which is imported. The turf fire of the country kitchen is a pleasure to be sought and enjoyed; the open fire on the hearth is the symbol of the heart of the home and it is there the best stories are still told.

There is a close relationship between town and country and a great many of the old traditions have been carried over into urban life. Some surface sophistication may be seen, but there is little change in the basic way of life for the majority of Irish people are only a generation or two away from farming stock.

The domestic arts of spinning and weaving have never died out; for centuries, they have contributed to the incomes of families dependent on farming on far-from-fertile soil and on fishing. While the standards of living have risen substantially, the traditional crafts have been fostered; the growing market for Irish tweed in the fashion world has led to the development of a new approach to design. Similarly, the distinctive pattern knitted into the jerseys of west coast fishermen have caught the imagination of the fashion-conscious and provided an important source of income for home craft-workers. This extra income has raised their living standards but has done virtually nothing to change the character of the people—a welcoming people, slightly diffident and with a strongly characteristic form of speech. A number of them have never traveled in a train in Ireland, but have flown to America to see a son or daughter or grandchild. They accept the idea that the next parish to the west of them is America, and they make no great fuss of driving down to Shannon Airport and joining a flight passing through for Montreal, Boston, New York or Chicago. They will accept passage by jet rather more readily than they might accept a change in their own home. These journeys and other external influences make very little impact on the personality of the people, whether they are from the remoter villages of the west or from the cities and towns. They absorb the experience and adjust it to their own way of life.

Clothes and the Man

Irishmen, except the young generation, display little interest in clothes and it is most unwise to judge a man by the clothes he is wearing—women have a great deal more interest, but to meet a young woman in a farmyard in the morning and see her going to a horse show later in the day, or a party in the evening, provides a sharp contrast. The men in the rural areas, and a great many in towns, prefer tweed suits without being overly concerned as to whether they are pressed or not. Their appearance has little to do with their financial status. Stand around at a cattle fair or mart and watch a deal being done; the size of the money roll produced to settle the purchase surprises many a visitor. And it is cash which is preferred on these occasions—it is traditional, just as it is traditional to slap each other's palm to mark the close of a deal in the market.

Even in the cities, there is less formal wear than in most European countries. Women conform more closely to international fashion, but although they display the keenest interest in reports of new styles, there seems to be a slight time lag in the adoption of the fashions—perhaps a reflection of the conservative way of life. The sense of conservatism may sometimes seem stifling (Irish writers have said so on many occasions), but there is no strong reaction to it.

The Quickening Pace

Ireland—as most people who live outside it would expect—has some laws which might be described as "Irish". Among them is a concession of freedom from income tax for the works of resident writers, painters, sculptors and composers—irrespective of nationality—introduced in 1969. Naturally such a concession inspires the wrath of Irish actors and musicians who do not benefit from it. The "tax haven" has attracted a number of new residents—around 600 at the latest count, over half of them writers—who have found the quiet of Ireland a plus quality to the tax concession. It doesn't cost the Irish Government or taxpayer anything; without the concession most of these people would live elsewhere, and the country does derive some benefit through the spending of the "new" residents. What constitutes "work of artistic merit"—the qualifying phrase—is sometimes debatable but, on the whole, the scheme works passably well.

A living for literary men in Ireland is difficult. Some teach, some present TV and radio programs or work as journalists; others lecture and—possibly the best rewarded ones—take posts as visiting professors or writers-in-residence at American universities. But they maintain a high output and are respected—if not remunerated—by their fellow Irishmen who are also their severest critics: after all, that is what happened to Brendan Behan. Strangely the most popular of the media—TV and radio—do the most for the arts which might be regarded as a minority interest. For 35 years—until his death in 1974—the poet Austin

THE IRISH SCENE

Clarke contributed a weekly poetry program to Radio Telefís Eireann, discovering in the process such artists as the Ulster poet the late W. R. Rodgers, a Presbyterian minister by occupation.

The Abbey Theatre has emerged from its Celtic Twilight induced by its founding parents. W. B. Yeats and Lady Gregory. But their influence is not ignored: the men who followed the Plough and the Stars—emblem of James Connolly's trade unionists in the 1916 Easter Rising—might not have accepted it, but the nationalism of the Abbey Theatre in its early days was a major influence on the movement towards Irish independence. Today the Abbey is a poetic theater, after passing through a "kitchen comedy" period, rather than a theater of realism. The whole scope of drama is, fortunately, encompassed in the Dublin theaters. Hilton Edwards and Micheál MacLiammóir, founders of the Dublin Gate Theatre are ageing but their influence is still felt; little theaters, although constantly financially insecure, are experimenting in drama which helps to keep Ireland alive as a well of dramatic influence.

Young men like Colm O Briain, named as Director of the Arts Council (An Chomhairle Ealaíon) in 1975, moving to the post from work in television and the theater, are stimulating new interest in all areas of the arts. Modest but helpful subsidies for cultural projects are ensuring that the younger generation of artists and experimenters in the arts—in the widest sense of the term—are being encouraged.

Irish television—a single channel service to be expanded to two channels during 1977—has been restricted in funds and therefore has been able to do little to develop new talent. In current affairs, reporting and discussion, however, it has made an important impact on Irish life.

In many parts of the country, largely through cable-relayed services, Irish viewers can also receive the programs of BBC and the British commercial service of ITV which gives them an edge on their fellows located in single-channel areas. When the Minister for Posts and Telegraphs proposed that the new second channel should be introduced solely for the purposes of re-broadcasting the service of BBC-1 to the entire country his suggestion was defeated—on a survey—by about two to one.

While Ireland has always had plenty of singers and a good musical tradition it is weak in light entertainment, and despite the number of Irish comedians—among them Dave Allen in recent years—there is comparatively little humor on the Irish air.

Women frequently have a higher educational status than men, although they have been seemingly disinclined to use it—except

THIS IS IRELAND

in education. They apparently preferred to accept the matriarchal role in the home and few of them have entered politics. Now the equal status of women has been recognized by the government, if not yet by all the male population. The "Women's Liberation" movement revealed that there are some outstanding personalities among Irishwomen and they have led public discussion on a number of the formerly "taboo" topics such as birth control, family planning and divorce. The principle of equal pay for equal work for men and women has been conceded, and the women of modern Ireland will ensure that it is implemented.

There is some quickening of pace in the Ireland of today, but it has not been permitted to disturb the comparatively even tenor which is so much a part of the charm of Ireland. The younger generation have reacted to the changing tempo with a more questioning approach to life than their parents, sometimes appearing to their seniors as showing insufficient care for national responsibilities. But the attitude of the young, and many of the middle-aged, is reflected not in the rejection of past glories and the achievements of their forebears but in the acceptance of them as being in the past: "What now?" is their question.

The impact of modern life is being absorbed and "relaxed" is still a one-word summary of the average Irishman's approach to life. His tempo may be slower than that of his American or European contemporaries—it may even aggravate them at times —but when efficiency and productivity in technical spheres are demanded they are forthcoming. It's just that the normal pace of life is more leisurely—as I said, it's "relaxed"

IRISH HISTORY

A Fabric of Disharmony

by

KEVIN DANAHER

(The outstanding authority on Irish folklore, Caoimhín Ó Danachair—as he is called in Gaelic—has written and lectured on his subjects for diverse audiences throughout Europe and America. He is presently Lecturer in Irish Folklore at University College, Dublin.)

Ireland was already an island, cut off by the sea from Europe, when the first human inhabitants arrived, sometime about eight thousand years ago. These first pioneers were mere hunters and gatherers of food, squatters on the seashore and the river banks, but even they must have possessed the skill to make boats fit to brave the sea and the courage to set out on a venture of some peril. Before many centuries had passed, they were followed by other settlers with cattle and dogs, with a knowledge of how to clear patches of scrub and forest in order to till the soil and raise crops. These early settlers were derived from the old Paleolithic stocks of western Europe; they have left to the Irish of today the physical heritage of paler skins and a higher proportion of light-colored eyes than the people of any other area in the world. So began the continuous and profitable occupation of a land which offered much to primitive settlers—welcoming beaches, navigable rivers leading deep inland, lakes teeming with fish, woods full of game and with no dangerous animals (except wolves), with a fertile soil and a mild climate.

Of the way of life of these Neolithic farmers through some thirty centuries we know very little, the archeologists can tell us something about their dwellings and their burial methods, and we can see fragments of their pottery and their stone tools and weapons in our museums. But even the simplest facts concerning their daily round, even the language spoken by them, must remain a mystery.

It was discovered that Ireland was rich in copper and in gold—copper for bronze tools and weapons and gold for coveted ornaments and jewelry. Bronze tools and gold ornaments from Ireland were traded abroad, and the remote and primitive island began to make some stir in the trade and commerce of western Europe, sending out pedlars and merchants and attracting the adventurous, the skilled and the greedy to its shores. Irish bronze and gold objects from this early metal-working period have been found scattered all over western Europe.

Cult of the Megaliths

About the same time as the first knowledge of metals, there came into Ireland one of the most remarkable phenomena in the history of the spread of culture, something analogous to the coming of Christianity more than two thousand years later. This was the cult of the megaliths. During a period stretching over many centuries, huge tombs, mighty pillars and great ritual circles of massive stones were erected in all parts of the island, so solid and enduring that they still excite our admiration. These great stone monuments are, without doubt, the most wonderful and most revealing relics of Ireland's ancestors. Problems of planning, of engineering, of mechanics, of the organization, direction and support of hundreds of workmen—all of these were met and overcome. Whether they were built by conqueror or native lord, by king or priest or sect, the megaliths demanded a degree of scientific knowledge and a command of material and moral resources only to be found in a vigorous and highly developed community.

New cultural influences and new population elements continued to arrive. Especially noteworthy are the changes in the type and form of weapons and ornaments around 600 B.C. and the coming of a knowledge of iron and of art styles clearly derived from continental Celtic sources around 250 B.C.

IRISH HISTORY

When, how, and in what numbers Celtic speaking peoples first came into Ireland is not known. There is no indication of any large-scale invasion. Nevertheless, at some time during the millennium preceding the Christian era, Celtic-speaking people did come into the island in strength sufficient to establish in it, as the ordinary speech of the inhabitants, that branch of Celtic which is the direct ancestor of the Gaelic still spoken today.

Of all the lands of western Europe, Ireland alone escaped invasion by the Romans, although, as Tacitus tells us, the Romans did cast envious glances across the narrow sea from their bases in Britain. One legion, they believed, would be sufficient to conquer Ireland, but no expedition was sent and Ireland was left to develop in its own way.

Pre-Christian Society

Its society was based upon the small local kingdom, the extent of which was roughly that of a barony and the ruler of which, although he was called *Rí*, king, was no more than a petty lord. Above him was a hierarchy of kings of larger areas, all (in theory) under a High King of all Ireland. A centralized authority seldom was, or could be, enforced, while even the provincial and lesser kings were seldom certain of the support of the small, local kingdoms. Under the local kings were the free landowners, who owed him tribute and loyalty and owned the land in their own right, as individuals or family or other groups. The settlement pattern was dominated by the isolated holding, the homestead and land of the free farmer, of which the "ring-forts" of today are the remains. There were no towns or cities, no urban organization independent of the countryside. Besides the free farmers, there were bondsmen or peasant tenantry, who may have been as numerous as the free men, but who had a lower place in society.

Ireland at the beginning of the Christian era, although lacking in centralized political authority, was united by a common language, a common culture and a common tradition. Members of the learned and professional classes could pass freely from one kingdom to the next throughout the island. There were schools of poetry, of medicine and of law, with long courses of training and numerous grades of proficiency, and the learned men from these schools seem to have possessed somewhat of a sacred or magical character which raised them above the common men.

Poetry was highly valued, and the reciters of epic tales and of poems in praise of their patrons were richly rewarded. Medicine was based upon sound hygienic rules and much herbal lore, together with some skill in manipulation and surgery; indeed the patients under the care of these ancient physicians had a very much greater chance of survival and cure than the inmates of an eighteenth-century hospital in a great European city. Law was based on a long series of legal precedents and depended upon public respect for legal forms for its efficacy; there were no court officers, police or prisons, but the sacred character of the law ensured compliance with the judge's ruling or the ostracization of the offender who refused to submit.

Skilled artists and craftsmen were highly respected; a master gold-worker or weapon-smith might dine at the table of a king. Such examples of their art which survive (mainly metalwork) show a very high degree of technical skill and artistic taste.

Outside of the professional classes the social standing of the individual depended upon his property and possessions, descending from powerful and wealthy landowners to laborers, serfs and slaves. A woman might own cattle and moveable property in her own right, and retain the ownership after marriage; she could inherit her father's land for her lifetime if he had no son, the land reverting to a male relative after her death. Whether married or single, she could take legal action on her own account, and could testify against her husband in court. Monogamy was usual, although polygamy and concubinage were recognized, with legally-defined rights and privileges for both lesser wife and concubine. The lot of female slaves, however, was hard while paganism lasted—the *cumal* (slave-woman) was a recognized standard of value, equal to three cows.

Wars frequently occurred between the small kingdoms, but were little more than manly sport, while cattle-raiding was common, and the prowess of the successful cattle raider was lauded in the tales and poems of the time. Indeed, it appears that a king, on his succession, must prove his leadership and courage by a successful foray on his neighbors' herds. Greater kings tried to ensure the loyalty of their subordinates by taking hostages; a hostage was treated with all the honor due to his social position as long as the pact was kept, but could legally be slain if it was broken.

Christianity

Into this remarkable blending of culture and residual barbarism, this unique non-Roman civilization of western Europe, came in the fifth century a new force—Christianity. Many aspects of

IRISH HISTORY

Irish life must have appeared strange to the Roman-trained missionaries, and they, no doubt, had many misgivings in regard to their venturing into a society where the familiar forms of Roman law and organization were unheeded and the prestige and authority of the still-mighty Roman Empire disregarded. Nevertheless, their path proved an easy one, for the conversion of Ireland to the Christian faith was accompanied by two very unusual phenomena. In the first place, the people of Ireland accepted the new religion readily, even with enthusiasm. Not one single Christian martyrdom is recorded in the conversion of Ireland, nor, apparently, was there any persecution of the few reluctant pagans. In the second place, the Christian missionaries showed no hostility to the native forms of learning, and the traditional schools of literature, law and leechcraft continued to flourish side by side with the centers of Christian teaching. Before long, Irish monks and churchmen were composing poetry in the native language and granting their patronage to native artists.

In the centuries which followed, there was a great blossoming of monastic fervor, with hundreds of Irish men and women devoting themselves to the service of God as monks and nuns; while local lords rivaled each other for the prestige of endowing monasteries. These establishments were notable for the rigor and austerity of their discipline, with much prayer, fasting, hospitality and good works. But the things of the mind were not neglected. Far from it—the larger monasteries became great centers of learning with hundreds, even thousands of scholars enrolled. These schools taught not only Christian theology, but all the learning of the time, both Roman and Irish, with literature, classical learning, philosophy, astronomy, cosmography and other sciences.

Soon the tide was flowing outwards again, with Irish monks and scholars pressing into Britain and Europe, preaching the gospel, founding schools and monasteries; some were to become great bishops and abbots or the friends and counselors of kings, others to be mere wandering scholars disturbing foreign schools with their disputations.

Enter the Vikings

In the year A.D. 795, a terrible band from the sea came ashore on the island which is now Lambay, sailing away again with all the loot and captives they could seize and leaving behind only corpses and smoking desolation. These were the Norse Vikings, and year after year the raids continued, extending farther and

THE IRISH SCENE

farther inland all around Ireland until no place was safe. The monasteries were their special prey, and the precious objects given by pious or repentant kings and lords made a rich booty; Scandinavian museums today show a profusion of such objects excavated from Viking graves.

At first the light weapons and happy-go-lucky fighting methods of the Irish proved no match for the mail-clad and heavily armed raiders, who soon began to establish bases on the coast, some of which developed into towns. Dublin, Cork, Waterford, Wexford and Limerick began as Viking strongholds. Some of these fortresses grew into towns and their occupants began to turn from freebooting to relatively peaceful trading, while around them and up some of the river valleys, Norsemen and Danes began to settle as farmers on land more fertile than any they had known at home. Some of these settlements made alliances with local Irish kings, and there was intermarriage between the new settlers and the older population. At times, there was fierce and bloody warfare, with the Irish gaining skill and experience in the fighting methods of the newcomers.

Finally, more than two hundred years after the first raids, the Norse attempt to subdue Ireland was broken at Clontarf, in 1014, by King Brian. But so mixed had loyalties and expediencies become by this time that a large part of the Norse army at Clontarf was made up of Irish allies, while the valor of King Brian's Norse contingents contributed much to his victory. Both wings of the Irish army on that day were led by Norse chieftains.

In one sense the victory of Clontarf was a disaster for the Irish, for King Brian, the only leader powerful enough to weld the whole country into one strong unit, was killed in the battle, and for the next one hundred and fifty years a succession of kings from various provinces and ruling families tried in vain to set themselves up as supreme ruler. Political disunity and intermittent warfare continued. Nevertheless, there was a revival of prosperity, of learning and of the arts. Churches were built and new monasteries established in the continental fashion. A series of synods regulated church affairs; the most important, at Kells in 1152, finally established the hierarchy as Ireland knows it today.

At the end of the twelfth century a provincial king, Dermot McMurrough of Leinster, was driven from his throne because of his evil life. He appealed for help to Henry II, King of England, who gave him leave to enlist volunteers among his followers, and in 1169, some bands of Normans arrived in Ireland to support McMurrough's cause. Next year, larger bands

IRISH HISTORY

followed, and made war with such success that in a few months they had overrun the greater part of Leinster and Munster. Hot upon their heels came Henry II, loudly proclaiming his zeal for the reform of manners and morals in Ireland. He had provided himself with some form of authority from the pope; the authenticity of this has long been questioned, but Henry's acceptance by the Irish bishops indicates some form of papal approval, and most of the Irish kings and lords came to Henry at Dublin and submitted to him.

The English and Norman Role

Here began a fundamental misunderstanding that was to confuse Irish affairs for centuries. Henry claimed the feudal lordship, that is to say, the ownership of the land of Ireland and the right to let it to his nobles, Norman or Irish, in return for loyalty and service, and to deprive them of it if these were withheld. But under Irish law, the land was owned by individuals or groups, and the king or lord had no right whatever to take it from them. English law said that the subject must bow to the king's will and give up his land; Irish law said that the owner should resist, even by force, any such attempt to rob him.

For the next 350 years, Norman families held about half the land of Ireland, acquired by conquest, by marriage agreement, by royal grant or by mere swindling. In some areas, they ejected the old population and settled their own followers on the land. In other places, they accepted the common people as their tenants. These Norman lords had few ties of loyalty or tradition to any country or language and readily adapted to the new environment. Soon the English authorities were passing laws to force them to give up Irish dress, language and manners, and especially forbidding their intermarriage with the Irish, for the most part in vain, for there rapidly developed an Irish-Norman society in which nothing but the family name distinguished the son of a Norman father and an Irish mother from the son of an Irish father and a Norman mother.

Each succeeding English king claimed the Lordship of Ireland, but was too occupied with foreign and civil wars to back the claim with any real force, while on the other hand the quarrelsome lords and chieftains in Ireland never could be brought to unite in a completely independent Irish kingdom. Were it not for their rivalries, they might easily have achieved such a kingdom at almost any time between the beginning of the thirteenth century and the end of the fifteenth. A bid for the throne of Ireland

THE IRISH SCENE

was made in 1315 by Edward Bruce, brother of King Robert Bruce of Scotland, but he failed to get sufficient Irish support and was defeated and killed in battle after three years of bloody and devastating war.

Even after the defeat of Bruce, no real peace came to Ireland. The main cause of contention was the possession of lands. The great lords, whether of Norman or Irish stock, were constantly at each others' throats, and peace and order reigned only where the local lord or prince was strong enough to maintain it.

So things went on, with neither side prevailing, with much turmoil, but with much noble patronage of the church and of the arts and sciences. The area under the effective control of the crown shrank until, by the late fifteenth century, it consisted only of a small territory around Dublin, called the "English Pale" because it had to be fortified with a great bank and palisade to keep unwelcome visitors out, and the dubious loyalty of a few towns overawed by royal garrisons.

Henry VIII Wins Out

Peace and prosperity were returning to England under the stern rule of Henry VII. His son, Henry VIII, inherited a rich, strong and united kingdom, and was able to turn his attention to Ireland. At first he tried to win over the Irish lords of all shades of descent and tradition by what he called "sober ways, politic drifts and amiable persuasions", and in this he might well have succeeded but for two obstacles which proved insuperable. In the first place, he claimed the right of a feudal monarch to dispose the land of Ireland to those friendly to him, while ancient Irish law, which now had been adopted by many of the great Norman-Irish families denied his right to this.

Another great obstacle was the outcome of King Henry's break with Rome. Hitherto, the English kings claimed the lordship of Ireland through the pope's feudal grant, but Henry had sacrificed even the dubious legality of this. He now proclaimed himself King of Ireland by right of conquest, and faced the task of effectively conquering Ireland to make good his claim; his methods were to smash down all opposition and then to drive the "rebel" lords and landholders from their estates and grant these to his own loyal followers, whether Irish or English. This policy was continued by his daughters, Queen Mary and Queen Elizabeth.

The Reformation had made progress in England, and under Elizabeth all effective opposition to it was snuffed out. In Ireland, things were vastly different, for both Irish and Anglo-Irish remained steadfast in religious allegiance to Rome; during the long reign of Queen Elizabeth, her opponents in Ireland were fighting for religious as well as for political liberty, which in the atmosphere of the time, added new dimensions of bitterness and savagery to the struggle. Because there was still no unity of purpose or action among the great lords of Ireland, they were defeated piecemeal.

Elizabeth's death in 1603 coincided almost exactly in time with the extinguishing of the last vestiges of Irish independence; the conquest was complete, and the Irish, with their land desolated by war and racked by famine, their old lords banished or reduced to the status of petty squires, their trade and commerce destroyed and their religion forbidden, were left to the mercy of the conquerors.

A few years later, the surviving princes and lords of Ulster, who had been restored to their own estates by treaty, became fearful for their lives and secretly fled the country. This gave the government the excuse to seize vast tracts of land in Ulster, to eject the remaining landholders and to replace them with English and Scottish settlers, all stout Protestants and all loyal to the crown. This was the beginning of the "Ulster Question" which has bedeviled Irish affairs ever since.

Civil Wars

Ireland settled down to an uneasy peace, rudely broken in 1641 by a long-planned insurrection which had the dual goals of religious freedom and the restoration of the confiscated lands to their former owners. The first victims of the fighting were the new settlers of Ulster; most of these were driven from their holdings and many of them killed. For twelve years war raged, the combatants splintering into numerous factions. There were "Old Irish" who dreamed of independence, "Old English" who would give loyalty to the crown if their religion and their possessions were secure, Royalists and Parliamentarians who supported the rival factions in the English Civil War and Scottish settlers who followed the Covenant. In the various stages of the war, each of these parties was alternately allied to and fighting against each of the others. On no side was there unity of policy or action, until Oliver Cromwell finished the war by bringing his victorious Parliamentary army to Ireland and wiping out all opposition. This final stage of the war sank to a new depth of horror, with famine and massacre, enormous destruction of property, hundreds of homeless men, women and children rounded up and shipped as slaves to the Sugar Islands, and finally, with the wholesale confiscation of the lands of all who had opposed the Parliament.

The restoration of Charles II to the throne of England brought little relief in Ireland. There was a relaxation of active religious persecution, but those who had been loyal to the king's father were dismayed when neither lands nor position were restored to them. The Irish had greater hopes on the accession of Charles's brother, James II, who was a Catholic, and gave him their support in the civil war which developed between him and the other claimant to the throne, William of Orange. William poured troops and material into Ireland while the supporters of James were disappointed in their hopes of massive help from Louis XIV of France and, after two years of resistance, surrendered on terms which became famous as the Treaty of Limerick. This ambiguous document appeared to guarantee many rights and privileges, but within a very few years these were set aside and a code of laws—the iniquitous "Penal Laws"—was introduced which denied even the semblance of freedom to the Catholics (who formed the great majority of the Irish people), depriving them of all access to property rights, franchise, education, office or appointment, however humble. They bore heavily too on the "Nonconformists," those Protestants who did not accept the rule and discipline of the state church, denying them privilege, office and education unless they conformed.

The "Ascendancy" and Union

The eighteenth century began in Ireland with all power in the hands of that small section of the population which gave full loyalty to the English crown and the state church—the landowners and office-holders who became known as the "Ascendancy" and who used religious differences to hold wealth and privilege in their own hands and deny them to Catholics and Nonconformists. However, as the century wore on, a more enlightened attitude spread, partly because of the liberal ideas propagated by such men as Swift and Berkeley, partly because of continued discrimination on the part of Britain against Irish policies and Irish trade. Towards the end of the century, the realization of their treatment as "second-class citizens" brought a demand for legislative independence and free trade, and, faced with the threat of force, Britain yielded, and Ireland was declared an independent kingdom under the British crown. Trade, industry and agriculture began to flourish and the worst of the

IRISH HISTORY

Penal Laws were repealed or relaxed, while some of the Protestant Patriots went so far as to agitate for complete religious freedom for all denominations.

The French Revolution had its effect in Ireland, and a strong movement towards complete independence in an Irish Republic on the model of France began, in which people of all classes and all faiths were involved. This was opposed on all sides, by religious leaders who feared the spread of atheistic liberalism, by the wealthy anxious for their lands and possessions and by convinced or opportunist British loyalists. Matters came to a head in 1798, when the republican party, the United Irishmen, relying on the promise of help from France, came out in open insurrection, only to be defeated and crushed with great severity and much bloodshed. British statesmen now succeeded, by a combination of threats, promises and flagrant bribery, in getting the Irish parliament to vote itself out of existence, and in bringing Ireland under the direct control of the London parliament, in the Act of Union of 1800.

The effects of this upon Ireland were, for a time, delayed, as the Napoleonic Wars ensured a continued demand for Irish products. The coming of peace brought depression in Ireland, with rising population and falling resources and standards of living, culminating in the Great Famine of 1846-49, which caused the death or emigration of two and a half million people. Irish leaders became more convinced than ever that the only hope of their country's well-being lay in some form of separation from Britain.

A majority believed that this could be brought about by constitutional means and agitated for the repeal of the Union and for Home Rule, while a minority held to the doctrine that only physical force could win independence. Irish policies swayed between these two ideas, with constant demands for the one in the British parliament, and a series of insurrections and disturbances to achieve the other, both without success. Other agitation went on all through the century, in one attempt after the other, to improve the lot of the farmers, who were suffering under an outmoded landlord system characterized by rack-renting (demanding nearly the full value of the property annually) and eviction. This agitation grew to such proportions towards the end of the century that the British government was forced to yield and to introduce legislation which enabled the tenant farmers to buy out their holdings and become independent proprietors of their land.

During the late 1800s, men like Charles S. Parnell led Ireland in attempts to achieve Home Rule. But for the scandal of his

THE IRISH SCENE

involvement in a divorce in 1890, which split the Irish Parliamentary Party in two, Parnell and his followers might have succeeded, or at least hastened the day.

Partial Independence

The political agitation for independence continued into the twentieth century, and finally succeeded, on the eve of the first Great War, in having passed in the British parliament an act giving Home Rule—a limited degree of independence—to Ireland. Opposition to this measure now came to a head, with a strong body of opinion in the eastern counties of Ulster, spearpointed by the Orange Order, actively preparing to resist it by force of arms. This was followed by a movement among the Nationalists of the greater part of Ireland to arm and organize themselves to support the decision of the British parliament, by force if necessary. The months before the outbreak of the 1914-18 war saw three different armies in Ireland—the British army in solid occupation, the Ulster Volunteers pledged to resist Home Rule and the Irish Volunteers determined to enforce it.

Civil war seemed imminent, but the outbreak of the greater conflict gave British statesmen the opportunity of shelving the whole issue on the pretext of the prior claim of the war against Germany. Immediate and massive propaganda was put into effect in Ireland, calling for help for little Belgium and the rights of small nations, and hundreds of thousands of Irishmen of all shades of belief joined the British army.

One body of opinion, however, stood aloof from the war effort and maintained that its loyalty was to Ireland alone. This consisted of the convinced republicans and the socialists who were weary of starvation wages and bad working conditions. At Easter, 1916 these, although doubtful of universal popular support, came out in open insurrection, seized the center of Dublin and proclaimed an Irish Republic. Numbering only about one thousand men, they were defeated in a week of bitter fighting in which a great part of the center of the city was destroyed by fire and artillery. At first the public reaction was one of shocked hostility, but a long-drawn-out series of executions of the leaders, culminating in the shooting of the crippled MacDermott and of the socialist leader Connolly brought the inevitable reaction of sympathy and support. (Connolly was dying of gangrene from a leg shattered in the fighting and had to be propped up in a chair before the firing squad.)

For the next two years, the British authorities in Ireland

alternated between measures of coercion and conciliation, neither of which bore any fruit. Republican opinion spread and hardened, and was greatly stimulated by a misguided attempt on the part of Britain to force general conscription on Ireland, a measure against which the Catholic bishops and other influential people of moderate leanings pledged their support. Home Rule and the promise of it lost their meaning in the face of such coercion, and in the general election at the end of 1918, republican candidates won 73 out of 105 seats, while the Home Rule party (which had held 80 seats) only secured 6, the other 26 being gained by Unionists, nearly all in east Ulster. In the same year, Sinn Féin chose Éamon de Valera as head of a provisional government, confirming the concept of the republic proclaimed in 1916.

The Irish Revolution

The die was now cast. In January, 1919, those of the elected republicans who were not imprisoned met in Dublin, declared themselves to be an Irish parliament, ratified the 1916 declaration of an Irish Republic and pledged themselves to defend it by force if necessary. They appointed delegates to the peace conference in Paris to claim the rights of small nations for Ireland, but these delegates were refused a hearing. Some months later, the republican parliament was declared illegal by the British authorities and driven underground, where its various ministries continued to operate in secret in spite of all efforts to suppress them.

With two rival governments, a state of war was inevitable, and under the circumstances, this was a bitter and bloody little war, on the one side of ambush, assassination and attack on outposts, on the other of reprisals, executions, burning of property and imprisonment without trial. In most parts of the country, the populace gave active support to the republican forces. To counter this, the British authorities, in a mistaken policy which only panic can explain, reinforced their armed police in Ireland with terrorist bodies popularly known as the "Black and Tans" and "Auxiliaries", whose murderous savagery and indiscipline nearly put an end to all hope of a settlement. But moderate opinion in England, in growing shame at what was being done in Ireland, prevailed at last. In July, 1921, a truce and an invitation to discussion was offered to the Irish leaders and accepted.

A treaty which really satisfied nobody was proposed, and was accepted in the Irish parliament by a small majority. The main cause of dissatisfaction was the exclusion of the six northeastern

THE IRISH SCENE

counties from the jurisdiction of Dublin. These six counties were constituted into the separate state of Northern Ireland, in union with Britain but with limited local powers. The rest of Ireland became the Irish Free State, with dominion status similar to that of Canada. Uncompromising republican elements would have no part in this and challenged the new state in arms in a civil war which lasted for some months only, but left deep and lasting bitterness.

The two parts of Ireland went their different ways. In the Free State, the rivalries of the civil war gave birth to two main political parties which differed in hostility rather than in any fundamental or political belief. The inclusion in Northern Ireland of a large section of Nationalists (about one-third of the whole population), whose only purpose was unity with the rest of Ireland, brought about a permanent state of political incompatibility between a majority pledged to maintain the state and a large minority determined to abolish it.

In the Free State, the party defeated in the civil war came to power in 1932 and began to undo, by constitutional means, the objectionable aspects of the 1921 Treaty, ending in 1938 with the introduction of a republican constitution. In World War II Ireland (as the erstwhile Free State was now known) remained neutral. The preparation to resist possible invasion by either of the belligerents had one good effect—the old hostilities of the civil war were largely forgotten in the face of the new danger.

The period since World War II has seen the tentative growth of the conviction in both parts of Ireland that the old bitterness can lead only to futility; that social, cultural and economic advance for the people is of more importance than harping on past ills. Behind the banner headlines of terrorist activities there is a painfully slow, crippled progress towards intelligent joint action in many fields, even in the most disputed area of all, politics.

A WAY WITH WORDS

Music—and Blarney in Irish Literature

by

TERENCE DE VERE WHITE

(*Literary Editor of the* Irish Times, *Mr. White is the author of many books on national cultural figures, as well as eight novels. His most recent literary work is a volume of short stories,* Big Fleas and Little Fleas.)

As everything must start somewhere, it has become the custom to date the beginning of modern Ireland at Easter Week, 1916. Now, whatever case may be made for the proposition that the seeds of the republic's constitutional growth were planted in those reckless and heroic days, little came of them that relates to the arts. The whole of history teaches us that art is to be found buried in the folk or that it is a flowering of an ordered polity and an established state. Admittedly the finest art of Italy was brought to life in city states with strife at the gate or in the streets; but the vitality of the Italy of that period defeats all attempts at categorizing. Genius was omnipresent in the air, and, whatever dangers they ran themselves, potentates not less than popes were able to

THE IRISH SCENE

some extent to protect as well as to patronize the artists they employed.

Yeats and 1916

One poem for which greatness may be claimed *did* arise from the ashes of 1916. William Butler Yeats, who had been led into politics by Maud Gonne, wrote *Easter, 1916* and other verses on this theme. But it was not a spontaneous tribute to the Rising. Yeats had despised MacBride, whom Maud Gonne had unaccountably married. Yeats' pride was mental, and a certain carefulness dictated all the actions of his life. It was observable in his dress—that of a poet, but a very well-cared-for poet. He had no regard for the poetical accomplishments of Pearse, Plunkett and MacDonagh, three of the executed republicans; and he had not taken any notice of them, accordingly. But now, they had braved and suffered death, all dying with courage. It was possible to see why Maud Gonne, the woman, had preferred MacBride, the man of action to Yeats, the cautious dreamer. Brooding over this and the thought that perhaps the Bastille had been stormed without his having been consulted, much less having been requested to participate, Yeats, after six months, produced his doubts and self-questionings in imperishable lines.

He wrote of these men whom he had "passed with a nod of the head or polite meaningless words" while he was on his way to a club, otherwise preoccupied.

After reflecting on the three men, he climbed to heights he never exceeded anywhere else in his work:

> The horse that comes from the road,
> The rider, the birds that range
> From cloud to tumbling cloud,
> Minute by minute they change . . .

And then he asks himself (as others did and do still), "Was it needless death after all?"

And then, like Horace and Shakespeare in the same train of thought, he does all the poet can, knowing it will endure longer than the noblest of the actions of men:

> I write it out in a verse—
> MacDonagh and MacBride

A WAY WITH WORDS

> And Connolly and Pearse
> Now and in time to be,
> Wherever green is worn,
> Are changed, changed utterly:
> A terrible beauty is born.

No apology need be made for dwelling on the only work of great art to which the whole revolutionary movement gave birth. But that is not to say that the core of Irish modern literature is to be sought elsewhere than in the national revival.

Gaelic Revival and the Abbey Theatre

George Russell (known as "A.E.") who was concerned only with Ireland's heart ticks, regarded politics, lay and religious, unsympathetically. He would have us go back to the founding of the Gaelic League in 1893 by Douglas Hyde and Eoin MacNeill for the beginnings of the "Gaelic Revival". Hyde, the son of a Church of Ireland parson from Roscommon, learned Irish from the cottagers near his home. A classical and Hebrew scholar, versed in French and German, he confessed to his examiners in Trinity that he dreamed in Irish. His *History of Irish Literature,* first published in 1899, was reprinted in 1967; it is to be recommended as an excellent introduction, not only to its subject, but to the imaginative life of Ireland, without which its scenery would only entitle Cathleen Ní Houlihan to call herself Heidi's little sister, as tearful as she is unpredictable.

But Cathleen is much more than that; she has, in Yeats' words, "the walk of a queen". Hyde explains the fable enshrouded in the story of her origins, and introduces the strange wealth of literary materials in which history and myth have become so inextricably involved. Part of the confusion came from the efforts of medieval monks who falsified the mythology to give it a Christian atmosphere. Moreover, we have the counter-weight of the bardic tradition, a word-of-mouth literature, liable also to manipulation. There is nothing like it except in Greece; Ireland's tragedy was that she never produced a Homer to give the material a final shape or that she never possessed the settled state in which a Virgil might have enshrined the beautiful saga of Cuchulain or the legend of the Children of Lir (to take only two subjects that we have to read in imperfect literary forms). The legend of Deirdre attracted the writers who grew up with Hyde. Yeats

THE IRISH SCENE

wrote a short play on this lovely theme; and it may well be the most effective of all his attempts at playwriting.

Synge also tackled Deirdre; but in Synge, comedy was as strong as tragedy. Yeats claimed to have won him for Irish literature by sending him from Paris to the West of Ireland, where he lived in a cottage and wrought that language of his which is a sort of idealization of the English spoken by those who think in Irish. It sounds horribly false when imitated by other writers.

The Playboy of the Western World is Synge at the height of his powers, and it is funny to recall that this once shocked Irish audiences in Dublin and the United States. A revival in the new Abbey Theatre of Dion Boucicault's *The Shaughraun*, rapturously received by an audience that had lost faith in the theater founded by Yeats and Lady Gregory, surprised many people by its anticipations of Synge.

Boucicault (1820-90) was as popular in America as in his own country. His melodramas were treated with contempt by Yeats and his friends, but they were full of what Yeats sadly lacked as a dramatist. Not only Synge, but Sean O'Casey and Brendan Behan owed their liveliness to Boucicault's example.

Mention of O'Casey brings us to Dublin. While Yeats and Synge are firmly embedded in the soil of the west, O'Casey was a Dubliner to the marrow. His forte was his marvelous ear for Dublin speech. He is the faithful recorder of the fast-disappearing slums and the inimitable speech of the dwellers there. Behan is very much second-best, not so rich a mine for the student of the subject to explore as Myles na gCopaleen (Brian O'Nolan), who died in 1966. *At-Swim-Two-Birds* is the name of his best-known book, but his best work was done for the Cruiskeen Lawn column in the *Irish Times*.

Of its kind, nothing could be better than the Joxer-Captain Boyle dialogues in *Juno and the Paycock*. This play and *The Shadow of a Gunman* are all that the drama has to show for the turbulent years 1916-22. They reflect the atmosphere of the times with complete authenticity.

Denis Johnston, ten years later, caught the spirit of disillusioned post-revolutionary Dublin in *The Old Lady Says No*. But without Micheál MacLiammóir in the leading role, this play might not seem as good as it did to two generations of Dubliners.

The Abbey in its fine modern theater has not particularly distinguished itself. The performances have been uneven, and it has sought to widen its range by performing the kind of classics which used to be the monopoly of the Gate Theatre, founded

A WAY WITH WORDS

by Hilton Edwards and Micheál MacLiammóir. The Abbey actors are more at home in such productions as Brendan Behan's *Borstal Boy,* than in Shakespeare. The Abbey also runs an experimental theater—the *Peacock*.

The most successful playwrights of recent years have been Brian Friel, but mainly in the United States, Hugh Leonard, with a large local following, Father Forestal, who has confined his offerings to the Gate, and John B. Keane, who has the broadest provincial appeal.

Apart from the Abbey, other Dublin theaters are the Gate, which plays for safety with Wilde and Shaw, finding small audience interest in experiment, none at all in gloom; the Project Theatre with mid-day experimentation; the Focus, which tackles Ibsen with no qualms and limited resources. Dublin is still without a concert hall.

Shaw, Wilde and Joyce

George Bernard Shaw lived so long that he stretched (almost) from Goethe to Genet. He wrote so much that he is the despair of all students. Shaw will live as certainly as Swift; he had everything a writer can ask for, except poetry. Burn all but a handful of his plays and you are left with the best comedies in England, with plays that will live with Congreve, Sheridan and Wilde. Wilde, as many forget, was Shaw's contemporary, and he wrote only one perfect play—*The Importance of Being Earnest*. Mention of his name should recall the gallant and theatrical woman, his mother, who, under the name "Speranza", wrote much indifferent verse, but collected a splendid volume of folklore. (The latter, however, is a task that a native government has tackled seriously. The Folklore Commission is very active.)

Joyce requires no introduction. His name is on the lips of every literate visitor to Dublin, and Joyceana is keeping many a student, grant-endowed, working away in Dublin libraries. What will be his ultimate place in letters? The novel, it has been said, was never the same after he completed *Ulysses*; but Virginia Woolf, and before her, Dorothy Richardson, had discovered the "stream of consciousness" technique for themselves. Joyce may not seem such a freak in the future as he did to contemporaries; his obscenity will fit naturally into the freer-speaking age which he anticipated by a few decades. His short stories achieved a new realism, but they will be read in the context of a remarkable crop of work by Irish contemporaries.

Finnegans Wake will always be a curiosity, genius over-reaching itself for lack of new subject matter.

In their separate ways, Yeats and Joyce were contemptuous of their Irish contemporaries. When Joyce mellowed, he saw good in some of them, but from the start, he pitched himself against Yeats, the one man whom he regarded as a foeman worthy of his steel. Yeats, it may be said, was unfailingly kind to Joyce.

Joyce was never discouraging to James Stephens, even speaking of employing him to finish the so-hard-to-be-comprehended *Finnegans Wake*. In *The Charwoman's Daughter,* Stephens wrote the most enchanting fairy story that ever slums gave birth to; as a poet he is like Allingham, from Ballyshannon, Co. Donegal —high in the ranks of the small, or small in the ranks of the great, whichever mode of classification you prefer.

Poetry

Of recent years there has been a revived interest in Irish poetry, which is likely to grow. Thomas Moore was aware of this poetry when he wrote his pleasant songs, and James Clarence Mangan brought the inspiration further. Douglas Hyde in his *Love Songs of Connaught* caught the very spirit of the originals.

That will hardly be bettered; but since Hyde's time, the late Frank O'Connor in his *Kings, Lords and Commons* produced a magnificent English rendering of the old Irish poets. (It was banned for a time in Ireland!)

With a renewed interest in things Irish, greater attention will be drawn to books like Daniel Corkery's *The Hidden Ireland*. Corkery, who lived (not surprisingly) in Cork, was a good friend to the young Frank O'Connor and the young O'Faoláin.

Formerly, a student might read books on history and about the Irish renaissance without realizing that there existed a living tradition which went underground, and was thus denied literary expression in those circles where cultural fashion is created. A start to uncover it was made forty years ago when George Thomson and Moya Llewelyn Davies translated Maurice O'Sullivan's *Twenty Years A-Growing*. Maurice O'Sullivan was a young Civic Guard who had been reared on Blasket Islands off the coast of Kerry. An even better book followed—*The Islanders,* by Tomas O'Crohan, who had never left the islands. This was translated by Robin Flower.

Corkery concentrated on the poets of Munster, and in his introduction he made his purpose clear: his book, he says, "will not, in any way, replace Lecky's (historical) study of the same century [18th]; that book it will rather supplement, inasmuch as its province is that side of Irish life, the Gaelic side, which to him and his authorities was dark. He must have thought the Gaelic language a wayside *patois*, clearly not one of the permanent forces of the nation. . . . From his own pages, one would never feel that the soul of the Gael is one of the more enduring features of our national life."

In his translations, Frank O'Connor did much to carry on the good work of his mentor, and *Kings, Lords and Commons* received considerable and laudatory attention in Britain. It will be noticed, too, that while translations from the classics have thitherto been the stock in trade of young academic poets, more and more are making their first plunge into verse by translating from Irish originals.

Few can rival the late Louis MacNeice, yet the reputation of Seamus Heaney stands high, and no Irish poet since Yeats has had so much recognition outside Ireland. Heaney and the late Patrick Kavanagh, both farmer's sons, have shown a stronger talent than any of their contemporaries, although Thomas Kinsella and the late Austin Clarke run them a close second.

Among the younger poets, Michael Longley, Derek Mahon, Eavan Boland, Eiléan Ní Chuilleanáin, Michael Hartnett and, from the North, John Montague are all poets of a high standard.

Touring Ireland in Poetry and Prose

Frank O'Connor died before his last anthology (with David Greene) was published. It is entitled *A Golden Treasury of Irish Poetry A.D. 600 to 1200*. These are the writings appropriate to visits to Ireland's ancient remains, whether they be the mysterious grave chambers at Dowth, Knowth, Lough Crew and, most notably, New Grange, or the relics at Cong with the cairns commemorating the last battle (so it is said) between the ancient races of Ireland. They are helpful in visiting the churches at Glendalough, Mellifont, Tara or (less known) the Hill of Ushnagh in County Westmeath, where the Milesian kings held court, or at the more Europeanized Cashel, Ardfert, Ardmore, or the hill of Slane, where Patrick lit the Paschal fire to celebrate the spreading over Ireland of the message of the Cross. They will give you "the feel" of the land.

Poetry should travel in one's suitcase in Ireland. It will sweeten the visit to Lissoy in County Longford to read again Goldsmith's *Deserted Village*.

In the rich pasture land of Meath, driving past the green

hedges, take out the poems of F. R. Higgins, who died too soon; from the same county came Francis Ledwidge, only beginning as a poet when he fell in France in the Great War. Donegal has Allingham at Ballyshannon. And stand among the ruined churches, the stunted tower and gravestones innumerable, by Shannon side, near Athlone, and recall Rolleston's rendering of *The Dead at Clonmacnois*. Here are its opening and closing verses, from the Irish of Angus O'Gillan:

> In a quiet water'd land, a land of roses,
> Stands Saint Kieran's city fair;
> And the warriors of Erin in their famous generations
> Slumber there.
>
> Many and many a son of Conn the Hundred Fighter
> In the red earth lies at rest;
> Many a blue eye of Clan Colman the turf covers,
> Many a swan-white breast.

The Way That I Went, by Robert Lloyd Praeger, is a very individual account of the landscape, without history or politics, by one who had traveled every foot of the road. *Highways and Byways in Donegal and Antrim*, by Stephen Gwynn is a classic; while on Dublin, Maurice Craig's book is still the best.

Satire

Bernard Shaw made his living out of the English by ridiculing them. An Englishman who attempted to reverse the process, however, would find it hard to survive in Ireland. This touchiness is a sign of immaturity and lack of confidence. It explains why the Somerville and Ross stories are treated suspiciously by Irish critics and no worthy biographer dares tackle the marvelous challenge that Patrick Pearse's personality offers.

Frank O'Connor was one who was not inhibited by the common fears. His independence of mind is growing more common, and a resurgence of interest in Irish would encourage rather than set it back. For one thing, study would disclose the possible foundation of the Irish fear of being laughed at. One of the bards, of an almost sacrosanct fraternity, was killed for his satire, for the worst punishment an Irish chieftain could inflict on a rival was to commission a bard to compose satirical poems at his expense.

A WAY WITH WORDS

The late Oliver St. John Gogarty was the last bard (if self-appointed). His lyrics won public praise from Yeats, but Gogarty was really better known for the sort of verse that is still circulated privately; even his serious verse is best when it has a bawdy tang.

He could parody Keats' "Silent upon a peak in Darien" with "Potent behind a cart with Mary Anne". But he could do much better than this; there is something of Joyce's gentler genius in Gogarty's poem that begins:

> I will live in Ringsend
>   With a red-headed whore,
> And the fanlight gone in
>   Where it lights the hall-door;

and ends

> And up the back garden
>   The sound comes to me
> Of the lapsing, unsoilable
>   Whispering sea.

That conveys a side of Dublin which Joyce has made world-famous, that must be set off against not only the image of the land of saints and scholars but the Ireland of donkey-carts, red petticoats and "the little people".

The Novelists

It is possible to argue that novel writing in Ireland died with the decay of the Anglo-Irish. If we treat Joyce as outside any category, then, in the writer's opinion, the best Irish novels since George Moore are *The Real Charlotte*, by Somerville and Ross of the *Irish R.M.* fame, and *The Last September*, Elizabeth Bowen's evocation of life in the big house during the Black-and-Tan days. She wrote it before going to London and becoming part of the wider literary scene.

When creative writers turn to other things, it is generally a sign that the spark has died. In middle life, Seán O'Faoláin took to history, travel and essay writing, having engaged international attention by his novels and stories. Frank O'Connor before his premature death was becoming increasingly absorbed by archeology and ancient Irish architecture. Liam O'Flaherty simply gave up.

Elizabeth Bowen stood out from her Irish contemporaries by equal achievement in the novel and the short story. The men have beaten her with vital autobiographies, but she had the last laugh. Her adult life gave the blood to her stories. The two Corkmen, O'Connor and O'Faoláin, drew too heavily on early recollection—their late emotional experience did not seem to help with copy. But, then, they began life by going to confession to priests, while Miss Bowen was a Protestant. And George Moore used mischievously to hold forth that no Catholic writer has produced a great work of art since the Reformation. Seán O'Faoláin is one of the Irish writers who have established a name in the world. He owes it principally to his first novels *Bird Alone* and *A Nest of Simple Folk*. But his admirable autobiography, oddly titled, *Vive Moi*, published in 1966, is a true and excellent picture of life in Cork; it can be set against Frank O'Connor's more colorful story of the childhood of a poorer child in the same city at the same time. In *An Only Child*, O'Connor is carried away by his worship of his mother.

These two and Mary Lavin have published short stories in England and America. Liam O'Flaherty, who has been silent for decades, wrote early stories of undoubted genius.

Neither Kate O'Brien's hugely popular *That Lady*, nor her early success, *Without My Cloak*, are likely to weather the years as the Bowen novels will. And only time itself can tell how the work of Seán O'Faoláin, Mary Lavin, Benedict Kiely, Mervyn Wall, Frank MacManus, Brinsley MacNamara or Lord Dunsany will fare. Of all their output, the book which I feel is most likely to stand the test is Dunsany's *The Curse of the Wise Woman*.

A New Generation

Of the younger writers, Edna O'Brien, after a sensational start with two splendidly funny, naughty books, *The Country Girls* and *The Lonely Girl*, which made her reputation and turned her into somewhat of a sex symbol, has never recaptured her first, fine, careless rapture. John McGahern, with *The Barracks* and *The Dark* established himself as a novelist of great possibilities. *The Dark* was more sexually explicit than was usual in Ireland. His third novel, *The Leavetaking*, though highly praised in some quarters, displayed a certain ingenuousness that was disappointing. Aidan Higgins, who lives abroad, has not yet followed up the success of *Langrishe Go Down*. Thomas Kilroy, with, first a play, and then the novel *The Big Chapel*, has staked a claim in this open field.

But the writers that have sold best in recent years are James Plunkett with *Strumpet City*, a serious treatment of life in Dublin

A WAY WITH WORDS

in 1913. Close behind came Christy Brown, the malformed slum child, whose courage is prodigious and whose facility for language remarkable. His novels are a pastiche of Joyce, but closer to the kitchen sink. Also on the best-seller list has been Eilís Dillon's historical novel, *Across the Bitter Sea*. But none has written so good a novel as *Tarry Flynn*, by Patrick Kavanagh, the poet, when he first came to Dublin.

EATING AND DRINKING

Which is Mostly the Latter, and Why Not?

Ireland is a farming country noted for its meat, bacon, poultry, and dairy produce. The seas around it are full of fish, and so are its innumerable rivers and lakes. Add game in season, fresh fruit and vegetables, and you have a well-stocked larder. In fact the food is unsurpassed, and the cooking, which used to be the weak spot, is catching up with it.

It is the beef that most people go for, and the steaks are famous, but the mutton is excellent, and when there is spring lamb, it deserves attention. Salmon, trout and lobsters come fresh from the rivers or the sea, and the Dublin Bay prawns come from . . . guess where?

Oysters (only eaten "when there's an 'r' in the month") are ushered in every year with an oyster festival at Clarinbridge on Galway Bay; the Guinness to go with them is easily come by in Ireland, either by the bottle or on draught. (Another excellent ancillary to oysters—or to smoked salmon or prawns—is Irish wholemeal bread.) With the price of other crustaceans soaring, the humbler shellfish like mussels and periwinkles are gaining favor.

If you can find them, usually in a country restaurant, it is worth while trying more typically Irish dishes such as corned beef and carrots, boiled bacon and cabbage, or the traditional

EATING AND DRINKING

Irish stew. Other local delicacies are crubeens (pig's trotters), colcannon (basically a mixture of potatoes and cabbage cooked together), and soda-bread. Sometimes you may come across a soufflé flavored with carrageen, which is made from a variety of seaweed. And don't forget the ever-present and ever-delicious bacon.

Dublin is full of restaurants, besides those attached to the big hotels; most of them are small and not all are in fashionable areas. Outside Dublin there are very few well-known restaurants; except in the bigger cities like Belfast, Limerick and Cork, they are mostly in the hotels.

Dining out is not a habit of the ordinary Irishman. Even in Dublin a surprising number of men go home to their midday meal; for them, dinner is at midday, and the evening meal is known as "tea". It is a substantial tea, not differing much from any other meal except that tea is drunk with it, and this is the "high tea" that you see listed by some hotels as an alternative to late dinner. With a hearty breakfast, a good midday dinner, and a steak or chop for tea, it is no wonder that the intake of calories per head in Ireland is among the highest in the world.

On Being a Tea-too-taler

Tea-drinking is an Irish habit. Tea is drunk at all times of the day, and the tea is excellent if you like it hot, sweet, and strong. You can get good tea anywhere. Coffee is a more debatable proposition; there are many places where you can get really good coffee, and some that specialize in it, but in places where everybody else seems to be drinking tea, it is wiser to drink tea too.

One form of coffee that calls for special mention is Irish coffee. This life-saving invention consists of a glass of black coffee to which is added plenty of brown sugar and a measure of Irish whiskey, all topped off with a layer of cream. The cream is carefully poured (often over the back of a spoon) so as to float on the top. You don't stir it. You drink the hot whiskey-coffee through the cool cream, and the effect is unique.

As for drinking, that is a serious matter, and the visitor who takes it seriously will lose a lot of enjoyment if he merely goes on ordering the drinks he is used to at home. You can get almost any drink but the two staple ones are the distinctive Irish products, whiskey and stout.

Irish whiskey (correctly spelt with the "e") is generally straight pot-still whiskey, and it has a characteristic flavor, different from that of Scotch, bourbon, or rye. It is not drunk until it is at least seven years old—that is to say, it is not bottled until it has been at least seven years maturing in the wood—and it can be got ten, twelve, fifteen or even twenty years old. Drinkers differ about this question of age as much as about their habitual brands; a *Power's* man seldom ventures on *Jameson*, and a *Jameson* drinker seldom tries *Power*.

Jameson and *Power* are the two big Dublin distillers; there are other popular brands distilled in various parts of the country. For instance, Cork has its *Paddy* and Tullamore its *Dew* (with its accompanying liqueur, *Irish Mist*); *Old Bushmills* comes from the far north; *Midleton Reserve* is an Irish blend that's lighter in flavor than traditional Irish, while *Hewitt's* is rather akin to Scotch. The thing to remember about all of them is that they are best drunk neat, or with a little water. Also remember that the measure used in the republic is rather larger than that used in England—an Irish double is about equal to three English singles.

Getting Stout (and Stouter)

Even more popular than whiskey, though it has not so long a lineage in Ireland, is stout, and stout in this connection is almost synonymous with *Guinness's* Dublin stout. There are other stouts that have their following, but the most all-pervading is undoubtedly the black brew that comes from the two-hundred-year-old brewery in St. James's Gate.

Stout comes both in bottle and on draught; the really popular drink is the draught pint. The pint is rather more than half-a-liter and is quite a lot of drink, though most Irish drinkers seem to be able to drink quite a lot of pints. The pint is served slowly; the foam must be given time to settle and the glass filled up again. Stout can't be splashed out like beer!

Without doubt, Guinness tastes better in Ireland. Especially in a modest pint-house, which almost invariably charges the basic price, though you may pay more in the superior surroundings of the modernized lounges, road-houses and hotels.

All this applies to Dublin and to most parts of the republic, though there are places where the pint bottle replaces the draught pint, and places that are traditionally attached to ale. Once the Guinness was transported in wooden casks or barrels to be stored in the basements of pubs, but that day has gone and special metal kegs—known universally among Irish pub-men as "iron lungs"—have replaced the casks. A great part of the Midlands used to be served with the casks carried slowly on canal barges

EATING AND DRINKING

to "ports" on the River Shannon where, it was said, "It never tasted better."

Guinness is dominant, but in Cork and many parts of the South if you ask for stout it is probable that you'll get the Cork brew—"Murphy's" . . . and it's good. Stout drinkers in Ireland are traditionalists!

Getting back to Guinness: they have taken a number of small local breweries of ales under their wing, and while St. James's Gate in Dublin—the stout brewery—is headquarters and the home of Phoenix Ale, McArdle's Ale (a fine strong brew) still comes from Drogheda on the River Boyne, Cherry's from Waterford; Smithwick's (particularly good on draught) from St. Francis Abbey Brewery in Kilkenny; and, if you are a light beer drinker, Harp Lager is the most popular in its class; it is brewed in a Guinness plant in Dundalk.

It is not really necessary to have a taste for stout, porter or Irish whiskey to find a good deal of pleasure in visiting Irish pubs. For one thing, they have every kind of drink available, including, very often, a half-dozen different ales on draught. But apart from this, the atmosphere of a good pub is itself one of the features of the Irish scene, and experiencing it is one of the ways of enjoying a holiday in Ireland.

Ould Wans and Singing Pubs

Like the restaurants, the pubs in Ireland are more varied than they used to be; they cater for all classes, and for women as well as men. Not so many years ago, the typical Irish pub was a place of dark wood and austere furniture where women were not welcome, except for the "ould wans" who drank their bottle of stout in obscure little compartments known as "snugs". Now you are more likely to find a lounge bar with well-padded seats and contemporary pictures on the walls and with table service, but with women of all ages persisting in perching on stools at the bar.

It is not always easy now to find a traditional Irish pub. They are apt to be modernized almost overnight. Many were so redecorated years ago—in Dublin, for instance, *Davy Byrne's* in Duke Street off Grafton Street, known to all readers of Joyce's *Ulysses*. On the other hand, *Mulligan's* in Poolbeg Street, scene of the bitter story "Counterparts" in Joyce's *Dubliners,* is practically unchanged (at the time of writing), and is, incidentally, an excellent house for a pint.

In a category of their own are the singing pubs, where the drinking provides an added attraction to the song. Sometimes

THE IRISH SCENE

the patrons themselves do the singing, but the boom in folk music has brought in the custom of engaging professional ballad singers and groups, often highly accomplished. The best-known of these resorts is the *Abbey Tavern* at Howth, on the northern tip of Dublin Bay.

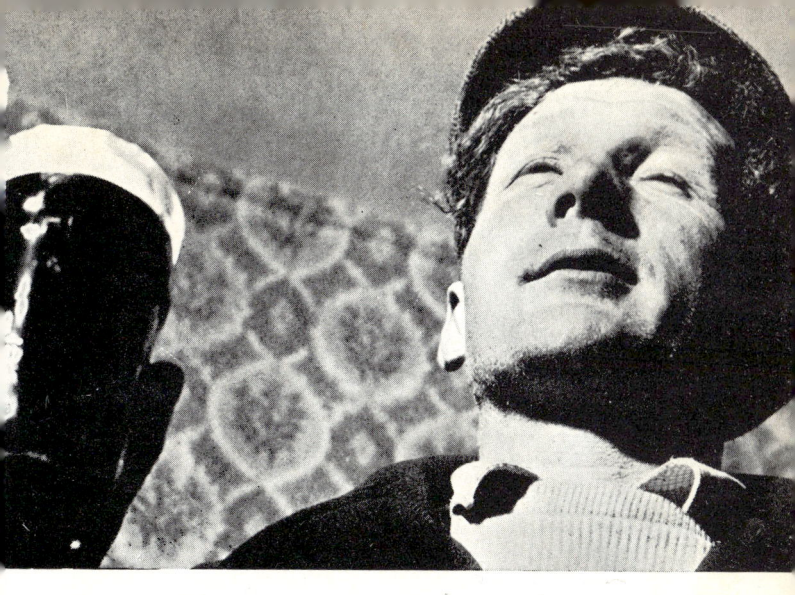

Great ballad singers, are the Irish, typified here at the Kilkenny Beer Festival; and as a toast in a Dublin "singing pub", what else but the national beverage, Guinness.

Across the river Liffey, Liberty Hall dominates the site of the old Hall, shelled out in the 1916 Easter Rising bombardment of Dublin.

Ready for a fast getaway from Dublin's famous Custom House, or for a leisurely tour, cabbies still wait on today's traveler.

You can live like a lord in one of Ireland's luxury castle hotels, such as Dromoland, or take to the road in a quaint horse-drawn caravan and explore the quiet byways of the countryside.

Drama in Ireland is at its best at the Abbey Theatre, where Synge's The Playboy of the Western World *is regularly performed.*

One of several castles offering hospitality to the visitor, that at Bunratty, near Shannon Airport, is famous for its medieval banquets.

Whether you visit Ireland for pageantry or for peace and quiet, you'll want to get away from Dublin's skirling pipes to quiet roads like this one in County Cork.

Hurling is the most popular Gaelic game, and the most dangerous.

THE SPORTSMAN'S PARADISE

A Formula of Horses, Fish, Fowl and Water

by

GARRY REDMOND

(*A former rugby player who tried Gaelic football and hurling at school, the author was sports editor of the* Irish Press *for several years. Now News Editor of* Radio Telefís Eireann (Irish National Broadcasting Service), *he also writes for the London newspaper,* The Observer.)

What distinguishes Ireland as a sporting country is not merely its achievements (though these are considerable for a nation so small) nor even the great variety of facilities it offers (and these are often unrivaled) but the character of the sporting atmosphere, primarily expressed in the universality of participation. Irish people have an unusual sporting sense—possibly something inherited in the race-memory from a war-like history, or from long association with the soil, or further back, from the ancient legends of Fionn and the Fianna, those great mythological huntsmen and heroes.

It is impossible to define its origins, but equally impossible not to feel it in the air. Wherever there is talk of golf or fishing, of horses or greyhounds—or any of a hundred-and-one national

THE IRISH SCENE

and international sports—you will find knowledge, appreciation, insight, and most of all, a willingness to talk, analyze and argue the toss. Your Irish sportsman, no matter what the sport is, invariably has participated at some age or other; as often as not, he is ready to back his instinctive judgment with a bet. This total involvement uniquely flavors any Irish sporting occasion, producing a sense of identification rarely found elsewhere; and this extends far beyond the particular day and place. Assessment, forecast, prognostication develop for days, even weeks, before the "off", then linger on in inquest and speculation long after the thing is over and done with, lost or won. If you come into a sporting company, you'll quickly find yourself directly involved, not only in the affairs at hand, but in a wider range of thoughts, theories and arguments. So, a day's fishing, or golfing, a day at Croke Park—for one of the big hurling or Gaelic football games —or at the races may give you more inside access to the mind and heart of Ireland than you'll get in a year of reading histories —or even guide books!

The widespread notion of Ireland as a "sportsman's paradise" derives principally from Ireland's pre-eminence as a country producing horses, fish and game. These merits in turn derive from accidents of geography, geology and climate; but the way they have been developed and the spirit in which they are indulged are unique—and Irish.

Angling

Éist le glór na h-abhann agus gheobhair breac, goes an old Irish saying. "Listen to the sound of the river, and you'll get a trout." It sounds like a fisherman's tale and you'll hear these wherever anglers meet. For so small a country, Ireland possesses enormous possibilities for the fishing visitor; so great, indeed, that their mere description is in danger of sounding like the fisherman's tale to end them all. There are thousands of miles of rivers, innumerable smaller lakes apart from the big inland "seas" of Loughs Corrib, Mask, Derg, Conn and Neagh and the Lakes of Killarney. The central limestone lowlands are traversed by deep slow rivers and in the mountains near the coast are upland loughs and myriad tumbling streams—a bewildering variety of waters offering salmon and trout to challenge the angler's art.

Brown Trout

For most Irish anglers, "fishing" means trout fishing, and

THE SPORTSMAN'S PARADISE

Ireland offers unrivaled sport in the pursuit of brown trout. They are found in every river and stream, in all lakes, big or small. As no rod license is required to fish them, they give some of the finest and cheapest angling in the world. They vary greatly from place to place in size, rate of growth, coloring and habits; all depends on the presence or absence of limestone. Thus, the fastest-growing brown trout are found in the clear limestone lakes of the Central Plain, principally in Loughs Sheelin, Derravaragh, Owel, Ennel, Arrow and Carra. They average over 2 lb. and may be as much as 4 lb. Trout of 8 lb. and upwards are regularly taken on the fly.

The less alkaline lakes like Corrib, Mask, Conn and Derg have trout averaging from 1 to 2 lb.—often much tastier than the bigger ones. And the flavor of a trout cooked on the open fire after a few hours on the water have sharpened your appetite! For the record if not for the pot, these last lakes also offer fast-growing, fish-eating Ferox-type trout which often reach over 30 lb. and are caught by spinning or trolling.

On the big lakes, you can have wet-fly fishing in March, April, early May and September and dry-fly angling in the summer evenings. Blow-line dapping with the natural mayfly is an uniquely Irish form of angling on these lakes—a form of madness, some say. The mayfly has as great a fascination for fishermen as for the fish and if the conditions are right, you'll hear of enormous catches and wonderful sport on midland and western lakes.

Trout fishing is free on many big lakes, such as Corrib, Mask, Carra, Conn, Arrow, Derg and the Lakes of Killarney. An enormous range of river and lake waters is controlled by the Inland Fisheries' Trust, a state-sponsored body set up for the purposes of preservation and research and operating in conjunction with local angling clubs; for a fee of £1 you can fish all the trust's waters. Minimum sizes are prescribed in most districts (usually 8 in. to 10 in.) and by some fisheries, and in a few cases, bag-limits are enforced. Brown trout fishing in all districts is prohibited before February 15. Many of the angling associations control lakes and stretches of rivers, and most are open to visitors who can get day tickets.

In the republic, the rainbow trout, native to the Pacific coast of North America, though introduced in the early years of this century, is not as widely distributed as in other countries. Experimental stockings have been made in a number of waters though and there is now good rainbow fishing in parts of Galway, Sligo, Kerry, Clare, Cork, Cavan and Offaly.

THE IRISH SCENE

A final cautionary word about the weather. There are often cold spells in spring which affect the fishing. Similarly, in summer we often get long hot spells, when the water in shallows and near the surface becomes quite warm and sends trout down in search of cooler conditions. So, a great deal will depend on the weather—as on the individual angler's skill.

Salmon Fishing

Salmon enter all Irish rivers and most streams of any size flowing into the sea. The sight from the bridge by the new cathedral in Galway of salmon queuing nose to tail, fin to fin, waiting to go up into Lough Corrib, is surely one of the timeless wonders of all Ireland. The salmon's mysterious ways offer the game fisherman good sport from the first of the year right through to mid-October. The Liffey opens on January 1, literally in the dark of winter morning. The Bundrowes in County Donegal also opens on January 1, so the New Year angler sneaking a few days on to his Christmas break can reasonably get some salmon fishing in mid-winter.

Some rivers have good spring fishing—March and April are often the best—though there usually are fair numbers of fish in some waters as early as January. So-called "spring" salmon are fish which will have spent two years at sea and are from 8 to 12 lb., according to the river. Bigger fish, which have been three or even four years at sea and may run from 15 to 30 lb. plus, are common in some rivers. And most "spring" rivers also have fresh-run fish in summer and autumn—but it all depends on where you are; local knowledge, which will be gladly shared, is best.

Note, by the way, that some rivers fish well right from the official opening day, but that others may have only a few clean fish until later in the season. In many waters, therefore, kelts (or spent salmon) may be numerous early on, and as these are protected by law, they must be returned alive to the water.

Among the best of the spring rivers are the Boyne, the Slaney, the Nore, Suir and Munster Blackwater. For summer salmon fishing, the best waters are the smaller lake and river systems of Counties Kerry, Donegal and Connemara.

Most Irish rivers can be fished from the bank or by wading; but on some big rivers, a boat is needed in some stretches. The usual methods are fly-fishing, spinning, prawning and worming. On some rivers (or certain sections of particular rivers), lures

THE SPORTSMAN'S PARADISE

other than fly or other specified methods are prohibited by local rule at fixed times of the year. In some cases, the use of a gaff with rod and line is forbidden, and here the angler will need either a tailer or a net—and, of course, don't forget the "priest" (club) to kill your fish on the bank.

The finest salmon fisheries are, of course, preserved, but in many of them day tickets can be had. Others are owned by hotels and reserved for guests, either "for free" or for an additional charge. There is free fishing (apart from hire of boats) on a number of lakes, for instance Loughs Corrib and Boliska (County Galway); Conn and Cullin (County Mayo); the Lakes of Killarney and Loughs Caragh and Currane in County Kerry; and in County Donegal on Loughs Fern, Gartan and Gweebara Lough. Parts of the Barrow River are free; so, too, are some of the upper reaches of the Nore; and there is a great range of "ticket waters" from Kerry to Donegal and throughout Mayo and Connemara.

Much fairly good to excellent river and lake fishing is controlled by salmon-angling clubs, some of which also have rights to a certain number of rods for the season or on special days each week on privately-owned fisheries. Visitors can often avail themselves of these facilities through daily, weekly or monthly tickets.

Sea Trout

Sea trout—or, as they are called in Ireland, white trout—abound in the little lakes and smaller rivers around the coast, particularly in Donegal, Connemara, Kerry and West Cork. In some places, they run as early as May, but their best months are July, August and September. They don't run very large—$\frac{1}{4}$ lb. to 2 lb. (the current Irish record is 14 lb. 3 oz.)—but you can catch a lot of them, and they're a highly spirited fighting fish. As with salmon, the best sea trout fishing is preserved, either by private owners who let it by the month, week or day, or by hotels which reserve it for their guests. Some angling associations control good sea trout fishing and there is good free angling for sea trout on certain lakes, as, for example, in Lough Currane and Caragh Lake in Kerry and also on some rivers. Many coastal streams are free and offer good sea trout, particularly after flood. Sea trout can in some places be caught in salt water and such fishing is, for the most part, free—an outstanding example is the mouth of the Moy, near Ballina in County Mayo; but here again, local knowledge and direction are your best guides.

FISHING CENTERS OF IRELAND

○ COARSE FISHING
● SEA ANGLING
✱ SALMON FISHING

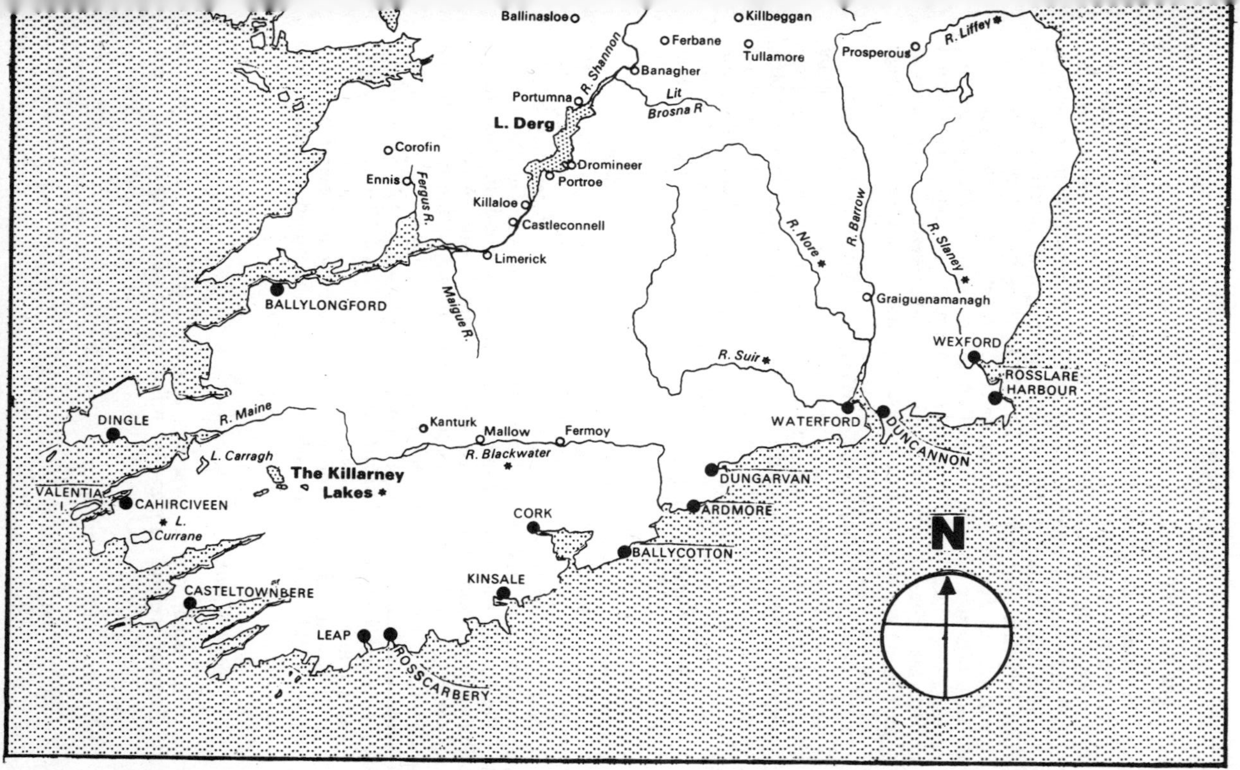
Ballinasloe
Killbeggan
Ferbane
Tullamore
Prosperous
R. Liffey
R. Shannon
Banagher
Portumna
Lit
Brosna R
L. Derg
Corofin
Dromineer
Ennis
Fergus R.
Portroe
Killaloe
Castleconnell
R. Nore
R. Barrow
R. Slaney
Limerick
Maigue R.
BALLYLONGFORD
Graiguenamanagh
WEXFORD
R. Suir
ROSSLARE
HARBOUR
R. Maine
DINGLE
Kanturk
Mallow
Fermoy
WATERFORD
DUNCANNON
L. Carragh
R. Blackwater
The Killarney
Lakes
DUNGARVAN
VALENTIA
I.
CAHIRCIVEEN
ARDMORE
CORK
L.
Currane
N
BALLYCOTTON
KINSALE
CASTELTOWNBERE
LEAP
ROSSCARBERY

Sea Angling

Although its exploitation is relatively recent, sea angling in Ireland has developed to the stage that it offers some of the most exciting and rewarding sport in Europe. The waters around Ireland's deeply-indented 2,000 miles of coastline teem with a remarkable variety of fish which may be got either from the shore or in boats. Ballycotton in County Cork is one center known to sea anglers for 50 years or more. In recent years, the sport has been organized by the formation of the Irish Federation of Sea Anglers, which now promotes a number of big international festivals. These have produced remarkable results; every season brings new record catches, new specimens, and new knowledge of this fascinating game.

In addition to Ballycotton, Westport, Achill and Kinsale, in particular, have acquired a cosmopolitan flavor from the many continental fishermen who come for deep-sea sport. It's a great experience to join the armadas that go out in search of conger, skate, monkfish, tope, blue shark, porbeagle and thresher. It takes a strong head and stout sea legs to cope with the combination of a rolling Atlantic swell under you and the powerful aroma of the "rubby-dub" mixture of oil, bran and fish offal which is the shark's peculiar delicacy.

There is also wonderful surf fishing, particularly for bass, on quiet, uncrowded beaches. Bass usually come between 3 lb. and 7 lb., except that if you run into a "school", some will be around $1\frac{1}{2}$ lb. or less. Bass of over 10 lb. are frequent. Their best season is June to September, but in many places they can be caught from mid-April to the end of October. On the Dingle Peninsula, the bass fishing is particularly good in November, December and March. Bass abounds from County Wexford on the southeast corner (traveling westwards) round to the north of the Dingle Peninsula. The Irish record bass (16 lb. 6 oz.) was caught off the Giant's Causeway on the northeast coast. Bass which measures less than 14 inches must be returned alive to the water as a conservation measure.

It is also advisable for sea-anglers coming to Ireland to bring their tackle with them rather than send it on in advance: this sounds pessimistic, but it may save delays.

Coarse Fishing

In recent years, overseas anglers have been astonished to discover Ireland's miles and miles of coarse fishing waters teem-

THE SPORTSMAN'S PARADISE

ing with pike, perch, bream and rudd. To fishermen used to returning catches alive to the water, the abundance and fighting strength of Irish coarse fish (a generic term covering many fish not bred for improvement) will be surprising: for this reason, and because Irish species come big, the visiting angler should use stronger gear when fishing here. The central and north midlands provide the best coarse fishing in slow-moving limestone rivers and lakes, especially in Cavan, Monaghan, Longford, Westmeath and Upper Shannon. As these parts are off the main tourist track, the fisherman will often have the quiet countryside all to himself.

Over forty centers are now organized, with local associations to help the angler. Apart from *The Anglers' Information Service* of Bord Fáilte, *The Irish Specimen Fish Committee* records all notable fish taken in Irish waters and about 65 percent of all claims ratified come from people living outside Ireland.

Debt in the Afternoon

Racing, inevitably, is in purely quantitative terms the most widespread Irish sporting interest. The fame of the Irish thoroughbred is world-wide. Limestone beneath Irish grass, they say, has produced the marvelous specimens of animal that have put Ireland's name in the international records wherever horses are raced. Maybe limestone in the bone has given your Irish racegoer his love and judgment of good animals, and, further, has ingeniously brought the sport of kings to the reach of the common man. The Irish Racing Board, a state-sponsored body, with the long-standing Irish Turf Club, regulates Irish racing, plowing back money levied on the betting to improve facilities for racegoers, owners and trainers alike.

The Curragh track, set on the great rolling plain of Kildare, is the Newmarket, Ascot, Chantilly and Longchamps of Ireland all in one. On its fine galloping track are staged the Irish classics —*1,000 and 2,000 Guineas, Oaks, Derby* and *St. Leger,* which attract the cream of Irish and overseas three-year-olds. The *Irish Sweeps Derby,* reconstituted in 1962 through the sponsorship of the world-famous Irish Hospitals' Sweep, is now one of the richest classic races in Europe. (It was, incidentally, the first race to be televised live by satellite to the U.S.A.) It is run at the end of June or beginning of July and attracts a crowd of nearly 50,000 people, a wonderful occasion demonstrating not only Irish sport at its best, but also Ireland's flair for organizing a vast, significant social and sporting occasion.

THE IRISH SCENE

Throughout the summer flat-race season, regular fixtures at the Curragh, Phoenix Park, Leopardstown and many provincial tracks offer wonderful sport, within the reach of most pockets. The holiday meet at Galway—scene of the famous *Galway Plate* and *Galway Hurdle* races at the end of July—is a long-standing institution. Likewise the Phoenix Park meetings in Dublin's *Horse Show Week* in August.

Hitting the Jackpot

In winter there is steeplechasing and hurdling, with the rich *Irish Sweeps Hurdle* at Christmas the biggest event of the season. It is in Ireland that leading jumpers prepare for the big Cheltenham and Aintree prizes—and a day at Navan, Leopardstown, Naas, Mullingar, Mallow, Gowran Park, Limerick or "The Junction" will provide racing at its best, among knowledgeable, keen-eyed racing folk. The structure of the Irish betting system, too, provides painless method of extraction and a good chance of fortune. The "tote" method of mechanical betting is easy to operate; variations include the "forecast," "tote double" and the "jackpot", in which you try to nominate in advance the winners of four races. The jackpot has often paid four-figure dividends for 25 pence, so you've a chance of making more than your holiday expenses! In addition to the tote there are the bookmakers, a colorful and characteristic part of the racing scene. Betting with the "books" at the track offers the heady pleasure of the floor of the Stock Exchange, the Bourse or Wall Street plus an unparalleled line of Joycean wit and repartee which no slot machine can give. And if you can't get to the course, you can still race vicariously through the betting shops, the licensed offices at which you can have your afternoon flutter from afar.

Two great institutions of Irish racing are absolute "musts" for Easter and spring visitors. The first of these is Fairyhouse, on Easter Monday and Tuesday: the annual fixture of the Ward Union Hunt Committee, a marvelous holiday event, held every year in County Meath, barely twenty miles from Dublin. There you will see the *Irish Grand National* and other jumping races featuring the cream of the year's steeplechasing crop. At the end of April is held Punchestown, annual meeting of the Kildare and National Steeplechase Committee, a great 'chasing carnival, traditionally regarded as the ultimate in point-to-pointing. Time was when this was the hosting of all the point-to-pointers, but changing economics have made it more of a regular race meeting. Yet it remains a gloriously gay and lively fixture—peer-

THE SPORTSMAN'S PARADISE

less Punchestown! It is traditionally the climax of the point-to-point season (from late January to mid-April), in which all the leading hunts clubs throughout the country hold their own meetings over ditch, wall, bank and fence courses; they are small, but to true enthusiasts significant and intimately sociable gatherings, at which you may expect to see the future stars of the 'chasing world take their first competitive steps.

Hunting Informally

Hunting in Ireland has had an astonishing revival, especially in the way it is attracting more young riders. It's no longer necessary to own your own mount: experienced horses can be hired and transported to meets, and most of the major hunts welcome visitors. The Galway Blazers, the "Killing" Kildares, the Scarteen "Black-and-Tans", and the Ward Union are famous wherever hunting is known. Whether over the stone walls of Galway or the banks and ditches of Kildare or Limerick, in pursuit of fox or stag or "drag", Irish hunting retains all its great atmosphere, life and color. Hunting is less formal in Ireland than elsewhere; as one hard-riding country gentleman has said, "You come to follow the hounds, not to be a bloody fashion show!" So, it's how you *go*, not how you *look* that counts.

In several areas, the hunting visitor can arrange an all-expense stay at small hotels, which will organize mounts, transport and special terms for temporary membership. In all, Ireland has 41 recognized harrier packs, two staghound packs and 32 packs of foxhounds—plus 10 groups of foot beagles. Cub hunting, to train newcomers—equine, canine and equestrian—usually starts in August or September and the season proper runs from November until April. Subscriptions for the whole season vary among packs from around £10 to £50, and cap money for each meet ranges from 50p to £5.

The Horsey Set

The quality of Irish horses and riders is known, too, in the international show-jumping scene, and the annual *Horse Show Week* in August, at the Royal Dublin Society's famous enclosure at Ballsbridge, is a unique social and sporting festival in which the horse is undisputed king. Climax of a week of competitions which regularly attract leading riders from Britain, the continent and America is the *Aga Khan Challenge Trophy* (Nations Cup) on the Friday of this wonderful week.

THE IRISH SCENE

Apart from the great Dublin Horse Show, there are, for show-yard enthusiasts, local gymkhanas all over the country, and in mid-August another important occasion is developing at Punchestown—the *Irish Olympic Horse Trials,* an international three-day event and dressage test, which is a reminder that Ireland won the world team championship at the 1966 Burghley Horse Trials.

So, you're keen, in this land of the horse, to do a bit of riding or hacking yourself? Almost everywhere, you'll find yourself not very far from a riding school or stables where you can hire a mount for a couple of hours and have a go over the "sticks".

In some places, also, you can arrange pony-trekking or trail-riding holidays, an ideal, lazy way to spend a few days among the quiet hills and valleys, and really get off the beaten track. The rates vary, but generally they're all-inclusive, to cover horses, feed, accommodation, grooms and so on. Any riding school or stable will point you in the right direction.

Shooting

Ireland offers much to the game shot, though the old notion of Ireland as a shooting paradise must be amended. There are wild duck, snipe, woodcock, pheasant, grouse, plover and geese; but in recent years, stocks have been depleted by a variety of causes (land division, reclamation and forestry development, for instance). In some cases, one fears, the depletion has been caused by indiscriminate blazing-away by many foreign guns who have come to believe that the shooting on Ireland's wild and lonely hills and bogs is free. There has even been slaughter of non-game species—thrush, blackbird, starlings and so on; as though anything that flies can be shot! Local gun clubs and private owners preserve and conserve the best shooting; so, if you want shooting, proceed with caution. Cartridge suppliers (usually the local angling shop) or your hotel will advise you.

Golf

For variety of courses, from tiger links to verdant, amiable inland park courses, Ireland offers golfers some of the finest and cheapest sport in the world. In all, there are over 200 clubs affiliated to the Golfing Union of Ireland. In Dublin there are nine courses, and another 19 in the county including the famous

THE SPORTSMAN'S PARADISE

Portmarnock links (which has housed the British Amateur Open, the Dunlop Masters', the Canada Cup and Alcan championships) and Royal Dublin, both less than half an hour from the city center. On one of the major championship courses in June or August is the Carroll's £15,000 event, a big professional competition which attracts the stars from the British tournament circuit.

Cork City has four clubs; and all the famous championship courses are within striking distance of the main centers. Big amateur title events are played each year, and there is no more truly golfing spirit to be found than among the crowds at, say, Rosses Point for the west of Ireland, at Lahinch for the south, or at Royal Portrush, or for that matter, at Royal County Down, Baltray, Rosslare, Tramore, Little Island, Killarney or wherever the tournament is.

Most clubs welcome visitors and by standards elsewhere, green-fees are still low; no fee at all is needed to enjoy the sporting welcome the merest stranger will find from the club's honorary secretary right through to the youngest urchin-cut caddy (though nowadays, caddies tend to be a dwindling breed). So, whether you want to watch or play, Irish golf is full of possibilities—a golfing holiday will introduce you not only to some superb scenery, but to some of the most sporting and friendly acquaintances to be met in many a day's march. Some of the world's finest golf, incidentally, is played in the bar—Ireland's 19th Hole is open to all; so, if play is rained off, just keep your head down and follow through!

Going to the Dogs

Another Irish institution which has become an industry is the greyhound. The export of greyhounds to America, Britain and Europe has given an old sport new life and the winter visitor will enjoy the unique atmosphere of Ireland's many coursing meets, held from late October to February. The "open" coursing, in which the dogs course hares flushed out of the winter pastures by teams of beaters, has been largely superseded by "park" coursing, in which the hare is released from an enclosure and the dogs are "slipped" after it to the "escape", though a few traditional open meets still survive. From Liscannor, in County Clare, to the *Irish Cup* at Clounanna, County Limerick, and the *National Meeting* at Clonmel, in February you'll find exciting sport at local spots all round Ireland.

From early spring until late autumn, you have greyhound racing at tracks in Dublin, Belfast, Cork and almost every major

THE IRISH SCENE

town. Here the dogs chase the electric hare round a floodlit track, over distances from 525 up to 700 yards. It is a tense, quick-fire sport which combines much of the magic of racing with a curious sense of ritual. The meetings are at night and the floodlit track assumes something of the hypnotic fascination of the gaming-table's green-baize—particularly as you can win quite a tidy sum on the tote, the mechanical betting system which is just like that at horse racing. A night "at the dogs" at Shelbourne Park or Harold's Cross in Dublin, or Dunmore or Celtic Parks in Belfast, or at any of the provincial tracks is an experience to stir the old pulse; moreover, there is no better place to rub shoulders with the man in the street.

A curious canine rite peculiar to Cork and South Kerry is drag-hunting. Here, terrier packs race cross-country style after an aniseed trail laid in advance—hence "drag", for the scent is put down by dragging a sack or some anointed lump of meat the night before. Hundreds follow on foot as the packs from various clubs race helter-skelter over a course of up to eight to ten miles. Enquire at the local pub. It's worth watching even if you don't follow.

For Water-Lovers

Sailing and rowing regattas are a picturesque part of Ireland's summer scene. The Royal Cork Yacht Club is the oldest in the world—founded in 1720. There are sailing clubs all round the south and east coasts from Baltimore to Portrush in the north of Antrim. In Dublin, the big center is Dún Laoghaire, where the armada of boats from ocean cruisers to dinghies is now counted in hundreds—the regular races are a wonderful sight!

In recent years, Ireland's wonderful inland waterways have been highly developed; sailing and cruising on the Shannon and its lakes offer uncrowded pleasure for the waterman who wants to get away from it all. It's possible to go by boat from Dublin right through the heart of the midlands and either south to near Limerick (Killaloe, on Lough Derg is now a water-sport center) or north up the Shannon to Carrick-on-Shannon. On this marvelous chain of rivers and lakes, holidays are available on comfortable, slow-moving converted barges—an idyllic escape from the crowds.

Rowing club regattas like the *Trinity Regatta* in May, on the Liffey at Islandbridge, or the *Metropolitan* on the Blessington Lake, or any of the championship events at Belfast, Coleraine, Drogheda, Carrick, Carlow, Waterford, Cappoquin, Cork, Limer-

THE SPORTSMAN'S PARADISE

ick or Galway provide splendid spectacle and social gaiety at the "afterwards" parties.

Many small harbor towns stage local regattas in which the racing is in seine-boats, skiffs or currachs—the remarkable lath-and-canvas craft in which the traditional fishermen of the west brave the Atlantic—instead of the slender river-racing "fine" or "clinker" outriggers. It's less sophisticated, but a wonderfully real and atmospheric sport—a regular community carnival. The currach races, which are often held at Salthill in Galway, attract thousands.

Hurling and Football

Summer visitors may think the time out of joint if they hear talk of football: this is Gaelic football, which, with hurling, is Ireland's main national summer game. From early June to September, county teams compete in the *All-Ireland Championships* and the big games—a *Munster Hurling Final* or the *All-Ireland Semi-Finals* and *Finals* at Croke Park, Dublin—are huge sporting occasions which reach out to every part of the community.

Both games call for fifteen-a-side. Hurling, in which a leather ball or *sliotar* is hurled with a *camán* (an ash-stick with curved broad striking base or *boss*), is perhaps the most thrilling, certainly the fastest field game in the world.

Gaelic football is faster than soccer or rugby or the American grid-iron version. As in hurling, scores can be got by getting the ball either under or over the bar, and as there are no stoppages for injuries, it can be a superb, quicksilver spectacle. Traditionally the All-Ireland Hurling Final is at Croke Park on the first Sunday in September, the Gaelic Final at the same great ground on the last Sunday in September. So if you're in Dublin then, don't miss either.

Odds and Ends

For off-beat, out-of-doors activities, Ireland is the place to come. Rolling mountains, hills and valleys are open to all; the walker or scrambler—even the rock-climber—will find a congenial countryside beckoning. *An Oige*, the Irish branch of the International Youth Hostel Association, has many hostels amid the choicest walking country; a note to An Oige, 39 Mountjoy Square, Dublin 1, will get you full information.

For mid-winter visitors, there are the rugby internationals at

THE IRISH SCENE

Lansdowne Road. Though the leading soccer teams (mostly part-time professionals) may not be as accomplished as the full-time paid players of Britain and the continent, they provide exciting football—and an afternoon at Dalymount Park in Dublin, or Windsor Park, Belfast, or at any of the provincial grounds, will bring one close to the man-in-the-street fervor of this universal game.

Through the benefit of the North Atlantic Drift—that curious northerly branch-line of the Gulf Stream—open-sea swimming, particularly on the south and west coasts, is perhaps the most exhilarating in northern Europe. Quiet coves and beaches, little rocky inlets of golden sand and blue-green water can, if you judge the angle of the wind, outdo the Mediterranean. And a high-tide morning at the Forty Foot—the rocky inlet near Sandycove, beyond Dún Laoghaire, where James Joyce set the opening chapter of *Ulysses*—will provide the swim of a lifetime.

If you play tennis, bowls (lawn-style and outdoor, not the American indoor tenpins style), pitch-and-putt you'll find facilities in most of the big centers.

The Key to Sporting Ireland

Is túisce deoch ná scéal—"Have a drink first, then let's talk," is the practical advice of an old Irish saying. So, the sportsman, whether hunter, shooter, fisher, golfer, birdwatcher, camper, caravaner, sailor, bowler or what not, should make a point of seeking out the local pub. The Irish tavern is not merely to be regarded as a local filling station in the national network of drink providers—more than the "local" anywhere else, it is a place of chat and sociability, where you will find in the wealth of information, advice and guidance, the immediate key to whatever sporting problem you face. The pub, particularly in small country towns and villages, is the nerve center of the community and represents, as it were, a chapel of ease in the whole sporting liturgy. If you come to Ireland on a holiday and don't establish a base in the local "boozer", your journey, no matter how many monuments you tick off, how many fish you kill or how many holes you play, may well have been in vain—and remember *Bould Thady Quill*!

SHOPPING IN IRELAND

Where "Home-Made" Means "Best"

Ireland has long held a high reputation for her tweeds and hand-made lace, but the visitor today will find a great deal more to entice him to shop all over the country, for Ireland is a country of craft workers who produce a wide range of items of quality in both modern and traditional styles.

The Irish Tourist Board, in order to retain the high standards of Irish craft goods, has accepted over six hundred special lines of souvenir items, all of which are characteristic of Ireland and no place else. There has also been concern to ensure that not only is the variety wide but also that the price ranges suit the pockets of budget-conscious visitors. Apart from the city and country shops, the airport shops at Dublin, Cork and Shannon have good stocks.

The Cloth of Kings

Tweed is, however, almost an automatic purchase with most visitors to Ireland. Irish tweed comes in a variety of weights, from the gossamer, cobweb tweed used for blouses, stoles and evening wear, to the enduring, tough type used for sportswear and outerwear. One can have a jacket or suit made to measure in tweed at reasonable prices within a matter of days. The visitor can watch the fabric being woven at the various tweed centers in the capital or provinces, and can select his own designs to be woven specially for him. Pre-packaged tweed lengths for skirts, also in a range of fabric weights, are perfect gifts for those at home.

Rivaling Harris for its fame as a producer of tweed is Donegal. It is an age-old cloth, with a history that goes far back into the romantic mists of Irish legend, making splendid the High Kings of Ireland and sailing in the capacious holds of Brabant merchantmen to warm the rich burghers of medieval Europe.

The people of Donegal, proud and stubborn, suffered want and deprivation for centuries. Then, about a hundred years ago, from the craft of weaving that had clung tenaciously to life, sprang the chance of prosperity for the incredibly poor peasants of the area. A series of brilliant and commercially-aware reformers tapped the age-old subconscious of the people and created a cottage industry which, in the last eighty years, has become a world-ranking tweed producer.

The work is still, basically—and literally—in the hands of "out-workers", people who weave in their own homes. The factories produce the designs, finish the woven cloth by the latest, most scientific, methods, and ensure the even quality of the total output, but the tweed that is made into jackets and skirts and proudly worn all over the world, is still the product of the Donegal Handwoven Tweed Association. It is the case of a craft treasured by the people of Donegal for centuries, coming to the rescue of their descendants in the hour of their greatest need.

Beauty from Necessity

One of the most popular (and certainly one of the most practical) things that you can buy in Ireland would be something knitted on Aran. No one would call Aran the gentlest island in the world, but as a place for invention and skill, perseverance and determination, there are very few to beat it.

The Aran fisherman lives with death and exposure as his everyday companions. He fishes from a wee, fragile craft called a *curragh,* a fantasy construction of canvas and wickerwork, that needs a degree of skill to handle second only to steering a kayak through rapids, and perhaps not even second. The seas he rides are violent and often shark-infested, beaten with cold, driving rain. The answer that the fisher families came up with was the Aran sweater, which might just keep out sharks, and has no trouble whatever in repelling wind, rain and cold.

SHOPPING IN IRELAND

Aran sweaters are created by a people who are not only hardy but very religious, and so the *bainin*, or raw, unbleached wool, is knitted into garments that use religious symbols and folk motifs in their patterns. The Tree of Life, the Honeycomb (standing for thrift and thought to be lucky), the Sea-house, Blackberry—all are patterns in the almost sculptured, deeply-knitted work that so characterizes the Aran method.

You can, of course, get garments which are called 'Aran-Knit' in many parts of the world, but the true, native produced garment, so redolent with oil that it is waterproof, is worth traveling all the way to Ireland to find.

For the home knitter who would like to combine tweed with a personal touch, there are skirt packs available that come with co-related, ready-balled wool.

Beauty from Flax

Linen has been an Irish fabric for centuries, at least as far back as the thirteenth, and possibly way further back than that. It is one of the crafts of the ancient world, as the delicate fabrics found in Egyptian tombs testify, and found its way to Ireland, quite early on, like so many good things.

But the linen industry really got started in Ireland during the reign of Charles I who, through his favorite, Stafford, took an interest in the matter. They appointed Louis Crommelin, a refugee Huguenot and a skilled weaver, to act as "industrial consultant". The British Isles, in general, owe a tremendous debt to the Huguenots. They were weavers *par excellence,* who, driven from their homes because their Protestant faith did not sort with the vicious bıgotry of the age, found asylum and a totally new field for their endeavours in Britain.

Crommelin was obviously a man of great skill and imagination, who traveled around the countryside showing the Irish farmers better and cheaper ways of growing the flax from which linen is made. He found ways to improve the quality of the flax seed, engineered machinery to work the looms, using the abundant water power in the streams of Ireland, and even introduced a fairer way of measuring the yarn which was on sale in the local markets. Not content with all these very basic improvements in the newly growing industry, he realised that much depended on the wives of the farmers that grew the flax. They were the backbone of the cottage industry, since not only did they help with the actual making of the cloth, but they also did the bleaching, using buttermilk and a lye that was produced in a way that seems medieval today, namely dissolving the ash from burnt seaweed in water. Needless to say, there are more convenient, if less colorful ways of doing it today.

Of all the linen that leaves the mills of Ireland, the "damask" is the loveliest. The name probably came from the Syrian city of Damascus, which was a vital center in the Middle Ages for trade in lovely fabrics, brocades and silks. Damascus also gave its name to the process of "damascening", which is the inlay of steel with precious metals; rather like a metal brocade, in fact. It is the damask table-cloth which has carried the fame of Ireland's linen industry all over the world, and its manufacture is a long, intricate process. Not least is the preparation of a series of cards, very like computer cards, which control the rise and fall of the warp threads in the machine, and so allow the design to take shape in the cloth. There are two kinds of damask, single and double. The double is the more desirable, as it usually has more threads to the square inch, and therefore better durability.

Nowadays, Irish linen manufacturers do not use linen fibers only. They also produce cloth which is a combination of linen and other, often man-made, fibers. It is worth making quite sure exactly what the composition of the cloth is before buying. Fabrics that have no linen in them at all are sometimes advertised as having "the linen look".

Lace and Rugs

Irish lace and Irish crochet is now high fashion all over the world. Delicate hand-made blouses and dresses in Irish crochet cost considerably less in Ireland than anywhere else, and all the beautiful rose, shamrock and Clones knot patterns are used. Lace collar and cuff sets also feature old Irish designs, and craft lace work has developed considerably once again, despite the long hours of hand work involved.

Knitted goods from Irish hand craft workers include accessories and soft furnishing items. Aran wool handbags and carry bags, ties, gloves, scarves and cravats are only some of the lines you will find in the stores. Tweed is another fabric which has moved into the home. Irish tweed scatter cushions, rugs, table mats, tweed-piece pictures of Irish scenery, bed covers, lightweight dressing gowns which pack into a small space, are some of the many objects especially popular.

Rugs for the home come in Irish fleece, Irish calf skin, Lumra, tweed and Irish mohair. Batik wall hangings are one of the newer gift lines; these are based on traditional Irish

SHOPPING IN IRELAND

designs in brilliant colorings. You will also find good examples of traditional Celtic designs embroidered on cushion covers of bainin.

Pottery and Marble

Pottery, both useful and ornamental, comes in quantity and has considerable individuality. A charming novelty, too, are the crested door knobs with heraldic emblems which would give an individual look to any home.

Gifts in Irish marble are another appealing range of craft souvenirs. These include ornaments such as ashtrays and bookends, statuary and carved pieces. Really beautiful jewelry in Irish silver, inset with Connemara marble, includes such items as cufflinks, pins, brooches, pendants and bracelets in hundreds of designs. Jewelry, particularly, has much to offer the shopper—copper work is of high quality, and Irish marcasite and semi-precious stones are widely used by craftworkers who specialize in jewelry with a charmingly traditional influence. There are many beautiful pieces in enamel set in silver- and copper-work, as well as intricately-worked beaten silver designs decorating bracelets and necklaces. Here, especially, one cannot but be impressed by the use of old Irish designs, some taken from the ancient Book of Kells, others given a very skillful modern interpretation by modern craftsmen. The Tara Brooch, a reproduction of the famed brooch in the National Museum, is a well-liked model, but you will find other variants in different parts of the country.

Silver and Glass

Irish silver is a highly prized gift and whether it is antique or modern, you will find much to choose from, not only in the many reliable antique shops (a number of whom specialize in old Irish silver), but in the more modern silversmiths' or gift shops, where souvenir pieces are on sale. The silver "potato ring", in fact a ring for holding a dish, is a characteristically Irish nineteenth-century piece and many are very beautiful examples of the silversmith's art. The sturdy blackthorn stick or *shillelagh*, one of the earliest Irish souvenirs sought by the visitor, is cheap to buy, as are briar pipes and smoking accessories of Irish woods.

Many visitors are enchanted by the range of souvenir dolls dressed in national costume and in their travels like to add to their existing collections. Ireland has them, too—the clothes completely authentic in design and content, the regional outfits accurate in every detail.

Ireland is proud of its tradition in glass, notably Waterford glass. All over Ireland, this beautiful cut glass is on sale, but again, in the country's capital, in its main shopping thoroughfare, Grafton Street, some of the big stores make a specialty of displaying it. If glass takes your fancy, there is also a good selection of Dublin and Galway crystal; and within the past few years the production of Tyrone crystal has been developed in the North and some excellent craftwork is available.

If you are a sports enthusiast, you will be well taken care of with equipment for your particular interest, particularly if you hunt or fish. Practically every town near a good river or good hunting country contains a well-equipped sports stockist.

Small lines to pack in the corner of a suitcase include attractive woodcarvings, crested and enameled keyrings, paper knives, all of them keenly priced and well designed. Souvenir prices range from about 25p to £85, according to the Irish Tourist Board, for the items they have accepted as being up to their standard of quality and design. You can still find the vulgar-looking leprechauns and garishly-painted Irish cottage style of souvenir for sale—but with the wide selection of real craft lines offered, the visitor can easily avoid the commonplace lines imported from outside the country.

The Country Crafts

We have talked about many products of Ireland, lace, knits, tweed, pottery, and you must be realizing that, to support such a varied output, there must be hundreds upon hundreds of people, working quietly away in the depths of the country, using their talents and inherited skills to create attractive, functional work. And you would be right, there are. It is not just the tweed weavers of Donegal who have turned the crafts of their fathers to good account. All over the country there are craftsmen and women drawing on centuries of knowledge and expertise. Here are a few of the places to go to find some of these artists at work.

In the Rosses, on the Atlantic shore of Donegal, nearly every girl and her mother knits whatever she is doing, whether just sitting or walking behind her cows. To them, knitting is just a normal human process, with the needles merely an extension of their fingers.

We have mentioned the sweaters of Aran, but they have

SHOPPING IN IRELAND

another craft there, the making of colorful belts, called *crios*. Just as with the patterns in the sweaters, the colors and design have deep significance, bestowing magic protection on the wearer.

Basket weaving is not the kind of craft that many travelers take much interest in, usually because the end products are too bulky to carry home. Maneuvering a large basket under the seat of a transatlantic jet calls for a very special kind of dexterity. Which is a pity, because Ireland, land of streams and lakes, is an ideal country for growing rushes, the basic component of baskets.

However, basketry does not only produce baskets; table mats, dishes, attractive statuary, all can be made from *scirpus lacustries;* the basket rush. St. Brigid, patron saint of spinners and weavers, has a lovely cross called after her, made of woven rushes. In Wicklow the weavers use split oak and hazel saplings instead of rushes, and this craft often goes hand-in-hand with wood carving. Ian and Imogen Stuart, a young woodcarver and his wife, live in the forests of Wicklow, looking out over the valley to Glendaloch, and produce lovely work in an art form that has provided beauty and practicality for centuries.

At Carley's Bridge in Wexford, there is a pottery that has been in the same family for more than four hundred years, the clay being thrown on the same wheel by generation after generation of the same dexterous clan. By contrast, there is a fairly new pottery in Terrybawn, County Mayo, where Grattan Freyer has set up his workshop. Using local clay (it's always the very best sign of a true craftsman that he will set up shop near to the sources of his materials) he has already made quite a reputation with his work.

All this activity needs some direction, and the Kilkenny Design Workshops were set up to work on the pressing problems that the opening markets for craftwork of quality caused. Their aim was that "through the association of Irish craftsmen and designers with their opposite numbers from abroad, a 'school' of characteristic style will in time emerge". Already it seems as if it is a goal that is not unattainable. But even with such good intentions, there is a lot left to do before the craft revival in Ireland grows to full development.

Even so, there are many lovely things already being produced all over the country that could well become your family heirlooms of the future.

THE
FACE
OF
IRELAND

DUBLIN

A Capital with Character

by

EDWARD F. MACSWEENEY

The capital of the Republic of Ireland has maintained its air of Georgian elegance and absorbed the newer developments without disturbing its balance. The River Liffey flows through the heart of the city from west to east, flowing out of the misty distances of the Phoenix Park district, past the elegant frontage of the Four Courts and the Custom House to a port which almost reaches the city's main thoroughfare—O'Connell Street, one of Europe's broadest. Dublin University (Trinity College), founded in the sixteenth century on the site of an old monastery, lies at the city's heart. Behind the new buildings there are still streets where the eighteenth century lives on. This is reflected in the manners of the people, their pace is more leisured than in most capitals; they have a courtliness and a friendliness which is not a face for the tourist, but their natural way of life.

The feeling of background is emphasized through the preservation of the buildings of the past—virtually every main thoroughfare has such a reminder. O'Connell Street is dominated by the impressive General Post Office, which has more historical than architectural significance, for it was the headquarters of the insurgent forces in the Easter Rising of 1916. At the top of

THE FACE OF IRELAND

O'Connell Street and its continuation, Parnell Square, the noble town house of the Earl of Charlemont has become an art gallery, overlooking a green square and the Garden of Remembrance of the heroes of the Irish War of Independence.

Dublin Castle, a link with former British rule of Ireland, has been preserved; parts have even been rebuilt. It is no longer a seat of power, but the offices of part of the civil service, with the state apartments and ornate St. Patrick's Hall reserved for occasions of state. Only one building of any considerable height has been permitted in the city—the 17-floor tower block associated with Liberty Hall, headquarters of the country's biggest trade union.

Sea-Water and Liffey-Water

By most standards Dublin is a small capital; the population is around 900,000, most of whom live within a radius of 12 miles of the city center, that is, an area bounded by Howth Head on the northern side of Dublin Bay and the seaside resort of Bray on the south. To the west and south the ring of the Dublin Mountains and Wicklow Hills make the visitor conscious that the countryside is only a step away—from many of the center city points, the passer-by catches glimpses of the hills which seem to be just at the end of the street. The surging tide of the Liffey under the city's nine road bridges is a reminder that the waters of Dublin Bay and the Irish Sea are just a mile or two down the riverside quays, and just a mile or two up the river to the west, at Islandbridge on the edge of the city, is one of the Liffey's salmon fisheries.

College Green may have no green, because it ceased to be a fair green long, long ago, but St. Stephen's Green, a few hundred yards away, is an open park strictly preserved for the people. One of Dublin's best hotels borders St. Stephen's Green, on whose south side are the headquarters of the Irish Department of External Affairs, located in Iveagh House (a fine mansion given to the government by a member of the Guinness Brewery family, the second earl of Iveagh). Nobody is in Dublin for long without being aware of the Guinness family and its brewery, which borders the south side of the River Liffey near the main rail terminal at Heuston (Kingsbridge) Station. The brewery is on the regular list of "sights" for the visitor, but the family's influence is wider than that of a successful commercial enterprise largely because of their interest in the arts.

Dubliners are very conscious of the arts. The city has two

DUBLIN

art galleries—the National Gallery, and the Hugh Lane Gallery of Modern Art. But it is the arts in the broadest sense that concern the Dubliner—he will be fiercely critical about a new building, without much knowledge of architecture; scathing or eulogistic, mostly the former, about a new play, novel or painting by a fellow-Irishman. Critical or not, the Dubliner is intensely proud of the artistic output of his fellows.

History of Dublin

Dublin's history dates from the second century, when Ptolemy marked it down on an ancient map in A.D. 140 as Eblana. Its excellent harbor gives the city its name, derived from the Irish words *Dubh Linn* meaning "dark pool", so called because of the blackish color of the Liffey waters emptying into the sea. In ancient times it was also known as *Baile Atha Cliath*, "the town of the ford of the hurdles", and this is the name by which the capital is known in Irish (Gaelic) today. The name derived from the fact that just above the harbor point there was a ford which spanned the Liffey, leading to one of the five great roads of old Ireland coming from Tara, the seat of the ancient Irish kings. Today, Father Mathew Bridge stretches across the Liffey on the site of the old ford.

Curiously enough, Dublin as a town was not established by the Irish at all, and did not become an Irish settlement until centuries later in history. Viking raiders plundered the coast during the eighth and ninth centuries, and the Danes used Dublin as a central naval base for their sea raids. The wooden settlement the Scandinavians founded on the site of present-day Dublin grew in importance when trade routes opened for the Norsemen in their maritime empire. The Danish power remained intact until the Battle of Clontarf on Good Friday, 1014, when the Irish led by Brian Boru won the day.

The Irish victory was short-lived, however, for the Anglo-Norman invasion took place in 1169. The Normans took Dublin by storm, making the city their headquarters for the conquest of Ireland. The rest of Dublin's long story is one of battles, conquests, massacres, and turbulent and tragic turns of events crowding one upon the other. The British hoped to make Dublin the clerical and governmental center of a country they tried to control for the seven hundred long years until the Irish finally won their independence in 1921.

During medieval English rule and in Elizabethan times, Dublin saw many adventurers pass through, like Lord Essex in his expeditions against the Irish leader, Tyrone. Later, the city threw its lot to the Royalists and opposed Cromwell, who took Dublin in the seventeenth century. Even today Dubliners remember bitterly that Cromwell stabled his horses in the magnificent St. Patrick's Cathedral. Later still, Dublin's population sided with James II against William of Orange. In Restoration times, the city took on a new importance, and many of Dublin's attractions such as St. Stephen's Green and Phoenix Park date back to this era.

The Golden Age

Dublin flourished gaily in the 18th century, when it was considered one of the most glittering of all contemporary European cities. Many great buildings were erected during that time as prominent architects added to the light, grace and charm of the place by building the Georgian mansions that today line St. Stephen's Green, Merrion Square, and other nearby streets of the city. People of note from all parts of Europe came to hear and see such theatrical greats as Garrick or Mrs. Siddons in brilliant plays. The world premiere of Handel's *Messiah* with the composer himself conducting was held in 1724 at Dublin's old Musick Hall, Fishamble Street. And Dublin's great literary figure, Dean Jonathan Swift, secretly wrote his Drapier Letters, political dynamite for the English, which fanned the embers of a city smoldering with undercurrents of revolt. In 1782 England recognized the independence of the Irish Parliament of Grattan, and during the brief period of conciliation that followed, some of Dublin's great monuments were erected—the Four Courts and the Custom House among them.

By and large, the history of Dublin has been inseparable from the history of the struggle for Irish Independence. Today, in its complete freedom, Dublin wears a new look. Reconstruction and development have taken place since independence and Dublin has asserted itself as a progressive capital city while preserving the best of the past.

Exploring Dublin

Dublin has a character to see, as well as places and things, and it is worth while to approach sightseeing in an unhurried manner. Adjust your pace to the leisurely tempo of the city and you will get more out of it.

For a quick once-over to get your bearings, try one of the

DUBLIN

city tours run by the bus company (CIE) from Busarus (Central Bus Station) near the Custom House. They touch main points and the well-informed couriers are interested in the city and like to ensure that their guests, which is the way they see their passengers, enjoy the tour. Once the main reference points are in your mind, the rest is easy. Dublin isn't a sprawling city, so sightseeing is best done on foot and by the regular bus services which cross the city, most of them passing either through or across O'Connell Street.

O'Connell Bridge, one of the nine road bridges spanning the Liffey between Heuston Station (near Phoenix Park) and the port, is a good reference point on which to base tours. Just beside the dark granite Ballast Office at the south side of the bridge, where Westmoreland Street joins the quays, there is a quick-reference "talking guide/map" to check your bearings. O'Connell Bridge is named for the famous nineteenth-century orator and parliamentarian and has an unusual characteristic—it is broader than its length. The River Liffey nears the end of its 80-mile journey from the mountains of Wicklow here, just before entering Dublin Bay and the Irish Sea.

Going Down O'Connell Street

On the north side of O'Connell Bridge, the statue of Daniel O'Connell ("The Liberator"), the work of sculptor John Henry Foley, dominates the traffic flow. You may notice in the figures around the base of the statue some puncture marks, made by the bullets which flew around this street in 1916 during the Easter Rising. Moving northwards, the General Post Office (invariably referred to as the GPO) is on the left. On the open space in the middle of the road before the GPO, now an island of flower beds and cobble stones, stood the most famous of all Dublin's statues—the 134-foot Nelson Column. It was blown up (or down) by some never-identified persons in the early hours of a morning in March, 1966. There is, on this safety island, another reference guide/map as well as an information kiosk for the bus and rail services, and (usually) some of Dublin's traditional flower sellers.

Turn off to the left along Henry Street, a good popular shopping street, and then take the first turning to the right to see Dublin's famous and colorful Moore Street, with its lines of stalls down both sides of the roadway. Most of the stalls sell the same things—fruit, flowers and vegetables, although some specialize in fish or chickens. The pitches are traditional with generation after generation of women succeeding each other, but

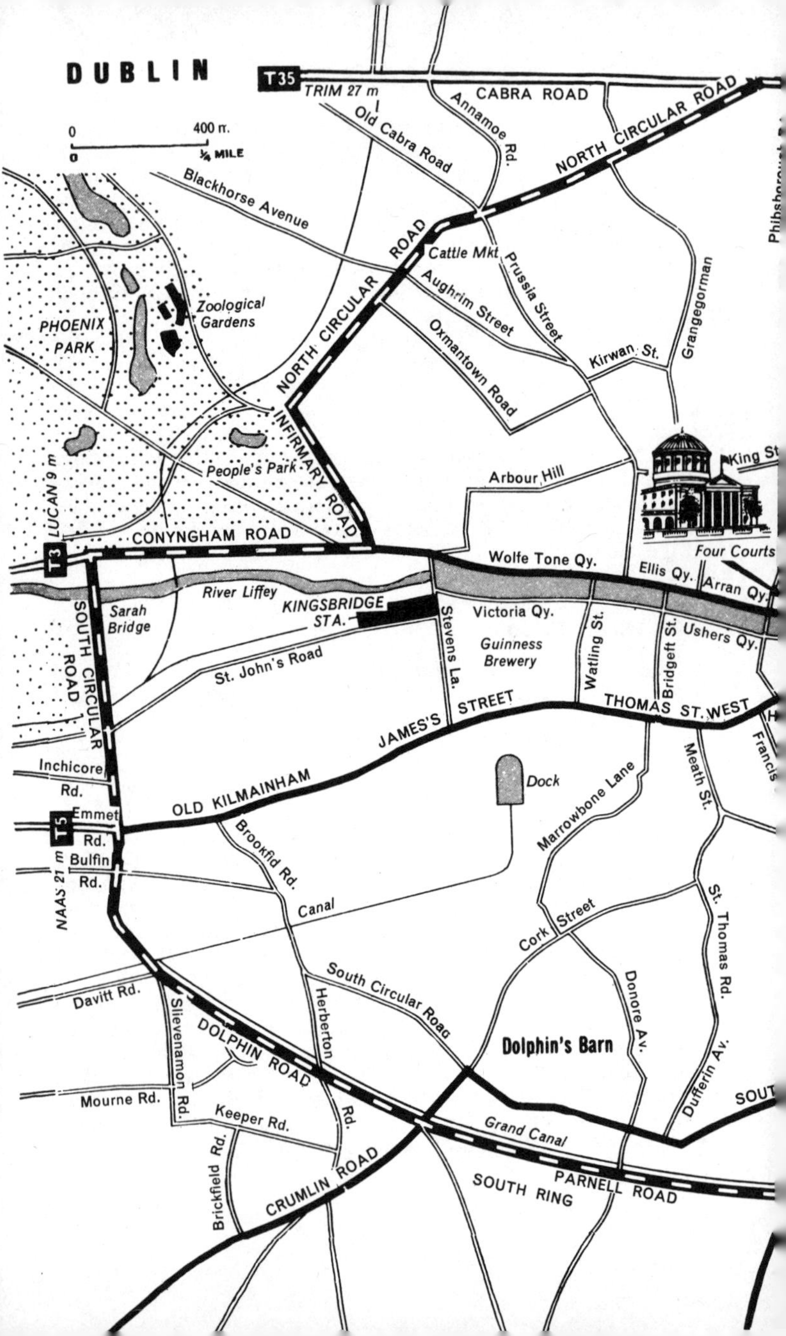

DUBLIN
0
400 m.
0
¼ MILE
T35
TRIM 27 m
CABRA ROAD
Old Cabra Road
Annamoe Rd.
NORTH CIRCULAR ROAD
Phibsborough
Blackhorse Avenue
Cattle Mkt
Prussia Street
Aughrim Street
Zoological Gardens
PHOENIX PARK
Oxmantown Road
Kirwan St.
Grangegorman
INFIRMARY ROAD
People's Park
King St
Arbour Hill
LUCAN 9 m
CONYNGHAM ROAD
T3
Four Courts
Wolfe Tone Qy.
Ellis Qy.
Arran Qy.
River Liffey
KINGSBRIDGE STA.
Sarah Bridge
Stevens La.
Victoria Qy.
Ushers Qy.
Guinness Brewery
Watling St.
Bridgeft St.
SOUTH CIRCULAR ROAD
St. John's Road
JAMES'S STREET
THOMAS ST. WEST
Francis
Meath St.
Inchicore Rd.
OLD KILMAINHAM
Dock
Marrowbone Lane
T5
Emmet Rd.
Bulfin Rd.
NAAS 21 m
Brookfld Rd.
Canal
Cork Street
St. Thomas Rd.
Davitt Rd.
South Circular Road
Donore Av.
Slievenamon Rd.
Herberton Rd.
DOLPHIN ROAD
Dolphin's Barn
Dufferin Av.
Mourne Rd.
Keeper Rd.
Grand Canal
Brickfield Rd.
CRUMLIN ROAD
SOUTH RING
PARNELL ROAD
SOUT

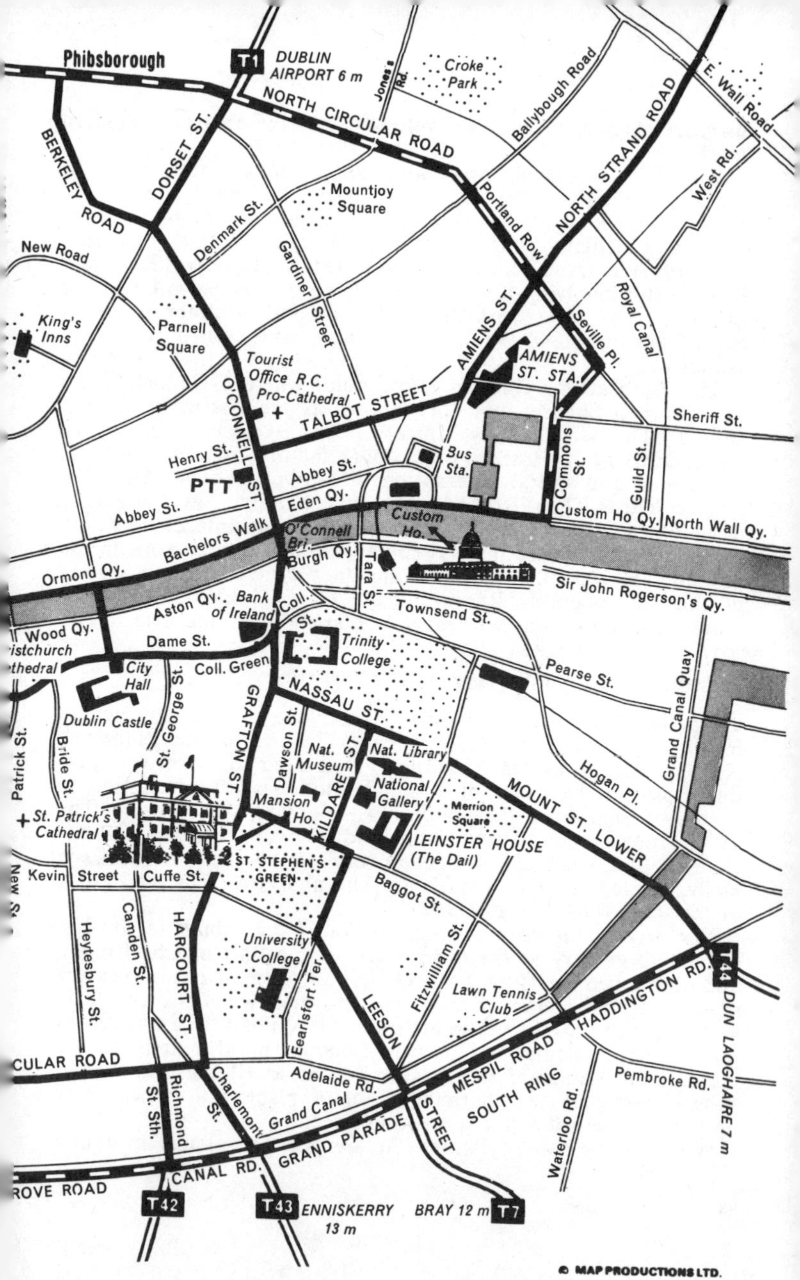
Phibsborough
T1
DUBLIN AIRPORT 6 m
Jones's Rd.
Croke Park
NORTH CIRCULAR ROAD
Ballybough Road
NORTH STRAND ROAD
E. Wall Road
West Rd.
BERKELEY ROAD
DORSET ST.
Mountjoy Square
Portland Row
Denmark St.
New Road
Gardiner Street
King's Inns
Parnell Square
AMIENS ST.
Seville Pl.
Royal Canal
AMIENS ST. STA.
Tourist Office
R.C. Pro-Cathedral
O'CONNELL ST.
TALBOT STREET
Sheriff St.
Henry St.
PTT
Bus Sta.
Commons St.
Guild St.
Abbey St.
Eden Qy.
Custom Ho.
Custom Ho Qy.
North Wall Qy.
Bachelors Walk
O'Connell Bri.
Burgh Qy.
Tara St.
Ormond Qy.
Sir John Rogerson's Qy.
Aston Qy.
Bank of Ireland
Coll. St.
Townsend St.
Wood Qy.
Dame St.
Trinity College
ristchurch thedral
City Hall
Coll. Green
Pearse St.
Dublin Castle
St. George St.
GRAFTON ST.
NASSAU ST.
Grand Canal Quay
Patrick St.
Bride St.
Dawson St.
Nat. Museum
KILDARE ST.
Nat. Library
Hogan Pl.
National Gallery
Mansion Ho.
Merrion Square
MOUNT ST. LOWER
St. Patrick's Cathedral
LEINSTER HOUSE (The Dail)
Kevin Street
Cuffe St.
ST. STEPHEN'S GREEN
New St.
Baggot St.
Camden St.
HARCOURT ST.
Heytesbury St.
University College
Fitzwilliam St.
Earlsfort Ter.
LEESON
Lawn Tennis Club
HADDINGTON RD.
T44
DUN LAOGHAIRE 7 m
CULAR ROAD
Adelaide Rd.
MESPIL ROAD
Pembroke Rd.
Charlemont St.
Grand Canal
SOUTH RING
Richmond St. Sth.
STREET
Waterloo Rd.
CANAL RD.
GRAND PARADE
ROVE ROAD
T42
T43
ENNISKERRY 13 m
BRAY 12 m
T7

THE FACE OF IRELAND

they are threatened with redevelopment of the area as a modern market.

Back on O'Connell Street and still heading north, note the statues, including a monument to Charles Parnell, leader of the Irish Parliamentary Party in the British House of Commons in the 1880s and virtually "uncrowned king of Ireland" until his parliamentary star waned after he was cited as co-respondent in a divorce suit involving Kitty O'Shea. The statue is a good example of the portrait-style work of the Dublin-born sculptor Augustus Saint-Gaudens (1848-1907), whose fame was earned mostly in America.

The Ambassador cinema, at the point where O'Connell Street joins Parnell Square, was once known as the Assembly Rooms. Built by Dr. Bartholomew Mosse (1712-1759), to help finance his Rotunda Lying-In Hospital (next door), the first maternity hospital of its kind and still an internationally-famous training center for gynaecologists. The Rotunda Hospital building was originally designed by Richard Cassels in 1751; the chief interest is within the main door, where there is some beautiful stucco work in the baroque-like chapel. Just behind the cinema, in an upstairs section of the old Assembly Rooms, is the Gate Theatre founded by Hilton Edwards and Micheál MacLiammóir in the late 1920s.

Parnell Square and Playwright's Territory

Up the slight rise of Parnell Square, one of the few inclines in the city, there is the impressive Garden of Remembrance (1966), designed by Daithi Hanly. "Dedicated to those who gave their lives in the cause of Irish Freedom" is the inscription in Irish and English on the granite walls flanking the entrance. The 25-ft. bronze group of four swans and four humans, depicting the children of Lir (an old changeling folk tale), is the work of Oisin Kelly, erected in 1971 to mark the 50th anniversary of the signing of the truce with Britain in 1921.

Just around the corner is Charlemont House, built in the late eighteenth century as the town house of the Earl of Charlemont, and now called the Hugh Lane Gallery of Modern Art in memory of one of its benefactors who was drowned when the *Lusitania* was torpedoed in 1915. The architect, Sir William Chambers, was the builder of Somerset House in London; he also designed for the earl the Italianate Renaissance Casino at Clontarf (northeast suburb), which looks charmingly out of place, but is now very properly preserved as a national monument.

While at the top of Parnell Square you are almost in James

Joyce territory, for he mentions the church at the corner, "Findlater's Church", the Abbey Presbyterian Church, with its graceful spire; and Eccles Street, where his character Bloom, also in *Ulysses*, lived. Joyce himself went to the Jesuit College, Belvedere, in Great Denmark Street, just across the road from the square. Playwright Seán O'Casey wrote all his famous Abbey plays: *The Shadow of a Gunman, Juno and the Paycock, The Plough and the Stars* and *The Silver Tassie* at 422 North Circular Road, not far away. The house has been rehabilitated in recent years and is now named Seán O'Casey House in honor of the onetime construction laborer who became Ireland's greatest modern playwright. Brendan Behan (1923-66), Ireland's rumbustious house painter/playwright, lived part of his childhood in nearby 14 Russell Street; a plaque unveiled in 1974 marks the house. Mountjoy Square still preserves some Georgian buildings and No. 15 is the library of the Irish Georgian Society (open weekdays 2-6 p.m.).

While on this side of the city, take a No. 19 bus headed for Glesnevin and visit the 50 acres of the Botanic Gardens, purchased in the eighteenth century from the poet Thomas Tickell. The Yew Walk is still named Addison's Walk for Joseph Addison, politician, pamphleteer, essayist and poet, who once had a house nearby; Dean Swift walked here with his "Stella", and playwright Richard Brinsley Sheridan, author of such classic plays as *The Rivals, The School for Scandal* and *The Critic*, was another who enjoyed the air of the gardens.

If you are interested in roses, take a No. 44A or No. 30 bus from the city center to St. Anne's rose garden by the sea at Clontarf. Based on an old 265-acre garden of the Guinness family, it has been planted with over 10,000 rose bushes and more are added each year.

Marlborough Street and the Liffey

Downtown again, and headed south, the Catholic Pro-Cathedral (St. Mary's) is just behind O'Connell Street in Marlborough Street. Built in the first quarter of the nineteenth century, it has a massive portico with six doric columns copied from the Temple of Theseus in Athens.

Lower down Marlborough Street is the Abbey Theatre. The first Abbey was developed on this site in 1904 from a disused Mechanics' Institute and part of what had once been the City Morgue. The old theater was burned down in 1951, and the new building was opened on July 18, 1966.

THE FACE OF IRELAND

A few paces further on down Marlborough Street brings you to the Liffey again. Away to the left, beyond Butt Bridge, named for the nineteenth-century politician Isaac Butt (leader of the Irish Party before Parnell), is the Custom House, designed by James Gandon (1743-1828) who influenced much Irish architecture in the eighteenth century. Because there is an ugly overhead railway bridge nearby, you'll have to walk along the quay to get the best view, passing on the way the new Liberty Hall. Built on the site of an old building of the same name which was the headquarters of James Connolly's Irish Citizen Army (freedom fighters with the Irish Volunteers), Old Liberty Hall was the place where the Proclamation of the Irish Republic was printed in secret. The main front of the Custom House is one of the most dignified to be seen in Ireland; only the external shell remained after it was burned out in 1921, but it has been skillfully restored. In the gardens on the north side (the back of the building) there is an 18-foot-high bronze group known as the Custom House Memorial, a modern work by the Breton sculptor Yann Renard-Goulet, now an Irish resident.

Turning your back on the docks and heading west towards Phoenix Park along the quays, you are likely to be tempted to browse at the secondhand bookshops, and pause to admire the remarkable metal bridge, a toll footbridge built in 1816 (Dubliners still call it "Ha'penny Bridge", since the charge was a halfpenny) to provide access to the Crow Street Theatre on the site where St. Michael and St. John's church stands, on the south bank of the river. The riverside road leads to another of James Gandon's architectural contributions to Dublin's historical beauty, the Four Courts, main seat of civil justice and meeting place of the High Court and Supreme Court.

West to Phoenix Park

This is the route that leads on to the Phoenix Park (1,760 acres of it); the brewery you see across the river is, of course, Guinness's. On the way, there's a detour up Church Street to St. Michan's, which is very close to the Four Courts. The organ in St. Michan's was reputedly used by Handel when he visited Dublin. St. Michan's main interest for visitors is in the vaults (contact the sexton at the gate lodge). Here are bodies which have been interred for centuries yet have not decomposed; the skin is brown and leathery in appearance, but still intact, presumably because of some characteristic of the atmosphere.

The land which now constitutes Phoenix Park was seized from

the priory of the Knights Hospitaller in the seventeenth century and turned into a royal deer park. Later, a home for the king's representative, the viceroy, was built here—it is on the right of the main road and is now known as Arus An Uachtaráin, the official residence of the president of the republic. The residence of the United States ambassador is on the left of the main road and other establishments within the park, the largest enclosed park in Europe, are a Garda Síochána (police) depot, the offices of the Ordnance Survey, founded in 1874, the Papal Nunciature and the Zoological Gardens. The deer still roam free in the park, but the old duelling grounds—generally called the Fifteen Acres—now provide sports pitches for all ball games instead of a killing ground. A short distance away, the visitor can watch polo (without charge) or relax in the flower gardens known as the People's Gardens. The Zoological Gardens, internationally known for the breeding of lions (animals whose sex life seems to thrive in captivity) is one of the world's finest.

The tall (205 feet), needle-like obelisk in the park is the Wellington Monument, a tribute to the first Duke of Wellington, who was born in No. 24 Upper Merrion Street, Dublin, in 1769. Sunday around noon is a good time to visit the park; there is usually a full program of Gaelic games in progress, horse riding, polo and model aircraft flying. The River Liffey, just below Phoenix Park, is the course for the rowing clubs, and nearby is the renowned Salmon Pool Fishery. The Phoenix Park racecourse is just outside the northwestern gate of the park.

South of O'Connell Bridge

Westmoreland Street, a short, wide thoroughfare leading from the south side of O'Connell Bridge, opens up an area full of interest to the visitor. The street is dominated at the river end by the Ballast Office and the other by the façade of Trinity College on the left and the Bank of Ireland on the other. Several airlines and the Irish Sea passenger shipping services have their offices on Westmoreland Street, and at the junction with College Street and College Green, there is a statue to Thomas Moore, poet (*Lalla Rookh* and other works) and author of many Irish songs now known as Moore's Melodies; Moore was born on the south side of the city at 12 Aungier Street, now a bar. Oscar Wilde was christened in nearby St. Mark's church in 1856. The church has been deconsecrated and will be used by Trinity College as an auditorium.

THE FACE OF IRELAND

Trinity College

College Green—once known as Hoggen's Green and then outside the walls of the City of Dublin—is the wide, traffic-busy area in front of Trinity College, which everyone who visits Dublin has on the "must" list. The original charter name of the College is "The College of the Holy and Undivided Trinity of Queen Elizabeth near Dublin". It was founded in 1591, but none of the original buildings of the Augustinian priory (which was on the site earlier) remains. The facade is in the Palladian style, with some fine stone carvings. On the lawns in front are the statues of two of the university's many illustrious alumni—statesman Edmund Burke (1729-97) on the left and poet Oliver Goldsmith (1728-74) on the right, both by John Henry Foley (1818-75) who was also responsible for the statute of statesman Henry Grattan facing the college from the safety island in the middle of the street.

Once within the arched entrance, you stand in cobbled Parliament Square. The atmosphere is that of a different age from the bustle of the streets outside. The building on the left is the chapel (built at the end of the eighteenth century): its "twin" on the right is the Examination Hall, which has a very graceful interior with ornamental plaster work, fine acoustics and is sometimes used for recitals. In the center of the square is the Campanile or bell tower, which is said to mark the center of the original priory church. Students' apartments surround most of this area. The Graduates Memorial Building on the left houses some of the college groups, such as the College Historical Society, of which many famous men have been members. The block known as the Rubrics is the oldest part of the college and was built around 1700. Male students reside in college apartments, if there are any vacant, but the girl students live elsewhere, mainly at Trinity Hall, and must be out of the grounds by a specified hour each night. Many of the students are from overseas. For most visitors, the high-vaulted first-floor room of the Library is the main objective of the visit.

The Book of Kells

Ireland's largest collection of books and manuscripts is housed in the Trinity College Library, which is entitled to receive without charge a copy of all books published in Britain or Ireland. The principal treasure is, of course, the *Book of Kells,* the beautifully illuminated manuscript gospel dating from the eighth century; this superb example of the art of illustration came to the college from the old Columban Monastery of Kells, County Meath; it is not certain whether the monks of the monastery were responsible for the work, although it was in their possession for many years. In order that it may be preserved from the light, it is screened when no visitors are present, and each day a fresh page is turned. Each leaf has its own beautifully rich detail inscribed in colored inks made by a secret process; all are worth scrutiny. Because of the fame of the *Book of Kells*, some of the other treasures may be overlooked on a quick visit; they include the *Book of Armagh*, a ninth-century copy of the New Testament which also contains St. Patrick's Confession, and the *Book of Durrow*, a seventh-century gospel book from another Columban monastery in Offaly.

Of the collection from outside Ireland, the treasures include an early book printed by William Caxton; a first edition of *Dante's Divine Comedy* and four Shakespearean folios. Among the busts around the walls is that of Jonathan Swift, later to become the celebrated Dean of St. Patrick's Cathedral; he was a student from 1682 to 1689. The Library also has the Brian Boru harp; it is known as Brian Boru's harp, although scientists say it was not made until the fifteenth century (and Brian was killed at the Battle of Clontarf four centuries earlier). Today it is used as the official symbol on Irish State documents and on the obverse side of Irish coinage. In a slightly different position, it is the trade mark of Guinness's stout!

Merrion Square

If you leave Trinity by the Lincoln Gate (the back gate), you are close to the birthplace of dramatist Oscar Wilde at 21 Westland Row, and another house (No. 1 Merrion Square) where he spent his childhood with his father, Sir William Wilde, a distinguished eye specialist, and his mother, the writer Speranza. Wilde was an alumnus of Trinity College. Another building to note on Westland Row is the attractive frontage of the Royal Irish Academy of Music, at No. 36.

Merrion Square is the most complete of the surviving examples of the Georgian squares of the eighteenth century. It is not surprising to find that in such a pleasant setting the Royal Institute of the Architects of Ireland have their headquarters, at No. 8. Famous men of the past who lived on the square include Daniel O'Connell (No. 58), the **poet-playwright William Butler Yeats** (No. 82) (born in Sandymount Avenue three miles away) and the

THE FACE OF IRELAND

thriller-playwright Sheridan Le Fanu (No. 70). The green space in the center, once intended for a cathedral, was presented to the citizens in 1973 by Archbishop Dermot Ryan. Along the west side of the garden, facing the roadway, there is the attractive surviving part of the Rutland Fountain.

The National Gallery

The National Gallery, on the west side, was originally financed by public subscriptions in the nineteenth century to honor a railway pioneer, William Dargan, the man whose statue is on the lawn outside the building. It has been considerably enlarged, the latest addition having been opened in early 1968 to house part of the gallery's remarkable collection. Near the gallery entrance is a statue of George Bernard Shaw, which is particularly appropriate as the gallery gets one-third of his royalties under the terms of the Shaw Bequest (the British Museum and the Royal Academy of Dramatic Art in London get the rest). The royalties from such stage productions and films as *My Fair Lady* have helped to finance the purchase of several major works in recent years, including the Giovanni di Paolo painted gold altar cross.

The gallery has one of the best collections of old masters in Britain or Ireland: the late Sir Alfred Chester Beatty, whose Chester Beatty Library collection of Oriental manuscripts and miniatures may be visited at No. 20 Shrewsbury Road, gave the gallery a fine collection representative of the Barbizon school, and also works by Corot, Boudin and Meissonier. The collection of water colors by the nineteenth-century English painter, Turner, are only on public display in January to protect them from fading, but they may be seen on request by visitors at other times of the year.

The open space next to the gallery, known as Leinster Lawn, is the back garden of Leinster House (whose entrance is in Kildare Street), meeting-place of the Dáil (Chamber of Deputies) and Seanad (Senate). Beyond it is the Natural History Museum of the National Museum, which contains a very large collection of Irish birds and animals of the past and present. Next door are the offices of the Prime Minister and Cabinet.

Just across the narrow Merrion Row, at the top of Merrion Street, is an attractive cul de sac known as Ely Place, the one-time residence of many famous Irishmen, including orator John Philpot Curran (1750-1817), writer George Moore (1852-1933) and Oliver St. John Gogarty. Ely House, on the left, was built in the eighteenth century for the Earl of Ely and is now the headquarters of the Knights of Columbanus. The doorway is worth noting as a fine example of a well-preserved Georgian entrance, complete with its flanking lamps which replaced the old torch holders. The new Gallery for the Royal Hibernian Society at the end of the cul de sac should be open by this year (1977).

St. Stephen's Green

A short street, Hume Street, leads from Ely Place to St. Stephen's Green, another Georgian Square which has lost much of its character, although a sharp public campaign a year or two ago promoted a better official attitude towards conservation of distinguished houses. The Green is the place to idle for a while, as there are plenty of seats and plenty to see. Its well-wooded walks have been kept up and there is a children's playground as well as a long artificial lake and a large population of duck and wildfowl. The bridge across the lake is a meeting place for students from University College, part of which is on Earlsfort Terrace leading off the south side. Band concerts and displays of Irish dancing are a frequent summertime attraction in the ever-popular Green.

As nearby University College buildings were too cramped for the increasing student intake, most faculties have been transferred to a new campus at Belfield, Donnybrook, about two miles away. The grounds at the back of the college were once the gardens of Iveagh House (St. Stephen's Green), the headquarters of the Department of Foreign Affairs; these link with No. 86 St. Stephen's Green, a building of fine exterior with some beautiful stucco work, which was the Catholic University of Ireland when it was established in 1853 with John Henry Newman (afterwards Cardinal Newman) as its rector. When the university did not obtain recognition in Britain, most of its faculties declined, but were revived in a University College; at a later stage the poet and Jesuit priest, Gerard Manley Hopkins, was one of the professors, and among its students were Patrick Pearse, Éamon de Valera (later to become President of Ireland), and James Joyce. "86" as it is known to generations of students is now the home of most of the societies of University College. University Church, next door, is somewhat Byzantine in character and its founder, Newman, is commemorated by a bust in the nave.

Along this side of the Green there is the English Language Studies Institute (No. 100), one of several internationally-recognized centers where foreign students come to learn English.

THE FACE OF IRELAND

(Dublin's claim to speak the *best* English is recorded as far back as 1764 in *Hibernia Curiosa*!)

A short distance away to the east of St. Stephen's Green is another of Dublin's jealously preserved Georgian Squares, Fitzwilliam Square; the green space in the center is reserved for its residents. Where St. Stephen's Green joins Merrion Row there is an old Huguenot Cemetery (1693), a reminder that many Huguenots fleeing from persecution in France in the sixteenth and seventeenth centuries found refuge in Dublin where, among other activities, they introduced poplin weaving.

There is plenty to be seen in the streets which lie between College Green and St. Stephen's Green. Here runs Grafton Street, fashionable shopping center, with half a dozen streets branching off—Duke Street and Anne Street both attract with their little boutiques and antique shops. Famous old Dublin silver and Waterford glass can be found in this area. There is a good range of Irish copperware jewelry and some interesting examples of modern Irish design in brooches. A narrow turning to the right, halfway along Grafton Street, has a small notice directing you to St. Teresa's, an interesting Carmelite church, retaining its eighteenth-century characteristics. See *The Dead Christ*, by sculptor John Hogan.

Dawdle around the shops, the *Bailey Bar* or *Davy Byrne's* across the way, and then move through to Dawson Street, where the Royal Irish Academy has an extensive collection of old Irish manuscripts. Short lunchtime concerts are a feature at St. Ann's Church next door. Tombstones in a tiny churchyard behind St. Ann's record famous Dubliners of the past. It is reached through a lane from Molesworth Street.

Mansion and Leinster Houses

Nearby, slightly back from the roadline, is the Mansion House, official residence of the lord mayors of Dublin since 1715. Here the lord mayor receives distinguished guests. Public rooms in the Mansion House include the Round Room, used for exhibitions, concerts and other functions, and notable for the display of family crests of former lord mayors.

Molesworth Street leads from Dawson Street to Kildare Street; the building now facing you is Leinster House, standing back from Kildare Street in a large quadrangle. Leinster House was built for the 20th Earl of Kildare (Duke of Leinster) to the designs of Richard Cassels, the foundation stone being laid in 1744. The Senate now meets in one of the reception rooms,

DUBLIN

while a former lecture theater, built during the Royal Dublin Society's occupation, is used for the Dáil Chamber. Internally, considerable structural work has been necessary, but the impressive frontage, so reminiscent of the White House in Washington, has been preserved. Visitors may be shown over the house when the chambers are not in session; if you do go through it, take a look at the wonderful Irish handloomed carpets. The Dáil is elected by direct vote of the people on the proportional representation basis, the Senate—60 members—is elected on a vocational basis, with six additional members elected by the universities and 11 nominated by the Taoiseach (Prime Minister). Members of the Dáil, known as "Teachtaí Dála" (usually shortened to "TDs"), represent 42 constituencies with 144 representatives. General elections must take place at least every five years; the President is elected by popular vote once in seven years and may run for a second term.

National Library and Museum

The buildings flanking Leinster House, when you face it, are the National Library on the left and the National Museum on the right, both in the heavy Victorian manner.

The National Library has an important collection of Irish books and manuscripts and micro-films of Irish manuscripts in libraries abroad. In a corner behind the library is the National College of Art.

There are, in this area, several commercial art galleries which present exhibitions of modern painting by Irish and other artists; in some of these, interesting old prints and maps can be purchased as souvenirs.

The National Museum's Irish Antiquities Division is the section you'll be likely to want to see most, because here is a fine collection of ornaments from the bronze age onwards. "Must see" pieces include the Tara Brooch and the Ardagh Chalice (both eighth century), the Cross of Cong, the Lismore Crozier and the Shrine of St. Patrick's Bell (all twelfth century). This division of the museum is very attractively laid out and among the ornaments on display, you will notice a number of collars and other gold pieces which have inspired some of the jewelry produced in Ireland today. Among the more recent material, look at the fine Irish silver and glass. The Irish Folk-Life and Military History sections are both worth your time too.

Trinity College and College Green dominate one end of Dame Street. Out of sight at the other end, up Lord Edward Street and around a slight bend in the road, Christ Church Cathedral is the dominant feature. Starting from College Green, go into the Bank of Ireland, designed in 1729; walk through the dignified portico with its Ionic columns and ask one of the uniformed staff to show you where Ireland's parliament of long ago met, before the Act of Union of 1800. Henry Grattan was a great figure of the parliament that sat here. Conversion into bank offices has not destroyed the character of the interior, and the main interest is in the former House of Lords, now the boardroom of the Court of Governors. This has a magnificent chandelier said to consist of over 1,200 pieces of glass, two tapestries by John van Beaver and the mace of the House of Commons; its House of Lords counterpart is in the National Museum, and the throne in the Royal Irish Academy.

Dame Street today is the center of the business community of Dublin, although No. 3 was, in 1822, the site of Daly's Club, famous for its gamblers (today, the site is appropriately occupied by an insurance company).

On Anglesea Street, the Stock Exchange may be seen in action from the Visitors' Gallery by permission of the secretary. Just opposite the short street which leads into the Lower Yard of Dublin Castle is one of the city's famous old theaters, today known as the Olympia.

Dublin Castle

Dublin Castle has a history dating back to the thirteenth century, but the only parts of the old Norman building surviving are the Record Tower on the southeast side and part of the Bermingham Tower (southwestern corner). It was from the Bermingham Tower that one of the most dramatic escapes in Irish history took place on Christmas Eve, 1592, when the Donegal chieftain, Red Hugh O'Donnell, made his getaway from the castle across the Wicklow mountains. During its long history (the Danes had a fortification on the site before the Normans came) the Castle was the jail of many famous prisoners, as well as being the former seat of British government in Ireland.

The castle provided many apartments for courtiers, servants and soldiers, as well as the Viceroy's Residence and State Apartments. Most of the rooms have been converted into offices for government departments, and a major reconstruction project was completed in 1967. The nineteenth-century Chapel Royal (now the Church of the Most Holy Trinity) is an attractive gothic building with some fine carvings on the exterior by Edward and

DUBLIN

John Smyth; the interior has some interesting woodcarving. You will notice the remarkable coincidence that, while each succeeding viceroy or lord-lieutenant had his coat of arms emblazoned on one of the stained-glass windows, the last remaining window was filled with the arms of the last lord-lieutenant! Prints of Malton's *Views of Dublin* give a very good impression of what the castle and Dublin looked like in the eighteenth century; they are now auction room gems, but small reproductions can be bought reasonably. In the upper Castle Yard are the State Apartments, including St. Patrick's Hall, which is now used for the inauguration of the president of the republic and the associated rooms are used for state receptions.

Across the courtyard is the Genealogical Office, one of the most attractive buildings of the castle complex. From this office, crowned by Bedford Tower, were stolen the Irish crown jewels, on July 6, 1907, on the eve of a visit by King Edward VII and Queen Alexandra. Neither the jewels nor the thief were ever found. The office has an interesting heraldic museum and provides the facilities for tracing family histories.

If you go out into the street through the gate in the north ride (a triumphal arch), you will be beside the City Hall, center of municipal government. The domed rotunda is now a gallery of statuary, including some by John Hogan. Not surprisingly, they are of great Irish figures of the past. To see more of Dublin's history, a visit should also be paid to the Dublin Civic Museum, located a short distance away in the old City Assembly House, South William Street, one of the streets running parallel to Grafton Street.

Christ Church Cathedral

From the City Hall, the road rises up the hill of Lord Edward Street. Before you reach the top you will see Christ Church Cathedral, located at what was the center of the first settlement of the city. The first church was built in 1030 by the Danish king, Sitric, but underwent many successive constructions and reconstructions, the oldest remaining part being the crypt. In history, the cathedral is generally linked with the name of its twelfth-century bishop, Laurence O'Toole, the patron saint of Dublin; his heart is preserved among the relics of the cathedral.

The buildings were at various times used as a meeting place of parliament (1559) and as law courts before the Four Courts were built across the River Liffey. The present cathedral has an impressive nineteenth-century dignity, but its interior holds many relics of the past, including the reputed tomb (in the south nave) of Strongbow, leader of the Anglo-Norman invasion of 1170. There is a graceful covered bridge linking the cathedral with the Synod House across St. Michael's Hill.

Within a few hundred yards from Christchurch Place, the scene of considerable clearance of old buildings in 1967, are St. Patrick's Cathedral, Marsh's Library and Tailors' Hall. Tailors' Hall is located in Back Lane and is the only remaining hall of one of the ancient guilds of Dublin. Its preservation is important because so few buildings of the period remain; close by is St. Audoen's Arch, only remaining gate of the old city walls.

St. Patrick's Cathedral

At 7 Hoey's Court, in the immediate area, Jonathan Swift was born on November 30, 1667; as Hoey's Court has greatly changed since Swift's day, there is little point in visiting it, but walk on down Patrick Street past the pleasant St. Patrick's Park to St. Patrick's Cathedral, with which he was associated as dean. Legend links the site of the cathedral with St. Patrick, and there was a church dedicated to St. Patrick on the spot in pre-Norman days. A quarrel between Archbishop Henri de Londres and the dean and chapter of Christchurch Cathedral in the thirteenth century was responsible for raising St. Patrick's to the status of a cathedral, and despite vicissitudes in the intervening years, it holds that status today. It is 300 feet long, the longest church in the country, a fact Oliver Cromwell's troops found useful for the stabling of their horses. The old chapter door in the south transept has a hole cut in it, dating from the ending of a quarrel between the earls of Kildare and Ormonde in 1492; the hole was cut so that they could shake hands before meeting.

The querulous, satiric Swift, whose pulpit is in the northwest corner of the north transept, was dean of St. Patrick's from 1713 to 1745. A graduate of Trinity College, he became closely identified with Ireland's political life, expressing his views in such writings as the *Drapier's Letters*; he is more generally remembered outside Ireland for *Gulliver's Travels* and *A Tale of a Tub*, a satire on corruption in religion and education. He died in 1745; his grave is in the south aisle. There is, over the robing room door, the Latin epitaph he wrote for himself, which says, in part (as translated by W. B. Yeats): "Jonathan Swift, for thirty years Dean of this Cathedral, lies here, where savage indignation can no longer rend his heart. Go traveller, and emulate if you can him who did a man's part as the inflexible upholder of

DUBLIN

liberty." Nearby is the grave of his beloved Stella (Esther Johnson, 1681-1728).

Marsh's Library, which adjoins St. Patrick's Cathedral, owes its name to Archbishop Narcissus Marsh, who created the country's first public library in 1702. Well worth visiting.

A Last Round-Up

Where else? Well, to Shaw Street, where playwright John Millington Synge (*Playboy of the Western World, Riders to the Sea*) was born, or to Synge Street (No. 33) where George Bernard Shaw (*Pygmalion, Saint Joan, Arms and the Man*) was born. Neither will tell you much about the man, nor will the birthplace in Pitt Street, where opera composer Michael Balfe (*The Bohemian Girl*) was born. On the north side of the city, the grim bulk of Mountjoy Prison may remind you that the jail provided source material for *The Quare Fella* by Brendan Behan.

The Grand Canal is used as a recreational waterway for holidays aboard cruisers. A walk along the tree-lined canal bank from Portobello towards the center of the city passes the headquarters of *Bord Fáilte* (Irish Tourist Board) at Baggot Street Bridge; turning away to the right over the bridge will lead you to the United States Embassy, a circular structure (1964) designed by the American architect J. Johansen. In the same Ballsbridge district are the exhibition halls and showgrounds of the Royal Dublin Society, center for the Spring Show (May) and the Dublin International Horse Show (August). Nearby, on Lansdowne Road, is the Rugby Football Stadium.

THE ENVIRONS OF DUBLIN

Trips Not Beyond the Pale

Accessibility is one of the great advantages of the many vacation areas of Ireland. Within 50 miles of Dublin there is a wonderland of contrasts, from the silver strands (the Irish call a sandy beach a strand) of County Wicklow, to the brooding hills inland, the rich plains of County Meath (once the seat of Irish kings) and the age-old passage graves of Newgrange. Bright, bustling resorts and quiet fishing villages, remote valleys and lakes are all within little more than an hour's drive from the city in an area which stretches from Dundalk and the shadow of the Mourne Mountains in the north down the coast to Arklow in the south and inland to Mullingar.

The area is conveniently served by public transport from Dublin; bus tours from Dublin encompass County Wicklow as far as Glendalough in the southwest and the Boyne Valley to the north; bus tours are also based on Bray for the Wicklow district.

Inside the Pale

Most of the places described in this chapter come within what was once called the Pale—the part of Ireland in which English law was formally acknowledged. The Pale was created after Henry II subdued the Norman nobles in the twelfth century and named his son John, "Lord of Ireland". Its boundaries varied

THE ENVIRONS OF DUBLIN

but roughly included Dublin, Kildare, Meath and Louth; as an entity, the Pale disappeared in Elizabethan times, but it long continued in Irish minds as the stronghold of English rule. The term Pale gave rise to the expression "outside the pale", an indication that somebody was excluded—outside the law. Ruins of old castles suggest the borders of the area, which never extended into Wicklow, the county to the south of Dublin; here, the wild mountainous country made law enforcement virtually impossible for centuries and there were frequent raids down from the mountains into what are now the suburbs of Dublin, such as Rathfarnham, where the Jesuit House of Studies, Rathfarnham Castle, was once an Elizabethan castle.

Exploring the Environs of Dublin

It is easy to become sidetracked in Ireland, but in exploring the environs of Dublin, it is a good plan to make your tours within three triangles, the first taking in the east coast north of the city, inland to County Cavan and then southeast back to Dublin. To the immediate north of Dublin city, Howth Head dominates the arm of Dublin Bay, with a fishing port on its northern side.

Howth Castle, a short distance from the harbor, has a garden famed for its beauty when the azaleas and rhododendrons are in bloom: gardens open to the public for a small admission fee. There is a legend that when the Irish sea-raider Gráinne Ní Mháille (Grace O'Malley) was returning from a voyage, she called at Howth and sought food and shelter for her crew. She was refused and in revenge her crew kidnapped the young heir of the St. Lawrence family, later releasing him on the promise that Howth Castle would never be barred to the hungry traveler. The family obeyed the command and the Gaisford St. Lawrence family honors the tradition by setting a place at their table each day for the unexpected guest.

There are a number of early monastic settlements both on the mainland and the off-shore islands. The Danes forced one group of monks from Holmpatrick to flee with the relics of their founder, St. Mochonna, across Dublin Bay to found a new monastery on the south side, at the place which became known as Monkstown. Ireland's Eye, another monastic home, is an attractive islet for excursions from Howth.

North from Howth

Portmarnock, a little to the north, has a long, golden beach which makes it popular with Dubliners; the beach featured in aviation history as the point of departure for the late Sir Charles Kingsford Smith in his monoplane *Southern Cross* on his trans-Atlantic flight from east to west in 1930. To golfers, Portmarnock is known for its championship course.

Malahide Castle, the throne of Lord Talbot de Malahide, has a background dating back to Norman days; it has been in the hands of the family since that time, except for a brief period during the Cromwell regime. It was here that a remarkable collection of James Boswell's private papers was discovered by American researchers. One batch, including the manuscript of Boswell's *Journal of a Tour to the Hebrides*, was found in a box which was supposed to contain croquet equipment, and still later (1939), yet another batch was found when an outhouse was being cleared. These have provided some of the most valuable social history of the eighteenth century, the first being *Boswell's London Journal 1762-1763*, which was published in 1950. The series has been appearing from Yale steadily since then.

The castle with its 265 acres of land was sold in 1976. It had been offered to the Irish government by Lord Talbot de Malahide before his death in 1973 and by the executors but the government was unable to acquire it. The property is expected to become a community center. The contents of the house containing many Boswellian relics were sold in 1976.

Visitors to London, Ontario, will see replica on a small scale of Malahide Castle because one of the members of the family was a founder of London and established his headquarters there.

Birds, Swords and Oliver Plunkett's Head

The largest island off the County Dublin coast in this area is Lambay, a bird sanctuary and the home of Lord Revelstoke. Permission to land on the island, where Lord Revelstoke rears Connemara ponies, must be obtained by writing to the Steward, Lambay Island, Rush, Co. Dublin. The house was designed by Sir Edwin Lutyens.

The coast road winds through a series of small and popular resorts as far as Balbriggan, where it joins the main road from Dublin. If you travel the main road instead of following the coast, the route passes through Swords, where the end of the main street is dominated by the ruins of an archbishop's fortified castle which dates back to the thirteenth and fourteenth centuries. Moving on north and approaching Drogheda, several more sandy beaches are passed, including Bettystown, where the

THE ENVIRONS OF DUBLIN

Tara Brooch, a fine example of early Irish metalwork, was found in the sands in 1850.

The Irish name for Drogheda is Droichead Átha, "the Bridge of the Ford". The town has bitter recollections of sieges in the seventeenth century, including its capture by Oliver Cromwell in 1649, when his troops massacred some defenders and transported others to the West Indies. Only one of the gates of the town walls remains, this being St. Lawrence's Gate in St. Lawrence Street; it is well worth seeing. The ruin of the seventeenth-century Augustinian Abbey consist of a tower and an arch spanning Abbey Lane. In Upper Magdalene Street, a two-story tower is all that remains of a Dominican Priory founded in the thirteenth century. The castle-like building on an eminence in the town (Millmount) was once part of the defenses of Drogheda.

The imposing gothic-style Roman Catholic Church, St. Peter's, in the main street, has a shrine housing the head of sainted Oliver Plunkett, Archbishop of Armagh, who was hanged, drawn and quartered at Tyburn (London) in 1681; the door of his cell is preserved outside the church. He was canonized a saint in 1975.

Side-trip to the Boyne Valley

Drogheda is a good place to make a diversion into the Boyne Valley, known to historians for its antiquities and to anglers because the Boyne is one of the best of the early salmon rivers in the country. A short distance inland along the Valley of the Boyne, William of Orange defeated James II for the crown of England in 1690; the area is well sign-posted to indicate the different phases of the battle and positions of the troops. The valley leads into Meath, where you will find Tara, once the seat of the High Kings of Ireland.

The various earthworks at Tara have been identified through the twelfth-century *Book of Leinster*. At Cormac's House stands the *Lia Fáil*, the Coronation Stone of the Irish Kings. Tom Moore's ballad, *The Harp that Once Through Tara's Halls*, has over-romanticized the spot. You will need a map or courier to identify sites. The period of Tara of the Kings covered the early centuries of the Christian era; it had considerable significance as far back as 2000 B.C., as archeological researches have shown, and it was also associated with the legendary queen Maeve. On the Hill of Slane, within sight of Tara, St. Patrick kindled the paschal fire on Easter Eve in A.D. 433 in defiance of a royal decree, thus furthering the strength of Christianity in Ireland, pagan until that time.

THE FACE OF IRELAND

There is far more to see at the passage graves of Newgrange, a short distance away. Identified as the *Brugh na Boinne* (Palace of the Boyne) of ancient Irish tales, Newgrange was constructed as a communal tomb and is regarded as the most important of its type in western Europe. The mound is 280 feet in diameter and was originally surrounded by a circle of standing stones (12 of them remain); it covers about an acre and the entrance, a 62-foot-long passage, faces south. This passage leads to a cruciform chamber off which there are recesses which presumably contained the cremated remains which have disappeared during the long history of Newgrange. The curb stone and other stones are carved with elaborate patterns; oddly, there are few concentric circles inscribed on the stones at Newgrange, although they predominate at nearby Dowth. Newgrange was first raided about 1,000 years ago by the Danes and it has been continuously open since A.D. 1700. A display center helps to interpret this prehistoric wonder; it contains a collection of casts of decorative stones at Newgrange and other related monuments in the area, together with a site map showing the origin and distribution of passage graves in Europe.

The custom of building megalithic tombs is believed to have originated in the western Mediterranean area; it is assumed that some of the early Irish passage-grave builders came from Spain and also from Brittany in northwest France. Radio-carbon estimations and other evidence show that the passage graves in Ireland (there are about 150 altogether) were constructed about 3,000 years ago.

Meath

While in this area (it is sometimes called Royal Meath) remember that it is great hunting country and has been for centuries; there are records of hunting carved on many old monuments, including one at Kells, County Meath. There are five High Crosses at Kells, the most important being the Market Cross (carved with religious scenes) in the center of the town. This is one of the most beautiful of the many Celtic crosses in the country, though at one point in its history (1798), it was used as a gallows on which to hang rebels. There is a Round Tower which has lost its conical top near the Church of Ireland. There are over 90 such towers in various stages of preservation in Ireland —they were built as watch-towers and places of refuge for monks from the ninth to twelfth centuries. The doors are usually at least 10 feet from ground level; the towers are invariably 100 feet high or taller. Kells is of course, the place from which the *Book of Kells* was brought to Dublin's Trinity College.

Trim is dominated by the 70-foot walls of King John's castle; the largest Anglo-Norman fortress in the country. It was originally built by Hugh de Lacy in the twelfth century, but "modernized" about 100 years later. The moat which was dug around the castle could be filled from the River Boyne to give it complete isolation. Two miles south of Trim is the village of Laracor, where Jonathan Swift was rector from 1699 until his installation as dean of St. Patrick's in 1713. Between Trim and Laracor are the remains of Stella's Cottage, where Swift's "Stella" (Esther Johnston) lived.

North of Drogheda

North of the Boyne from Drogheda there is the little fishing village of Clogherhead, a good place for sea anglers. Inland, the ecclesiastical ruins at Monasterboice recall a monastery that was a great seat of learning until about the twelfth century. Muireadach's Cross dominates the entrance to the graveyard; it is one of three elaborately carved High Crosses and is the most important of the monastic remains which include a Round Tower, reportedly the highest in Ireland (although it has lost its top), and two churches—the south church is ninth century and the other was built about four centuries later.

Three miles away, Mellifont Abbey (1142) was the first Cistercian monastery in Ireland. A large part of the abbey church is still standing and the outline of the cloisters can be seen. The Chapter House ceiling is worth seeing and so is the remarkable decoration on the octagonal lavabo. The Cistercians have a modern foundation known as New Mellifont a few miles away at Collon. It was in Collon that the nineteenth-century admiral, Sir Francis Beaufort, inventor of the wind measurement system still in use today and known as the Beaufort Scale, was born.

Little of historical interest remains in Dundalk, at the north end of County Louth, but the sister of the Scots poet, Robert Burns, is buried in St. Nicholas's Church, a building which incorporates part of the thirteenth- and fourteenth-century churches.

Dundalk is the base for exploring the Cooley Peninsula, which juts out into the Irish Sea, separating Dundalk Bay from the deep inlet of Carlingford Lough to the north. This area was the scene of some of the legendary deeds of the boy hero Cuchulain, including the famed "Cattle Raid of Cooley," one of the best-known of all the folk tales of ancient Ireland. This tells of a four-day battle for a great bull coveted by Queen Maeve of Connacht —some say a black bull, some say a red, but all agree that it was a mighty battle. In the Cooley Mountains, the legends tell of the burial place of Bran, the mastiff of the giant Fionn Mac Cumhaill (Finn McCool), and a signpost points to the "Long Woman's Grave"; another, with less association with legend, indicates the Proleek Dolmen, near Ballymascanlon. Dolmens, of which there are many in various parts of the country, were simple megalithic tombs consisting of a large capstone on three or more supporting stones (the capstone at Proleek is estimated to weigh about 50 tons).

Along the north side of the Cooley Peninsula, there are views of the Mountains of Mourne across Carlingford Lough, and in Carlingford itself there is plenty of evidence of the town's importance in earlier centuries. King John's Castle here is a fortress of the thirteenth century and Taaffe's Castle, well preserved, dates from the sixteenth century. The ruins of the fourteenth-century Dominican Abbey include a fine gothic arch beneath an impressive square tower. The Mint is typical of a fortified town house of 400 years ago, while the nearby Tholsel, once a gate in the town wall, also served as the town jail at a later period. The peninsula is well worth making a detour to cover, remembering that in completing the circuit you are at the border with Northern Ireland, and should be sure to check on the current situation before setting out.

Inland to the Lakes

Inland from Dundalk lie the little hills of Monaghan, a county of lakes and rounded mountains with the Slieve Beagh range bordering it to the north. They say that there are more than 180 lakes in Monaghan, all of them teeming with fish; Monaghan and its neighbor Cavan are two of the most popular counties in Ireland for coarse angling and there is shooting around Lough Egish and the Creeve lakes, Shantonagh.

Patrick Kavanagh (1904-67), the plowboy who became one of Ireland's most distinguished poets, is buried at Inniskeen, where he was born.

Castle Leslie at Glaslough is a 1,500-acre estate with a mansion built on the site of a seventeenth-century building. It is mainly Italian in style, with a fountain from Sienna and pillars from ancient Rome. There is an Italian walled garden which, like the house itself with its art treasures and its mementos of the Churchill and Wellington families, may be visited. An 18-hole

THE ENVIRONS OF DUBLIN

golf course designed by Robert Trent Jones has been laid out in the grounds of the estate.

Many of Cavan's lakes are linked with the River Erne, which provides fishing right from the hills of Cavan to the sea at Ballyshannon in County Donegal. Monaghan town has a Market House dating back to 1792, and near the town of Cavan in Lough Oughter, on the site of a crannog (an artificial island), is the finest remaining example of an ancient Irish circular tower fortress. It was built by the O'Reilly clan, which once ruled this territory. Virginia is one of the prettiest villages in Cavan, with a golf course overlooking Lough Ramor, full of fish.

Maria Edgeworth and Oliver Goldsmith

Moving south into County Longford, Edgeworthstown (also known as Mostrim) is a reminder of the famous nineteenth-century novelist, Maria Edgeworth. Not far away is Ballymahon, on the River Inny, and the country associated with Oliver Goldsmith (1728-74) who was born nearby. This is the area of his *The Deserted Village*; a number of places associated with his writings can still be identified, including the house at Edgeworthstown (Ardagh House, now a convent), where he is said to have had the adventures which he subsequently used in the play *She Stoops To Conquer*.

In Longford town, St. Mel's College, a seminary, has an interesting museum. St. Mel's Cathedral is a nineteenth-century building of considerable grace. Castle Forbes, three miles northwest, is the home of Lord Granard—the grounds may be viewed if you write ahead for permission.

Westmeath is part of the great cattle-raising country, with Mullingar as its center. Once a stronghold of the Anglo-Normans, its importance changed to that of market center and touring base for the Westmeath Lakes. Visit Castlepollard to see Tullynally Castle, ancestral home of the Earls of Longford; two 1,500-year-old boats from the nearby lake are in the stables.

From Mullingar back to Dublin across the plains, the road passes through Leixlip. The salmon leap which gave the town its name has disappeared in the creation of a reservoir, but a modern fish-pass facilitates the salmon on their up-river journeys. Lucan, closer to Dublin, was once famous for its spa. The remains of the home of Patrick Sarsfield, one of Ireland's most distinguished generals of the Jacobite Wars, are in the grounds of Lucan House.

This journey in through the western suburbs of Dublin completes the largest triangle of the three in our "environs of the capital", yet none of the places mentioned is more than two hours' driving from the city.

West from Dublin

A second triangular tour embraces a journey westward to Maynooth, the center of Roman Catholic secular ecclesiastical education in Ireland. On the Dublin side of the town is Carton, a fine eighteenth-century mansion in extensive grounds; once the home of the Dukes of Leinster, it is open in summer, Sat. and Sun. 2-6 p.m. In the town itself, the remains of the thirteenth-century Geraldine Castle are at the end of the street leading into St. Patrick's College. The college has a most interesting museum open to visitors during the vacation period; the exhibits range from vestments presented by the Empress Elizabeth of Austria to electrical devices invented in the course of researches by members of the faculty in past generations. The architecture is varied, as the college has been considerably enlarged since it was founded in 1795.

Carton House at Maynooth, with its 1,000 acres of walled demesne, was put on the market last year (1976) by its owners, the Nall-Cain family who had acquired it in 1949. Carton, a Palladian mansion, was another of the works of the ubiquitous Richard Cassels and was built in 1739-47.

Three miles from Maynooth on the way to Celbridge is an astonishing 140-foot-high obelisk known as Connolly's Folly, built in 1740 to provide work after a hard winter on the orders of Lady Louisa Connolly. Celbridge was the home of Dean Swift's second romantic association, "Vanessa" (Esther Vanhomrigh).

One of the most perfect Georgian houses in Europe is at Castletown, Celbridge; it was built by an Italian architect, Alessandro Galilei, in 1721–28 for William Connolly, speaker of the Irish Parliament, and decorated by the brothers Francini and other artists. Castletown House was in the possession of the same family from the time it was built until 1965; it is now the headquarters of the Irish Georgian Society. Its furnishings are Georgian. As it is only 13 miles from Dublin, it is well worth the slight detour.

Further to the south, the main road from Dublin to Cork passes through Naas, once the seat of the kings of Leinster and now an important horse-training center, and on to Newbridge, with the imposing buildings of Newbridge (Dominican) College on the right of the road. Newbridge is an industrial town with

THE ENVIRONS OF DUBLIN

rope, carpet and cutlery works. A short distance beyond is The Curragh, a plain of 12 square miles with the Curragh Racecourse—the headquarters of Irish racing and the venue for the Irish Derby—on one side and on the other, the training depot of the Irish Army. If you are out early enough in the day, you will see strings of racehorses at exercise; trainers have the right to train their horses on the plain but only for a specified time each morning.

Donnelly's Hollow and Kildare

On the left of the Curragh plain is a small depression known as Donnelly's Hollow; it is marked with a small obelisk commemorating the fact that here, on December 13, 1815, the Irish giant Dan Donnelly fought and defeated the English boxing champion, George Cooper. The bone of Donnelly's mighty right arm is exhibited in the *Hide-Out* at Kilcullen on the edge of The Curragh, together with some other unusual curios.

The main road across the plain drops down into Kildare, where St. Brigid, the patron saint of the county (and, with St. Patrick and St. Columcille, one of Ireland's patrons), founded her nunnery in the sixth century. The cathedral, although extensively reconstructed in the last century, retains many features of the older buildings on the same site, including an unusual carving with a skull and crossbones. Kildare Castle, scene of fierce fighting in Elizabethan and Cromwellian times, is in ruins. The nearby Round Tower has battlements in place of a conical top—an embellishment certainly not conceived by the monks who first built it. At Kildare, pay a visit to the Japanese Garden at the National Stud; the entrance is not through the elaborate main gate of the Stud, but down a side road. The garden was devised by Lord Wavertree in 1906 and made by two Japanese, Eda and his son Minoru, with the help of 40 assistants, a job which took four years. It depicts the symbolic story of the life of man in plants, shrubs and flowers and the tale is well explained by the guides. Open March-October, small admission fee.

Further down the road on the way to Monasterevin, there is an odd thatched cottage—odd because, at a distance of 40 miles from the coast, its walls are covered with shells. At the entrance to the town of Monasterevin are the gates of Moore Abbey, a mansion on the site of an old Cistercian abbey. At one time it was the home of Count John McCormack (1884–1945), the famous Irish tenor, but is now an institution under the care of the Sisters of Charity. This is the town through which the Grand

Canal passes on its way from Dublin to link with the River Shannon at Shannon Harbour. The waterway is used recreationally and motor cruisers can be hired at towns such as Tullamore for use on both the canals and the Shannon. There's a museum of old steam engines and transport at Stradbally, Co. Laois, open May through Sept., daily 2–6 p.m.

A Side-Trip to Athy

A line of the canal from Monasterevin goes south to Athy. White's Castle in the main street was built by a sixteenth-century earl and has a tower in an excellent state of preservation, dominating a bridge over the River Barrow. The Dominican Church here is a "must see", as an example of contemporary church architecture; built in the shape of a fan, it has a remarkable peaked roof. In an agricultural area, Athy has several prosperous industries, including a peat moss factory which produces a valuable horticultural aid as an associated product to the cutting of peat (turf) for fuel. To the south, Kilkea Castle, the oldest (twelfth-century) inhabited castle in Ireland, is now a hotel. Barberstown Castle at Straffan also dates from the twelfth century; it has recently been restored. Moone, eight miles east of Athy, has a famous High Cross (17½ feet) with 51 sculptured panels depicting scenes from the scriptures.

On to Abbeyleix

Returning on the main road to Cork, the view is largely of thousands of acres of bogland. South along the road, the dark gray walls of the republic's only convict prison on one side of the road and the bright modern appearance of hospitals on the other are slightly incongruous entrances to the town of Portlaoise.

Southernmost point on this tour is Abbeyleix, a charming town of stone houses associated with the family of Viscount de Vesci, who owns an Adam-style mansion built in the late eighteenth century on the traditional site of the ancient abbey which gave the town its name. The surrounding forests are well developed and are one of the most important examples of private forestry in the country. The estate gardens, with thirteenth-century monks' bridge still in use, are open to the public in summer.

Turning northwest on another leg of the triangle, it is worth visiting Birr (Offaly) to see an interesting example of a country town which developed in Georgian days. It used to be called Parsonstown, after the Parsons family. One of their descendants

THE ENVIRONS OF DUBLIN

was made Earl of Rosse, and distinguished himself for astronomical researches, building in 1845 what was then the world's largest telescope. It was set up in the estate of Birr Castle; some parts of it may still be seen by the public. According to one seventeenth-century surveyor, Sir William Petty, Birr is the centre of Ireland, but since the title was given to at least three other places, the claim is regarded as a little dubious. (The ancient meeting place of the four great provinces—Ulster, Munster, Leinster and Connacht—at the Hill of Urnagh, County Westmeath, has been given the title and so has a hill two miles northeast of Glassan in the same county. Yet another Westmeath hill, Knockcosgrey, near Kildare, has the "honor").

At Tullamore, Durrow Abbey is the site of a monastery where the famous *Book of Durrow* (now in Trinity College Library, Dublin) was written. Now drive across the midlands and the Bog of Allen to Trunk Road 3, and back to Dublin.

South of Dublin

The southern area of the environs of Dublin provides first a run down the east coast with the Irish Sea rolling in on a mixture of sandy and rocky coastline. The railway out along this coast was the first in Ireland, being completed as far as Dún Laoghaire (then Kingstown) in 1864. On the way, it passes a small bathing spot called Salthill, named for a plant which once existed here to extract salt from the sea. Monkstown, just at the back of Salthill, still has the remains of a castle built by monks to defend their farms, but they lost the castle to General John Travers, an Irishman who commanded Henry VIII's artillery. It changed hands several times and was once held by the Cromwellian General Edmund Ludlow (1617–93), the man who signed Charles I's death warrant. Ludlow has the credit of restoring the castle and planting its gardens, including a Yew Walk, of which there are still some trees left near the ruins of the castle.

Dún Laoghaire, "the fort of King Leary", is the terminal for the car ferry from Holyhead (Wales). The harbor was built during the nineteenth century, largely by convict labor, with stone quarried from the nearby Dalkey Hill. Dún Laoghaire harbor is one of the top sailing centers around the Irish coast and stages regular races and regattas. Immediately behind the harbor, Moran Park is a recreation center for tennis and bowls.

The end of Dún Laoghaire's long promenade is marked by the Martello Tower, associated with James Joyce; it is now a Joyce Museum, and apart from its associations with one of Ireland's most controversial writers, is worth visiting because it is one of the few Martello Towers open to the public; these towers were built during the Napoleonic Wars to resist a French invasion which never came.

Bulloch Harbour, around the corner from Joyce's tower, is associated with the monks of St. Mary's Abbey, Dublin, and of Monkstown (they built a castle here to defend their fisheries). The remains of Bulloch Castle are now incorporated in an institution run by Carmelite nuns.

On Dalkey Island, just off shore, remains have been found indicating that it was inhabited as long ago as 2500 B.C. Dalkey, one-time home of George Bernard Shaw, overlooks a long crescent bay edged with sand and backed by Killiney Hill, which is topped by a small obelisk of a type to be found in several parts of Ireland. They were built as relief works during the famine years.

Bray and Arklow

Bray, at the southern end of the bay, has a dual personality as a town; it has several industries and Ardmore Studios, the main film-making center in Ireland, in addition to its role as a resort and gateway to County Wicklow, the "Garden of Ireland". No. 1 Martello Terrace, Bray, was the home of James Joyce between 1888 and 1891. Over Bray Head (you can walk around it in an hour) is Greystones, a quieter resort which has a considerable reputation among sea anglers; boats are available in the harbor to fish the off-shore banks, and there is also good sport to be enjoyed fishing off the uncrowded beach. In fact, uncrowded and unpolluted beaches are characteristic of the Irish coast. The Silver Strand and Brittas Bay are two other sections of the coast between Wicklow town and Arklow, which is a flourishing resort, with the biggest amusement center in the country. Boats may be hired for trips on the bay or up the attractive Avoca River.

Arklow has a new (1976) maritime museum which is worth a visit. Some exhibits are slightly macabre, including two bottles of wine salvaged from the wreck of the Pomona which sank in 1859 en route from Liverpool to New York with the loss of over 300 immigrant passengers. Believe it or not the bottles are still full! They were recovered from the wreck in 1975. See also the multicolored figurehead of a schooner built in the town in 1880.

Four miles from Wicklow town, the informal botanic gardens at Mount Usher, Ashford, have trees and shrubs from many parts of the world. Open to the public on Sunday afternoons.

THE ENVIRONS OF DUBLIN

From Dublin to Glendalough

The inland areas of southwest Dublin and Wicklow counties are attractively mountainous. The road out of Dublin rises through Rathfarnham. The ruins to be seen on Mountpelier Hill nearby are those of the Hell Fire Club, a resort of eighteenth-century sporting bloods, according to local legend.

Look back over the city of Dublin and away to the north—on a clear day, the mountains of Mourne (80 miles distant) can be seen; on all other sides stretch mountains, peatland and valleys, with an occasional lough. At Kilakee Mountain, you join the start of the Military Road, a roadway built across the mountains in an endeavor to suppress the uprising of 1798 and control the territory. The road is now a modern highway but still retains its old name; it leads on through wonderful scenery past Glencree and the Sally Gap to Laragh and Aughavanagh.

The color of the Wicklow Mountains suggests Irish tweed, being all shades of brown, flecked with whitish grey of granite outcrops, the gold of the gorse, purple heather and the contrasting greens of the hillside forests and small fields filled with sheep and lambs. This is a favorite place for painters, the week-end artists as well as the professionals.

Glendalough

Glendalough (Valley of Two Lakes), reached from Laragh, was first discovered by a hermit monk, Kevin, in the sixth century. His route across the mountains still exists and is known as St. Kevin's Road. A great monastic city grew up in the valley. At one time, there were seven churches in it, all in an area on the shores of the lakes.

In the ninth and tenth centuries, Vikings found the valley and plundered the churches; English troops raided it in the fourteenth century, but each time some of the buildings were repaired and the monastic life continued, until the suppression of the monasteries in the sixteenth century. The cathedral is the largest of the ruins, but St. Kevin's Church (often called St. Kevin's Kitchen) is the best-preserved (apart from the almost perfect Round Tower) and is an example of the early Irish barrel-vaulted oratories with a high-pitched roof of stone. The gateway to the area is the only existing example of this type of entrance arch and was the original gate to the monastic city.

Glendalough is a valley with one road out—the way you came in, although for walkers, there are magnificent hill walks. Despite the romantic beauty of County Wicklow, it has a past as a mining county (gold was mined there in the long ago, and more recently lead and copper). Avondale forestry school plantations include trees planted in 1779 by Samuel Hayes who built Avondale House, later the home of Charles Stewart Parnell. The house, which contains Parnell relics, is open for visits, Monday through Friday.

Russborough House and its collection of paintings valued at £30 million—one of the most valuable in the world—was handed over to an educational trust for the Irish nation in 1976 by its owner, diamond/copper magnate, Sir Alfred Beit. The collection includes works by Vermeer, Velasquez, Goya, Franz Hals, Gainsborough, Rubens and Murillo. Russborough House was the scene of an £8 million art robbery in 1974, but the 19 stolen paintings were recovered undamaged in a farmhouse in County Cork a week later. The house is to become an arts center; it will be open to visitors, but check with local tourist office for current information on times.

Powerscourt Gardens (the house was destroyed by fire in 1974) near Bray, are open Easter through October. The Powerscourt Waterfall is 400 feet high, the highest in Britain or Ireland. Russborough House, designed by Richard Cassels, is one of Ireland's finest Georgian houses; its impressive façade can be seen from the main road. Blessington Village was a one-time staging post for the coach-and-four service from Dublin; it has Georgian dignity and is located near Blessington Lake (also known as Poulaphuca Lake from nearby Poulaphuca Waterfall), which provides facilities for water sports as well as supplying Dublin with 20 million gallons of water a day. The area is to be developed as a wild life sanctuary. The regions described above are quite simply beautiful; it is a happy fact that the Irish appreciate their own scenery and know how to use their natural resources without spoiling the countryside.

THE SUNNY SOUTHEAST

Wexford, Waterford, Kilkenny and Carlow

The Irish call the southeast corner of their country "the sunny southeast" and the people who live there produce statistics to prove it; as the Irish Meteorological Service has one of its main weather stations at Rosslare in County Wexford, they are in a good position to substantiate their claim of more than an extra hour of sunshine daily.

The coastline shares with its northerly neighbor, Wicklow, a number of sandy beaches; the Saltee Islands, about three miles off the coast, are the biggest bird sanctuary in the country. The four counties are rich in history—the Rising of 1798 had its origins in Wexford and its stories are still told and retold; many of Ireland's best-known ballads have arisen in this corner of the country. The history of the people of the area stretches back to pre-Christian times and the largest dolmen in Ireland, dating from the Bronze Age, is to be seen at Browne's Hill in Carlow—its capstone weighs more than 100 tons.

Although the southeast, particularly along the coast, is known primarily as one of Ireland's playgrounds, the entire area is rich in history, and its people have preserved a sense of that history. They do not live in the past, but they are aware of its legends and traditions; this characteristic may enhance your interest in a visit here.

THE FACE OF IRELAND

Kilkenny —the Marble City

Kilkenny is a good starting point because in the "Marble City", the visitor gets an immediate sense of the past. The tag "Marble City" is derived from the black marble (from nearby) which is used for decorative purposes in churches. Looking across the River Nore, the skyline of the city reminds us of its history—the great bulk of the castle and the towers and spires of the churches overshadow the twentieth century, yet down in the narrow streets of the city, the old buildings do not look out of place among their newer neighbors.

The city, now with around 11,000 inhabitants, has existed in the Valley of the Nore from the sixth century, when St. Canice founded a monastery where the cathedral stands today; the city gets its name from Canice—in Irish, Cill Chainnigh, literally "Canice's Church", anglicized to Kilkenny. The Normans came in the eleventh century and built the first castle overlooking the river. There has been a castle on the site ever since; it was the property of the earls of Ormonde until 1966, when it was transferred to a local committee and then the State, which is carrying out restoration work. The Great Picture Gallery has been one of the priority tasks in the restoration.

The former stables have already become the Kilkenny Design Workshops, a government-sponsored project in which designers from overseas work with and train Irish designers. The workshops cover a range of ceramics, woven textiles, woodturning, printed textiles and silver and metal work. Designs and prototypes are produced for commercial firms. W. R. Grace Studios, built with a grant from the Grace Foundation of New York, are used by textile designers. Some work is on exhibition, and worth seeing.

Kilkenny's castle was the hub of activity in medieval times when several parliaments were held in the city. One of these, summoned in 1366 by the Duke of Clarence (son of King Edward III of England), passed the infamous Statute of Kilkenny. It forbade the Anglo-Normans to intermarry with the Irish, use the Irish language, dress or surnames or allow Irish clergy into their churches. The Irish were banished from the city (there is still a district across the river known as "Irishtown"). As the law extended to all areas under Anglo-Norman control, similar "Irishtowns" are to be found in other cities.

The General Assembly of the Catholic Confederacy made Kilkenny its "capital" in 1642. Dissensions and compromise finally broke up the confederation, and Kilkenny became a royalist stronghold which surrendered in March 1650, after a

THE SUNNY SOUTHEAST

five-day siege, to Cromwellian forces. They proceeded to act in their accustomed fashion and broke "down all the windows, and carried away every bit of glass, and all the doors of it, that the hogs might come and root, and the dogs gnaw the bones of the dead".

The cathedral was reconstructed in succeeding centuries and is now bordered by streets whose names recall the ecclesiastical character of the neighborhood—Bishop's Hill, Vicar Street and Dean Street. The style is Early English, with a squat but imposing tower; there are also remains of a 100-foot Round Tower in the churchyard. The twelfth-century Kilkenny marble font is worth seeing, and there are a number of medieval tombs. The library (founded 1693) has an impressive collection of ancient books, including a Sarum Missal (1498) printed by Caxton. Contact the Librarian if you wish to see this priceless library.

Merchants and Witches

In Parliament Street is a perfect example of a Tudor merchant's house, the only one remaining in the city. The well-head in the courtyard carries the coat of arms of the Rothe family and a memorial slab. In looking around the house, glance upwards to see the fine workmanship in the roof timbers. In this restored house, the Kilkenny Archaeological Society (founded in 1849 and the oldest Irish body of its kind) has found a home for its regional museum. It is open to the public, May through September. The Courthouse across the street dates back to the sixteenth century; it was later the city jail.

Where Parliament Street meets St. Kieran's Street, you will find the home of the fourteenth-century witch, Dame Alice Kyteler, the daughter of a Norman banker. She was convicted "of sorcery and magic, of heresy and of having sacrificed to demons". The sentence was whipping through the streets and burning at the stake, but Dame Alice's influential friends assisted her to escape and she fled to England. Her servant and other accomplices were burned at the stake outside the Tholsel in High Street, a building with an unusual cupola arched over the footpath.

Nearby are the ruins of thirteenth-century St. Francis Abbey, which has given its name to the adjoining brewery. This abbey was at the northeast corner of the old city wall; over at the northwest junction was a Dominican friary of the same period. The church has been restored and is still in the possession of the Dominicans—the window of its south transept is something to

THE FACE OF IRELAND

note. Nearby is the old Black Abbey, or Trinity Gate, the only remaining gate of the old walled city. Shee's Almshouse (1594) is another of the representative buildings of the past; it is in Rose Inn Street on the way to St. John's Bridge, which provides the most imposing view of Kilkenny castle.

Kilkenny College (1780), on the right of John Street, is the successor of St. John's College, where Jonathan Swift (1667–1745), William Congreve (1670–1729) and the philosopher Bishop George Berkeley (1685–1753) were educated.

Kilkenny Arts Week is an unusual event which is staged in August and embraces virtually the whole city.

South from Kilkenny

To the southwest of Kilkenny City is the once-fortified town of Callan, the home place of Edmund Ignatius Rice (1762–1844), founder of the Irish Christian Brothers, an influential teaching order in Ireland (and with colleges in the U.S.A., South America, South Africa, India and Australia). Callan was also the home of Ireland's most famous diarist, Humphrey O'Sullivan, who was born in County Kerry about 1780 but settled with his father in Callan where he became a school teacher. For many years he kept diaries in Irish which are now in the Royal Irish Academy in Dublin and have been translated into English by a Jesuit, Father Michael McGrath.

Ten miles across country from Callan to the east is Thomastown, named for Thomas Walsh, a thirteenth-century seneschal of Leinster. Thomastown Castle, another of the castles which Cromwell's troops destroyed, was sufficiently restored to become an eighteenth-century 50-guestroom luxury inn, where the amenities included a pack of hounds (the Kilkenny Hunt today has its headquarters in Thomastown), an outdoor theater and a bowling green. The Mount Juliet Stud at Thomastown is one of the most successful in Ireland. In the grounds is buried the horse Tetrarch, the most famous two-year-old of all time. (The Irish have a pleasant habit of saluting distinguished sporting animals of the past and in the neighboring county of Waterford there is a monument, near Dungarvan, to Master McGrath, a greyhound that won the Waterloo Cup—the blue riband of coursing in England—on three occasions in the last century).

Focal point for the visitor in this neighborhood are Ireland's finest monastic ruins, Jerpoint Abbey, about two miles outside Thomastown, a Cistercian foundation of the twelfth century. The oldest sections are the chancel and transepts, in Hiberno-

THE SUNNY SOUTHEAST

Romanesque style. The architecture represents several centuries, including a fourteenth-century window, fifteenth-century cloisters and a battlemented square tower built at about the same time.

Two miles to the north of Thomastown, off the Kilkenny-Thomastown road, is the Legan Castle Studio, which specializes in designing and casting mosaic panels in addition to other graphic design activities.

The River Nore at Bennettsbridge, southeast of Kilkenny, has been providing power for Mosse's Flour Mills since 1503. It's not only the smallest mill in Ireland but its products include a mix which makes the famous Irish brown bread. One of the family, Dr. Bartholomew Mosse, founded the Rotunda Hospital in Dublin in 1751.

North of Kilkenny

Dunmore Cave, about seven miles north of Kilkenny, is not only interesting to cave explorers, but easy of access for the not-so-energetic. The caves have been known to be in existence since early Irish history and skeletal remains found there confirm that big battles once took place in the neighborhood. In one of the group of interlinked caves is the so-called Market Cross, a stalagmite column of great size.

To the northeast of Kilkenny City (27 miles) is the town of Carlow (pop. 7,700). Industrially progressive, it is the site of the first of Ireland's beet sugar and food processing factories. Its history has been particularly stormy, as it was an outpost of the English Pale and a fording place of the River Barrow. The last great battle was fought here during the Rising of 1798, when over 600 of the insurgents were killed, most of them being buried in a nearby gravel pit which is marked by a Celtic design memorial cross. The gothic-style Cathedral of the Assumption has John Hogan's monument to Bishop James Doyle (J.K.L.).

Captain Myles Keogh, who died with General Custer at Little Big Horn in June 1876, was born at Orchard House, Leighlinbridge, 9 miles from Carlow; there's a small museum to his memory at Clifden Castle nearby.

County Wexford

Across country to the southeast lies Gorey (in County Wexford), a major battleground of the 1798 Rebellion. Here the road from Dublin is joined; it continues south to Enniscorthy, a town which developed beside a castle on a hill which guarded the limit

THE FACE OF IRELAND

of the navigable waters of the River Slaney. The English poet Edmund Spenser (1551-99), author of *The Faerie Queene*, lived here at one time; at another, the castle was a jail. Now, it houses the regional museum, with an important folk section. The capture of Enniscorthy by the insurgents of 1798 inspired a major revolt in the country; the biggest engagement of the subsequent fighting took place on nearby Vinegar Hill. Enniscorthy's nineteenth-century cathedral (St. Aidan's) was designed by Augustus Pugin and its tower largely composed of stones from a ruined Franciscan Friary nearby. The fine memorial in the Market Square of Enniscorthy recalls the priest-leader, Father John Murphy, and his pikemen—it is the work of Oliver Sheppard.

The road south runs parallel to the River Slaney into Wexford (pop. 11,000), passing by Ferrycarrig, a narrow river gorge which still bears signs of its one-time military importance as a defense of the river entrance.

Wexford is identified by the historians as the Menapia of old; the town's name is a corruption of the Norse *Waesfjord*, "The Harbor of the Mud Flats", because the River Slaney was even wider than it is today when the early raiders came. In the seventeenth century, it was the naval base of the Catholic Confederation of Kilkenny. Cromwellian forces captured the town, but in 1798 the insurgents pushed the English garrison out and kept them out for nearly a month.

The town has lost its seaport character, but memories of the old sailing ship days are recalled by the Ballast Bank, a stone bank a short distance off shore where the ships which arrived light to collect cargo dumped the ballast from their holds. The Quay runs from the new bridge the full length of the town, broken by a Crescent, which is dominated by William Wheeler's bronze statue of Commodore John Barry, the father of the American navy. This memorial to the commander of the *Lexington* in 1776 was presented by the United States in 1956. (Barry was born at Ballysampson, about nine miles away, and the site of his birthplace is marked by a plaque.) A former lightship, the *Guillemot*, is moored to the quay and houses a floating museum.

St. Martin and the Tufted Ducks

St. Martin is the patron saint of Wexford fishermen, but they never put to sea on Martinmass Eve, November 10. Once in the last century they were said to have defied the tradition and the night brought disaster—over 80 men were drowned.

THE SUNNY SOUTHEAST

The narrow streets of the town create a problem for traffic—at one part of the main street, you can stretch out and shake hands with a man on the opposite footpath—but a one-way street system and a good deal of friendly tolerance keep things moving.

This corner of Ireland is a refuge for many species of wildfowl which migrate there. Half the world's population of Greenland white-fronted geese winter at Wexford; shelducks, mallard and tufted duck all breed on Wexford polders—known as the North Slob, a wildlife refuge, and the South Slob. There is rough shooting in the southeast, but these sanctuaries are strictly preserved.

Much of the old port traffic of Wexford has gone to New Ross, up the River Barrow from Waterford, but Wexford has made up the loss with a car assembly plant, a cheese factory and tweed weaving; it also has status as an historic touring center.

The late autumn Opera Festival, staged with top international singers in a small restored-Regency theater (the Theatre Royal), is a "must" event of the Irish social season and attracts a number of overseas visitors. Basically for opera, it has a wide range of fringe events, from sailing races to singing pub competitions, that provide a cross-section of Irish life at its most relaxed.

Mumming in Wexford

Another Wexford entertainment to be sought is Mumming. This is invariably a stylized dance or mime play performed by men; it is archaic in origin (somewhat similar forms are to be found in some districts of rural England). The participants wear a sash, usually green, with an orange rosette at shoulder and waist, sometimes with a harp embroidered on the sash. Each man carries a stick of an ash tree smoothed to the appearance of a sword blade. Sometimes the participants wear a hat or other insignia to identify the character they are portraying—a Turkish fez for the "Grand Signore" or a plumed hat for "Prince (or Saint) George" (invariably the tallest of the group). The characters in the Mumming plays hereabouts are virtually the same as those noted by folklorists in Britain, for there is no doubt that the Mumming in Wexford is English in origin, but there is also a version in which the characters are Irish heroes of the past, from St. Columcille (replacing St. George) to Father Murphy, the priest-leader of the 1798 Rising (naturally to be found in any hero-tale of the Wexford area).

Mumming is becoming a rare thing and this is one of the few places left to see it.

The town of Wexford slopes sharply up from its Main Street, in which you will find the homes of Jane Frances Elgee (the poetess "Speranza", who became Lady Wilde, mother of Oscar Wilde), and of the explorer Sir Robert McClure (discoverer of the Northwest Passage between the Atlantic and the Pacific), both now incorporated in the buildings of an hotel and a bank.

Of the old walls of the town, only the Westgate Tower remains. The nearby ruins are those of Selskar Abbey, a one-time Augustinian priory; the Church of St. Selskar (Sepulcher) is on part of the site and makes use of the old priory tower. Like the Augustinians, the Franciscans established themselves comparatively early in the history of the town and the present Franciscan Church in John Street is on the site of the original foundation. Beneath the altar of St. Francis are the relics of a Roman boy martyr, St. Adjutor, who was murdered by his own father; they were presented to an Irish family by Pope Pius IX in 1856. St. Iberius's Church, in the Main Street, has an unusual façade.

Hemmed in by shops and a market building in the center of the town is a square which still bears the name Bull Ring, because it was here that the Normans staged their bull-baiting competitions. Main interest of the ring today is the fine bronze statue of a Wexford pikeman of 1798 by Oliver Sheppard.

South of Wexford Town

Since the earliest days of recorded history, the southeast has had associations with Wales, the link in modern times being through the little port of Rosslare Harbour, terminal of the passenger- and drive-on-car-ferry from Fishguard and from Le Havre (France). This is a major entry point and the road system fans out from Wexford to give speedy access to the scenic areas of the south and southwest.

Within five miles of Rosslare is Lady's Island, on an almost totally enclosed inlet of the sea; it is linked to the mainland by a causeway and has been a place of pilgrimage for centuries. The pilgrimages now take place between August 15 and September 9. The ancient monastery on the island was dedicated to the Blessed Virgin—hence the name, Lady's Island. A mosaic from a former Fishguard-Rosslare ferry, found in a shipbreaker's yard, is now in St. Patrick's Church, Rosslare Harbour, as a memorial to all who died at sea in the area in World War II.

The flashing light six miles out to sea off this coast guards the notorious Tuskar Rock, a danger to shipping but a great place for anglers, sharing the latter role with the Splaugh Rock off the same coast. The last-named is noted for its bass fishing, while men who fish around the Tuskar not only bring back stories

THE SUNNY SOUTHEAST

of the big fish that got away, but the big fish themselves—usually skate, plaice, cod, tope and mackerel.

Kilmore Quay, not far from the rather dismally-named Forlorn Point (the Irish alternative is better—Crossfornoge), is one of the rapidly developing fishing ports around the Irish coast; the development, however, has not spoiled its quiet character. For the visitor the main interest is the facilities it provides for sea anglers and the boat service, weather permitting, to the Saltee Islands, which lie five or six miles south.

There is a name hereabouts which may puzzle visitors who have visited the famous Tintern Abbey on the River Wye in Monmouthshire, England. There is a Tintern Abbey in this part of County Wexford, named for the parent house, from which it was founded many centuries ago. Stones from the old abbey have since been used to build a local bridge and a church and part of the old building is embraced in the residence still known as Tintern Abbey.

New Ross and J. F. Kennedy Park

New Ross, 23 miles to the northwest of Wexford town, is a major inland port on the River Barrow and, to the pleasure of the growing number of people who like to take a holiday cruising on inland waterways, it is linked to Dublin and to the Shannon through the Grand Canal and the Barrow Navigation. Narrow streets are characteristic of its medieval nature. Most of the older buildings have disappeared. The Tholsel (Municipal Offices) is worth a visit because its treasures include old silver maces and the original charter granted to the town by James II. The town is called New Ross to distinguish it from the place now known as Old Ross, about five miles to the east, which it supplanted (because of its riverside location) in medieval times.

The road south on the left bank of the River Barrow leads to Dunganstown and the cottage where the great-grandfather of President John Fitzgerald Kennedy was born; Kennedy relatives are still living in the house. The memorial of Ireland and Irish-American groups to the late president is a £200,000 park bearing his name at Slieve Coillte, near Dunganstown. When the project is completed, 270 acres will be an arboretum in which it is planned to have 6,000 species of trees and shrubs from all parts of the world. It will be used as a training center for botanists and foresters and international meetings of silviculturists.

English monks settled at Dunbrody Abbey at Campile, about 10 miles from Dunganstown, in the twelfth century, but they

THE FACE OF IRELAND

seem to have surrendered their foundation to St. Mary's Abbey, in Dublin. Although the abbey was suppressed in the sixteenth century, the buildings are still sufficiently well-preserved to warrant a visit. The low tower is typical of religious establishments of its kind, and there are some elaborately-shaped windows of considerable beauty.

The county boundary separating Wexford from Kilkenny and Waterford runs down the middle of the River Barrow, which can only be crossed in this area by the bridge at New Ross, or, much lower down at the fishing village of Ballyhack, by passenger ferry to Passage East. Ireland's only remaining windmill (built 1846, restored 1971) is in the village of Tacumshane in South Wexford.

County Waterford

Crossing the Barrow into Kilkenny at New Ross, the road leads southwest to Waterford City (population 28,000).

The district to the west, South Kilkenny, is an important apple-growing area which extends into Waterford. If there is time to make a detour, take in the village of Kilmacow, where there is a modern mural covering 80 square yards of wall in the local parish church. It is the work of Father Aengus Buckley, an Irish Dominican whose murals include one at St. Joseph's University, Philadelphia, on the theme of hunger.

Two of the "sister rivers" of this southeast area, the Nore and Barrow, join before reaching New Ross; united at the Barrow, they flow south to join the Suir at Cheekpoint, on the seaward side of Waterford. Edmund Spenser, in his *Faerie Queene*, saluted all three of the rivers, but his special tribute was for ". . . the goodly Barrow, which doth hoord Great heapese of Salmons in his deepe bosome".

As the road enters Waterford, it makes a sharp turn over the River Suir to the quays which front the city itself; on the way, part of the old defenses may be seen near the railway station. It is a prospering port, as its busy quays indicate, with a number of major industries including the famous Waterford glass factory. Here, the ancient craft of glass-making has been revived with success in recent years. This craft is well worth taking time out to watch.

Danes gave the city its name (Vradrefjord, later anglicized to Waterford), although the Irish name is Port Láirge (in English, "Lairge's Landing Place"). The Danes were eventually pushed out by the Anglo-Normans and it was in Waterford that their great Norman leader Strongbow allied himself to the Irish by marrying Eva, the daughter of the King of Leinster, Dermot MacMurrough, thus considerably increasing his personal power in the country. Strongbow and Eva are buried in Christ Church Cathedral, Dublin.

From King John to Fort Sumter

Almost 1,000 years ago, Reginald the Dane landed in Waterford and built a circular guard tower with walls 10 feet thick and a low conical roof. Reginald's Tower is still standing, having served in succeeding centuries as a fort, a royal residence, a mint, a magazine for ammunition, a prison and a police barracks. Since 1955, it has been a civic museum of considerable interest, displaying many of the archives of the city's history. Waterford received a royal charter from King John in 1205, ten years before he signed the Magna Carta in England. Henry VII had also rewarded the loyalty of the city by granting it the motto *Urbs Intacta Manet Waterfordia*, which is still on the city coat of arms; what happened to the money he presented at the same time is not recorded!

The City Hall, built on the Mall in 1788, has a group of unusual exhibits, including two of the flags carried by the Irish Brigade at Fredericksburg and the uniform, sword and medals of Brigadier-General Thomas Francis Meagher (1823-67). Meagher was born on the Quay (a plaque on one of the buildings marks the site); he was an active "Young Irelander" and one of the founders of the Irish Confederation. Captured in the Rising of 1848, he was sentenced to death but the sentence was commuted to transportation: he escaped in 1852 and in America fought in the Civil War at Fort Sumter and Fredericksburg. Subsequently, he was appointed governor of Montana, but was drowned in the Missouri River in 1867.

Blue-blooded Glass

In the City Hall, after looking at the Meagher Collection, look up at the Waterford glass chandelier—its "twin" is in the Hall of Independence, Philadelphia.

Waterford was also the birthplace of Father Luke Wadding (1588-1657), a Franciscan, educated in Portugal, who became president of the Irish College at Salamanca, Spain, before founding St. Isidore's College for the Irish Franciscans in Rome. During a crowded life he wrote a number of works on history

THE FACE OF IRELAND

and philosophy and collected a library of 5,000 books and hundreds of manuscripts for the college.

Charles Kean (1813-68), one of the greatest actors of the London stage in his century, was another native of Waterford and so was the composer of *Maritana*, *Lurline* and other operas and operettas, William Vincent Wallace (1814-65). This link with the opera of the past was the inspiration for the latter-day Festival of Light Opera in Waterford, which brings together each year many operatic societies from England and Wales (as well as Ireland). On O'Connell Street, the Chamber of Commerce building is a good example of Georgian architecture, both in external appearance and for the fine staircase and ceilings within.

Don't pass up a visit to the famous Waterford Glass Works (check for times of free tours). Informative guides lead the way so that you can see the skill of glass blowing, polishing and cutting. There is an excellent lobby display, but no glass is sold on the premises.

Cathedrals and Mansions

There are two cathedrals, Roman Catholic and Church of Ireland; the original architect of both was the same man, John Roberts. Christ Church Cathedral in Cathedral Square near the City Hall is mainly nineteenth century, but there are some remnants of the ancient crypt which can be seen if the verger is contacted. St. Olaf's, in the same area, was a Danish church, later rebuilt by Normans. It has some beautifully carved black oak in its pulpit and a bishop's throne.

A tower is virtually the only remains of the thirteenth-century Franciscan Friary, which retains the name "French church" since its use by a Huguenot colony in the eighteenth century. The tower of the Dominican Priory (St. Saviour's) is the only major surviving part of the original foundation which dates back to 1266, but its treasures include a small oak figure of the Blessed Virgin known locally as "Our Lady of Waterford". Treasures in the Cathedral of the Holy Trinity, on Barronstrand Street just off the Quay, include a collection of cloth of gold vestments dating from pre-Reformation times; they were found during the demolition of the old Christ Church Cathedral nearly two centuries ago and presented by the Church of Ireland bishop to his Roman Catholic counterpart. The altar plate includes fine silver and gold craftsmanship from the seventeenth and eighteenth centuries.

Two big houses, Mount Congreve and Curraghmore (the latter owned by the Marquis of Waterford), are in the immediate neighborhood. Interest in Curraghmore is centered in the charm of the valley which forms part of the 10-square-mile estate, but there are also a collection of statuary and a Shell House. The gardens at Mount Congreve overlook the River Suir and are famous for an eighteenth-century conservatory (to be seen by appointment).

East of Waterford

If you take a swing along the estuary of the Suir and on to the coast of Waterford Harbour, you will find the pleasant village of Passage East. Cheekpoint Hill nearby provides sweeping views of the countryside, the Comeragh Mountains to the west and the Blackstairs Mountains to the northeast, as well as down the harbor to Hook Head on the Wexford side of the river. The headland saw its first beacon fire lit as a warning to shipping in the year 500.

Passage was the landing place of Strongbow, who arrived in 1170 with over 1,000 men; in the following year, the local waters must have been even more crowded, for Henry II arrived with a fleet of 400 ships and 4,000 troops.

Not far south of Passage are the ruins of Geneva Barracks, infamous in Irish hearts since the 1798 rebellion. The Barracks got its name from its original use, a home for a colony of immigrant goldsmiths and silversmiths from Geneva, who were invited to Ireland under a government-sponsored scheme in 1785. The scheme was a failure and the buildings were converted into military use and as a prison for the insurgents. The ruins, which overlook Waterford Harbour, are marked with a tablet.

Our road ends in the pleasant fishing village of Dunmore East; it is a village in name, but is in actuality a thriving fishing port, whose harbor is crowded with boats during the herring season. Most of the catch is exported, as are the substantial catches of lobsters and crayfish, regularly flown to Paris from Cork Airport. Despite the exports, there is invariably a fresh lobster or some other attractive fish dish to be enjoyed by the visitor. The little sandy coves and rocky inlets make it a good get-away-from-it-all holiday spot, and there is plenty of sport for sea anglers.

A popular resort on this coast lies just across Tramore Bay, at Tramore, where the beach is three miles long and suitable for bathing at all states of the tide. At the west end of the beach, the coast takes a sharp turn to form an arm of the bay and changes from a sandy shore to rocky cliffs—the Doneraile Cliffs,

THE FACE OF IRELAND

with a well-surfaced pathway barred to cars. The path leads on to the setting for one of Ireland's most popular legends. On the Great Newtown Head, at the end of the Doneraile Walk, stand three white pillars, on one of which is "The Metal Man", an iron figure of an old-time sailor with an arm pointing out to sea. It is said that if a young woman hops round the base of the pillar three times on one foot, she will be married within the year—and you will see them hopping away!

Across the bay on Brownstown Head, two more pillars can be seen as another warning, distinguishing Tramore Bay from the entrance of Waterford Harbour, which lies further east.

Local history goes back to the bronze age and there is a good example of a dolmen, one of the burial places of the period, at Knockeen, three miles from Tramore. Tramore today, however, is keenly conscious of the present, and its entertainment center, lively race meetings in the summer and other diversions justify its claim to be a seaside resort which has backed up its natural assets with intelligent development.

TIPPERARY

The Heart of Ireland's Dairyland

Just before World War I, Jack Judge, an Englishman, who so they say, had never been to Tipperary, wrote a song which has been sung around the world ever since: *It's a long way to Tipperary*. That may have done Tipperary a disservice by suggesting remoteness, for it's only 112 miles from Dublin and just over 50 from Cork, and even less from Shannon. To the traveler, Tipperary may be the inspiration of songs, but to the Irish, Tipperary is the county of hurlers and footballers, the breeding ground of fine horses and greyhounds and the heart of a great dairying area. Guarded on the south by the Knockmealdown and the Galty (sometimes Galtee) mountains and on the west by the Shannon and Lough Derg, it is great country for sportsmen, for mountaineering and cave exploration. It is also great for the traveler with a sense of the past and for the relaxed tourist who wants to enjoy the scenery. The main road from Dublin to the south and southwest passes diagonally through Tipperary, but it's a mistake for the traveler to hurry through an area which is both storied and scenically satisfying.

Tipperary has been the birthplace of many famous and infamous Irishmen. Buffalo Bill Cody was the son of emigrant parents from Tipperary, and Australia's famous Robin Hood-style bandit, Ned Kelly, was also a child of a Tipperary parent. There's one story that says Ned Kelly's mother was a sister of Buffalo Bill's father. And it may well be true, for the people

THE FACE OF IRELAND

of Tipperary traveled widely. For a picture of the county in the past, it's worth reading *Knocknagow,* by the nineteenth-century writer, Charles J. Kickham.

Exploring Tipperary and Beyond

Tipperary's historical background is emphasized almost as soon as the traveler crosses the county line—on driving in from Dublin, the remains of St. Cronan's Abbey, built in the twelfth century on the site of a monastic settlement five centuries earlier, dominate the entrance to the town of Roscrea. The west door of the abbey wall is a particularly good example of Hiberno-Romanesque architecture, with three arches within each other; and with sculptured heads and an ecclesiastical figure over the center (reputedly St. Cronan, the original founder of the monastery). One of the treasures of his original abbey is the illuminated gospel book, the *Book of Dimma*, which is now in the library of Trinity College, Dublin. Just across the road from the abbey, there is one of the familiar Irish round towers, but without its top, because it was blown off during the Rebellion of 1798, when a cannon was hoisted up the tower in order to command a better field of fire. There is an unexplained carving of a ship about 25 feet from the base.

In Castle Street, the castle is an imposing thirteenth-century structure, with some later additions, a reminder of the one-time strategic importance of the town. Nearby is a pleasant Queen Anne house. The Franciscan Friary in Abbey Street, founded in 1490, has been partly incorporated in the nineteenth-century Roman Catholic Church (St. Cronan's); the gateway to the church is part of the salvaged building.

Not far from Roscrea (about two miles east), there are remains of another church on what was once an island in a strange lake which disappeared just over two centuries ago—Loch Cré, the lake from which *Ros Cré* (Roscrea) got its name. The one-time island was a land of mystery and legend for centuries: to the Irish it was *Inis na mBeo*, "Island of the Living"; to the Anglo-Normans it was "Insula Viventium", the island on which there is no death, a reference to the belief that on the island the dead could not decay.

Thurles

Journeying south to Thurles is pleasant driving. The town itself is bounded by the Silvermines and Devil's Bit mountains—

there is a gap in the hills, clearly seen from the main road, which they say was bitten out by the devil in a fit of anger. Thurles is the seat of the Roman Catholic archbishop of Cashel, and his cathedral is a nineteenth-century Irish architect's interpretation of the Romanesque style. It is reputed to have been inspired by Pisa Cathedral.

Thurles (pop. 6,000) is the birthplace of the Gaelic Athletic Association, Ireland's biggest sporting body, which was founded at a meeting in *Hayes's Hotel* on November 1, 1884, during which Archbishop Thomas William Croke (1824-1902), a priest who was born in Cork and became bishop of Aukland, New Zealand, before returning to Ireland as archbishop of Cashel and Emly, was named patron. He is honored by a memorial in Liberty Square and by the naming of the GAA's main stadium in Dublin as Croke Park.

The one-time military importance of the town is recalled by the fifteenth-century castle keep guarding the south side of the bridge over the River Suir and another near the center of the town. There's another castle which was never completed two miles north of the town—it was the idea of a wealthy man named H. G. Langley in the nineteenth century to build a castle in the imposing style of Warwick Castle in England, complete with a moat filled with water and a drawbridge. The project came to a halt when well advanced because a piece of falling masonry killed the man with the money.

Near Newport, and close to the Slieve Felim mountains are the Clare Glens (named for the family, not the county), an interesting plantation of trees, all named, and strange rock formations.

Holy Cross Abbey

The remains of Holy Cross Abbey, beside the river just over four miles from the town on the road to Cashel, are worth an excursion for historic and scenic interest. The abbey was founded in the twelfth century by Donagh Cairbreach O'Brien, king of Munster, for a community of Cistercian monks, and had in its keeping a fragment of the Cross. The shrine became a place of many pilgrimages for centuries and the buildings were constantly being reconstructed. There is a most impressive east window of fine craftsmanship in the chancel, and on the right side of the chancel is a *sedilia*, a wall seat used by the celebrant and his assistants during High Mass, which is of finely carved black marble. It is considered to be one of the best examples of this

THE FACE OF IRELAND

work in Ireland. The age-old interest in hunting is seen in a mural in the transept, which shows three men on a stag hunt. When the monastery was suppressed in 1536, the lands became the property of the Earl of Ormonde. His family (the Butlers) were given the relic which gave the abbey its name; today it is in the Ursuline Convent at Blackrock, Cork. Holy Cross Abbey has been restored to replace an existing parish church.

When the Cistercians returned to County Tipperary in modern times, they established themselves at Mount St. Joseph's Abbey, near Roscrea, where they have an important college, a model farm and the only silk farm in Ireland, growing their own mulberry bushes to feed the silkworms.

The Rock of Cashel

Heading south across a plain, with the River Suir not far away on the west side, we see the Rock of Cashel, topped by its famous buildings of the past, dominating the landscape. Officially, it is St. Patrick's Rock, and unofficially, it is said to be the piece of rock that the devil spat out when he took the bite from the Devil's Bit to the west of Templemore: unfortunately for the legend, the Devil's Bit Mountain is sandstone, while the Rock of Cashel is limestone. But the legend is more entertaining than the geological fact that the Devil's Bit gap was worn away by a glacier in the Ice Age.

The town-name Cashel (pop. 3,000) derives from the Irish *caiseal* (a stone fort) and that was the basic concept which led to the establishment of the group of buildings on the rock. The kings of Munster held it as their seat for about seven centuries and it was here that St. Patrick plucked the shamrock which he held up in explanation as he preached the doctrine of the Trinity, an action which has given to Ireland the emblem which is universally recognized as essentially Irish.

Brian Boru, the great warrior king who defeated the Danes at the Battle of Clontarf (Dublin), visited Cashel to be crowned King of Munster. The reputed Coronation Seat of Brian and the other kings is now the great stone base of the Cross of St. Patrick, high up on the rock.

There is an atmosphere of life about the Rock of Cashel because the buildings from a distance have a remarkable appearance of being complete. You enter by way of an old Dominican Friary with a beautiful thirteenth-century window. The full value of the visit is in the astonishing group of buildings and the view of the surrounding countryside. The Round Tower is the dominant

TIPPERARY

feature from far off, because it is in perfect condition and 92 feet high, but only slightly lower in height is the old castle, 80 feet high and with walls so thick that they have passages inside them. St. Patrick's Cross, standing on the green patch just within the gateway, is believed to have been carved from a single block of stone.

Cormac's Chapel was built by Cormac, who was both a king and a bishop in the twelfth century; it is stone-roofed, vaulted and richly carved. Some of its features are unusual in Irish church architecture of the period and may be the result of continental European influence, notably a carving of a beast being attacked by a centaur.

The cathedral is thirteenth century, a cruciform building with high lancet windows typical of the period and an adjoining building which was probably the archbishop's residence. There is a roof walk on the top of the central tower, 127 steps up.

The cathedral was burned down in 1495 by Gerald, Earl of Kildare, who explained his action to King Henry VII with the excuse that he had thought the archbishop was inside! Another of the archbishops, Dermod O'Hurley, was martyred in St. Stephen's Green, Dublin, in 1583. Cromwellian troops damaged the cathedral, and it was repaired, although subsequently abandoned in 1748 because the archbishop of the time could not reach it in his coach from the town below.

Don't hurry through the buildings on the Rock of Cashel—it's easy to absorb the atmosphere and picture the men who lived here in the long ago if you take the time to wander through them slowly. It's also pleasant to rest on the short grass outside and look out across the quiet plains of Tipperary.

Down in the town of Cashel, there is another memory of its ecclesiastical past in the former *Archbishop's Palace*, just off the Main Street on the right-hand side, now an hotel. On the left of the same street, *Grant's Castle* is another hotel with a history; built in the fifteenth century, it was used as a prison and a place of execution before becoming a printing works and subsequently an hotel.

South of Cashel

One of Ireland's most famous bloodstock farms, Vincent O'Brien's Ballydoyle House Stud, is four miles out of town on the Clonmel Road. If you've a special interest, you can make an appointment for a visit.

The modern importance of Cahir (pop. 1,700), next town

on the road south, is as a marketing and sporting center. The original name, *Cathair Duin Iascaigh*, means "Fortress of the Fish Abounding"; the fortress (or its successor) is still there, and so are the fish. There was a fortress on the spot as early as the third century, but the present castle dates from 1142. Extensive restoration work has kept the castle in good preservation and a visit is worth any traveler's time because the castle is used as an "interpretive center" which explains aspects of architectural, historic and environmental interest. The center is equipped with an audio visual unit and its program "Stone Upon Stone", lasting 12 minutes and including over 500 color slides, tells the story of man's impact on the Irish landscape and shows the evolution of architecture in Ireland.

Charles Bianconi

It was to Cahir that the Italian immigrant Charles Bianconi operated his first transport service in 1815. Bianconi, who arrived in Ireland in 1802 as an apprentice picture-mounter and seller of prints, opened a shop in Carrick-on-Suir in 1806. Later, he used a gig to get around the county to drum up business because the ordinary mail coaches were too expensive and covered only a few routes. This gave him the idea of starting a service of his own—the first trip was by a two-wheeled outside car (known today as a jaunting car) which carried the mails and a couple of passengers the 12 miles from Clonmel to Cahir for 1s 6d (then about 50c) each. His operation developed until he was using coaches carrying up to 19 people and drawn by four horses, and the aggregate mileage on his route network was up to 4,000 miles a day. His home, Longfield House, is at Goold's Cross, 20 miles northwest, and is preserved (since 1970) by the Irish Georgian Society. (Period aquatints by M. A. Hayes of Bianconi's coaches are a good buy as a souvenir.)

The River Suir both north and south of the town is rich in salmon and in beauty; about 10 miles of fishing are available to vistors at reasonable rates. On one of the stretches is the charming Swiss Cottage, a meeting place for romance built by a one-time earl of Glengall who had an imposing Georgian mansion (now an hotel) in the town. It's a pleasant town for the traveler interested in angling or hunting (there are three hunts groups meeting within easy reach of the town). Because it is a good base town, a break from the main south road can conveniently be made to explore to the east of the county to Clonmel and the Valley of Slievenamon.

TIPPERARY

East to Clonmel

Clonmel (pop. 11,000) is Tipperary's chief town and because of its location on the River Suir was the subject of many water-borne raids in its early history. Later it became a walled town (its rebuilt West Gate still straddles a main road), and part of the old wall is still around St. Mary's (Church of Ireland) Church.

The author of *Tristram Shandy*, Laurence Sterne (1713-68), was born in Clonmel, the son of an English officer serving in the town; George Borrow (1803-81) was another English novelist who lived in Clonmel while his soldier father was on duty there; Borrow's work reflects rather more of the atmosphere he absorbed in Ireland than that of Sterne. The Town Hall on Mitchell Street has some very interesting civic regalia including swords and silver maces and a gold mayoral chain. Every new mayor is bound to add a fresh link.

A once-famous Weslyan chapel designed in the Greek style by Victorian architect William Tinsley, a native of Clonmel, has been converted into a little theater. The building had been unused for some years and the purchase and conversion have both preserved a beautiful building and provided an entertainment center.

Horse-breeding and greyhound-breeding are two considerable industries in the area and within the town there is a large cider plant which uses the apples from the orchards of the south. Not for nothing is the Irish name of the town *Cluain Meala*, "honey meadow".

To the northeast is Slievenamon (2,368 feet), an impressive viewing point associated with the delightful story which gave the mountain its name, literally, "Mountain of the Women". The legend says that the fairy women (or maybe just the beautiful girls of the district) were enchanting Fionn and his warriors, the Fianna, and finally Fionn agreed to marry the girl who won a race to the top of the mountain. The winner was Grainne, daughter of King Cormac, a woman later to be famous in the legend of Diarmuid and Grainne, the hunted star-crossed lovers of Ireland.

In the southeast of County Tipperary, Carrick-on-Suir (pop. 5,000) has a fine example of an Elizabethan fortified mansion, with the keep of an earlier castle beside it. The mansion was built by an earl of Ormonde, known as "Black Tom", for a proposed visit by Queen Elizabeth I. Nobody knows why the visit was called off, but "Black Tom" spent his money for nothing, except to provide a mansion which is still worth seeing.

THE FACE OF IRELAND

Mountains and Caves

For mountain-climbers, Carrick-on-Suir shares with Clonmel the claim to be the best town for exploring in the Comeragh Mountains, over the border in County Waterford. Clonmel is the undisputed center for the Knockmealdown Mountains, which form the county line with Waterford; they are best approached through the village of Clogheen. There's a fine road up the mountainside through Clogheen to the Vee Gap, passing on the way a cairn of stones known as Grubb's Grave. Grubb was a Quaker living in nearby Castle Grace and his death-wish was to be buried on the mountainside in an upright position facing towards the plains stretching to the north. He got his wish. Whether you propose to continue over the mountains into Lismore or not, it is worth driving to the top of the Vee Gap for the magnificent view of County Tipperary to the north and County Waterford on the south.

If you're staying on in Tipperary, journey westwards from Clogheen to the next village of Ballyporeen, because just north of this spot are the famed Mitchelstown Caves. They are called this, even though Mitchelstown is 10 miles away over the border in County Cork. In one of them, the Old Cave, the Sugan Earl of Desmond took refuge after an unsuccessful rebellion in 1601, but he was betrayed by a relation and died in the Tower of London. During the War of Independence (1921), the caves were again used by men "on the run" and the local landowner's house was burned down by the military because they suspected him of allowing the insurgents to shelter there. The caves form a fascinating network, some miles in extent, with interest for the amateur and plenty to attract the attention of the experts. The guide lives near the entrance to the caves.

To the north, the Galty Mountains and Galtymore (3,018 feet) bar the way to the Glen of Aherlow and Tipperary town, which lie beyond yet another range of hills. There are a number of pleasant hill walks on the southern slopes of the Galtys, but for people who want something a little more exciting, there are rock faces on the northern side.

The Way to Tipperary

The route to Tipperary is either through the mountains, between the Galty and the Ballyhoura mountains to the west, or back by way of Cahir. For the traveler driving eastwards, it is easy to recall how this was once the pass between Tipperary's

TIPPERARY

plains and Limerick and the scene of many a bloody battle, and how it became the hiding place (there are many small caves in the Galty Mountains) for men outlawed for their part in activities against the occupying forces. The road through the glen meets the trunk route in the village of Bansha, where Canon John M. Hayes (1888-1957), founder of *Muintir na Tire,* the important Irish movement for rural community development, was parish priest from 1946 until 1957; he is buried in the graveyard beside the church.

Turn northwest to Tipperary (pop. 5,000), the great dairy center of the rich pasture lands of the Golden Vale. It was here that Canon Hayes formed the first guild of Muintir na Tire in 1931. The history of the town is unspectacular. It was the birthplace of many famous men of the past, including the Fenian leader John O'Leary (1830-1907). William Hazlitt (1778-1830), the essayist, lived for a time nearby before his family moved to America and then back to England; Sir William Francis Butler (1838-1910), a British army officer who resigned his command because he was sympathetic to the Boers during the South African War, was born not far away; he wrote many books, including *The Wild Northland* and *Red Cloud*.

To the west of Tipperary is the village of Emly, which at one time had considerable ecclesiastical significance; an important church was founded here by a contemporary of St. Patrick, St. Ailbhe, whose name was joined with that of Patrick in the original naming of the Rock of Cashel. Ailbhe's Well is still visited in the neighborhood and an ancient cross in the graveyard beside the Roman Catholic church is supposed to mark the saint's burial place.

North of Tipperary

For centuries the existence of silver, lead and zinc in the appropriately-named Silvermine Mountains, south of Nenagh, has been well known; the lodes have been mined with varying degrees of success through history and are now being successfully exploited by an Irish-Canadian company operating under a license from the Irish Government, which controls all mineral rights in the country.

Nenagh (pop. 4,000) is the principal town of North Tipperary. The dominant feature of the town is the 100-foot-high circular keep of Nenagh Castle, one of the best examples of this type of structure in Ireland; it was once part of a much larger castle built in the thirteenth century. The top of the castle was reconstructed about 1860, but all its characteristic features remain, including winding stairs within the thickness of the walls to give access to the battlements at the top of the structure. Damer House, an excellent example of pre-Palladian architecture, within the walls of the Norman castle, has been leased to the Irish Georgian Society for 99 years and preservation and restoration work is being undertaken. The house bears the name of its builder, Joseph Damer, who married in 1714 and purchased the castle the following year. Used as a barracks for most of the nineteenth century and a school more recently, its future purpose will probably be as a museum and associated meeting rooms. It contains a very fine carved staircase and some original mantels. See it if you can.

Four miles northeast is a three-ringed earthen fort of prehistoric times with its stone gate piers still in position.

To the southwest of Nenagh the village of Ballina (don't confuse it with the town of Ballina in County Mayo; it's pronounced differently) is one of Tipperary's contact points with the River Shannon at the southern end of Lough Derg, the longest of the Shannon lakes.

The most important of the Lough Derg harbors in this area is at Dromineer, a few miles to the north of Ballina and five miles from Nenagh. The Lough Derg Yachting Club at Dromineer is one of the oldest in Ireland and the village is noted for its amiable hospitality to visitors who are interested in water sports. There are frequent cruises on Lough Derg from Dromineer, Garrykennedy Quay and Killaloe; the lough is an inland sea 25 miles long from Portumna in Galway to the limit of inland navigation at Killaloe at the southern end. Scenically, the shores and the many lake islands are beautiful, offering plenty of picnic sites. Warnings are issued by the Lough Derg yachtsmen to the inexperienced; they ask that the advice of the local men be heeded, as they know the waters and such things as the "Scarriff Breeze", which blows across from the Clare shore and can be dangerous. There's more advice to be got from the local fishermen—at the north end of the lake, for example, coarse fishing from the banks is particularly good at Munster Harbour, Connacht Harbour and Hayes's Island. The size of Lough Derg pike is almost legendary.

North to County Westmeath

Exploration of the northern sector of this area is most easily made from Athlone (pop. 10,000), which is astride the River Shannon and takes its name from the river crossing, *Ath Luain*,

"Ford of Luan", Luan being a one-time innkeeper beside the crossing. There is an older name, *Ath Mor*, "Great Ford", but there's no doubting the town's importance through the centuries as the dividing line between the eastern and western provinces. It was the scene of many battles; the first "modern" defenses of the crossing were built in the twelfth century. The existing castle, known as King John's Castle, was built by John de Gray in 1210 and is known today both by its old name and as Adamson's Castle, for Brigadier George Adamson, who fought in the Irish War of Independence.

Just below the castle is the pier for joining the waterbuses for tours on the Shannon River. While Athlone is a major point on the Shannon most of the cruiser hire operators are based up-river, but there are some at this point including *Athlone Cruisers* from whom boats may be hired on a weekly basis.

From Athlone, an armada of a hundred or more small craft sets out every July for the north, through Lough Ree, for the Shannon Boat Rally, but there is so much space on the Shannon that the waterway is never crowded and the anglers and the peace-and-quiet seekers are not disturbed.

Old Athlone

On the Leinster (eastern) side of the Shannon, the old character of Athlone is shown in the narrow streets approaching the river and its bridge. The nineteenth-century St. Mary's Church, in the center of the town, stands beside the tower of an older church which, according to tradition, has one of the bells from the old ecclesiastical settlement at Clonmacnois, lower down the river. (Its second bell comes from the Tholsel, or Market House.) Near the riverside is the Franciscan Friary and the remains of a thirteenth-century foundation of the same order. On the outskirts of the town are the remains of fortifications built in the early nineteenth century in preparation for a French invasion which never happened. In the neighborhood, too, there are eskers showing the track of the glaciers of the ice age across this part of the country.

Famous sons of Athlone include Count John McCormack (1884-1945), the great Irish tenor, whose birthplace on The Bawn, off Mardyke Street, is marked with a plaque. There is a fine portrait bust in bronze of the singer (unveiled 1970) by Cork sculptor Seamus Murphy on the promenade beside the Shannon. T. P. O'Connor (1848-1929), Nationalist member of parliament,

THE FACE OF IRELAND

journalist and litterateur, was born in the house marked with a plaque in The Square.

Clonmacnois

Clonmacnois, one of Ireland's most important early monastic settlements, is 13 miles south of Athlone (about nine miles by river). It was founded about A.D. 548 by St. Ciaran, who died a few months later, when only 33. The first settlement grew rapidly into a large monastic city and medieval university. None of the original buildings remain; the earliest structures to be seen were built in the ninth century, among them Temple Ciaran, a cell just over 12 feet long, reputed to be on the place where Ciaran built his original oratory. Enter the area at the parking place, where the road reaches the site from Shannonbridge.

On the right is the South Cross, dating from the eleventh century. Walking to the right, the first building you see is Temple Doulin, a restored ninth-century church, and adjoining it, a seventeenth-century church (Temple Hurpain). Next is the twelfth-century King's Church (Temple Ri), which is on a rise in the ground and has an interesting east window.

To the north is Temple Ciaran, where the saint is reputedly buried at the end most distant from the door. The largest building of the group (facing towards the entrance again) is the cathedral, originally founded in 904 by Abbot Colman and King Flann. There has been considerable restoration work in later centuries.

Nearby there is a remarkable gallery of ancient carved grave slabs, and beyond them a refuge tower, O'Rourke's Tower, built between the tenth and twelfth centuries. About 500 yards on the east of the main settlement is the Nun's Church, built in the tenth century and an outstanding example of Irish Romanesque architecture at its best. The monks of the settlement produced many famous books, including *The Book of the Dun Cow*, now in the Bodleian Library at Oxford. Metalworkers produced great works, and the masons have left the results of their skill as stone carvers for the traveler to see centuries later. Because of its artistic and material wealth, Clonmacnois was raided many times in its history, by everybody from the Vikings to the English, and it was finally despoiled in 1552. Restoration work has been well done to preserve the past so that it can tell its story through the stones.

There's a pilgrimage to Clonmacnois on September 9 each year.

A few miles down river is Shannonbridge, a village with a single street and an imposing stone bridge across the Shannon

TIPPERARY

into the west. Shannon Harbour, still further south, is the Shannon's link with the Grand Canal and the waterway to Dublin, a well-known meeting place for yachtsmen.

The little town of Banagher (pop. 1,000), 13 miles downriver from Shannon Harbour, is in the heart of angling country, located almost halfway between Lough Ree and Lough Derg. Remains of old defenses built to command the river crossing are still to be seen, but most of Banagher's links with the past are peaceful: novelist Charlotte Brontë (1816-55), writer of *Jane Eyre*, spent her honeymoon at Banagher in Hill House; another English novelist, Anthony Trollope (1815-82), was stationed in Banagher when he was a postal service official, and in this district he found the material for his Irish novels, *The MacDermots of Ballycloran*, *The Kellys and the O'Kellys*. It was Trollope who later wrote in his autobiography of the peace of mind he found in Ireland—he wasn't the first to make the discovery, and he is certainly not the last!

THE CHARM OF THE SOUTH

Cork and Kinsale, Bantry and Blarney

County Cork, heart of the Province of Munster (an historical geographical area with no political significance today), is the largest county in Ireland, with 2,880 square miles stretching from Limerick and Tipperary down to the Atlantic. Over mountains and through valleys of much charm, like the Blackwater and the Lee, Cork extends to the coastline, rugged rocks alternating with sandy beaches, lying southwest of County Waterford and east of the mountains of the Kerry border. (For reasons of convenience we have overlapped the county boundaries; "The South" in our book, therefore, embraces the part of County Waterford west of Tramore.)

There is a strong feeling of regional loyalty and an almost fierce pride among the people of Cork, which has contributed many leaders to Ireland in the past as well as in the present. The ear of the stranger will detect a different note in the voice, a lilting sound to which it is easy to become attuned. History jostles with modern times, industry with a leisurely way of life—there is a sense that Cork has an age-old character and is unlikely to be perturbed by changes; it will absorb them all and adapt what is best. This is one of the most prosperous areas in the country, industrially and agriculturally, although you may wonder in the western section of the county how a living may be earned on certain remote farms.

THE CHARM OF THE SOUTH

If you are lucky, you may see road bowling, a game that is peculiar to this part of the country. It is deceptively simple to watch: it consists of a contest between two players to throw a 28-ounce iron ball along a roadway over a distance of two or three miles with, of course, the least number of throws winning. The matches are known as "scores" and there is often high betting on the participants.

The gentle breezes of the south and its uncrowded roads have inspired a leisurely way of looking at the countryside by horse-drawn caravan, Romany in external design, but with modern conveniences on board and a horse that knows the roads. A growing number of young people like to explore the Lee and the Blackwater, both of which give access to large tracts of the south, by canoe.

Whatever your interest, from canoeing to conversation, you can find it in the south, and don't expect to go to bed early if you get into an evening conversation for if "the talk" is good, nobody minds the time. A word of warning, however: the trains and the buses do run on time. Enjoy the atmosphere, the food and the drink and most important of all, relax in the part of Ireland which knows best how to do just that.

Exploring the South

Because the City of Cork, with its population of 120,000, is Ireland's third largest city (after Dublin and Belfast) and the county center, it is the most convenient focal point for visitors to the south. It is also a place with a certain charm that captures interest even before you get your bearings. The popular reference point for Corkonians giving directions is "The Statue", John Henry Foley's statue of Father Theobald Mathew (1790-1861), a superior of the Capuchin Friary in Cork, who led a nation-wide temperance crusade.

"Ivernia" is the old tribal name for the region of Cork and Kerry; the Ivernii were reputedly the chief tribe in Ireland in the second century. The shortened name for the Cork/Kerry Regional Tourism Organization is just "Ivernia"—you will find the office on Patrick Street if you want any local aid or information.

When late in the sixth century, St. Finbarr (you'll find the name also written Fin Barre) came down the valley of the River Lee he built a church on the south bank and established a school. Legend says that he came down to slay the last dragon left in Ireland. Finbarr found a marshy place where the Lee reached

THE FACE OF IRELAND

sea level and the waters divided to form a mile-long island, which is now the heart of the city. Today, Cork has spread up the steep hillside of the valley, making it a bowl-shaped city, the Lee below arched with numerous bridges.

Through the centuries the city earned the name of "Rebel Cork", a title of which it was justly proud and which it maintained until after independence in 1922. Cork's role in the final phases of the fight for independence cost the lives of two lord mayors—Lord Mayor Thomas MacCurtain was assassinated (his name is remembered in MacCurtain Street) and his successor, Terence McSwiney, died in Brixton Prison, London, after a hunger strike of 74 days. The bitter days of 1920 are responsible for much of the new building in the city, for a large area, including most of Patrick Street and the City Hall, was burned down by British auxiliary forces.

The rebuilding has given Cork a fine City Hall, with a dignified façade of dressed limestone overlooking the South Channel of the Lee. The public auditorium associated with the building is the center for the International Choral Festival each spring, and many other events during the year, including the informal Festival Club associated with the International Film Festival in June. This festival is primarily for documentary and short films, but there is a feature section also, to attract filmgoers. The festival is less exotic and more good-humored than most of its kind.

When on the south side of the city, visit St. Fin Barre's Cathedral. There has been a church on the site for 1,300 years, but the present building was erected in the second half of the last century.

To the west of St. Fin Barre's, on Western Road, is University College, Cork, founded in 1845. Originally established as a Queen's College (Victoria was the queen), it is now one of the constituent colleges of the National University of Ireland. The buildings are attractive and dignified examples of nineteenth-century university architecture, with some modern additions. The college library and associated collections include a number of Ogham stones. Ogham was the early Irish form of writing and the inscriptions on the stones are usually of a commemorative character.

The Bells of Shandon

When in Patrick Street, which was originally built in 1789 by covering in a channel of the Lee, turn north over St. Patrick's Bridge and then left along Camden Quay to Pope's Quay and

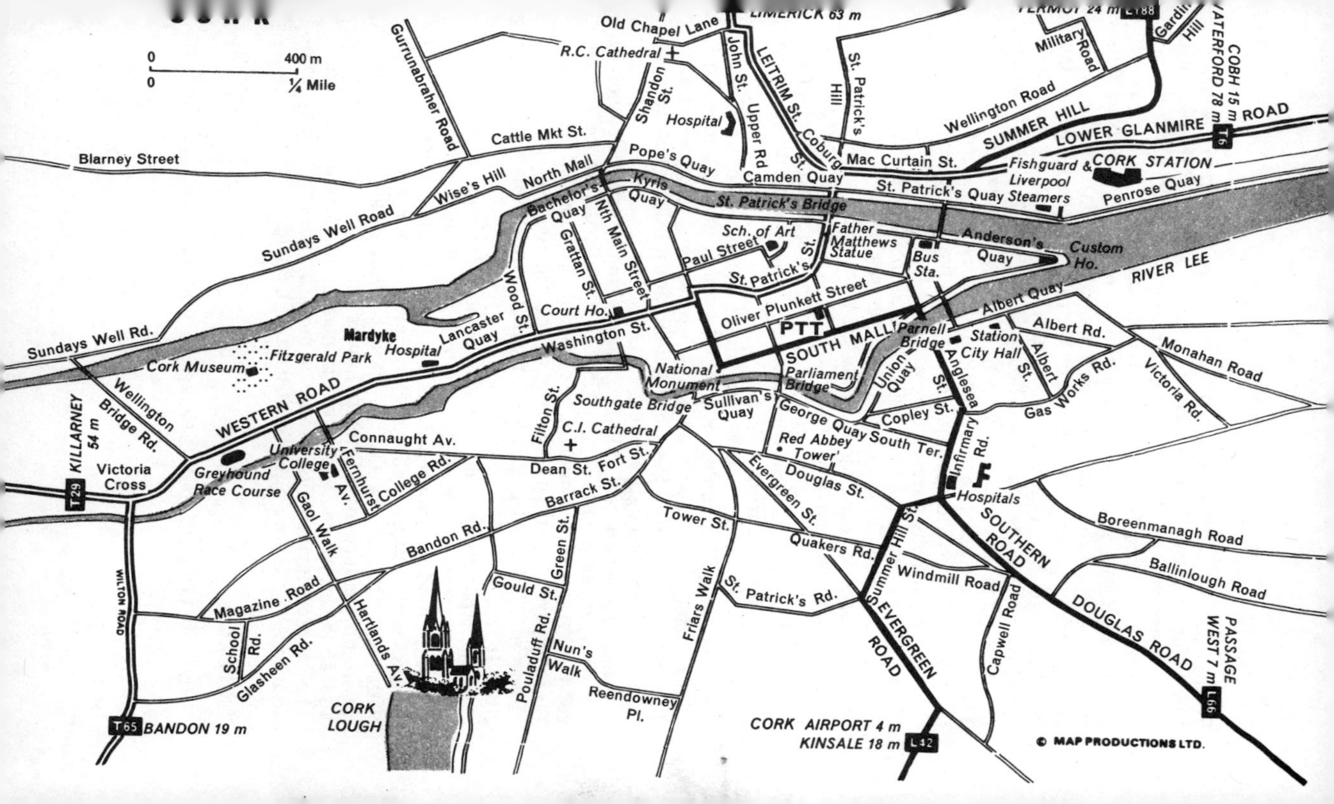

0
400 m
0
¼ Mile
LIMERICK 63 m
COBH 15 m
WATERFORD 78 m
T6
ROAD
LOWER GLANMIRE
SUMMER HILL
Military Road
Wellington Road
St. Patrick's Hill
Old Chapel Lane
R.C. Cathedral
John St.
LEITRIM St.
Shandon St.
Hospital
Upper Rd
Coburg St.
Mac Curtain St.
Fishguard & Liverpool Steamers
CORK STATION
Penrose Quay
Gurrunabraher Road
Cattle Mkt St.
Blarney Street
Pope's Quay
Camden Quay
St. Patrick's Quay
North Mall
Wise's Hill
Kyrls Quay
St. Patrick's Bridge
Bachelor's Quay
Sundays Well Road
Nth Main Street
Grattan St.
Sch. of Art
Paul Street
St. Patrick's St.
Father Matthews Statue
Bus Sta.
Anderson's Quay
Custom Ho.
RIVER LEE
Wood St.
Court Ho.
Oliver Plunkett Street
PTT
SOUTH MALL
Albert Quay
Parnell Bridge
Station
City Hall
Albert Rd.
Albert St.
Monahan Road
Victoria Rd.
Gas Works Rd.
Sundays Well Rd.
Mardyke
Hospital
Lancaster Quay
Washington St.
Fitzgerald Park
Cork Museum
National Monument
Parliament Bridge
Union Quay
Anglesea St.
Copley St.
Wellington Bridge Rd.
WESTERN ROAD
Southgate Bridge
Sullivan's Quay
George Quay
South Ter.
Infirmary Rd.
Filton St.
C.I. Cathedral
Red Abbey Tower
KILLARNEY 54 m
T29
Victoria Cross
Connaught Av.
University College
Fernhurst Av.
Dean St.
Fort St.
Douglas St.
Hospitals
Greyhound Race Course
College Rd.
Barrack St.
Evergreen St.
SOUTHERN ROAD
Gaol Walk
Green St.
Tower St.
Boreenmanagh Road
Bandon Rd.
Quakers Rd.
Summer Hill St.
Windmill Road
Ballinlough Road
WILTON ROAD
Magazine Road
Gould St.
St. Patrick's Rd.
Friars Walk
EVERGREEN ROAD
Capwell Road
DOUGLAS ROAD
School Rd.
Glasheen Rd.
Hartlands Av.
Pouladuff Rd.
Nun's Walk
Reendowney Pl.
PASSAGE WEST 7 m
L66
T65
BANDON 19 m
CORK LOUGH
CORK AIRPORT 4 m
KINSALE 18 m
L42
© MAP PRODUCTIONS LTD.

THE FACE OF IRELAND

St. Mary's Dominican Church to see, on the Lady Altar, a fourteenth-century Flemish figure of Our Lady of Graces. This small figure was originally in the Dominican church at Youghal, where it had been found on the beach embedded in a piece of wood which was apparently part of the mast of a wrecked ship (possibly one of the ships of the Spanish Armada). In this hilly area of the city, too, is the famous 120-foot Shandon Steeple, the bell tower of St. Anne's Church, built on the site of a church destroyed when the city was besieged by the Duke of Marlborough (then John Churchill) for William of Orange in 1690. The steeple, shaped like a pepper-pot, houses the famed Bells of Shandon. The odd device on the top of the steeple is a gilded fish. The eight bells were cast by an Abel Rudhall, of Gloucester, England, who also made the bells for St. Fin Barre's Cathedral.

St. Mary's Pro-Cathedral, in the same area, is another example of gothic architecture, this time dating from 1808, with later and rather elaborate interior decoration by George Richard Pain. Incidentally, if you think you have Cork forebears, you might care to check at the presbytery here, for their records of births and marriages date from 1748.

There's one thing in common about the churches in Cork— they have excellent choirs, to hear the voices of the young Cork children singing in church on a Sunday morning is quite pleasing. The natural voices of the Cork people are musical, and in song they are particularly attractive.

Returning down the hill and across the North Channel of the river, make a visit to the Cork Art Galleries, housed in the red-brick Crawford Municipal School of Art, located in Emmet Place, just off Lavitt's Quay. Part of the building was the Custom House in 1724; it has been an art gallery under varying auspices since 1832.

Most exploring around the city is best done on foot, cutting through narrow streets with their old-style houses and breaking out into modern thoroughfares such as Patrick Street, Grand Parade and South Mall. Modern architecture often contrasts with the old, as in Grand Parade, where there are some eighteenth-century bow-fronted houses near the South Channel, and at the other end, an open-air market in Cornmarket Street. The market, incidentally, is still named for the Coal Quay (pronounce it "Coal Key"), where it used to be held.

Old Cork

Just off Grand Parade you are in the oldest part of the city.

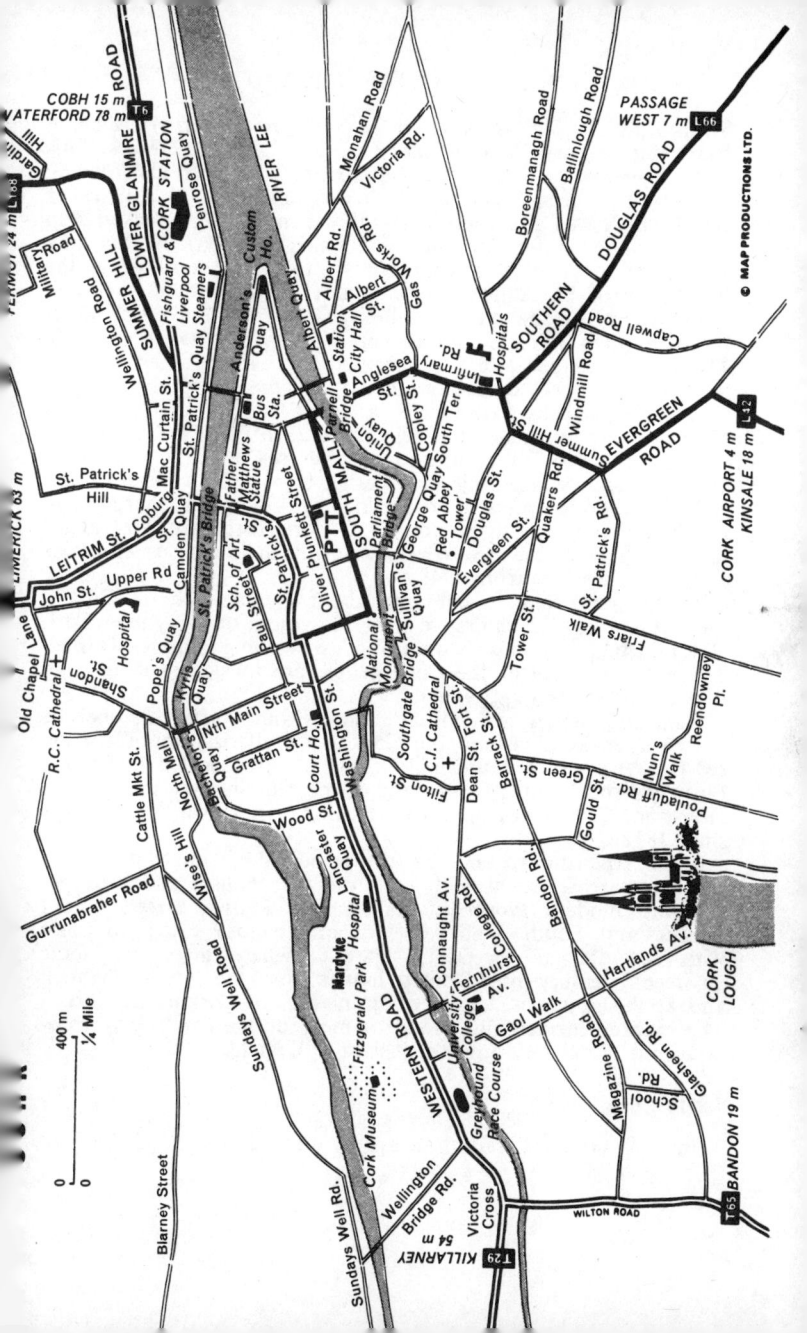

THE CHARM OF THE SOUTH

The Mercy Hospital (Peter's Street) incorporates the old Cork Mansion House (1767) and contains some fine stucco ceilings which may be seen if you ask permission. Returning to the Grand Parade, there is, at the junction with South Mall, an architecturally exuberant gothic monument to some of the Irish patriots of the eighteenth and nineteenth centuries—Erin is under the canopy and the statues are those of Wolfe Tone, Thomas Davis, Michael Dwyer and O'Neill Crowley. South Mall is the commercial and legal district and in the Munster and Leinster Bank Building there are roof-supporting marble pillars from Old St. Paul's Cathedral, London.

One church which it is suggested should be included in a tour of the city is the Church of Christ the King (1930), at Turner's Cross about two miles from the city center; designed by Barry Byrne of Chicago, it was the first break from traditional church architecture in Ireland.

Cork, like Dublin, has a long brewing tradition. The Cork Porter Brewery, as it was originally known, was in operation in the early seventeenth century; in 1791, it was taken over by three partners—William Beamish, William Crawford and Richard Barrett. Today, the brewery, still known as Beamish's, is part of United Breweries of Ireland, Ltd., and a new plant has been built on the old site in South Main Street. Tours arranged.

William Penn (1644-1718), the founder of Pennsylvania, was born in County Cork and spent his boyhood here; he became a Quaker at the meeting house in Cork City then in Nile Street (it is now called Sheares Street, for two United Irishmen executed for their political associations).

The central island, which is the heart of Cork, ends at a point downriver overlooked by the Custom House and the offices of the harbor commissioners. From the Port of Cork, in 1838, sailed the first steamship to make the westbound crossing of the Atlantic. The *Sirius* made it in the record time of 17 days. As the local people will remind you, if you mention the feat, the *Sirius* was commanded by a Corkman, Captain Roberts.

Downstream to Cobh

Cork Harbour has found a new and vital role, as a base for oil exploration off the south coast. At the entrance to the Upper Harbour is the river port. A waterside power station is a dominant feature on the city's edge, but immediately beyond it on the south bank is a long tree-lined promenade and on the north bank the main road and railway to Cobh (pronounce it "cove") run parallel to the river for some distance beside the slopes of the fashionable Tivoli and Montenotte districts. A short distance down river, Blackrock Castle is a dominant south bank feature; its original purpose was to guard the entrance to Cork. Built in the sixteenth century and rebuilt in the last, it is now a first-class restaurant. William Penn is reputed to have stayed here before sailing for America.

The Lee flows eastward into Lough Mahon, past Little Island (famous for its golf course) and then breaks into channels again to create Great Island, on which Cobh and its shipyard are located. Cobh (then called "Queenstown") was at one time an important British naval base, the fleet anchorage being in the vast land-locked harbor known as the Cove of Cork. During World War I, it was a base for the U.S. Navy, which also established a seaplane station at Aghada on the eastern shore of the harbor, near the location of the republic's only oil refinery. Many of the buildings on Haulbowline, one of the islands off Cobh, were built by convict labor for naval use. Today its old fortifications are still partly occupied by the Irish Army; another part of the island is used as a cattle quarantine station. Two other forts at the entrance to the harbor are now known as Fort Davis and Fort Meagher. Nearby, the Irish Naval Service has its headquarters on the headland.

Many of the emigrant ships of the last century sailed from Cobh, but today it is only an occasional cruising port of call for liners, and there are no longer tears, as in days gone by, when families broke up as numerous young people left to seek their fortune across the ocean. The best view of Cobh is from the sea. Its West Beach is the waterfront and it is dominated from the hillside by the gothic revival St. Colman's Cathedral. The building and decoration took from 1868 to 1919 and much of the cost was subscribed by Americans. There is a 17-ton carillon of 47 bells in the tower; regular recitals are given by the carrillonneur—it is worth making a point of hearing a performance.

Many of the victims of the sinking of the liner *Lusitania* (torpedoed off the Old Head of Kinsale, May 7, 1915) are buried in the cemetery of the ruined Clonmel Church, about two miles from the town. The impressive Lusitania Memorial is on the waterfront, and a short distance away is the one-time headquarters of the world's oldest yacht club, the Royal Cork, which dates back to 1720. It is now an educational establishment.

Cobh has become a deep-sea angling center; apart from fishing within the harbor area, blue shark, tope and ling are caught beyond Roche's Point.

THE CHARM OF THE SOUTH

Cloyne and Ballycotton

When on this side of the River Lee, explore further to the east, to take in Cloyne, with another St. Colman's Cathedral, on a foundation dating from the thirteenth century. St. Colman himself founded the first church in Cloyne. The present building has undergone a number of changes, but it is still in use as the cathedral church of the Church of Ireland diocese of Cloyne. A fine view of the neighborhood can be enjoyed from the tower (there are a wooden stairway and platforms inside)—the key is at the verger's cottage beside the cathedral.

Tucked into the side of a cliff a few miles to the southeast, traveling by way of Shangarry (William Penn's family once lived here) to look in on the local pottery, is Ballycotton, long famous as a deep-sea angling center. Off shore is a steep island dominated by a lighthouse, where the Atlantic sweeps around the headland to become calm in the wide expanse of Ballycotton Bay.

Along the Blackwater

Go on now from Ballycotton to the west bank of the River Blackwater, at its estuary at Youghal (pronounce it "yawl"). Incidentally, the river is reputedly the best in Europe for roach fishing (it is locally known as the Munster Blackwater because there are two other rivers of the same name in Wexford and Meath); it is at its most beautiful around Lismore.

It is said that Phoenicians established the pottery industry here 200 years before the birth of Christ, and the tradition still exists. The name Youghal (pop. 5,000) means "Yew Wood" and there are still a few yew trees to be seen. Organized invasions, raids and pillaging by pirates all struck Youghal at various times. Some of the raiders came from Spain and Algeria, but none was able to settle; a relic of one of the Spanish ships, the ivory figure of Our Lady of Graces, now in the Dominican Church in Cork, is as much likely to be a relic of a shipwreck of this time as from a Spanish Armada vessel. In the main street there is a beautifully carved statue of the Madonna and Child by the Cork sculptor Seamus Murphy, based on the ivory figure. It's a busy corner, so best park some distance away.

Richard Boyle (1566-1643), the remarkable English lawyer who became the first earl of Cork and who had a major role in Lismore's history, is buried in the Church of St. Mary, sited on an old church and dating back to the thirteenth century, although considerably restored at various times. Myrtle Grove is the best-known of all the buildings in the town; it is a good example of Elizabethan domestic architecture and it was in the garden here that Sir Walter Raleigh (who was Mayor of Youghal at the time) is reputed to have planted the first potatoes in Europe and smoked tobacco to the astonishment of his servants. The house is still occupied as a private residence and is not open to the public.

On the main street you literally pass through one of the principal remaining architectural features, the Clock Tower, which straddles the street. This eighteenth-century replacement of an earlier gate has served as a jail during its history; it is now a museum and display center for local crafts as well as a tourist information office. Local crafts, by the way, include the handmade lace known as *Pointe d'Irlande*.

Tynte's Castle is a 400-year-old tower; also, parts of the old town walls are still to be seen, including the Water Gate (also known as Cromwell's Gate, because he passed through it when he landed at Youghal in 1649). Youghal provides an interesting example of how events become absorbed in local folk history; film director John Huston used Youghal for the New Bedford harbor scenes in his film of *Moby Dick,* so today, one of the popular bars is known as *Moby Dick's*. Youghal's interest for the visitor is mainly historical, but its long sandy beach and recreational facilities make it a popular seaside resort as well.

A Side-Trip to Dungarvan

About 30 miles to the east is the prosperous little port town of Dungarvan (pop. 5,200), a rapidly developing angling center which has boats available for shark and inshore fishing. Five miles away is Helvick Head (230 ft.), which is interesting to visit, not only for its scenery, but because it has a monument commemorating the landing of a group of 200 Irish-Americans with arms and ammunition to take part in the Fenian Rising of 1867.

In this area, at An Rinn (Ring), there is a college for the teaching of Irish, so the language is very much alive both here and in the neighboring village of Ballynagaul. Ardmore, 15 miles from Dungarvan, is another of the Irish language centers of County Waterford; it was here that St. Declan founded a monastic settlement in the seventh century. His Oratory, with some modern reconstruction, is an interesting example of an early church, just over 13 feet long and under nine feet wide, with a high-pitched roof; the reputed grave of the saint is at the southeast corner of the building. The Round Tower is well preserved and is unusual because it bears some grotesquely carved heads in the interior (most round towers were severely practical in their structure and lacked ornamentation of any kind). There's a local tale that St. Declan's Stone, a glacial boulder on the seashore, cures the rheumatism of persons who crawl under it; there may be doubt about the legend, but it is apparent from remains at Temple Dysert, another of the ruins, that there was a Holy Well and pilgrims bathed in the waters.

The Knockmealdown Mountains

When you're in Ardmore you are 37 miles from Cork, if you plan to return directly by the main road through Youghal and Midleton (where there is the largest pot-still in the world: it holds 36,000 gallons of spirits).

We recommend, however, going up through Cappoquin and The Vee on the top of the Knockmealdown Mountains to cut across a corner of Tipperary from Clogheen. It's worth stopping off at Cappoquin to look at a particularly odd piece of architecture, Dromana Gateway, described variously as "Hindu-Gothick" and "Brighton Pavilion" architecture. With a pale green onion dome on top of a gothic arch, flanked by slender minarets, it looks astonishingly out of place in rural Ireland. It is the only gateway of its kind in the country and stands beside a bridge over the River Finisk. Now owned by the Forestry Commission, it was carefully restored in 1966.

Near Cappoquin is famed Mount Melleray. A landowner in County Waterford, Sir Richard Keane, gave the monks a stretch of wild, unreclaimed mountain land, here on the Knockmealdowns, then treeless and a wilderness of bog, boulders and gorse. The first monks moved in to a cottage on the mountainside in 1832 and since that time, the Abbey of Mount Melleray, named for the mother house of the order at Nantes (from which the monks had been driven by the religious persecution in France), has expanded considerably. The monks have progressively reclaimed more land and created an important 500-acre farm; they have built their monastery and their church and a seminary. There are two churches, one the enclosed church of the monks and the other for public worship. The abbey church is largely built of stone from the ruined Mitchelstown Castle. From the public church, there is a stairway leading to a gallery from which the enclosed church may be seen, with the Great Cross hanging from the roof and the stalls of the monks along the sides. There is a guesthouse at the abbey at which men may stay. There is no charge (the guest leaves whatever offering he wishes) and there is a neighboring guesthouse for women. The monks are Cistercians bound by the strict rule of silence, but the guest master is absolved from the rule during his period of office. Virtually all the needs of the community and the guests are met with the produce of the monks' mountain farmlands.

Lismore and The Vee

To the west, historical Lismore dates back to the seventh century when it became a major ecclesiastical and educational center, but its character was destroyed through the centuries of raids and counter raids. Lismore Castle and grounds, belonging to the Duke of Devonshire, stand on the banks of the Blackwater. The castle itself is of eighteenth-century construction incorporating parts of earlier castles on the site. The entrance gate is thought to have been a chancel arch from a twelfth-century church. The lands were once owned by Sir Walter Raleigh, who sold them, with other Irish estates, to Richard Boyle, later to become known as the "Great" Earl of Cork, a man who defeated much plotting at the court of Elizabeth I of England to survive and receive an earldom (1620) and become High Treasurer for Ireland (1631). The Lismore Estate passed to the Devonshire family in 1753. The estate owns extensive fishing rights and enquiries should be made to the Estate Office, Lismore, for salmon, sea- and brown-trout fishing. Lismore Castle Gardens are open to the public in summer.

If you drive along the road to Clogheen, it will take you up the Knockmealdowns to The Vee, a gap in the mountains which presents one of the most impressive views of the country, across wooded mountain slopes to the plains of Tipperary on the north and east and the Galty Mountains, peaked by Galtymore (3,018 ft.) in the northwest. There is a large parking area at the top.

After The Vee and Clogheen, drive into the dairy town of Mitchelstown (pop. 2,700), noted for its butter and cheese. The extensive College Square is worth a visit, for it still has a nineteenth-century atmosphere; the college was not an educational establishment but a home for aged gentlefolk.

The road south from Mitchelstown leads up to the western end of the Kilworth Mountains by Kilworth Camp, an Irish Army center; there are fine views of the neighboring country-

THE CHARM OF THE SOUTH

side before the road descends into Fermoy (pop. 3,250), which was originally built as a "garrison town"—a major center for British forces—in the eighteenth and nineteenth centuries. Part of the old military barracks remains but a considerable section is now devoted to industrial uses. There is an impressive bridge over the River Blackwater. Talk angling around here and you'll be among friends, for Fermoy is the center of the Lower Blackwater Fishery.

Drive on through Watergrasshill and Sallybrook as the road falls towards sea level, running beside the Glashaboy River. At Riverstown, turn 400 yards off the main road at the signpost indicating Riverstown House, at Glanmire. The house was built for Dr. Jemmett Brown, Bishop of Cork, in 1745 and contains some very beautiful stucco work by Paul and Philip Francini. It has now been restored and some furniture of the period introduced, including a hunting table from Doneraile Court (in the same county) and Irish Chippendale chairs. Open to the public in summer.

The road follows the course of the valley, past one of the many roadside shrines you'll see in Ireland depicting the Apparition of the Virgin Mary to Bernadette Soubirous at Lourdes, and swings to the right into the City of Cork again.

All Blarney

Blarney Castle is, of course, a must but don't rush the visit—absorb the atmosphere of Cork for a while before making the five-mile excursion to kiss the famous Blarney Stone.

Queen Elizabeth I of England is credited with giving the word "blarney" to the language, when, commenting on the unfulfilled promises of Cormac MacDermott MacCarthy, Lord of Blarney at the time, she is reported to have remarked: "This is all Blarney; what he says, he never means." Whether you intend to kiss the stone and achieve the gift of eloquence or not, the view from the battlements of the square tower is most impressive. The Kissing Stone is set in the battlements, and to kiss it, the visitor must lie on the walk within the walls, grasp a guard rail, lean his head back and touch the stone with his lips. It sounds dangerous, but it isn't, and it makes a first-class picture!

Nobody is certain how the Elizabethan comment developed into the legend that the gift of eloquence may be derived from the Blarney Stone, but it is not unlikely that the stone itself had some significance in the MacCarthy Clan—such as, perhaps, the stone on which the chieftain sat to be formally installed—and was subsequently built into the battlements during reconstruction work. Reconstruction was necessary because Blarney, like many other Irish castles, was the scene of battles on more than one occasion. The castle is open daily all year.

Trees in the neighboring Rock Close are reputed to be 3,000 years old and among the oldest in the world. There are caves and a staircase which is supposed to grant your wish, if you walk down it backwards! And in the Blarney Lake, the MacCarthys are reputed to have dumped all their treasure in an effort to hide it from raiders—it has never been recovered! The little village of Blarney outside the castle estate is pleasantly attractive.

Romantic Kinsale

Kinsale (pop. 1,600), a harbor town 18 miles southwest of Cork city, combines an image of the past with a very active present as one of Europe's top deep-sea and wreck-angling centers. (A short detour on the way will take in the famous pottery at Carrigaline, which is worth a visit.)

Kinsale Harbour, where the River Bandon finds the sea, is deceptive; from the shore it looks exceedingly small and crowded with boats. It was a seventeenth-century shipbuilding center and royal docks for the British navy and some of the old slips are still to be seen. Many old buildings are worth seeing for their character, including a number with slate-hung walls. The narrow streets on sloping hills emphasize the compact nature of the once-walled town.

1601 is one of the best-remembered dates in Irish history, for it was at that time the Irish and Spanish forces met in the Battle of Kinsale against the English. The harbor sheltered a whole Spanish fleet for ten weeks and 4,000 Spaniards seized the town. The Spanish were forced to surrender early in 1602; Kinsale then became an English town, in which the Irish were forbidden to live within the walls. The battlefield was in the neighborhood of the old highway to Cork and is very well signposted. During the period of Kinsale's naval history, the buccaneer Dampier sailed from here in 1703 on board *The Cinque Ports,* a 90-ton vessel; among his shipmates was Alexander Selkirk, who was later to be marooned on the lonely Pacific island of Juan Fernandez and be immortalized in William Cowper's poem *The Solitude of Alexander Selkirk* and, more popularly, as the *Robinson Crusoe* of Daniel Defoe's novel.

In the excellent museum in the seventeenth-century Market

THE CHARM OF THE SOUTH

House (later a courthouse) you will see the famous Kinsale hooded cloaks (sometimes handed down from generation to generation). Models of ships built at Kinsale and relics of the naval and military history of the town, as well as its civic charters dating back to Elizabethan days and examples of Kinsale lace, are also preserved in the museum.

There is a jumble of architectural styles in the town which emphasizes its mixed history, including a richly ornamented mansion in the French tradition on the Long Quay and the somber Norman character of St. Multose Church, with its imposing tower. In the porch of the church are the town stocks, where the local wrongdoers were confined. The interior has many memorials to the old families of Kinsale and a limestone font not later than the seventeenth century. The story is told that the damage to the stone arch of the west door was caused by Cromwell's soldiers, who sharpened their swords on it.

Desmond Castle in Cork Street is generally referred to as the French Prison. Built in the reign of Henry VII, it was used as a jail for French prisoners-of-war during the Napoleonic Wars. The Carmelite Friary in Abbey Street dates back to the fourteenth century, and close by are the ruins of Holy Well and a seventh-century burial ground.

Just beyond the town, at Summer Cove, there is good swimming. Kinsale's popularity as a yachting and angling center attracts many foreign boats during the summer, particularly as bunkering and supply facilities are excellent and there is a truly Irish atmosphere of hospitality at the clubhouse of the Kinsale Yacht Club at the oddly-named sector of the town called Scilly.

Near the Old Head of Kinsale, southwest of town (it overlooks the site of the sinking of the *Lusitania*) is a fine example of a large three-ringed fort; excavations here have shown that it was occupied 1,300 years ago.

Along the roads in this area you are likely to meet the horse-drawn caravans, which are a popular and relaxed way of exploring the countryside and the seaside, with its pleasant resorts like Courtmacsherry (on a bay of the same name), and inland to Dunmanway and Macroom (the castle was William Penn's childhood home) and westwards to Bantry and Glengarriff.

West to Bantry

For the more hurried traveler there are several routes to West Cork, but the most attractive is from Cork up the valley of the River Lee, past the spreading lakes of Inchigeelagh to the Pass of Keimaneigh. Not far from the pass is Gougane Barra, the lake which is the source of the River Lee, located in a forest park. On an island in the lake, connected by a causeway to the mainland, was the cell of the sixth-century monk, Finbarr, who was later to found Cork. There is nothing of Finbarr's cell remaining, but there is an eighteenth-century church to which there is a pilgrimage on September 29 each year.

As the road nears the fjord-like indentations at the head of Bantry Bay it divides at the village of Ballylickey, the left fork leading on in to Bantry (pop. 2,200), where Spanish is a familiar tongue, because many of the Spanish trawlers fishing in the Atlantic use Bantry as their base.

On one of the largest islands, Whiddy, there are three nineteenth-century forts and the remains of a very much older fortification, the castle of O'Sullivan Beare. Part of the island is now the Gulf Oil storage terminal, served by 300,000-ton tankers. The warm waters of the Gulf Stream swing into the Irish coast at this point and give the whole district a mild climate in which sub-tropical plants flourish.

Bantry House on the shore of the bay is one of the "must see" houses in the country and is open to visitors from Easter to the end of October. Lawns and flower beds in front of the Georgian house emphasize the lush growth of the district. The best view of the house is from the water, but it is the interior which is of most interest. The house was the seat of the earls of Bantry from 1765 and is now owned by a great-granddaughter of the third earl; it was remodeled and extended in 1840. Famous for furniture, tapestries (including some reputedly owned by Marie Antoinette and saved from the sack of the Tuileries in Paris during the French Revolution) and *objets d'art*—the second earl was the great collector. Two fireplaces were originally in the Palace of Versailles and the furniture includes pieces of the Louis XV period and examples of Chippendale, Hepplewhite, Sheraton and Old Irish styles.

Baltimore and Garnish Island

The whole area south of Bantry is exciting, hilly country. There are no dramatic heights—Mount Gabriel (1,339 ft.), west of Ballydehob, is the highest—but the country is spectacular right down to the appropriately named Roaring Water Bay and Mizen Head, the most southerly point of Ireland, between Roaring Water Bay and Dunmanus Bay. Clear Island stands offshore from Baltimore on the east side of Roaring Water.

THE CHARM OF THE SOUTH

Baltimore is a small port with a long history, including the seizure of 200 of its inhabitants as slaves during a raid by Algerian pirates in the seventeenth century. Today, Baltimore is a sea-angling and sailing school center and ferry port for Sherkin Island, which has the ruins of an old Franciscan friary (fifteenth-century), and Clear Island, once the terminal point of the European telegraph service. It was the old telegraph station here that was the first place in Europe to receive news of the outbreak of the American Civil War; the news was received from an eastbound ship and flashed to European capitals long before the vessel reached port. Irish is the native language of the people of the island, but they've a welcome for the stranger. The lighthouse four miles to the southwest is the Fastnet, landfall for transatlantic liners and ocean yachtsmen.

Glengarriff is screened from Bantry by the bulk of Whiddy Island, and there is a 12-mile road between them. Top attraction at Glengarriff is Ilnacullin, or Garnish Island, which is open to visitors throughout the year. The once-barren island was laid out and planted as a garden about 50 years ago. Warmed by the Gulf Stream and enclosed by sheltering trees, the island has trees, flowering shrubs and plants from the Himalayas, China, South America, South Africa, Japan and Tasmania, all flourishing as luxuriantly as in their native climates. This collection was made by the Bryce family (the island is sometimes called Bryce's Island, although Annan Bryce gave it to the Irish nation). One section is an Italian garden of outstanding beauty and color. It was at Ilnacullin that George Bernard Shaw (1856–1950) wrote his play, *St. Joan*.

Glengarriff is a portal to the dramatic scenery of the southwest (to be explored in *The Southwest* chapter) and travelers to Kerry can continue northwest by the Tunnel Road (it passes through a short mountain tunnel), or, less directly, by heading southwest and making the crossing of the mountains by the long Healy Pass and exploring the lonely, impressive country of the peninsula.

Up the Sullane from Cork

The direct road from Cork to Killarney follows the course of the River Lee almost as far as Macroom. It is an attractive scenic route with the river and lakes.

There are angling and boating stations near Inniscarra and water-skiing at the village of Dripsey, which is more famous for its woolen and worsted mill. From Macroom, the road follows

THE FACE OF IRELAND

the course of the Sullane River to Ballyvourney, a village where the thirteenth-century wooden figure of St. Gobnat (sixth or seventh-century) is preserved in the local church. The remains of several buildings associated with Gobnat's religious foundation still exist, together with evidence that iron and bronze workers lived and worked here in the early days of their craft. The way on to Killarney lies over the Derrynasaggart Mountains with the bulk of Mullaghanish (2,133 ft.) away in the distance on the right of the road.

THE SOUTHWEST

Ring of Kerry, Rose of Tralee

The southwest consists of a series of tongues of land jutting out into the Atlantic: the Beara Peninsula, part in Cork and part in Kerry, with the Caha and Slieve Miskish Mountains forming its backbone; next, the Kenmare Peninsula and its Ring of Kerry; and then the Dingle Peninsula, dominated by Mount Brandon (named for Saint Brendan, the man the Irish claim discovered America long before Christopher Columbus was born). "The Dingle" points its long mountain-boned finger to the southwest and the lonely Blasket Islands.

Kerry was the first part of Europe to be sighted by Charles Lindbergh when he made his breath-taking solo Atlantic flight from New York to Paris in 1927; today, Kerry head, at the estuary of the River Shannon, is the landfall for transatlantic services on their way to Shannon Airport. There have been very strong links between the people of Kerry and the United States for generations—the emigration rate from the area was very high in the last century, and although today the number of emigrants is very much lower, the movement of people between the two countries is substantial.

Kerry is being "discovered" as a quiet land of peace and there has been an influx of semi-permanent residents, but they are

THE FACE OF IRELAND

easily absorbed in the wide and rugged countryside and along the many miles of sandy beaches, some of which are used for sand yachting. Watchful local authority is a check against any danger of spoiling landscapes by building or development. The landscape has a strong pictorial quality, a quality which is not formalized or stereotyped, for each bend of the road presents a new picture, a new interest.

While the scenic beauties are the prime attraction of the southwest, which embraces the whole area, from Glengarriff on Bantry Bay to the southern shores of the River Shannon, its resources for anglers and golfers are almost legendary. The well-developed road network makes sight-seeing easy, whether on the most famous of the routes—the Ring of Kerry—or on the less familiar excursions which have their own special interests.

Hotel development is just about keeping pace with the ever-growing number of visitors. At peak times in the summer, Killarney bursts with visitors. The early spring and late autumn are periods when there is less of a press on accommodation, and the everlasting beauty of the lakes and mountains is there in even more exciting colors from the flashing gold of the gorse in April to the rich and varied reds and browns and purple heather of October. Much of the beauty is created by the skyscapes; and the reflection of the clouds in the lakes even in the shorter days of early spring and late autumn gladden the eye and mind.

It's easy to make the mistake of thinking that Killarney and its lakes and the Ring of Kerry are all that the southwest has to offer. There's no doubt that it's all that you've heard and read—a land of magic, but don't miss out on the other aspects, bonus qualities, of a visit.

Killarney and the Muckross Estate

Some have called Killarney "heaven's reflex", and they might well be right. Killarney has been one of the world's favorite beauty spots for nearly 200 years since it was first "discovered" by an English agriculturist Arthur Young in the eighteenth century.

Killarney is a market town as well as a tourist center, and is not architecturally or historically distinguished in its buildings. Killarney's main interest lies outside the town and particularly in the area of its three main lakes in the valley, which runs southwards. Nearest the town is the Lower Lake (Lough Leane—5,000 acres) with its many islands and, on its eastern shore, Muckross Abbey and Ross Castle.

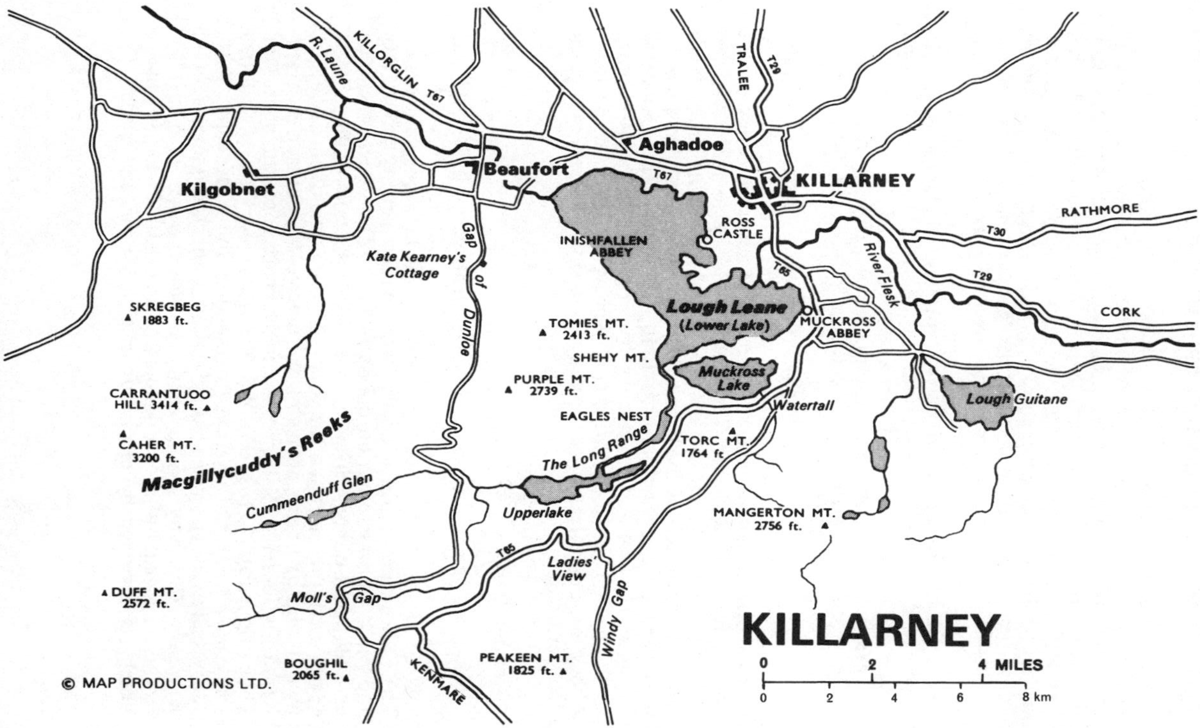
KILLARNEY
KILLARNEY
Aghadoe
Beaufort
Kilgobnet
KILLORGLIN T67
R. Laune
TRALEE
T29
T67
RATHMORE
T30
T29
CORK
River Flesk
ROSS CASTLE
INISHFALLEN ABBEY
Lough Leane
(Lower Lake)
T65
MUCKROSS ABBEY
Muckross Lake
Lough Guitane
Waterfall
Kate Kearney's Cottage
Gap of Dunloe
SKREGBEG 1883 ft.
TOMIES MT. 2413 ft.
SHEHY MT.
PURPLE MT. 2739 ft.
EAGLES NEST
CARRANTUOO HILL 3414 ft.
CAHER MT. 3200 ft.
Macgillycuddy's Reeks
The Long Range
TORC MT. 1764 ft.
Cummeenduff Glen
Upperlake
MANGERTON MT. 2756 ft.
T65
Ladies' View
Windy Gap
DUFF MT. 2572 ft.
Moll's Gap
BOUGHIL 2065 ft.
KENMARE
PEAKEEN MT. 1825 ft.
0 2 4 MILES
0 2 4 6 8 km
© MAP PRODUCTIONS LTD.

The Muckross Estate of 10,000 acres, a National Park also known as the Bourn Vincent Memorial Park, was presented to the Irish nation by its former American owners, Mr. and Mrs. William Bowers Bourn, and their son-in-law, Arthur Vincent. The latter was quoted, at the time of making the gift in 1932, as saying "I hope that Muckross will be made a real garden of friendship, and that it will be the greatest playground in the world—there is not another in the world like it, and I know them all."

To the left of the road before entering Muckross is an old churchyard in which is buried the remarkable Rudolf Erich Raspe (1737-94), author of *Baron Munchhausen's Narrative of his Marvelous Travels and Campaigns in Russia*; Raspe died while visiting Killarney as a geological adviser on the development of copper mines.

Cars are not allowed through the Muckross Estate, but quite a lot of people discover they can still ride a bicycle when they go to Killarney (bikes can be hired in the town) and this speeds up a visit in the demesne. The traditional way to make the trip is by jaunting car, and if they're lacking elsewhere in Ireland, there's still enough of them in Killarney. The driver, by the way, is known as a "jarvey" and his fund of stories adds a bonus to the tour. The route after entering the grounds is along the shore of the Lower Lake to Muckross Abbey, a ruined Franciscan Abbey of the fifteenth century, remarkably well-preserved and fully restored.

Colleen Bawn

Not far away is the ruined cottage which you will be told was the home of Danny Mann, the boatman in the story of *The Colleen Bawn*; the Colleen Bawn rock will also be pointed out. The Colleen Bawn (Ellen Hanly) was murdered many miles away and her body was found on the north bank of the River Shannon at Killimer, County Clare, in 1819. When Gerald Griffin (1803-1840) used the story as the basis of his novel *The Collegians* (one of the best Irish novels of the nineteenth century), he transferred the locale to Killarney—a much more romantic spot—and Dion Boucicault (1820-90) did the same for his melodrama *The Colleen Bawn*. The German composer Julius Benedict (1804-1885) followed on, when using the plot for his opera, *Lily of Killarney*. (But why spoil a good story for the sake of a fact?)

There's a narrow neck of land at Dinis Island—Dinis Cottage nearby is encircled by exotic sub-tropical shrubs and plants. The

THE SOUTHWEST

Meeting of the Waters can be seen from the pathway behind the cottage and a short distance away is the whirlpool called "O'Sullivan's Punch Bowl".

It's a good plan to explore the Middle and Lower Lakes by boat and Dinis Island is the place to pick one up, but it's advisable to arrange for it before starting the tour. The road swings left under Torc Mountain, continuing along the lake shore to Torc Waterfall (there's a path from the road up to the cascading 60-foot fall, which is kept constantly in spate by water from the Devil's Punch Bowl, high up on Mangerton Mountain, about five miles away). This road leads back into Killarney. While in the Muckross Estate, take time out to see the Folk Museum in nineteenth-century Muckross House—it provides comprehensive coverage of the folk history and crafts of Kerry and includes hand-carved furniture. The rhododendrons, bog garden and alpine garden are the most important features of the gardens. There is a special entrance to the estate for cars visiting Muckross House three miles out from Killarney on the Kenmare Road.

Tours from Killarney

One of the most popular of the Killarney tours takes in the Gap of Dunloe, the Upper Lake, Long Range, Middle and Lower Lakes and Ross Castle. This heads out westwards and then turns south to cross the River Laune, which drains the lakes (it flows into the sea at the head of Dingle Bay), past Dunloe Castle, a one-time fort, and into the deep gash in the Macgillycuddy's Reeks, with Purple Mountain (2,739 ft.) on the left and Carrantuohill (3,414 ft.). Ireland's highest mountain, distantly on the right. Cars can't pass through the celebrated Gap of Dunloe, so the journey is continued on foot, by pony or pony-drawn trap, and then by boat. Before Lord Brandon's cottage is reached, the bugler will certainly be on hand to demonstrate the odd echoes which bounce around the rocky hills. You'll also see Serpent Lake, where St. Patrick is said to have drowned Ireland's last snake. The Head of the Gap is 797 feet above sea level and as the path continues down towards the Upper Lake, there are fine views of Cummeenduff Glen (more popularly known as the Black Valley) before stopping off for a meal and joining the boats on the Upper Lake (430 acres).

The trip afloat enters the channel called the Long Range, passing the closely-wooded Eagle's Nest, backed by Shehy Mountain on the left and Torc Mountain to the right. When the rowers ship their oars, you are at the Old Weir Bridge, where the traditional skill of the Killarney boatmen shoots the boat quickly through the rapids and into the placid Meeting of the Waters. Dinis Island is in view, and there will be more stories about the Colleen Bawn caves, wave-scoured limestone caves on the north shore of the Middle (Muckross or Torc) Lake (680 acres) before you pass under Bricken Bridge into the Lower Lake (Lough Leane) and its thirty islands.

Killarney's racetrack and airstrip are on the flat lands on the shore near the island on which stands Ross Castle, terminal point for the boat trip. The castle is an imposing ruin; the keep dates back to the fourteenth century and there is a spiral staircase inside it; a trip up to the battlements is rewarded with a fine view.

Aghadoe, just beside the magnificently located golf course on the edge of the Lower Lake, is worth a special trip. Less than three miles out of town on the Killorglin Road, Aghadoe Hill is only about 400 feet high, but it provides a remarkable view. Close by to the east is Aghadoe Castle and the site of what is called Aghadoe Cathedral, the ruins of a small church with a romanesque doorway (reconstructed), which dates back to the twelfth century (although a church was founded on the site about 600 years earlier). A visit to Aghadoe is made primarily for the view (and the hotel); in the east are The Paps, to the southeast, Crohane is the dominant feature, and swinging towards the south, the bulk of Mangerton. The Lower Lake is in the foreground with Innisfallen Island in the distance, Mahony's Point just below the hill, and away to the southwest, the Gap of Dunloe. Innisfallen Island, with its history of monastic foundations back to the seventh century, was presented to the Irish nation by its American owner, John McShain, in 1973.

Innisfallen and the Mountains

An excursion to Innisfallen Island has a double interest. It's a small island near the northern shore of the Lower Lake with some unusual vegetation including a four-in-one tree—holly, ash, hawthorn and ivy growing as if from a single stem—and a holly tree, reputed to be Europe's largest. There was a monastery established here in the sixth or seventh century and the ruins of Innisfallen Abbey may still be seen near the landing stage. Between 950 and 1350, the *Annals of Innisfallen* were compiled here by a number of monks. The book is now in the Bodleian Library at Oxford, England. Another relic of the abbey, the Innisfallen Crozier, was found in the river at Killarney towards

THE SOUTHWEST

the end of the nineteenth century and is in the National Museum, Dublin.

There are a number of short tours around the neighborhood; the trip to Carrantuohill provides a thrilling view over a great part of the counties of Limerick and Cork with the Galty Mountains in Tipperary making a boundary line on the horizon. The best-known climb on Carrantuohill is from near Gortbue School at the mouth of Hag's Glen, which is reached from Beaufort village.

After Carrantuohill, the mountain that appeals most to climbers is Mangerton, but it isn't really a climb in the sense that mountaineers use the word. There's a signpost on the Kenmare road indicating the track. The sedentary can go up most of the way by pony. At just over 2,000 feet, there is the Devil's Punch Bowl, a deep, dark pool which feeds its waters to Torc Waterfall. A few hundred feet further on, and the full panorama which is the purpose of the trip is spread out. For the more serious climbers, there are some rock climbs on the cliff range on the southern side of the glen. Shehy Mountain, one of the Purple Mountain group, is the only spot from which you can view all three of Killarney's lakes at once. It's reached by way of Twomey's (also Tomies) Mountain, driving about four miles out of town on the road to Killorglin, then turning on the Gap Road and taking a turn towards the lake, then another to the right, with a walk to follow.

The magnificence of the vistas around Killarney is inclined to switch the attention from what is close at hand—the luxuriant growth of the woods and the profusion of saxifrages, ferns, acacia and arbutus, but take time to take a look at this natural botanical garden.

How did Killarney happen to be so beautiful? The mountains are old red sandstone and grit, and there are volcanic rocks and glacial boulders, limestone eroded by the action of time and water; the Ice Age made its mark on the neighborhood long, long ago, and left behind one of the world's most beautiful gardens. If there's movement that isn't human in the woods bordering the lakes, there is no need for surprise, as there are many red deer and Japanese *Sika* deer about.

"The Ring of Kerry"

The famous Ring of Kerry road (about 110 miles long) may be picked up from any of the towns on the road, but Killarney is the generally recognized base point and "The Ring" is usually traversed in an anti-clockwise direction—don't buck the tide, as it seems pleasanter that way around and the views are more striking. Except for the Laune River on the left and the distant views of the Macgillycuddy's Reeks, the first stage of the Ring is hardly dramatic. But after Killorglin, scene of the famous Puck Fair, the visual excitement steps up.

The time of great "diversion" in Killorglin is in mid-August; this is the period of the three-day Puck Fair. Nobody knows how or when it began, but nobody in the neighborhood would let it die out. The central event, the enthroning of a goat, has been suggested as a survival from pagan times, but whatever the truth of it, the he-goat, invariably a big one with be-ribboned horns, heads a procession in a large cage on a lorry. In the town center a high tower is built and the goat in his cage is hoisted up to preside over the fair, well supplied with food and water. There is a big cattle, sheep and horse fair with dancing and entertainment to follow far into the night, and on the third day down comes "King Puck" and the fun is over for another year.

Killorglin is the place to make a diversion from the formal tour, a turn left to make a detour around Caragh Lake, one of Kerry's best fishing spots, and loop back into Killorglin by way of the foothills of Carrantuohill; it adds about 25 miles to the trip, but it is scenically worth it.

Glenbeigh is the next village on the main road and worth a stop to have a look at Glenbeigh Towers (also known as Wynne's Folly) nearby.

Dingle Bay and Valentia Island

From here on, the road closes to the sea, with the hills rising on the left hand; parallel with the road is the remains of the old railway which ran to Caherciveen, almost at the end of the peninsula, through halts at points such as Mountain Stage, a name which came from the days when the stage coach was the only means of wheeled travel in the district. Dingle Bay is on the right of what is surely one of the world's most picturesque roads; luckily there are lay-bys to enable halts to be made for a general sharing of the beauty.

Cutting inland for a time the road passes Knocknadobat Mountain (2,267 feet) and reaches Caherciveen, near where Daniel O'Connell (1775-1847), the crusader for Catholic Emancipation, was born. If there is time, a visit to Leacanabuaile Fort, two miles outside the town at Kimego West, is interesting, because the excavation work shows the wisdom of its planners of long ago. Mountain slopes protect three sides and the single entrance to the ramparts of stone is on the east. There are chambers in which were found iron and bronze objects and millstones which date it in the Early Christian era.

Leaving the town for Waterville, notice the building on the right of the road. This is the Valentia Observatory, part of the Irish Government's meteorological service. At this point, another short detour runs to the road bridge for Valentia Island, formerly the Western Union cable station and terminal point of the first transatlantic cable. Valentia is developing as a deep-sea angling resort and an exciting spot for skin-divers. Boat trips can be made from here to the Skellig (Scellig) Rocks or the Blasket Islands from Derrynane pier, weather permitting. It isn't necessary to be an archeologist to appreciate Scellig Michael, a massive rock rising 700 feet out of the Atlantic nine miles off the mainland, but as a stimulant to the imagination, it's the experience of a lifetime. Early Christian monks built a settlement 600 feet up the rock and it is still reached by the steps they cut. The state of preservation of the beehive-shaped stone cells in which the community lived is remarkable after 1,000 years of Atlantic storms, and beside the cells, there are a church and two oratories. What happened to the monks? Nobody knows.

Divers have located the wreck of the *Santa Maria de la Rosa*, one of the Spanish Armada (1588) vessels which foundered off the coast in the Blasket Sound, with a reputed million-pound in gold on board. They've hauled up cannon balls and an anchor and follow up the hunt when weather permits.

Lough Currane

Whether your tour stays with the main road of the Grand Atlantic Route—and it's easy to see how it got its Victorian name—or uses the detour above, both the roads meet in Waterville, at the head of Ballinskelligs Bay. The town is sited on a narrow neck of land which separates the Atlantic from Lough Currane, one of the most fruitful and beautiful lakes in this lovely land.

Most important of the historic sites in the Waterville area is the strategically sited Staigue Fort, one and a half miles north of Castlecove, which is east of Waterville. This is in a remarkable state of preservation. Surrounded by an 18-foot-high stone wall, the fort encloses a circle about 90 feet in diameter. Entry to forts of this kind, built in early Christian days, was always by a single small doorway with a square lintel. The wall of Staigue Fort is 13½ feet wide at the base. On the inside of the wall, there

THE FACE OF IRELAND

are terraces reached by steps in the wall, which also has a number of chambers in which the defenders presumably lived and had their stores. There are other stone forts in the neighborhood but Staigue is the most important of the group.

There is an extraordinary number of flowering plants hereabouts, fostered by the mild winters (mean January temperature 44°F.), and many of them are of particular interest to the naturalist because they are not found elsewhere in northern continental Europe. Without checking the number of species the non-botanist can get pleasure from the overall impression of their beauty. Nature has been very successful with her "green thumb" in the wild garden of Kerry.

After leaving Waterville, a good lunch stop on "The Ring", you are headed for home. A stop on the lay-by cut into the mountain provides a viewing place for Deenish Island and Scariff Island, with a scattering of others. Far below, there is a faint roaring sound of water on even the quietest day; the views here and towards Lamb's Head in the southeast have a pictorial quality of great depth.

"Head of the Sea"

Excavations in 1967 near Caherdaniel on this section of the road overlooking Derrynane Bay revealed a wedge-shaped gallery grave, indicating that the area was inhabited over 3,000 years ago. This is near the spot where the patriot Daniel O'Connell, born on the other side of the peninsula, made his home at Derrynane House (open to visitors).

The road is now skirting the estuary of the Kenmare River as it heads through Sneem, where lived the "Father O'Flynn" of the ballad of that name. Riverside scenery predominates all the way from Parknasilla to Kenmare, with views of the Caha Mountains across the estuary. Kenmare (pop. 1,000) derives its name from the Irish *Ceann Mara* ("Head of the Sea"). Homespun woolens are a tradition in this district, and so is the lace which is made in the local convent of the Poor Clares. Two holy wells in the district are still visited by pilgrims: Our Lady's Well at Goramullin, one-quarter of a mile outside the town, and St. Finan's Well, near Kenmare Old Church. Before taking the road for Killarney go to see a prehistoric stone circle of 15 standing stones at The Shrubberies, about one-quarter of a mile southwest of Kenmare. The circle is about 50 feet in diameter, and in the center is a megalithic tomb.

If you came from Glengarriff when making for Killarney, the

next 20 miles of road between Kenmare and Killarney have been covered before, but it is a never-failing pleasure as it moves up Peakeen Mountain to Moll's Gap, where there is a souvenir shop, and then swings down to the woods and the lakes.

Few people leave Killarney without wanting to return, and it is the character of the climate that whenever a return visit is paid, there is always a change in the scenery—not a physical change, but that of the light and shade of the clouds, perhaps of a mist on a mountain. Long after you've left Killarney, long after you've gone from Ireland, the memory will flash back to a view, maybe a corner or perhaps a great panoramic sweep, and the image will come clear in the mind to renew the pleasure of one of the world's most beautiful spots.

Tralee

The third of Kerry's Atlantic-pointing fingers is the Dingle Peninsula, with the county capital, Tralee (pop. 12,000), as the gateway. Tralee is an industrial and commercial center, but it is immediately associated with the song *The Rose of Tralee*, composed by William Pembroke Mulchinock (1820-64) at Cloghers House, Ballymullen, which is just outside the town. Tralee has a Rose of Tralee Memorial surrounded by roses specially bred in the north of Ireland and named for "The Rose". Each year international competitions are held to select a girl as "The Rose" for the year. It's a big autumn attraction which embraces racing, music competitions and street dancing, not to mention all-round merry-making.

Don't miss the excellent "Siamsa" presentation in Tralee; it's a dawn-to-dusk sequence of happenings in rural Ireland of 50 years ago, presented by Siamsoiri na Riochta (The Merrymakers of the Kingdom).

The Dominicans were introduced into Tralee by an earl of Desmond in 1243 and some of the sculptured stones from their original foundation of Holy Cross Abbey are in the priory of the nineteenth-century gothic Dominican Church on Princes Quay. St. John's Roman Catholic Church is another nineteenth-century church, with a fine set of Stations of the Cross by Seán Keating and a modern statue of St. Brendan the Navigator, who was born at Annagh, near Tralee. The Ashe Memorial Hall is an admirable example of the attractive use of local materials.

Kerry is a land of many legends. Three miles south of the town at Glanaskagheen, there is a stone which is said to mark the grave of one Scotia, a daughter of a pharaoh. The girl came from Egypt with the prehistoric invaders of Ireland—the Milesians, it is said. The legends tell of a great battle at the foot of the Slieve Mish Mountains, a battle won by the Milesians but in which Scotia, a queen, according to the tales, was killed. (The glen now is a pleasant area for exploring on foot, pony-back or by car.)

Five miles northwest of Tralee is Ardfert, with its ruined cathedral dating from the thirteenth century; the village was a great ecclesiastical center from the time St. Brendan founded a monastery there seven centuries earlier. The cathedral, named in honor of Brendan, has examples of the Romanesque style in its architecture, while a short distance away, Teampall na Hoe has some unusual ornamentation in the early Irish manner. Teampall Griffin, also nearby, is from the fifteenth century. The Franciscan Friary is another well-preserved ruin.

The many ringforts in the district are an indication of the onetime importance of the center. It was at one of these forts (McKenna's Fort, also known as Casement's Fort), a mile west of Ardfert, that Sir Roger Casement was captured in April, 1916, on the eve of the Easter Week Rising, after landing from a German submarine on Banna Strand, a short distance away. Casement, who remained in the fort overnight, was captured by the local police and tried and executed for high treason in London on August 3, 1916. Robert Monteith, who had landed with Casement, evaded capture and escaped to America, where he died in Detroit in 1956. Casement's body was returned to Ireland in 1965 and buried with full military honors in Dublin.

Fenit is the port for the area, and is becoming known as a good center for sea angling, particularly for the angler who doesn't like the sea! (Big fish are hooked off the deep water pier!)

The Dingle Peninsula

The Dingle Peninsula does not offer the same well-developed facility as The Ring of Kerry for making a complete main-road loop around it, but the roads are good enough and the journey westwards beside the Slieve Mish Mountains is interesting. On the highest peak, Catherconree (2,050 feet) is a seemingly impregnable stone fort.

The glen beyond the village of Camp is *Gleann na nGealt* ("Glen of the Madmen"), getting its name because a type of watercress that was found there was reputed to cure madness. The main road continues straight ahead at Camp, and the trip

THE SOUTHWEST

west across the foot of a small peninsula takes in the village of Castlegregory.

The Dingle Peninsula was chosen by director David Lean for the making of his famous movie *Ryan's Daughter*.

The bulk of Brandon Mountain (3,127 feet) is ahead, Brandon Bay opening up on the right. This is where the astonishing sixth-century navigator Brendan (484-577) started his wanderings. Brendan was 59 when he started the voyagings which have given him a place in history, sailing out from what is now Brandon Bay in a currach (curragh) of wood and skins. From the records of the trip, it seems he reached the Shetland Islands off the coast of Scotland in three months, after landing at one time on the back of a sleeping whale, mistaking it for an island.

The first trip took several years and took him as far north as Iceland. On his return he built a new ship of wood and sailed in it with 60 companions from one of the Aran Islands off Galway. The records indicate an encounter with an iceberg, a landfall which was almost certainly Newfoundland or Labrador. Voyaging again to the west, Brendan made a landfall on white sandy beaches—was it Florida? Back in Ireland two years after his departure, he was appointed a bishop and established a monastery at Clonfert (Co. Galway), before making further short voyages to Wales and to the north of France, where he died in Brittany at the age of 93. Brendan's discovery of land to the far west of Ireland was recorded in medieval maps as an island: did he discover America? (Don't tell an Irishman that he didn't!) The way to the summit of Mount Brandon is an ancient track which is said to have been the saint's path and bears the name, The Saint's Road.

South With Scott

Another story of exploration turns up in the village of Anascaul, between Camp and Dingle, where the *South Pole Inn* recalls Captain Robert Falcon Scott's unlucky expedition to the South Pole in 1912. A local sailor named Thomas Crean was one of the party who found Scott dead in his tent after the return from the Pole. He later set up this bar. Relics of Crean's Antarctic days form a miniature museum in the tourist office in Dingle.

Dingle, westwards along the south coast, was once a walled town and a port with a strong trade with Spain.

At Tom Fitzgerald's sawmill there is a fine waterwheel, more than 150 years old and still in perfect working order.

Beyond the town there is an extensive Irish-speaking district and many archeological remains of considerable interest. Dunbeg Fort in the Fahan Group is one of the most important because it cuts off a triangular promontory and on the landward side is protected by earth ramparts, trenches and a great wall 22 feet thick. Beehive stone huts are common indications of the past. A few miles west of Ballyferriter there is a remarkable structure known as Gallarus Oratory, built of unmortared stone so well fitted together that it is still watertight after a thousand years or more. This is one of the soundest of the early Christian churches to be seen anywhere.

Dunquin, at the head of the peninsula, backed by Mount Eagle (1,696 feet) is a little village of essentially Gaelic traditions, with a charm that has to be encountered to be appreciated. A currach journey from here to the Blasket Islands is an experience, though the Blaskets can also be reached from Caherciveen and Waterville (across Dingle Bay) by boat. The great Blasket was abandoned by its few remaining inhabitants, who were moved to the mainland in 1953 after a succession of bad fishing seasons.

North Kerry

Although the traditional time for the "Wren Boys" is Christmas, they are likely to be encountered at festivals at other times of the year in North Kerry and West Limerick, particularly at the time of Listowel's race week in October. Persecution of the wren was a common tradition in many countries because the chattering of the bird is said to have betrayed St. Stephen, and in the south of Ireland it became a custom for groups of youths to visit houses on St. Stephen's Day (December 26).

In the old days they carried a dead wren, but today it is a bunch of feathers or ribbons tied to an evergreen branch. Instrumentalists accompany the group and in Kerry the traditional instrument of the area, a goat-skin drum known as a *bodhran*, is included. This has a strangely haunting sound and has been more widely used in Irish music in recent years. Apart from the traditional wren song, which invariably ended with a hint for money with which to "bury the wren", there are other ballads in the performance.

Listowel and its hinterland has been the birthplace of many writers and Listowel Writers' Week (in June) provides a Writers' Workshop, plays by Kerry authors and literary get-togethers.

The population of Ballybunion, on the coast to the northeast of Listowel, rockets sharply in the summer season, for it's one of the happiest unsophisticated spots around the coast. Irishmen

THE SOUTHWEST

like it for holidays because it has a championship golf course and also plenty of beach space for the family. Cave exploring by boat and on foot at low tide is a diversion along the cliffs; it's not difficult to believe the stories that are told of them being haunts of smugglers and chieftains-in-hiding.

Kerry Head, to the southwest of Ballybunion, marks the entrance to the River Shannon. Along the coast of the estuary in the opposite direction, at Tarbert, there is an early nineteenth-century fort commanding the approaches. A car ferry service operates from Tarbert across the estuary to Killimer on the County Clare (north) side of the river.

Inland, Newcastle West has the remains of a great castle of the Earl of Desmond, partly embraced in a modern residence but with one of the fifteenth-century halls still complete.

Between Newcastle West and Adare lies a district still known as the Palatinate, a remembrance of the days when Calvinist refugees settled there in the eighteenth century, after the French conquest of the German Palatinate. Some of the old names still exist, but in an Irish form as the community became absorbed with the people of Limerick. Adare itself has an unusual appearance for an Irish village, largely through the developments carried out by a nineteenth-century earl of Dunraven (the family seat, Adare Manor, is open most days). The town is attractively laid out with characteristics which suggest the English rather than the Irish countryside. But indications of its background before the nineteenth century are visible in a castle of the middle ages and the well-preserved ruins of a fifteenth-century Franciscan friary.

Ten miles up the road is Limerick and Shannon, or you can take the short cut to County Clare on the ferry from Tarbert (Co. Kerry) across the Shannon to Killimer (every hour).

SHANNON

Ireland's Atlantic Gateway

Sometime in the mid-1930s, a group of Irish engineers, surveyors and Army Air Corps officers were given the job of finding a site for a transatlantic air base which would be suitable for both land-based aircraft and flying-boats. (The experts hadn't made up their minds which of the two types would be the eventual answer to operating profitable trans-ocean services.) On the north shore of the River Shannon, at the junction with the River Fergus, in County Clare, the party located a large area of unproductive land with no high ground in the neighborhood and with a high degree of freedom from fog. The maps named the place as Kilconry and Rineanna.

Work on the base started in the autumn of 1936. By the winter of 1941-42, the land base at Rineanna was ready for use, but the name Rineanna disappeared, to be replaced by "Shannon". The debate about the merits of flying-boats and land-based aircraft was decided in favor of the latter and, on October 24, 1945, the first scheduled commercial transatlantic flight operated through Shannon.

Shannon was conceived as a facility, but this facility has grown into a major international shopping and industrial center and the base has created something quite new in modern tourism by refocussing attention on Ireland's past.

The estimate is that there are about 900 castles around

SHANNON

County Clare, from marvelous examples like Bunratty to crumbling old ruins. At the northerly limit of the Shannon region, on the shores of Galway Bay, one of the many castles is still occupied; known sometimes as Dun Guaire and sometimes as Kinvara, it stands with its foundations lapped by the waters of the bay. Here, too, the visitor from overseas (and the Irish too) find unusual entertainment, a recalling of the Irish plays, literature and music, with a meal to match.

There's more to see than the castles and their entertainments. Old crafts have been preserved throughout County Clare; opportunities to see them are provided on a stopover at Shannon. Some of the prehistoric monuments by the roadside have stories going back to the days when the world was young. In the north of the county, The Burren is one of the world's prime nature reserves, with a profusion of wild flowers and vegetation not found elsewhere. Each year, the strange rocky area of the Burren attracts visits from botanists from many countries.

Exploring the Shannon Area

Today, the jets sweep in from America and continental Europe to Shannon Airport, which has opened up an entirely new recreational area. Now you can fly into Shannon in the afternoon and dine in state in the manner of a medieval lord in the evening, taking a look at Ireland's earliest history in the meantime.

Because the accent on tourism in the Shannon area is on the switch-back in time from the jet present to the placid past, it is possible (but not advisable) to overlook the Shannon Industrial Estate, a customs-free zone beside the airport, providing factory facilities for overseas companies, who can import their raw materials, process them and ship them out again without customs duties. The project grew out of Shannon's *Duty-Free Shop*, the first of its kind in the world, which offers a range of international bargains for shoppers in transit or for mail order. Shannon shop purchases, by the way, aren't weighed with your baggage, a factor that counts when you're traveling on a limited baggage allowance.

Bunratty Castle

The organized tours out of Shannon are an admirable way of getting a quick, comprehensive view of the area. Bunratty is the premier attraction.

Bunratty Castle, as you'll discover from the top of the keep,

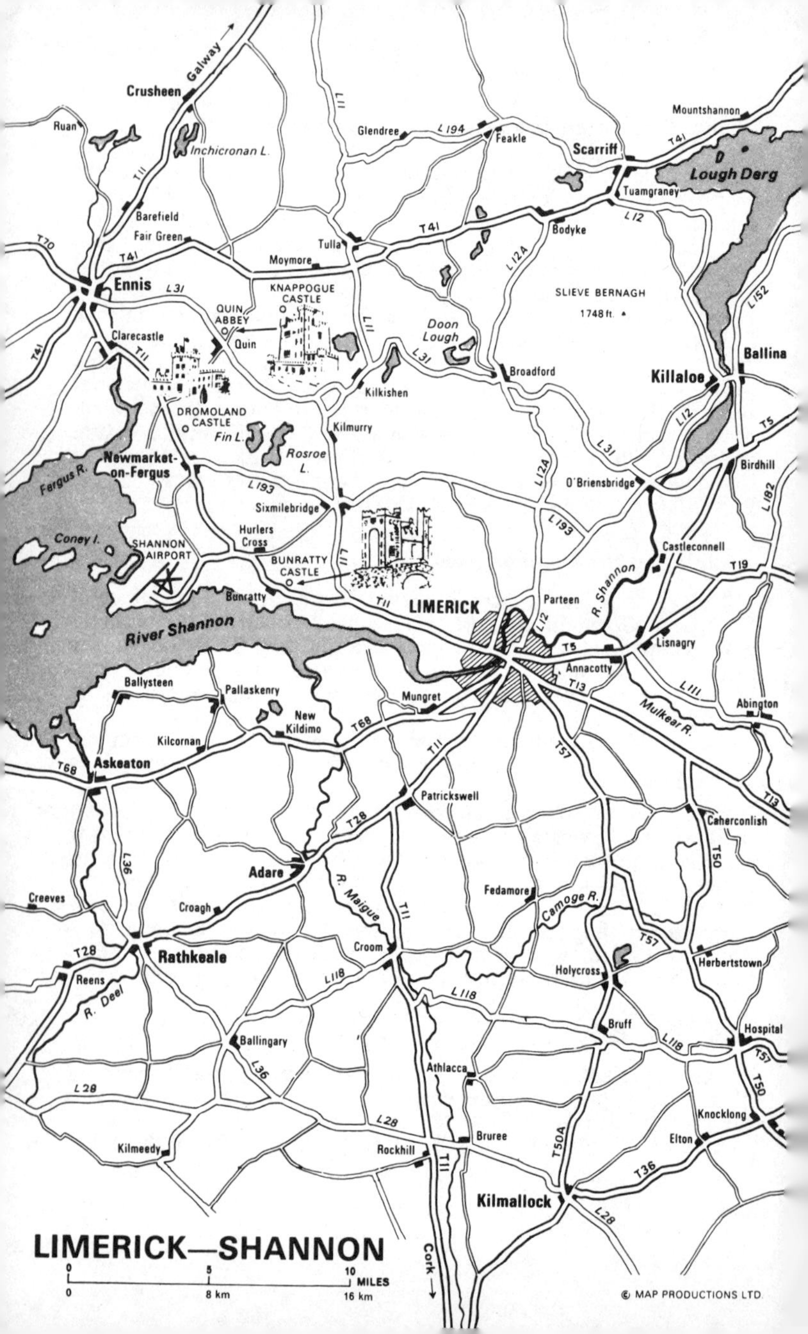

LIMERICK—SHANNON
0
5
10
MILES
0
8 km
16 km
© MAP PRODUCTIONS LTD.
Galway →
Crusheen
Ruan
Inchicronan L.
T11
Barefield
Fair Green
T70
T41
Ennis
L31
Clarecastle
T41
T11
QUIN ABBEY
Quin
KNAPPOGUE CASTLE
DROMOLAND CASTLE
Fin L.
Rosroe L.
Newmarket-on-Fergus
Fergus R.
L193
Sixmilebridge
Hurlers Cross
Coney I.
SHANNON AIRPORT
BUNRATTY CASTLE
Bunratty
River Shannon
T11
LIMERICK
L11
Glendree
L194
Feakle
Scarriff
Mountshannon
T41
D
Lough Derg
Tuamgraney
L12
Bodyke
T41
Tulla
Moymore
L12A
SLIEVE BERNAGH
1748 ft.
L152
Doon Lough
L31
Broadford
Kilkishen
Kilmurry
Killaloe
Ballina
L12
T5
L31
Birdhill
L12A
O'Briensbridge
L182
L193
Castleconnell
T19
R. Shannon
Parteen
L12
T5
Lisnagry
Annacotty
T13
L111
Abington
Mulkear R.
Ballysteen
Pallaskenry
New Kildimo
Mungret
T68
Kilcornan
Askeaton
T68
T11
T57
T13
Patrickswell
Caherconlish
T28
L36
Adare
T50
R. Maigue
Fedamore
Creeves
Croagh
Camoge R.
T57
T28
Rathkeale
Croom
T11
Herbertstown
Reens
R. Deel
L118
L118
Holycross
Bruff
L118
Hospital
T57
Ballingary
L36
Athlacca
T50
L28
L28
Knocklong
Bruree
Elton
Kilmeedy
Rockhill
T11
T50A
T36
Kilmallock
L28
Cork →

dominates a considerable area of the counties of Clare and Limerick; that's why it was built, located on the edge of a river which formed one side of its defense and filled the moat around it. Bought by Viscount Gort in the 1950s, it was restored to its medieval splendor under the guidance of John Hunt, Ireland's leading expert on the period, to give the place true character. Since 1962, therefore, visitors have been welcomed each night, by colleens in fifteenth-century dress, with the traditional "bread of friendship" (Irish brown bread and salt) before donning bibs and sitting down to the long tables under the presidency of an Honorary Earl chosen from among the visitors. Beakers of honey mead wash down unusual and very palatable food based on authentic recipes, while the serving wenches break off to sing a few ballads or pluck the strings of a harp and high pageantry prevails. Banquets should be booked well in advance as they are extremely popular.

Behind Bunratty Castle, the village of Old Bunratty has been created, a folk village having grown out of what was originally planned as a demolition job. A thatched farmhouse once typical of the area, was "transplanted" when it was found to be in the way of a runway development at Shannon Airport. It was reconstructed and furnished in its period and soon other houses were added to the village, which now has every area of the Shannon Region represented, from West Clare to the Golden Vale.

The forge is a replica of one from Athea in County Limerick, and the blacksmith is a skilled member of his ancient craft, still working to meet the needs of the neighborhood. There are other old crafts to be seen: the making of butter by hand in a "dash" churn, baking of delicious soda bread in a pot-oven on an open turf fire (you can get to taste the soda bread at one of the party-time tours) and lace-making. This is the village where time stands still; there's no museum atmosphere about it.

Knappogue Castle

Knappogue Castle, at Quin (about eight miles northwest of Bunratty), is the latest addition to the castle-circuit in Clare. Knappogue, literally "The Hill of the Kiss", was built in 1467 by an Irish chieftain; it now belongs to an American couple who have restored it. The Shannon people have leased the castle for 50 years for the presentation of medieval banquets and an entertainment in the form of a colorful pageant of Irish history. The menu differs from that of Bunratty, but is well in line with the traditional meals served at the castle 400 years ago. Fresh garden fruits and a mild cheese of a type first made in Knappogue long ago round off the meal. To drink? Mead from fermented honey, apple juice, clover and heather for a start, and then Beaujolais from casks in the Banqueting Hall.

Nearby is the recently restored (1975) Craggaunowen Castle, an example of a fortified home, typical of the fifteenth and sixteenth centuries. It has a fine collection of Irish antiquities.

Also worth visiting is the neighboring *crannog,* an ancient (600 B.C.) ringfort and lake dwelling, built on an artificial island; furnished in the period manner and reached by a wooden causeway. Not far away was found, in 1854, the greatest collection of gold objects ever discovered together in Europe.

Dun Guaire and Matrix Castles

Dun Guaire of Kinvara is about 40 miles from Shannon, and best reached on one of the Shannon-based tours (although if you're staying in Galway, it is sometimes possible to make a booking). Don't arrive hopefully without a booking—Dun Guaire is small.

The castle is on a rock, almost cut off from the shore, and was a defensive position as far back as the sixth century, when it was the fort of King Guaire. Dun Guaire, as the traveler sees it today, sheltered behind a defensive wall, is a sixteenth-century building.

Castle Matrix at Rathkeale was originally built in 1487 and was later confiscated by Queen Elizabeth I. After many vicissitudes the ruined castle was bought in 1970 by Col. Sean O'Driscoll, an Irish-American architect who restored it, and now features medieval banquets in traditional manner. It is claimed that the "Virginia Tubers" imported to Ireland by Sir Walter Raleigh were first planted in this area, thus giving rise to the large-scale potato cultivation in Ireland.

Limerick

Limerick, Ireland's fourth largest city, is the main center for the region. King John's Castle, beside Thomond Bridge, is an imposing piece of thirteenth-century architecture, still marked by the shot from the guns of the Williamite artillery. St. Mary's Cathedral (1172) in Bridge Street also bears some of the marks of wars gone by. Its interior is particularly interesting because of the fifteenth-century misericords, the carved embellishment

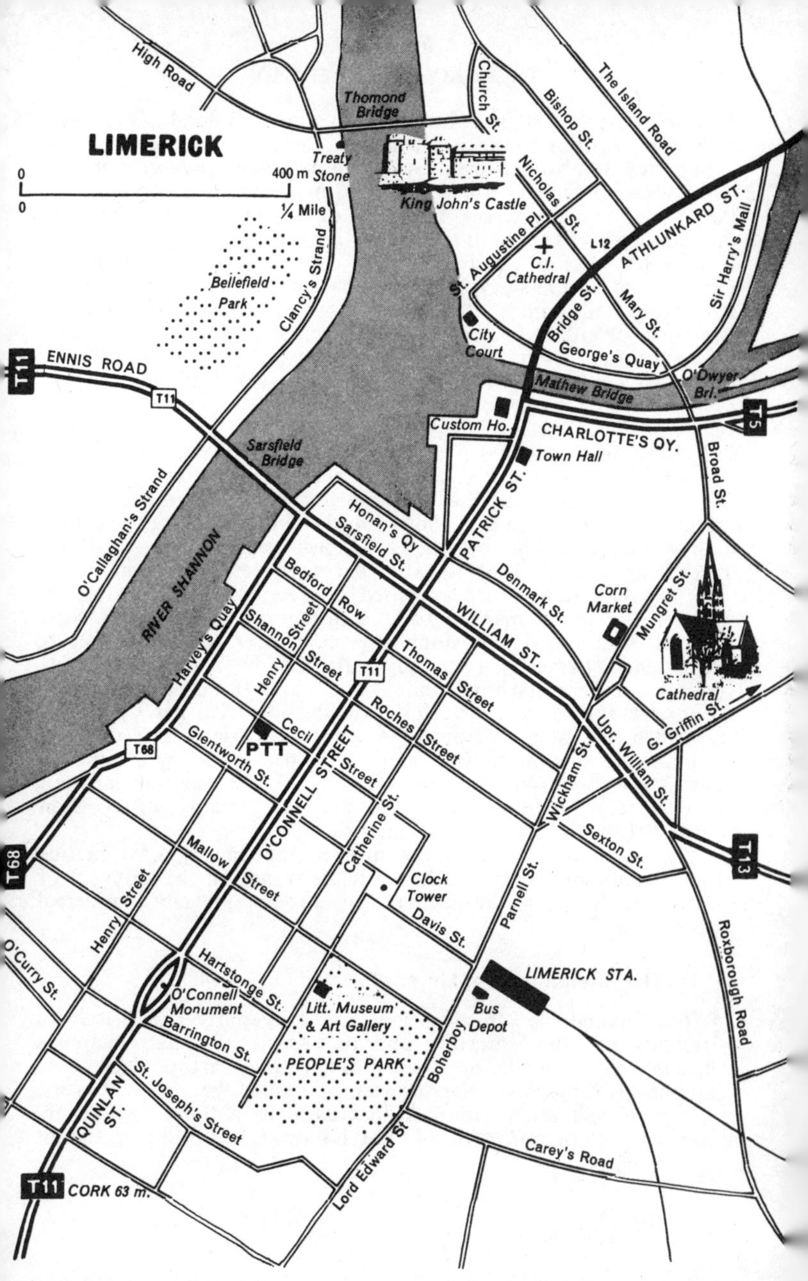

beneath the choir stalls, which are unique in Ireland. The view from the 120-foot tower is worth the climb to get there.

Limerick has some good Georgian buildings and an impressive Custom House at the Dublin end of the main thoroughfare. Pery Square suggests the Limerick of a century ago and the museum and art gallery in the nearby People's Park deserve a visit. The gallery has a good collection of Irish paintings and the museum covers the story of Ireland back to the stone and bronze ages. Included among the relics of the later centuries is the Limerick "Nail", a pedestal which formerly stood outside the Exchange (now part of St. Mary's Cathedral boundary wall) in Nicholas Street, on which Limerick merchants paid their debts, giving currency to the expression "Paying on the nail" as indicating prompt payment.

Francis Bindon (1690-1765) painter and architect, was among the city's most famous sons; of Limerick's daughters, probably the most colorful, and the one who achieved most international fame, was Lola Montez, born Maria Dolores Eliza Rosanna Gilbert in 1818. She became a Spanish dancer, captivated the mad King Ludwig I of Bavaria, exercised remarkable influence over the Bavarian Court, appeared in New York in a couple of flops in the 1850s, married for the third time, made a theatrical tour of Australia (horse-whipping a newspaper editor for reflecting on her character), returned to America in a few more non-successes before starting a new career as a lecturer and writer (*The Art of Beauty*, New York, 1858) and ended her days as a reformed character visiting the poor and sick. She died in Astoria, New York, in 1861, and is commemorated by a tablet in the Greenwood Cemetery in that city. A less spectacular, but more successful, Limerick actress was Ada Rehan, born Crehan (1860-1916); she, too, died in America.

The traditional craft of the district, the making of Limerick lace, is still continued as a home industry and in the Convent of the Good Shepherd; it is marketed through the city's principal stores.

Up the Shannon from Limerick

The Shannon is 240 miles long (the longest river in Britain or Ireland) and the waterway and its associated canals enable a journey to be made by boat through the heart of Ireland to Dublin or to the River Barrow and then south again to Waterford.

Up the Shannon from Ardnacrusha is Killaloe, where the Roman Catholic Church on the hilltop is supposed to be on the site of Kincora, once the residence of Brian Boru, High King of Ireland. Apart from the associations of the site with the long-ago ruler, the church has some fine stained glass windows.

The remains of St. Mo Lua's Oratory, which once stood on Friar's Island in the lake, have been re-erected beside the church; the island was submerged during the flooding of the reservoir for the Shannon power station's water supply. The Church of Ireland Cathedral of St. Flannan was originally built in 1182, and, as was usual in the Ireland of long ago, it was on the site of an even earlier church, probably St. Flannan's Oratory, which is in the churchyard, a small early church with a high-pitched roof of stone. The richly carved doorway of the cathedral, restored in 1966, is thought to have been the entrance to the tomb of King Murtagh O'Brien, a Munster monarch who died in 1120. There is a fine twelfth-century (east) window and the latest work on the cathedral has opened up a medieval barrel staircase.

For the more adventurous this is the center for water-skiing and power-boating. There are also good fishing and sailing on Lough Derg to the north, and there are plenty of places to be visited in the neighborhood, such as Balboru Fort and some low hills from which pleasing prospects of the shores and waterscape of Lough Derg may be enjoyed if you go pony-trekking. To the north are the long stretches of the Lough and the Shannon, navigable for small-craft cruising, a popular form of holiday in Ireland.

Lough Derg itself is 25 miles long and varies between two and three miles in width, with a number of islands, the most interesting being Holy Island (Inis Cealtra), which, as you'd expect, has the remains of a number of buildings covering six centuries from the seventh onward and including a cramped "Anchorite's Cell" about ten feet long by eight feet wide and never more than five feet high.

To the south of Limerick (12 miles), excavations at Lough Gur have shown that people lived here continuously from the neolithic period down to the late medieval period. Research has revealed lakeside dwellings, dolmens and stone circles (including the largest in Ireland, embracing an area 150 feet in diameter, with 30 standing stones), and finds of food vessels in the center have dated it a Bronze Age burial place. The profusion of relics of the long ago give it a strange atmosphere in these days, an atmosphere enhanced when somebody retells the legend of the last Earl of Desmond who disappeared in the fourteenth century

THE FACE OF IRELAND

and whose ghost is said to rise out of the lake on a white horse and ride across the surface, a feat which he must repeat every seven years until the silver shoes of his horse are worn out.

From Shannon to the Sea

Ennis is the county town and was once linked to the seaside resorts of the Clare coast by the West Clare Railway, a railroad which still has international fame through Percy French's ballad, *Are Ye Right There, Michael?* Michael was the driver of an engine on the West Clare Railway, which had not much of a reputation for punctuality, but a great reputation for the friendliness of its staff.

The last of the engines of the West Clare, the *Slieve Callan*, is now preserved in Ennis, and on taking a look at it there is almost a likelihood of truth in the tale that the guard sometimes called out: "First-class passengers keep your seats; second-class passengers, please get out and walk, third-class passengers get out and shove." Today, a bus service covers the area rather more efficiently.

Located on the banks of the River Fergus, Ennis Abbey, founded in 1241, has been very well restored and contains some fine sculptures which are unusual in Ireland—the key can be borrowed from *Mulqueen's* shop, beside the abbey grounds.

Ennis became Éamon de Valera's town—the New York-born teacher was reared in Bruree, County Limerick; he was first elected for the district in 1918 and continued as its representative until his election to the presidency of Ireland in 1959.

Harriet Constance Smithson (1800-54), the famous actress and the wife of the French composer, Hector Berlioz, was born in Ennis. (She died in Paris.) A famous son of the town was the artist William Mulready (1786-1863), the man who designed the first postage stamp.

Corofin and Lemaneagh Castle

Heading up the road northwest from Ennis for about six miles, there is an interesting stop about one and a half miles off the main road at Dysert O'Dea. The church which you see here was founded by St. Tola, and among its impressive survivals is the fine Hiberno-Romanesque doorway.

Corofin, the next village on the way northwest, is a regular stop on the medieval tours. Along this stretch of road, there is frequently a thatcher putting a new golden straw roof on a cottage; and on the left is a wheelwright's shop, where the traditional craft of making wooden wheels and shrinking iron bands on them is still practised.

North of the village, and on the left of the road, there is a primitive cross of pre-Christian times, known as the Killinaboy Sculptured Stone. It is a short stump with a transom across the top, on which are carved two heads looking up at the sky, the necks meeting in the center. It is believed to have been the local form of an idol of the late Celtic Iron Age of 2,000 years ago; somewhat similar idol stones have been found in the southeast of France.

In the same district is partly-ruined Lemaneagh Castle, interesting because it mixes two styles of architecture. It is a fifteenth-century tower castle with slit windows onto which a seventeenth-century fortified house was built. The result is a building of graceful proportions, with mullioned and transomed windows.

They're great story-tellers around here, and along the coast there are tales of the Spanish Armada and of shipwrecks. Spanish Point, for example, near Miltown-Malbay, gets its name from the burying place of the men drowned nearby when the ships were wrecked in 1588. Lahinch, a few miles up the coast, is famous for its golf course, but its neighboring village of Liscannor also has a claim to fame, because there was born John P. Holland (1841-1914), a one-time teacher who emigrated to Paterson, New Jersey, in 1872 and seven years later successfully invented and tested, in the Passaic River, the first submarine.

Northwest of Liscannor are the dramatic Cliffs of Moher, rising out of the Atlantic in a five-mile wall which varies in height from 440 feet to 700 feet at O'Brien's Tower; there is a sign indicating a car park and safe viewing spot just near the tower. The north of County Clare is known as the Burren, a strange desert of limestone covering 100 square miles, rising in terraces to over 1,000 feet; in some parts, there are lakes which seem to appear and disappear mysteriously, a phenomenon caused by the drainage beneath the limestone.

More Caves and Twin Wells

In the new Interpretive Center at Kilfenora the visitor can discover a great deal about the Burren which will help him to greater enjoyment of the area. It houses an array of Burren treasures such as moths, butterflies, rock formations, landscape models, flora and fauna, which can be seen and studied and interpreted by means of special lighting and visual techniques. There is also a good school of painting hereabouts.

For the caver, there are about thirty miles of caves and passages for exploring beneath this strange landscape, including a pothole (100 feet deep) at Pollnagollum, with a passage that takes the explorer past an underground waterfall. In the rugged countryside, there are stone forts and a number of dolmens, which have survived the centuries.

Ireland was once a land of many spas; most of them have been forgotten, but not Lisdoonvarna, where there are several springs. The principal sulphur springs are at Gowlane, one of the "Twin Wells", where a sulphur and an iron water flow out of the rocks within a few inches of each other. Lisdoonvarna is one of the liveliest towns in the country during its season. From the neighborhood of Lisdoonvarna, at Lough Quarries, the flagstones for the steps of some of London's most famous buildings were quarried, including Westminster Abbey, St. Paul's Cathedral and the Tower of London. Among the defensive works worth seeing within easy reach of the town is Ballykinvarga Caher, a dry stone (unmortared) fort about 150 feet in diameter and surrounded by a *chevaux de frise* of pointed stones, a deterrent to attack by cavalry and the forerunner of modern tank traps.

From Lisdoonvarna there is a main road leading northeast to the little village of Ballyvaughan, with a corkscrew on the road midway which provides an opportunity to get some fine distant views of romantic Galway Bay; an alternative route, by the west side of Slieve Elva, northwest of Lisdoonvarna, is a coastal drive with a view of the Aran Islands of Inisheer (the nearest) and Inishmaan. You then reach Black Head and turn east to drive beside Galway Bay through the villages of Ballyvaughan and Burren. Beyond, and just over the County Galway border, is Dun Guaire, today an hospitable northern outpost of the Shannon Region.

THE WONDERFUL WEST

Where the Next Parish is America

When the Irish speak of "the West", they embrace all the area west of the Shannon; the old province of Connacht itself includes the modern counties of Galway, Mayo, Roscommon, Sligo and Leitrim; for our purposes, it is convenient to deal with Sligo and Leitrim in our next chapter, the Northwest, but there may be detours across the county borders where the routes wander that way.

In the country to the west of Galway, which is the keystone of the area, the Irish way of life has been less anglicized than any other part of the country, and the Gaelic language has been preserved without dilution by a proud and hospitable people. The west has seen a substantial percentage of emigration of its people since the days of the Hungry Forties of the last century; many a shipload of families sailed out from Galway for American and Canadian ports. Today the emigration rate is down to a trickle, but the tradition of going away still persists in many families of Galway and Mayo and the young people want to see faraway places. Some do travel far, but many of them return to the peace that they can find nowhere else in the world.

Thatched Cottages Galore

The houses and the cottages may have an electricity supply

but the peat fire is a tradition; at all times of the year, the traveler will see the characteristic blue smoke rising from the chimneys of the low-built thatched cottages. The ancient craft of thatching with straw (or, in some places, a type of grass called "bent") is still carried on. No matter what road the traveler takes, there is certain to be a thatched cottage within a few miles, not retained as a tourist gimmick but because people of the older generation (and some of the young) prefer to live in them. The traditional cottage is a two-room single-story structure, sometimes with the fire on an open hearth and a chimney in the center of the building. Others have a chimney in the end wall and a slight projection known as an outshut, an indication that in the old days the main bed of the house was built in beside the fireplace.

Modern life has been absorbed and adapted in parts of the west, but it has not dominated the lives of the people. Some of them may work in factories, for the government has encouraged the establishment of new industries, but they have also maintained their old craft industries of knitting and weaving and the making of the canvas-covered boats called *currachs,* in which they ride the Atlantic waves.

Beyond Galway and to the northwest lies Connemara, a land of great beauty and loneliness, the place where you discover that mountains really can look blue and where the water in the bog streams is every shade from pale tan to a dark translucent brown, and white limestone punctuates the landscape. This is country which has attracted Ireland's finest painters, among them Sean Keating, Maurice McGonigal and Jack B. Yeats. And it has attracted many writers, too, including Jack Yeats's brother, William Butler Yeats (1865–1939), Abbey playwright and poet, who lived in an old tower which he restored near Gort. John Millington Synge (1871–1909) drew the inspiration for *Riders to the Sea* from the life on the Aran Islands, off the west coast, and for *The Playboy of the Western World* from other experiences in the west. Film-maker Robert Flaherty recorded the drama of the fishermen of the western waters in his picture, *Man of Aran* and a latter-day film-maker, John Huston, made his home in County Galway for several years.

Exploring the West

The west is a land of strange contrasts and color, moving from the limestone plains of the midlands to the rocky crags beyond Galway, a land of good stories and breathtaking views. Much

THE WONDERFUL WEST

of the 5,000 square miles of country which is embraced in the general term of "the west" is wild, yet in places there is rich land, while the deeply-indented coastline is as rugged as the people of the western isles of Aran. Beyond Galway, set between Lough Corrib and the Atlantic, is the romantic Connemara, beloved by painters.

Galway was known to the sailors of earliest times, but it began to grow up from its fort and fishing village status with the arrival of the Anglo-Normans in the thirteenth century. Not long afterwards, it became a walled city, the physical stones of the walls creating also a mental ghetto within which resided the Anglo-Normans, isolated from the Gaelic influence of the Irish, who lived outside. Remoteness from the rule of England allowed Galway to develop in its own way but the ruling tribes still tried to keep out the Irish; a local law stated that "neither O nor Mac shall strutte ne swagger thro' the streets of Galway". But, of course, the Irish took little notice of that and their raids became so effective that over the West Gate an inscription read: "From the fury of the O'Flahertys good Lord protect us."

Trading links with France and Spain developed through the centuries and contributed to the wealth of the city, and to some extent to the architecture—Spanish Arch and Spanish Parade are among the city's relics of the period. All through its long, stormy history Galway has shown a toughness of spirit and the Irish character here has always asserted itself.

Lynch's Law

The city is compact and easily explored on foot, using Eyre (Kennedy) Square, with its Great Southern Hotel as a base. Eyre Square was named for the Eyre family, who gave it to the city. They also gave it a five-foot silver mace in 1709; the mace and a seventeenth-century ceremonial sword were given to Mayor Edmund Blake, in lieu of money owed to him. Ninety years later, his daughter sold the heirlooms to an art dealer and, in turn, they were bought by American newspaper tycoon William Randolph Hearst for £5,000 ($14,000). Just before his death in 1951, he gave instructions that the regalia, then at his ranch home in California, should be given to Galway, and nine years later they were formally handed back to the city.

In one corner of the square there is a statue of a little man with a battered hat. This is Padraic O'Conaire (1882–1923), a Galway-born Gaelic storyteller of renown. The road to the left of the square leads past Lynch's Castle (now a bank), an interesting example of a restored tower house of the sixteenth century. The design is unusual in Ireland and it still bears the arms of King Henry VII of England and the Lynch family, famous among the old "tribes" of Galway. One of the family members added the word "lynch" to the language when he hanged his son (the executioner refused to perform the duty) for murdering a Spanish guest in his house. The gruesome event is commemorated by a marble stone set in a wall by a walled-up door, near the Collegiate Church of St. Nicholas, which recalls "the stern and unbending justice of the Chief Magistrate of this city, James Lynch FitzStephen, elected Mayor 1493, who condemned and executed his own guilty son, Walter, on this spot."

Columbus and the Clasped Hands of Claddagh

The neighboring church in Lombard Street, officially the Collegiate Church of St. Nicholas of Myra, dates back to 1320, with many later additions. Its interior is unusual because the aisles are wider than the nave. In this church, Christopher Columbus is reputed to have prayed before sailing for the west in the *Santa Maria*.

In the Middle Street, there is the nineteenth-century Roman Catholic Church of St. Nicholas, formerly the pro-cathedral, in which there are some panels of seventeenth-century carving taken from an earlier church. Nearby is the Gaelic Theatre, *Taibhdhearc na Gaillimhe*. It was in the adjoining streets that one of its actors and playwrights, Walter Macken (1916-67), set his first play *Mungo's Mansion*, for the Abbey Theatre in 1946. One of his most successful books, *Rain on the Wind*, was set in the Claddagh, the old fishing village of Galway. The gold Claddagh Ring in the form of two hands clasping a heart was a traditional heirloom in the village, being handed down from mother to daughter; the rings are still made and are one of the most distinctive souvenirs of the west, along with the handknits and tweeds.

In the old Claddagh section of the town is the Dominican Friary, on the site of a friary established in the fifteenth century. It is part of the Galway tradition that a priest from the friary should bless the sea at the start of the herring-fishing season in mid-August. The fishing fleet decorated with flags moves down Galway Bay headed by one carrying the priests; at the appointed spot the fleet stops, sails are lowered and the blessing ceremony performed.

The shoaling of salmon in the River Corrib can be watched from the Upper Bridge, and nearby, on the site of the old jail,

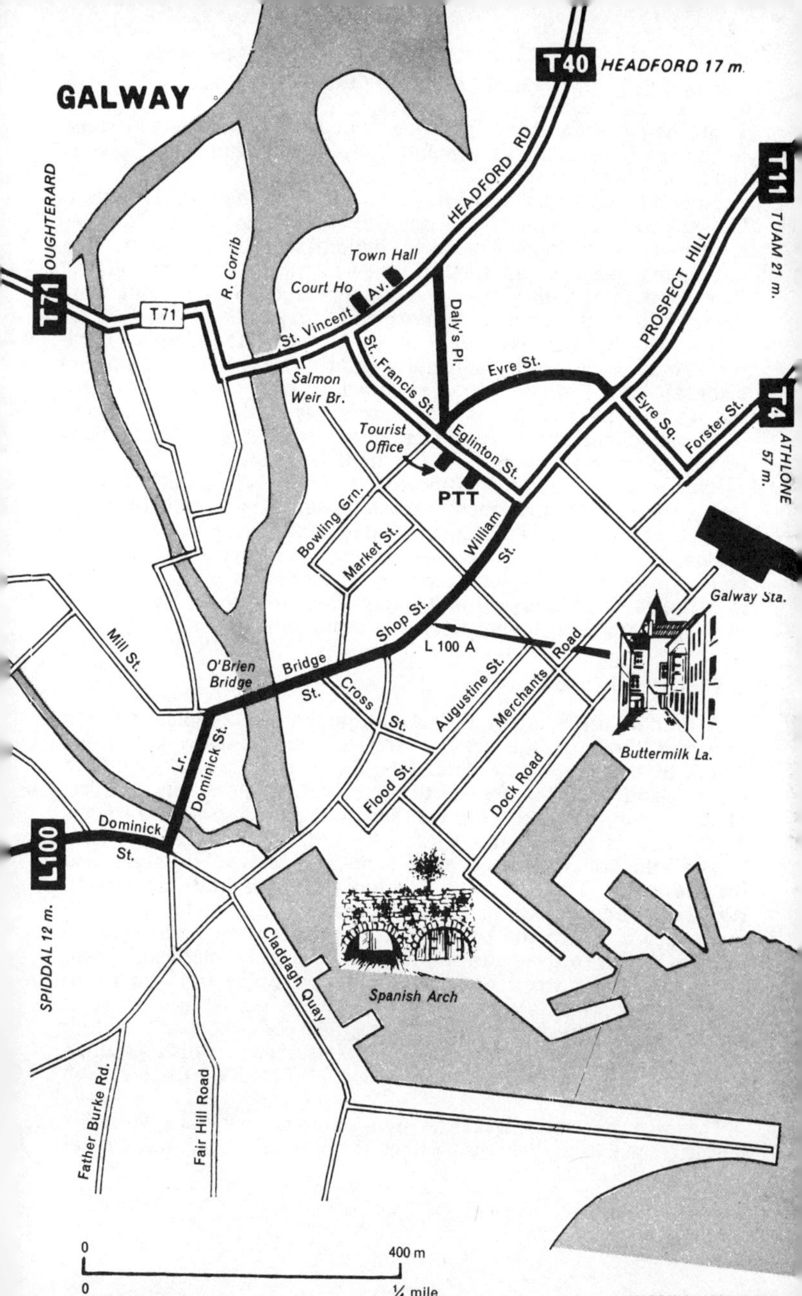
GALWAY
T40
HEADFORD 17 m.
T11
TUAM 21 m.
T4
ATHLONE 57 m.
T71
OUGHTERARD
T71
R. Corrib
HEADFORD RD
Town Hall
Court Ho
Av.
St. Vincent
Daly's Pl.
PROSPECT HILL
Salmon Weir Br.
St. Francis St.
Evre St.
Eyre Sq.
Forster St.
Tourist Office
Eglinton St.
PTT
Bowling Grn.
Market St.
William St.
Galway Sta.
Mill St.
Shop St.
L 100 A
Road
O'Brien Bridge
Bridge St.
Cross St.
Augustine St.
Merchants
Buttermilk La.
Lr. Dominick St.
Flood St.
Dock Road
Dominick St.
L100
SPIDDAL 12 m.
Claddagh Quay
Spanish Arch
Father Burke Rd.
Fair Hill Road
0
400 m
0
¼ mile

THE FACE OF IRELAND

is the new cathedral, an imposing structure of Galway limestone, in the shape of a cross surmounted by a great dome, and accommodating 3,000 people.

Not far from the cathedral are the buildings of University College, Galway, one of the constituent colleges of the National University of Ireland. The older buildings are in a Tudor style, more reminiscent of an English university town than Ireland, but they were only built just over a century ago. New buildings are being added to meet the continually expanding demand for higher education, a trend very much a part of the Galway tradition. As long ago as the sixteenth century, there was an important classical school which attracted students from all over Ireland, but it was finally suppressed, because of its strong Irish character, in Cromwellian times. At the modern University College, many of the subjects are studied in the Irish language.

Southwest of this area is the lively suburb of Salthill, with its long promenade, amusement park and dance halls, which attract a large number of young Irish holidaymakers during the summer season. Its high point is reached during the Galway Races at the end of July. Salthill's setting on the north shore of Galway Bay is particularly attractive, for it looks across the water to the blue hills of Clare and, to the west, the Aran Islands.

The Aran Islands

A tour of the West of Ireland would not be complete without a trip by one of the regular ferries from Galway down the length of the bay to the Aran Islands, 30 miles away. There are three islands: Inishmore, Inishmaan and Inisheer, the smallest of the group. The people are fisherfolk and subsistence farmers. Their land is rugged and with little soil, so the islanders have "made" the soil themselves with sand and seaweed to raise feed for the cattle. They fish the Atlantic waters in traditional craft, *currachs,* made of laths and tarred canvas which ride the waves easily and in which the traveler will be ferried ashore to land on Inishmaan or Inisheer; Inishmore has the only pierhead where ferries dock. Air strips have been built on Inishmore and Inishmaan, served from Oranmore (Galway) by Aer Arann. There is also a seasonal service from Shannon Airport. A recent feature is the folk museum established on Inishmaan, which is open April-October; contact Madame Roisin Ni Mheara-Vinard on the island.

The men invariably wear the style of dress they have worn for centuries, with a *bainin* (pronounce it "bawneen"), a white home-

THE WONDERFUL WEST

spun jacket of great wearing qualities. The costume also includes hand-knitted sweaters in intricate traditional patterns, heavy tweed trousers (usually supported by a *crios,* a long, colorful braided girdle) and *pampooties,* shoes of hide without heels. The women dress almost as simply. They spin their own wool and weave their own material to make most of their clothes. This work arises from their independence of spirit almost as much as through economic tradition; they do it because it is their way of life, not just as a gimmick to entertain the tourist. They are an hospitable people using the Irish language in their everyday speech, but speaking English freely to visitors.

Forts and Hermits

Prehistoric forts indicate that the islands have been inhabited since the world was young, certainly by the Firbolgs, the earliest people who lived in Ireland. The most famous of all the fortifications is Dun Aengus on Inishmore. Built on the edge of a 300-foot cliff, it is semi-circular in shape (it was originally circular, but half of it fell into the ocean before the recorded history of the fort). Regarded by archeologists as one of the finest prehistoric monuments in Western Europe, it was built with three rings of defense, and has an inner court 150 feet in diameter, surrounded by a wall of unmortared stone 20 feet high and 18 feet thick at the base. This is ringed by another wall and a 30-foot wide *chevaux de frise* of sharp-pointed stones about four feet high and set closely together. There are flights of steps on the inner side of the walls and from the top of the innermost ring, you can obtain a wonderful view of the island.

Dun Eochla, close to the village of Oghill, is a smaller fort, but it is in an excellent state of preservation. Dunchathair, on the southern side of Inishmore, about two miles from the village of Killeany, is believed to be the oldest of these Aran forts, but if you want to see the finest example still remaining in Ireland, you must cross to Inishmaan to see Dun Conor, dominating the highest point of the island. There are many other traces of Irish history on the Aran Islands, including a perfect example of an ancient stone dwelling, known as a *clochan,* on Inishmore.

The monks who wanted to lead the life of hermits in the early days of Christianity found the peace they sought on the islands. St. Enda, who lived in the sixth century, is believed to have been the first. There are remains of a number of monastic settlements still to be seen: Teachlach Eine (the house of Enda) is near the village of Killeany on Inishmore, and close by are the remains of the ninth-century church founded by St. Brecan. Teampall Bheanain, also hereabouts, is probably the world's smallest church, being ten feet nine inches by seven feet, although it is fifteen feet high.

Strange puffing holes are found on the islands, places where the sea has eroded the rock and roars in to create a fountain like a whale spouting, under some conditions of wind and tide. The Aran Islands are a place of mystery; islands which leave a deep impression on the traveler's mind long after the ferry has returned to the mainland.

Around Connemara

Connemara is rather vague in terms of geography but to say that it is the western part of County Galway lying between Lough Corrib and the Atlantic is close enough. Many people who have never seen it have heard of the Connemara ponies, the sturdy little breed of ponies which are seen at their best at the Connemara Pony Show at Clifden (August or September) and the Royal Dublin Society's Horse Show at Ballsbridge, Dublin (early August).

Many of the people of this sparsely populated district, like the Aran Islanders, use Irish as their everyday language, and there are important centers for the teaching of Irish at such villages as Carraroe and Rosmuc. The road westwards from Galway, through Salthill, begins to enter the region at Barna, the center for deep-sea angling on Galway Bay, and Spiddal, another language center and a good place to buy handknits and tweeds. The shore line at the mouth of Galway Bay, opposite the Aran Islands, is fretted into a number of inlets and islands.

Carna, on the big promontory between Kilkieran Bay and Bertraghboy Bay, is a center for Connemara ponies and the place to take a ferry to St. MacDara's Island, one of the holy places of the west; following an age-old custom, fishing boats dip their sails when passing it. Pilgrimages (usually followed by a regatta) take place in July and September.

Taking the Straight Road

The main road from Galway into Connemara is rather less interesting until it reaches the angling center of Oughterard, although it passes (on the east of the road) Ross House, birthplace of Violet Martin (1862–1915), who, as Martin Ross, was a partner in the Somerville and Ross authorship team. They wrote

THE WONDERFUL WEST

a number of stories of Irish life including *Some Experiences of an Irish R.M.* (1899), an "R.M." being a Resident Magistrate, the pre-Independence administrator of law at local levels.

Oughterard is the principal angling center for Lough Corrib, a lake 27 miles long and linked by the short River Corrib to the sea at Galway. Lough Corrib provides the best free-fishing in the country, whether it is for salmon, trout or the coarser fish. The lake is studded with wooded islands, and boats can be hired for excursions to them. Inchagoill ("Island of the Foreigner") is the most important for its ecclesiastical remains.

The road to Maam Cross runs beside a chain of lakes in a valley with the Maamturk Mountains (Lechavrea Mountain, 2,174 ft.) beginning to dominate the view in changing patterns to the northwest.

Near Recess, on the southern shore of Ballinahinch Lake, there is a castle which was once the home of the remarkable Richard Martin (1754-1834), a duellist of renown, known in youth as "Hair-trigger Dick". He became known in later years as "Humanity Dick" because of his interest in the welfare of animals—he was one of the founders of the Royal Society for the Prevention of Cruelty to Animals. Roundstone, an English corruption of the Irish name *Cloc an Ron* ("Rock of the Seal"), is a little harbor in the heart of Connemara, with long stretches of white sand and a special interest for botanists in the nearby countryside, particularly around Carrigamore Lake, where there are some rare heaths such as *Erica Mackaiana*.

Clifden and Kylemore

Clifden is the westernmost point of the Connemara tour. It is backed by the Twelve Pins, which change color with the light and the season, and faces the Atlantic—the next parish to the west, they say, is America. The village won a place in aviation history when Alcock and Brown, first men to fly the North Atlantic, landed at Derrygimlagh Bog (south of the town) after their flight from Newfoundland in 1919. The feat is commemorated in a memorial on high ground overlooking the bog where their converted bomber landed; a cairn of stones is near the landing place. Clifden is an ideal spot to idle on its coral strand, to explore and to fish.

A few miles northwest, you can get a boat to the offshore islands of Inishbofin, Inishturk and Inishark; the first-named has a monastic foundation by St. Colman and a fort built by the sea-queen Grainne O'Malley and the remains of Cromwell's Barrack (based on a much older fort).

Kylemore Abbey, once known as Kylemore Castle, is on the water's edge at Kylemore Lough, at the northern end of the Twelve Pins; it was rejected by Edward VII as an Irish residence because it was too big; today it is a convent of Benedictine nuns.

Killary Harbour is a few miles to the north; the eight-mile-long inlet, rather like a Norwegian fjord, was at one time a naval station. Leenaun, an angling village of charm, sits near the head of the harbor, with Aasleagh Waterfall nearby making a spectacular entry for the Erriff River into the waters. The small modern church at Creeragh, Connemara is worth a visit. Apart from an unusual exterior and stained glass it has fine examples of enamelwork and welded sculptures.

The wild and lonely area of dramatic beauty to the east of Leenaun lies at the south end of the Partry Mountains and stretches from the Maamturks to Lough Mask. It's part of Connemara but overspills to the north of it. It can be explored across country on foot, skirting the north side of the Devil's Mother (2,131 ft.) and passing between it and Maamstrasna (2,239 ft.) to join the road at the eastern end of Lough Nafooey, it's a distance of about ten miles as the crow flies.

Lough Mask and Ashford Castle

Lough Mask can be reached from Leenaun by driving southwest along the valley to the north of the Maamturk Mountains, and taking the left fork where the road divides to skirt the northern shore of Lough Corrib before heading north again through Clonbur, on the neck of land between the lakes of Corrib and Mask. Under this isthmus, underground rivers link the two loughs; a stream can be seen at such points as the Pigeon Hole at Cong. The name Cong comes from the Irish word which means "a neck". To the north is Mask, ten miles long and four miles wide, to the south Corrib, and a journey all the way to Galway by water, if you are so inclined. The country is well wooded and provides a contrast to the barer mountains to the west. As on the Corrib, the fishing on Mask is free; it is noted for the size of its trout, perch and pike.

Lough Mask House, on the eastern shore about four miles from Ballinrobe, was the home of Captain Boycott (1832-97), who was ostracized by the tenants, men refusing to work for him or deal with him; from this treatment the word "boycott" was added to the dictionaries. (He was forced to live under police

THE WONDERFUL WEST

protection and eventually to leave the country.) Recently Princess Grace of Monaco (the former Grace Kelly) bought the homestead from which her grandfather emigrated to America at Drimurla, County Mayo—a cottage and 35 acres of land—for £7,850.

Ashford Castle, now a luxury hotel set in magnificent grounds, has a history going back to the Norman De Burgo family who came to the west of Ireland in 1228. They built a castle at Cong and held it until the forces of Queen Elizabeth I seized it and subsequently built a fortress on the site. A look at the map shows why it was sought as a fortress—it commanded the pass between the lakes from the mountainous country of the Irish to the farms of east Connacht.

The Guinness brewing family purchased the property when it was sadly run down in the nineteenth century and Sir Benjamin Lee Guinness proved an excellent landlord, improving the land, building roads, planting trees and adding to the holding until it totalled 26,000 acres. The family added further to the buildings, and the western side of the castle built by the Guinness interests bears the coat of arms of a member of the family, Lord Ardilaun. The property remained with the Guinness family until 1939, when it was acquired for development as an hotel.

Royal Cong

It was on the lands near the castle that the Royal Abbey of Cong was founded in 1106. The Augustine abbey buildings spread over a considerable area; what is now the main entrance to the abbey site is a doorway from the village of Cong, a fine piece of gothic design. The remains of the abbey confirm records which speak of the large numbers of scholars and students who attended the abbey—3,000 at one time. There is a domestic note down by the river, where the monks had their refectory and kitchen. The nearby fishing house was designed over the river with a fish trap beneath the floor in which the fish were caught and held until needed for the kitchen. In the south wall of the refectory is the hatch through which food was passed to strangers who called at the abbey.

The abbey's great days were ended with its suppression in 1542 and the expulsion of the 1,000 monks who were there at the time; its treasures were taken by the invading forces and although some were given to Trinity College, Dublin, many of them were lost. One of the treasures that was not lost is the Cross of Cong which was made of oak, plated with copper and embellished with gold filigree work in Celtic designs. It was made at Roscommon, in the northwest of Connacht, in 1123 and subsequently taken to Cong, where it disappeared. It was only re-discovered early in the last century, in a chest in a house in the village. The Cross of Cong is now one of the great possessions of the National Museum in Dublin, where it is on display.

The land stretching to the east of Cong towards Tuam was the scene of great battles 3,000 years ago and there are a number of megalithic tombs which give credence to the tale. There is a "Giant's Grave", just off the main road a mile west of Cong; it is a tomb built of stones with an average thickness of eight inches; the lid of the tomb is a stone six by five feet. At the nearby village of The Neale is a stone which still puzzles the experts—it bears three figures, a human, an animal with a single horn on its forehead and an unidentified reptile.

At Headford, about half-way along the road back into Galway from Cong, there are some remains of a fourteenth-century Franciscan friary, which provide an interesting study of the planning of the buildings for a friary of the period.

South of Galway City

South of the city of Galway there is the little seashore village of Clarinbridge, location of Ireland's best-reputed oyster beds and scene of the inauguration of Galway's Oyster Festival each year in September. It's traditional that the Mayor of Galway takes the first oyster (and custom decrees that stout is the best drink to follow the oysters).

When in this area the place to visit is Thoor Ballylee, where the poet-playwright William Butler Yeats made his home for some years. He discovered the Ballylee Castle (official name) when visiting another of the literary figures who helped to found the Abbey Theatre, Lady Augusta Gregory (1852–1932), at her home at Coole House, Gort, a short distance away. Sadly, the house no longer exists. Thoor Ballylee, now a Yeats Museum, was one of the 32 Norman towers built by the de Burgo family. Yeats bought it for £35, a price which included two cottages and a walled garden. It is open to the public daily, April through October.

The seventh-century King Guaire, who lived in Gort and gave his name to the fort on Galway Bay, Dun Guaire (now the center for nightly medieval banquets and Anglo-Irish literary entertainment), in a less martial mood gave one of his relations the site for a cathedral about three miles south-west of Gort at

THE WONDERFUL WEST

Kilmacduagh. It was replaced in the fifteenth century by a new cathedral, which can still be seen. Don't worry about your eyesight if you have the impression that the neighboring Round Tower is leaning like Italy's Tower of Pisa—it is about two feet out of perpendicular.

Loughrea, on the shores of Lough Rea, a good fishing lake, is a pleasant little town, with St. Brendan's Cathedral beside the lake shore and the Diocesan Museum in the restored southeastern gate of the town; the cathedral has some good stained-glass windows.

County Roscommon

Some of the most interesting crannogs in the country are to be seen further north at Boyle in County Roscommon, where at least thirty, dating back to the Bronze Age, have been found in Lough Gara, together with many implements of the period. Boyle is also worth a visit to see some impressive ruins of a twelfth-century Cistercian Abbey beside the river on the north of the town. Lough Gara is linked with Lough Key by a short river; Lough Key forms part of the River Shannon system of lakes, the Shannon flowing south to form the eastern boundary of Connacht. Donamon Castle, near Roscommon town, dates back to the twelfth century. It now houses the Divine Word Missionaries.

Ballintober Abbey

Westward in County Mayo is one of the most historic of all Irish abbeys, Ballintober, just a mile off the main road between Galway and Castlebar. It is unique because it is the only royal abbey in Ireland or Britain that has been in continuous use for over 750 years. The abbey was founded near the site of a church which had been established by St. Patrick about 441. Patrick's visit is commemorated in the place name in Irish, which means "Homestead of the Well of Patrick". Twenty miles to the west is the famous pilgrimage mountain of Croagh Patrick, the scene of the oldest pilgrimage in the western world, held on the last Sunday of July every year. The pilgrim road which passed the abbey was called Tochar Phadraigh, "Patrick's Causeway"; excavations have shown that there was a guesthouse for pilgrims built over a stream and there are signs of burned stones which were heated and thrown into water to heat it for the weary pilgrims.

Ballintober was suppressed like all other religious establishments by Henry VIII, but although the monks lost all their possessions, they continued to live and worship here. After the Catholic Emancipation Act (1829) was passed by the British parliament, work was started for the restoration of the abbey. Father Thomas A. Egan renewed the drive for restoration during the early 1960s and by 1966, when the 750th anniversary of the abbey was celebrated, he achieved success, not only ensuring the continued life of the abbey but contributing to the knowledge and understanding of the monastic life of centuries ago. More than 1,000 stones were unearthed during the excavations, revealing the fact that there were two cloisters, one of the thirteenth century and one of two centuries later; both have been restored.

Westport House

Westport House, home of the Marquess of Sligo, which may be visited any afternoon between April and October, is built over the ruins of another castle; the dungeons still remain. The east front of Westport House of today was designed in 1730 by the German architect Richard Cassels and the house was completed by English architect John Wyatt about 1778. Wyatt also laid out the plans for the town. A well-stocked Zoo Park was opened in 1973 on the estate. There is a fine collection of paintings, Waterford glass, old Irish silver and many historic exhibits of outstanding interest in Westport House.

A road from Westport follows the north shore of Clew Bay through great hedges of fuschia around Mullarany; there's a fine view here from Lookout Hill, behind the hotel, across the bay, with its 365 islands (maybe more) to the towering church-topped peak of Croagh Patrick (2,510 feet) on the southern shore. Winding around the hills, the road crosses a bridge to Achill Island with its dramatic Croaghaun Cliffs (2,192 feet) overlooking Achill Head. The Atlantic Drive on the island is a noteworthy scenic tour, but much of the island is best explored on foot. The netting of basking sharks (they are harmless to man), which shoal in these waters from April to July, is carried out along the rocky shore of Keem Bay, the fish being speared from currachs and then towed away to a factory on another part of Achill for the extraction of oil. Less spectacular, but more likely to yield pleasant souvenirs, are the handknit and weaving industries. See Kildownet Castle, and the sandhill settlements on Keel Strand and west of Curraun House, which were occupied in the sixth and seventh centuries. Also of interest is the strange,

THE WONDERFUL WEST

deserted village of Slievemore, a group of houses, some still well-preserved, abandoned in the late nineteenth century, when a religious mission failed.

With 5,000 square miles of scenic countryside, dotted with the traditional thatched cottages, redolent with exciting historical associations and bursting with excellent fishing and some of the most attractive golf in the world, the West of Ireland is deservedly a place for some of the happiest holidaying you can find anywhere.

SLIGO AND THE NORTHWEST

Yeats Country and The Donegal Highlands

The northwest is a land of contrasts in scenery and activity, a rugged country with small fertile valleys, lakes rich in fish, a sea coast which changes from sharp cliffs to long beaches of white sand. The Atlantic bites deep into the 400-mile shoreline of mixed rocks, carving out Sligo Bay, Gweebarra Bay (where the waters of the Gweebarra River come down from the Donegal Highlands) Sheep Haven and Lough Swilly (on the northern shore with Lough Foyle, which lie on the other side of the peninsula headed by Ireland's northernmost point, Malin Head). The Atlantic has torn off islands—Arranmore (sometimes referred to as "Aran", so don't confuse it with the Aran Islands off Galway) and lonely Tory (which used to name its own "king"). Donegal is piled high with rugged mountains, Leitrim is holed with lakes, small and large, which make it one of the finest coarse-angling centers in Ireland, and Sligo has its seaside resorts and strong associations with the poet William Butler Yeats, who is buried, as he requested, in Drumcliff Churchyard, "under bare Ben Bulben's head"

Exploring the Northwest

Sligo is the dominant town of the northwest because of its

SLIGO AND THE NORTHWEST

ease of access from Dublin, Shannon and other ports of entry into Ireland; it's a busy commercial center, but within 15 minutes' driving, you are a world away from big cities and their bustle. There is a good network of roads through the region and little heavy commercial traffic, a factor adding to the pleasure of touring its spectacular views. Sligo is a good place to start, because you hear immediately of stories that are age-old and those that are modern.

Sligo is sited on the banks of the short Garavogue River, which links lovely Lough Gill with the Atlantic in Sligo Bay; it was the river which gave the town its Irish name, Sligeach, "The Shelly River". It began to grow in importance in the thirteenth century, when Maurice FitzGerald built a castle there with the intention of using it as a base for the invasion of Donegal, but it was destroyed several times by the O'Donnell Clan, coming down from the north, and by 1470 it was under their control.

Maurice FitzGerald also founded an abbey for the Dominicans here. The remains of it, in a good state of preservation, are to be seen in Abbey Street; some of the carving is very beautiful, excellent examples of the medieval sculptors' art. At St. John's Church on John Street there is a memorial in the north transept to Susan Mary Yeats, mother of the poet William Butler Yeats and his painter-brother, Jack B. Yeats (1871-1957).

Jack was born in Sligo and there is an important collection of his paintings to be seen in the Sligo Museum on Stephen Street. A number of paintings with Yeats family associations were given to the Sligo Museum by a New York stockbroker, James A. Healy, whose mother was an emigrant to America in 1884.

Yeats Country

The region has been immortalized by the poetry of W. B. Yeats and it's quite pleasant to pick up a book of his poems and seek out the places which inspired him. Take a boat up the Garavogue River into Lough Gill and see *The Lake Isle of Inishfree* and the many other islands of this Killarney-rivaling lake; or take a car for a circular tour around the lake shore, passing Aghamore and Dooney Rock, another place which Yeats commemorated, in *The Fiddler of Dooney*. A short distance outside the town on the north side is the little graveyard beside Drumcliff Church, where Yeats is buried under the monument for which he asked a limestone slab "quarried near the spot". On it is the epitaph which he wrote for himself:

THE FACE OF IRELAND

> Cast a cold Eye
> On Life, on Death,
> Horseman, pass by.

Yeats died in the south of France in 1939 and his body was brought home for a state funeral to his native place after World War II. The poet and his works are discussed by scholars and enthusiasts in Sligo every year in August at the Yeats International Summer School.

Among the places in the neighborhood of which Yeats wrote was a building on the north shore of Drumcliff Bay, Lissadel House. It is still owned by a member of the distinguished Gore-Booth family, with much interesting memorabilia, and can be visited every afternoon (except Friday) between May and September.

Nobody believes the stories about Sruth-in-Aghaidh-an-Aird ("Stream Against the Height"), but take a trip four miles east of Drumcliff to Glencar Lough and see for yourself. The waterfall has an unbroken drop of 50 feet, but it gets its name from the fact that when the wind blows from the south, the water is blown up into the air and gives the appearance of a waterfall that is going both up and down. It's best viewed when traveling towards Sligo from the direction of Manorhamilton.

The Battle of the Books

What was probably the first copyright action in history took place near Drumcliff at Cuildrevne between the followers of two monks. St. Columba had borrowed a psalter from St. Finian, but before returning it, Columba made a copy. St. Finian claimed both book and copy and the dispute was submitted to High King Diarmuid who ruled, in a Solomon-like judgment: "To every cow its calf, and to every book its copy." Since there was no court of appeal, Columba's followers went to war with those of Finian, and in the dreadful "Battle of the Books" (A.D. 561), more than 3,000 men were killed. In subsequent anguish, Columba sailed away from the north coast to the Scottish island of Iona. The Drumcliff district is full of interest—here you can see a finely-carved High Cross of the tenth century, a wedge-shaped gallery grave of prehistoric days, and climb to the bold tabletop head of Ben Bulben for a view of impressive beauty. There is considerable botanical interest in the flora on the mountain, which includes some rare specimens of saxifrages.

SLIGO AND THE NORTHWEST

Sligo and Donegal are rich in prehistoric monuments which indicate a large and active population as long ago as 2,500 years before the Christian era. At Carrowmore, a low hill about three miles southwest of Sligo town, there is one of the largest concentrations of megalithic tombs to be seen in Europe. There were at least 65 tombs in the immediate area, all of the passage grave type; many were obviously raided during the centuries since they were used. From them has come a collection of passage-grave pottery of the Neolithic period (the late Stone Age, between 2,500 and 2,000 B.C.), food vessels, stone balls, bone pins and charred human bones. Beside Carrowmore is the mountain of Knocknarea (1,078 feet), which is not difficult to climb. Here is the unopened cairn which is reputedly Queen Maeve's Grave (Miscaun Meadbh), a cairn 200 feet in diameter and 80 feet high. (There are other similar cairns nearer to Sligo on Cairns Hill.) Maeve (it's the Irish of "Mab") was queen of Connacht almost 2,000 years ago.

But to see the best example of one of the court cairns of the Neolithic Age turn off the Sligo-Bundoran road at Creevykeel (there's a signpost indicating the turn). The cairn here was excavated by a Harvard archeological expedition in 1935 and is regarded as the best example of its kind in Ireland. The basic feature, believed to have been used in the burial ceremonials, is the enclosure of a rectangular court, giving access to a gallery. Neolithic pottery, stone arrow heads and polished stone axeheads were among the finds here.

South of Sligo Town

You'll come across the story of Romulus and Remus again, near Ballymote in South County Sligo. Cormac MacAirt, one of Ireland's famed kings, was born at Kesh and nurtured by the she-wolf in a cave on the side of the hill. The tale appears in early Irish literature. Ballymote was clearly a place of importance long ago, for the ruins of its fourteenth-century castle cover a considerable area and are guarded by six towers. The castle was one of the gateways to the north. Franciscan friars once had an important friary in the town and in 1391 compiled the *Book of Ballymote*, a manuscript volume which is now in the library of the Royal Irish Academy in Dublin.

In the southeast of this region, near Carrick-on-Shannon, the beautiful Lough Key Forest Park on the Rockingham Estate is worth a detour. There's an unusual stone bridge, and also one of the best camping grounds in the country.

North of Sligo

When exploring northwards of Sligo, beyond Drumcliff, you will find much to interest you on Inishmurray Island (about four miles offshore at Grange), where the evidence of the people of the past includes a wall of unmortared stone, in places 10 feet high and up to 15 feet thick at the base. There's a group of about 40 rounded cursing stones and you will be told that nobody who counts them ever gets the correct answer twice in succession.

Traveling through Ireland, the visitor frequently sees buildings which seem mysteriously unrelated to their surroundings; invariably, they are the ideas of landlords of the past with grandiose ideas and the money to satisfy them. Classiebawn Castle looks as if it belongs somewhere else—Scotland, probably. Its exterior is in the story-book Victorian baronial style, made from stone ferried to the site at Mullaghmore from north Donegal, but it has no romantic or dramatic background except that it was being built for the third Viscount Palmerston (1784-1865), who was three times prime minister of England. He died before it was finished.

For a break in journeying, Bundoran is a pleasant resort. Once the grazing grounds of war horses, today the battling around Bundoran is limited to that on the championship golf course around the *Great Southern Hotel*. Bundoran is a good base for explorations into the Donegal mountains.

The lovely Lough Melvin, only about five miles from Bundoran, is a lake which strides the border between Northern Ireland and the republic. Between Bundoran and Ballyshannon, at Ballymacward Castle, lived the Colleen Bawn, whose elopement with Willie Reilly ended with her tragic death on the Clare coast many miles to the south.

Five miles inland from Ballyshannon, in the border village of Belleek, is a pottery famous for its lustrous chinaware. Visitors are welcome to see the craftsmen at work.

St. Patrick's Purgatory

A little to the north and still on the border is Lough Derg and St. Patrick's Purgatory, the scene of the most important of Irish pilgrimages, regarded as the most arduous of Christendom. The stories tell of St. Patrick spending 40 days of prayer and fasting in a cave on what is now Station Island, to expel the last evil spirits from Ireland. Nobody knows how long ago the first

SLIGO AND THE NORTHWEST

pilgrimages began, but the strict penitential exercises are performed by many thousands of pilgrims every year.

As nobody but pilgrims are allowed to land on the island during the pilgrimage season (June 1—August 15), you might want a note on the regimen. The pilgrimage takes three days and the pilgrims go barefoot throughout the period; food consists of a single daily meal of dry bread and black tea (no milk, but sugar if it's wanted). Water can be drunk at any time and it's often boiled and flavored with pepper and salt and generally referred to as "Lough Derg Soup". Pilgrims reach the island before three o'clock on the first day, maintain an all-night vigil in the basilica on the first night and sleep in a hospice on the second night. Apart from the devotions in the basilica, there are prescribed prayers at the crosses of St. Patrick and St. Brigid, and at each of six penitential "beds", the remains of the cells of the early monks on the island.

Donegal

Donegal was an early Viking settlement and the name is a corruption of the old Irish Dun na nGall, "Fort of the Foreigners". Part of a castle is near The Diamond, a square tower to which a Jacobean fortified house was added by the first of the English overlords, Sir Basil Brooke, about 1610. Until a few years earlier, there had been an important Franciscan friary, but it was destroyed; you can still see part of the church and cloisters.

The town has a greater importance than its size suggests, for here the main roads from the south, to West Donegal and to Derry in the northeast meet. If you take the northeast road, there is the companionship of a river for part of the way and the view of the Blue Stack Mountains to the north; then there is the wildness of the Barnesmore Gap between two peaks before you drop down into the valley to Stranorlar and its twin town of Ballybofey, across the River Finn.

A few miles north, in the village of Convoy, is one of the leading woolen mills in Ireland; it is worth a detour from the main road taking you to Letterkenny.

The main road runs to the east before heading north a short distance inland from Lough Swilly; beyond Newtowncunningham you can see a great fort, the Grianan of Aileach, dominating the countryside from the crest of an 800-foot hill.

There's a fine scenic road through the mountains of the Inishowen Peninsula with Slieve Snaght (2,019 feet), the highest point at its heart; if you're heading north to Ireland's northernmost point on Malin Head, stop off at Carndonagh to take a look at St. Patrick's Cross, one of the most important monuments of early Christian art (a distinction shared with St. Mura's Cross at Fahan near Buncrana). It was carved, probably 1,300 years ago, with interlaced ribbons on one face and with rudimentary human figures. The village of Malin is on Trawbreaga (Deceitful Strand) Bay, four miles north; Malin Head is eight miles beyond. Returning down the east side of the peninsula you can see relics of the association of this part of Ireland with Scotland in Culdaff, and the remains of a fourteenth-century castle.

At Muff you can rejoin the road for Letterkenny, the starting point for further exploration of the mountainous peninsulas.

Exploring the country from Letterkenny, up towards Fanad can be done on either side of the peninsula, but if you go up the east side, the route is by the shore of Lough Swilly to Rathmullan, a little port where a kidnapping in the sixteenth century contributed to one of the intensive wars between the Irish and the English. The old fort near the pier is one of a series of fortifications built along both sides of Lough Swilly in the nineteenth century, when the lough was a British naval base. If you've the energy for a climb, the view from Croaghan Hill (1,137 feet) gives a rewarding impression of the whole area, and if you choose to stay around, you'll find Rathmullan a pleasant little resort with opportunities for exploring the eastern side of the lough by taking the ferry across to Fahan.

The better-known seaside resort on the Fanad peninsula, Portsalon, is further north, reached by a scenic road over Knockalla Mountain. Apart from its pleasant aspect, there are some spectacular rock tunnels carved out by the sea; some are about 100 yards long and 15 or 20 feet wide with a 30-foot-high entrance. The most remarkable of them is the Great Arch of Doaghbeg, two miles north of the main group.

The Wild Shores of Donegal

Milford, the eastern "gate" to the peninsula, is at the head of Mulroy Bay; it offers scenery, fishing and shooting within minutes of the town; if you're just passing through, take a look at Bunlin Glen and the nearby Grey Mare's Tail waterfall. The Irish have a gift for descriptive names and you'll find them in many town names as well as at spots like this; they've also a more confusing habit of spelling the name of a town more than one way: Carrickart (also Carrigart), next village to the northwest on a tour in this area, is one of them. To be fair, the variations in spelling are usually the result of anglicization of the spelling of the original Irish name. There is still evidence here in the sandhills of many prehistoric habitations. Carrigart and the Rosguil Peninsula with Rosapenna and Downings (another of the two-name villages, for it's also called Downies), is a most attractive area. The district is largely Irish-speaking and the hand-weaving of tweed is a craft of long tradition among the people. The Atlantic Drive is a scenic road around the Rosguil Peninsula.

The legend of the harrying of Diarmuid and Gráinne as they pursued their unlucky love affair is strong in the district; several places will be pointed out as Diarmuid and Gráinne's Bed. These are usually chambered cairns or similar age-old tombs, but may well have been used by the fugitives of Diarmuid's time as they were in later years. There's one of these "beds" near Creeslough on the road to Dunfanaghy. Creeslough attracts the antiquarian, the angler and the historian.

Doe Castle and Horn Head

The nearby Doe Castle is a strong fort which was occupied until late in the nineteenth century. It was built as the stronghold of the MacSuibhne (MacSweeney) Clan. In the neighboring graveyard, on the site of a Franciscan friary founded by the MacSweeneys, was the burial place of many of the chieftains of Donegal. The MacSuibhne coat of arms and an elaborate cross on a grave slab in the eastern wall of the graveyard mark the grave of MacSuibhne na Doe, chief of the clan; the only other grave of its kind in Ireland is at St. Mary's in Killybegs, commemorating the chief of another branch of the clan, Niall Mor MacSuibhne of Banagh. The Capuchin Franciscan friars now occupy Ards House (Ard Mhuire) at Cashelmore, Creeslough, and will give permission for visits to the attractive grounds if you ask.

Compared to much of Donegal, you'll notice that this is comparatively low-lying country, but as you move towards Dunfanaghy from Creeslough, the breathtaking bulk of Muckish Mountain dominates the landscape to the southwest.

The cliffs of Croaghnamaddy and Horn Head, breeding ground of strange sea-birds, lie to the north and the seascapes live up to the impression of artists who have painted them. Sandy beaches at Port-na-Blagh, a golf course on the edge of a bay, and Marble Hill are all good reasons for pausing along this stretch of the coast. To the westward is Marble Arch, a great water-worn archway, while MacSweeney's Gun nearby can often be heard. It is a long tunnel eroded under the cliffs, in which the air makes a report like heavy artillery when storms surge in against the coast.

Falcarragh and Gortahork on the mainland are the heart of the Donegal *Gaeltacht* (Irish-speaking district), and there is an important Irish College, Coláiste Uladh, in the neighborhood. Of historical interest in the graveyard of Myrath is a gigantic stone cross reputedly cut from a single rock on Muckish Mountain and brought to its present resting place by St. Columcille. If you're planning to climb Muckish, Falcarragh is the nearest point, but you need to be in good physical shape to do it.

"Bloody Foreland"

When the sun is setting, its rays strike the headland on the northwest point of the Gweedore district and give it a dark red color, hence its name, "Bloody Foreland". Gweedore is both beautiful and rich in fishing, and excellent for mountain walks and climbs. Errigal (2,466 feet), the highest, is best approached from Dunlewy, and from the top (there are two summits 30 yards apart linked by a route called "One Man's Path"), the view embraces an exciting panorama of mountains to the east (the nearest are the Derryveagh range) and, to the west the Atlantic coast, with its many bays and islands. If your interests lie landward, explore the Poisoned Glen; if you're interested in hand-woven tweeds, Gweedore is the place to see them made. There's also an interesting craft industry of toy-making in nearby Crolly.

Burtonport is a great herring-fishing port and the place from which to visit Aranmore, three miles offshore.

This district is known as the Rosses and the land consists of over 60,000 rock-strewn acres, cut up by streams and with dozens of lakes of all sizes, many of which provide good angling. Dungloe is the main village of the area. To the southwest is a geological oddity, the Talamh Briste ("Broken Earth"), a chasm about one quarter of a mile long and only 12 feet wide—and the district, particularly around Lough Anure, shows tracks of the Ice Age glaciers.

The wide Gweebarra River is crossed on the journey south and the deep inlet of Gweebarra Bay opens up on the westward side of the road, which forks a few miles beyond, the right-hand road taking in yet another of Donegal's many headlands.

SLIGO AND THE NORTHWEST

The left-hand road brings you to Glenties, the meeting place of two good fishing rivers, the Owenea and the Stracashel; there's a big fish hatchery on the Owenea which is worth a visit. There's also one of the many detours which make touring in Ireland an especial pleasure; there's really no need to drive off into the mountains on what is called the Aghla Mountain Circuit, but it only takes you about 20 miles off the main road and it's worth the time. The road heads up the river valley with Aghla Mountain (1,961 feet) on the right and runs parallel with Lough Finn (also on the right) for about three miles.

The return journey to Glenties is made by a subsidiary road passing through the edge of a forest with Gaugin Mountain (1,865 feet) on the left, and the Lough Ea, a lake five miles further on.

Tweed Country

Ardara, a village on the Glenties-Killybegs road, is famed for its handwoven tweed, handknits and embroidery; a short distance outside the village, a right junction leads to Glencolumbkille, a small valley beside the coast which has both an historic and modern interest. As you'd guess from the name, it has close associations with St. Columcille. At Glencolumbkille, the saint is said to have captured and destroyed demons which evaded St. Patrick, by driving them into the sea. He founded a monastery and you will be shown his cell and other indications of his occupancy with that of his followers.

Modern Glencolumbkille preserves its legends and traditions —on St. John's Eve (June 23), bonfires light up the area—but it is also the location of an intensive co-operative effort by the small farmers of the neighborhood, inspired by Father James McDyer, an example which is being cited for other parts of the country. The Glencolumbkille group not only undertakes projects of mutual benefit to raise their standards of living, but has also undertaken the cleaning of the many ancient monuments of the district and similar public service activities. The four-house folk village portrays 250 years of Donegal architecture.

There is some hard climbing for the adventurous on the range of cliffs that are dominated by Slieve League, but courage and skill are rewarded by impressive views of the sea and of secluded loughs that can never be seen from the roads. The series of bays facing south along this section of the coast have a great natural harbor at Killybegs, an inlet of McSwyne's Bay. Killybegs is one of Ireland's major fishing ports and its fleet contributes substan-

THE FACE OF IRELAND

tially to the annual catch, some of which is processed locally. Killybegs has a second industry with a long tradition, the making of hand-tufted Donegal carpets; this is a craft industry producing work of high quality and characteristic design which you can watch being made. The district, particularly the village of Kilcar, is another noted center for local tweeds, embroidery and handknits.

Attempts to follow a logical sequence of exploring Ireland invariably become frustrated because some side attraction diverts all but the most determined from his planned path. This is particularly true in the northwest where the mountains and the valleys influence your way as the glaciers of long ago shaped the land into the varied contours which give it a special appeal today. There's a stone with a story at almost every turn of the road in the northwest; you may not believe all that you hear, but you'll enjoy hearing them—and, who knows, they may be true, for the memories of men and women are long in these parts.

FACTS
AT YOUR
FINGERTIPS

FACTS AT YOUR FINGERTIPS

AIR TRAVEL		MONEY	240–1
To Ireland	236, 237, 239	MOTORING	247–8
In Ireland	246–7	Car Hire	248
Airport Transport	262	PASSPORTS	235–6
Bonus Stopovers	236–7	SEA TRAVEL	237–8, 239
ANCESTOR HUNTING	257–8	SPECIAL EVENTS	229–31
BUS TRAVEL	246	SPORTS	253–5
CARAVANNING	250–1	STATELY HOMES AND	
CLIMATE	227	GARDENS	258–9
CLOSING TIMES	256	TAXIS	257
COSTS	227–8	TELEGRAMS	256
COTTAGE LIVING	244	TELEPHONES	256
CUSTOMS	239, 261–3	TIME	256
ELECTRICITY	257	TIPPING	242
FARMHOUSE LIVING	243–4	TOURIST OFFICES	231
HOTELS	242–3	TOURS	232–4
INFORMATION OFFICES	260	TRAVEL AGENTS	231–2
INLAND WATERWAYS	252	TRAIN TRAVEL	245
MAIL	255	WHAT TO TAKE	234–5
MEDICAL SERVICES	257	YOUTH HOSTELS	244
MEET THE IRISH	234, 260		

FACTS AT YOUR FINGERTIPS

PLANNING YOUR TRIP

DEVALUATION – INFLATION

Devaluation in some European countries with consequent rising taxes and costs throughout and possible inflationary trends to come, make accurate budgeting long in advance an impossibility. Prices mentioned throughout this book are indicative only of costs at the time of going to press (mid-1976). Keep a weather eye open for fluctuations in exchange rates, both when planning your trip and while on it.

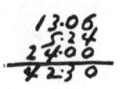

WHAT WILL IT COST? Although prices in Ireland have gone up considerably recently, as they have everywhere else, it is still one of the least expensive countries to visit and definitely good value for the money. On a very tight budget it can be done for around £7 a day.

A TYPICAL DAY

Approximate costs for one person's basic and miscellaneous expenses on an average day in Dublin:

Hotel with breakfast (first class)	£6.00
Lunch	1.50
Dinner	3.00
Transport (2 taxis, 2 buses)	2.00
Theater	1.80
Coffee (one)	.20
Beer (one)	.30
Whiskey (per glass)	.50
Cigarettes (American)	.60
Miscellaneous	.85
	£16.75

These prices represent the middle bracket; at the expensive level it's at least £21 per day; inexpensive as low as £7.

FACTS AT YOUR FINGERTIPS

Hotel rates range from around £2 for bed and breakfast in a farmhouse to £9.25 and up in a deluxe castle, and they vary as to season and location. (See pages 242-44 for details.)

Meals are not expensive (an Irish breakfast is a treat), and several of the better hotels have inexpensive coffee shops or grill bars where you can eat well for £1.25, less if you take the dish of the day (usually soup, main dish and coffee). Out of town the price is around 95p in a restaurant and in most small towns these are in hotels. Best buy for lunch is to follow the example of many of the natives and eat in one of the snack bars for about 90p; soup, cold plates, or a ham, beef or cheese roll (about 30p) which will keep you going for a long time. Dinner will cost what you want to spend, about £3.75 without wine, if you're doing yourself well, but you'll also get an excellent meal for £2.25. Wine is imported and covers a wide price range; a half-bottle of a very drinkable French wine still costs around £1.75; Spanish or Portuguese wine comes cheaper. Eating *à la carte* is more expensive than the *table d'hôte* meal which in most cases offers a choice of at least three main dishes anyway. A service charge is made in many restaurants, usually 12½%, and in this case a tip is not necessary unless you feel generously inclined. A small State tax is also added. Most package tours include both the service charge and State tax, so check the brochures for this.

WHEN TO GO. May through September are the most popular months for visiting Ireland. The country is unique in that it has no extremes of temperature and it is possible to go sightseeing even in midsummer without discomfort, or without having to take time off to rest up in the middle of the day. There's little or no snow in winter and the temperature at that period varies around 40° to 42° Fahrenheit. In high summer the average is between 60° and 65°, with some days on which it pushes up to 80°. The lush green of the countryside is not entirely due to the rain, although Ireland gets its share; the rich soil and the limestone rock contribute to the richness of the grass and for the rest, it is the warming wind in midsummer that gives the countryside its characteristic color.

Ireland is smog-free and virtually fog-free. Weather forecasting is good and when it does rain in summer, it will be showers that soon clear away. The Irish will say "it's a soft day" if it's raining—and that characterizes the rain itself, which is invariably gentle.

Avoiding the Crowds. Ireland isn't a crowded country, but during the summer the pressure builds up on accommodations. A good buy is an off-season trip, as most hotels have off-season rates (except at Christmas) and travel is easier. American travelers to Ireland have made the Irish hotels conscious of the need to keep the central heating at a good level during the winter months and the standard of warmth and comfort is good in the majority of top- and medium-grade establishments. *Córas Iompair Eireann* (usually referred to by its initials, CIE), the national transport company of Ireland, runs off-peak coach tours from early March to November, starting in Dublin or at Shannon Airport.

FACTS AT YOUR FINGERTIPS

Christmas is a good time to visit Ireland because the spirit of the season has been well maintained. A number of hotels organize special entertainments with activities that vary from a race meeting on the day after Christmas Day (St. Stephen's Day) to a cruise on the River Shannon and an island picnic, or hunting for the more energetic. St. Patrick's Week (including St. Patrick's Day, March 17) has special attractions as well as its parades. Participation in the Dublin parade is now an "in" thing for Irish-American groups who get a special place and honors.

WHERE TO GO. Ireland isn't a big country, by anybody's standards, just 32,605 square miles of it, and theoretically, you can visit any part of it in a day. But that would be a mistake, for you'd miss the atmosphere of Ireland, and that's a major part of the value of an Irish holiday. Speak in praise of one part of Ireland and you'll always hear an Irishman speak of another that he thinks you will like even more; everybody in Ireland has an enthusiasm for the country, an eagerness that isn't commercial, so take an Irishman's advice and go where he suggests—you'll be sure to enjoy your stay and get entertainment value out of it!

Dublin, the capital of the Republic of Ireland, is the best base because it's a lively city with a great many places of historical, cultural and sporting interest. Located on the east coast, it is within two miles of bathing places, and little more from fishing areas and hillsides from which you can look down over the city itself, across the wide plains of Meath or up the coast to the Mourne Mountains 80 miles away. Dublin is one of Europe's cities that has preserved its character and for the most part, its modern buildings have not destroyed the atmosphere; there are still quiet Georgian squares, for example, as well as modern hotel and office blocks.

Using Dublin as a base, it's easy to explore the east coast by visiting Royal Tara, seat of the ancient kings, and a 2,000-year-old grave cairn at nearby Newgrange in County Meath; or Glendalough, the deep Wicklow valley which was once one of the world's great seats of scholarship and where the remains of its seven churches seem a natural part of the landscape. You can travel over the border past the Mourne Mountains into Northern Ireland to its capital, Belfast, with its museums and art galleries; travel along the beautiful Antrim coast road; or visit the ecclesiastical capital of Armagh.

Take **Cork** for your travel center, and there is the sophistication of the republic's second city, with the lonely wild beauty of West Cork and Kerry less than an hour's drive away, and plenty besides the Blarney Stone to be seen and explored in the immediate neighborhood.

Killarney is a natural, not just for the lakes and the "Ring of Kerry" (the coastal drive around the peninsula), but for its sense of relaxation and the stories you'll hear.

FACTS AT YOUR FINGERTIPS

Partly because it is the entry port for many visitors, **Shannon Airport** is a touring center. A number of tours are made from the airport, for visits to the medieval banquets at Bunratty, Knappogue and Dun Guaire on a one-day and two-day basis and for longer Circuit-of-Ireland journeys (with some planned to take in a trip to Britain as well). Several tours are organized to start at Shannon and finish at Dublin, and vice-versa.

Whether you pick **Galway** as a base or not, you haven't seen Ireland unless you have walked through its narrow streets, seen its Spanish Arch and the cathedral where Columbus is said to have prayed (before his first voyage to America) or journeyed into Connemara to discover the truth of the blue mountains that the artists paint.

You might choose to use **Sligo** as a base, exploring northwards into the highlands of Donegal or eastwards into the country around Lough Erne; it differs in character from Killarney's lakeland, having its own special appeal.

SPECIAL EVENTS. January, at least six major *race meetings* at centers such as Thurles, County Tipperary; Naas, County Kildare; Leopardstown, County Dublin; and Gowran Park, County Kilkenny. There's at least one rugby *football* international match in Dublin; and the *coursing* (hunting hounds) of live hares is reaching its peak in the southern counties.

February. On *St. Valentine's Day,* in the Carmelite Priory in Dublin, the saint is honored with formal liturgical ceremonies—his body is entombed here. Limerick holds its festival of *Irish music and dancing,* Féile Luimní. Important pure-bred *cattle shows* and sales take place in Dublin, Cork and Belfast; the interesting *Punchestown Bloodstock Sale* sees the change of ownership of horses on their way to fame. *Coursing* for the Irish Cup takes place at Clounanna, County Limerick, at the end of the month.

March. St. Patrick's Day, March 17, is celebrated by a parade in Dublin, with guest bands from the U.S.; it is the day for the *Gaelic Football* and *Hurling Cup* finals at Croke Park, Dublin, but book well ahead. *Angling competitions* start. The finest dogs are seen at the *Irish Kennel Club's All-Breed Championship* in Dublin on March 17. The Dublin *grand opera season* opens this month.

Easter, whether it's in March or April, is the time of one of the biggest events of the racing season, the two-day *Irish Grand National* meeting at Fairyhouse, County Meath, about 12 miles from Dublin. Punchestown, another of the big meetings of the *racing* calendar, is an **April** event, and is a starred two-day meeting within 20 miles of Dublin. The *Challenge Cup Final* of the Football Association of Ireland (soccer) takes place in Dublin, and leadership of the *Gaelic Football League* is decided around the same time at Croke Park in Dublin. The *Circuit of Ireland International Motor Rally* takes place around Easter.

FACTS AT YOUR FINGERTIPS

May sees the opening of Ireland's agricultural shop window, the *Royal Dublin Society Spring Show and Industries Fair* at Ballsbridge. As the holiday season gets into swing, so does Ireland's pleasure in festivals. These range from the *International and Folk Dance Choral Festival* at Cork to a *Beer Festival* in Kilkenny and a *Maytime Festival* at Dundalk. The Feis Ceoil, the Dublin *musical festival*, takes up a full week in half-a-dozen halls in Dublin in the search for new singers and musicians.

June. Bundoran's *Lobster Festival* is a lively western seaboard occasion. *Fleadh Ceoil na hEireann is* Ireland's annual gathering of traditional musicians, singers and dancers, in both formal and informal sessions; this is held at a different venue every year and is linked to the first weekend of the month. Biggest of the month's fishing events is the *International Sea Angling Festival* at Westport on the Mayo coast. The Royal Horticultural Society of Ireland holds its important *Rose Show* in Dublin. The *Carrolls International Golf Tournament* is usually held this month. Cork's *International Film Festival* is a major event.

One of the richest horse races in the world, the *Irish Sweeps Derby*, is run at the Curragh, headquarters of Irish racing, 30 miles from Dublin in early **July**. The *Moy Festival*, named for the River Moy, is held in Ballina and appropriately salutes the salmon for which the river is famous. The *Shannon Boat Show Rally* finishes with the sailing of an armada of small craft up the Shannon from Athlone to Carrick-on-Shannon. The *Tour of Ireland* is an 8-day international cycle race. Another of Ireland's classic races, the *Guinness Oaks*, takes place at the Curragh late in the month. On the last Sunday in July, many thousands of *pilgrims*, some in bare feet, climb the stony slopes of Croagh Patrick (2,510 ft.) in County Mayo to honor Saint Patrick. In the West, you'll also find *pony races* at Oughterard in County Galway.

August. Dublin *Horse Show* attracts the best of Irish bloodstock and the crowds for the principal social-sporting event of the year, invariably in the second week of August. International jumping events every day for six days. The Royal Horticultural Society's *Summer Show* of flowers is held in conjunction with the Horse Show. Highly entertaining is *Puck Fair* in Killorglin, County Kerry, a mid-month event. The *Connemara Pony Show* at Clifden, County Galway, invariably attracts a cosmopolitan crowd, and apart from the ponies there is an exhibition of arts and crafts in the Gaelic tradition. The *Irish Exhibition of Living Art* is usually staged in Dublin. The shooting season starts, and the *Irish Antique Dealers* have their annual Fair in Dublin.

Late August or early **September** the *Festival of Kerry* elects a "Rose of Tralee". In Galway, the *oyster season* begins. Cork stages a vintage motor car rally. In the second half of the month there is the *Waterford International Festival of Light Opera*. The *Galway Bay International Sea Angling Festival* is a major sporting event of the month; the *All-Ireland Gaelic Football and Hurling Finals* take place in Dublin. Water sport includes the *Irish Open Water Ski Championship* on the Shannon at Killaloe and an

FACTS AT YOUR FINGERTIPS

international canoe race down the Liffey into Dublin. The September *Bloodstock Sales* in Dublin attract the men (and women) with an eye on a future winner. The *rugby football season* gets started.

October. Wexford holds its *Opera Festival* late in the month. International stars, designers, producers and conductors contribute to the performances in the tiny restored Georgian Theatre Royal. The festival also offers many "fringe" events and excellent hospitality. This is the month of Dublin's *International Theatre Festival*.

In **November,** the *hunting season* starts and continues through until April. *Racing,* which never really ends in Ireland, continues at eleven tracks, and there are trotting races in the south. Famous bloodstock sales are held at the Royal Dublin Society's grounds. The *Irish Rugby Football Union* gets going with hotly-contested games between the four provinces: Ulster, Munster, Leinster and Connacht.

December is a month with a character all its own. The build-up for *Christmas* is on and the personal feeling which the Irish have for the feast overcomes the commercial associations. *Racing* breaks off briefly in midmonth but resumes on December 26, with traditional meetings at Leopardstown (Dublin) and Limerick.

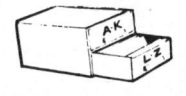

TOURIST INFORMATION OFFICES ABROAD. The *Irish Tourist Board* (Bord Fáilte Eireann) has its headquarters in Dublin, at Baggot Street Bridge, with information offices in O'Connell St., and Dawson St. Offices in *North America* are at: 590 Fifth Avenue, New York, N.Y.; 224 North Michigan Ave., Chicago, Illinois; 681 Market St., San Francisco, California; 510 West Sixth St., Los Angeles; 7 King St. East, Toronto, Ontario, Canada. In *Britain*: 150 New Bond St., London W1; 28 Cross St., Manchester 2; 6/8 Temple Row, Birmingham, B2; 19 Dixon St., Glasgow; also at 53 Castle St., Belfast. *Continental Europe* at: Rue Auber 1, Paris 9e, France; Munchenerstr. 8, Frankfurt/Main, Germany.

HOW TO GO. When you have decided where you want to go, your next step is to consult a good travel agent. If you haven't one, the American Society of Travel Agents, 711 Fifth Ave., New York, N.Y. 10022; ASTA, 130 Albert St., Ottawa, Ontario, Canada, or the Association of British Travel agents, 53-54 Newman St., London W1P 4AH., will advise you. Whether you select *American Express, Cook's Diners/Fugazy, Maupintour Associates, Columbus Associates,* or a smaller organization is a matter of preference. The *American Automobile Association,* 28 East 78th St., New York, N.Y. 10021 is also an authorized travel agency which can arrange all types of foreign tours. Travelers from Britain can get good buys through such operators as *CIE Tours International, CARA Ireland, Frames Tours, Swan-Ryan International* and *Emerald Isle Holidays.*

FACTS AT YOUR FINGERTIPS

A good travel agent can help you avoid costly mistakes due to inexperience. He can help you take advantage of special reductions in rail fares and the like that you would not otherwise know about. Most important, he can save you *time* by making it unnecessary for you to waste precious days abroad trying to get tickets and reservations.

There are four principal ways of traveling:

The *group tour*, in which you travel with others, following a prearranged itinerary hitting all the high spots, and paying a single all-inclusive price that covers everything—transportation, meals, lodging, sightseeing tours, guides. And here your travel agent can book you with a *special interest* group; thus you needn't spend a high proportion of your time trotting round museums if you would much rather be wandering round botanical gardens, and you will be among people with similar interests to your own. This is the least expensive way to go, if you don't mind conforming to a timetable.

The *prearranged individual tour* following a set itinerary, planned for you by the travel agent, with all costs paid in advance.

The *individual tour*, where you work out the itinerary for yourself, according to your own interests, but have your agent make transportation and hotel reservations, transfers, sightseeing plans.

The *free lance tour*, in which you pay as you go, change your mind if you want to, and do your own planning. You'll still find a travel agent handy to make your initial transport reservation and book you for any special event where long advance booking is essential.

TOURS. The number of package tours has sharply increased and they are now available not only for sightseeing trips but also for those with specialist interests such as fishing, hunting, castles, golf, horse-drawn caravans, barge cruising, skin-diving, pony-trekking and sailing. These tours take care of all expenses including transportation, accommodation, sightseeing, facilities and gratuities. You can get an all-inclusive deal, including your airline ticket from New York, on a 17-day Getaway tour of Ireland, Scotland, Wales and England for around $1,200. Most of the tours which include transportation to and from Ireland are packaged by travel agents in the U.S. and Britain. For example:

Aer Lingus have one-week tours of Ireland or Ireland and London for $150 land portion plus air fares of about $350; two-week tours at $280 for the land portion. Or TWA one-week tours at about $400-$500 including air fare and self-drive car. Or an Aer Lingus-Irish Fling Tours 15-day package for about $625 off-season or $800 in season including air fare.

It's worth shopping around for special offers. For example, if you are staying in Britain in the off-season, there's a deal which allows a married couple to fly to Dublin at a reduction of 50% on the normal fare for one person.

FACTS AT YOUR FINGERTIPS

Lynott "Irish Gannet" offers two weeks including rental of self-drive car and accommodation at choice of 57 hotels, spending first night at Clare Inn or Limerick Inn. Cost: off-season, $250 plus $341 return air fare; peak, $315 plus $436 return air fare, New York-Shannon.

Avoca does a two-week "Irish Spree", including self-drive car for two weeks (unlimited mileage), first night in hotel and rest in guesthouses during the peak season. Cost: $120 (double occupancy) plus air fare. Round trip fares from New York or Boston to Shannon are about $436.

Avoca also have a one-week "Super Spree" package, including self-drive car with unlimited mileage, shopping discounts, a castle tour, and seven nights' accommodation in first-class hotels. Cost: $135 off-season (double occupancy). Return air fare New York-Shannon, around $377.

Both *CIE* and the *Shannon Free Airport Development Company* can set up chauffeur-driven tours for small parties. A *four-day tour* for four works out at £150 (approx.). You'll like the Irish couriers: they're friendly, well-trained and informative without being too talkative, and when they tell a story, it's a good one! *Aer Lingus-Irish International Airlines* as well as *British Airways,* in conjunction with CIE, offer a number of tours starting at major British airports; the inclusive fare covers air travel by regular day-tourist flights to and from Dublin, reservations on the coach tour and all accommodation and meals. CIE also co-operate with *British Rail* and the two ferry companies operating across the Irish Sea, *British Rail* and the *British and Irish Steam Packet Company,* on similar tours using standard-class rail travel in Britain, and first-class boat travel to and from Dublin; if you are traveling independently there are good mid-week deals, such as the B & I Line's "Wednesday Special", which cuts costs from Britain.

If you've only time to hit the top spots, take a *Radio Train* trip to Killarney or Connemara; the all-in fare includes rail travel, seat reservation, lunch, high tea and a tour by jaunting car in Killarney or by coach in Connemara. The trains provide music interspersed with commentaries on places of interest along the route; both trips take a full day and there are departures for Killarney (from Heuston Station, Dublin) on several days a week, Connemara once a week (from Connolly Station, Dublin). All-in fares are about £11 and £9.50 respectively.

CIE's Rambler tickets at around £18 are good value: you can go anywhere anytime on any scheduled train for 15 days. For another £5 you can use any of the provincial bus services. If you want to include Northern Ireland in your tour, ask for an Overlander ticket which gives similar facilities all over the Republic and the North for about £25.

Several half-day and full-day tours are available to cover Dublin and the surrounding country, particularly the Wicklow Hills and northwards to the historic Boyne Valley. Departures (morning and afternoon) from Busarus (Central Bus Station) and full information is available from the CIE

FACTS AT YOUR FINGERTIPS

Information Kiosk in the city center, right on the traffic island near the General Post Office.

Shannon Airport has become a major touring center, both for its medieval tours embracing the historic area, and the banquets and entertainment at Bunratty Castle, Knappogue Castle or Dun Guaire Castle (at Kinvara, on Galway Bay). The one-day *Medieval Tour* at around £20 leaves the airport at 2 p.m., and visits the Old Ground Hotel in Ennis (home-baked apple tart and tea). The drive continues through County Clare, visiting a typical Irish pub, a wheelwright's shop and a couple of fishing villages and seeing remains of pre-historic Ireland before reaching the Norman fortress of Dun Guaire Castle for a medieval banquet and an Anglo-Irish literary entertainment. After a farewell drink, the party returns to stay overnight at Ennis. On the following morning, there's another sightseeing tour which takes in the 700-ft. Cliffs of Moher before reaching Shannon Airport for lunch, with time for some shopping at Shannon's famous Duty Free Store. *Two-day* tours out of Shannon cover Killarney, Blarney and Cork, and in *four days*, you can take in Dublin and Connemara. A seven-day "Wheelaway" tour from Shannon provides a self-drive auto, six nights with breakfast at first-class hotels and a medieval banquet at Bunratty Castle for around £40. Shannon is a good base for starting and ending tours if your time is limited and your itinerary is onward to, or returning from continental Europe.

SPECIAL INTEREST TRAVEL. There's a Meet-the-Irish scheme operating which puts visitors in touch with Irish people with kindred professional or social interests. These meetings are mainly arranged in Dublin and Cork, but with a little advance notice, contacts can usually be fixed in other centres. Contact *Bord Fáilte Eireann* (Irish Tourist Board), Baggot Street Bridge, Dublin 2.

Irish hospitality does not depend on this channel alone, as the many professional bodies in the country will be happy to set up contacts for overseas visitors.

WHAT TO TAKE. The summer temperature reaches the 80s at times, but the average at that time of the year is about 65°F, and the average in the coldest time of the year is about 41°F. The Irish are casual dressers—they like to be informal and comfortable; both men and women favor tweeds, which are available in all weights. Take a suit along and a sweater (but you'll be attracted by the Irish-pattern handknit sweaters which have a distinctive style and are a good buy). Take comfortable shoes for sightseeing, and a pair of overshoes as a precaution. As in most other places, it rains in Ireland, and a light rainproof coat and/or folding umbrella should be taken along. For the average visitor, there's not likely to be a need for formal evening wear, and a dark suit will do for most events for

FACTS AT YOUR FINGERTIPS

men, a cocktail dress for women. Women should also take along a wrap to ward off night chills and draughts.

Travel light. Whether you go by air or not, keeping under the airline free limit of 66 pounds of luggage per person (44 pounds in economy) makes sense. It simplifies going through customs, makes registering and checking baggage unnecessary, lets you take buses with room for hand baggage only, and is a lifesaver if you go to small places where there are no porters. The principle is not to take more than you can carry yourself (unless you travel by car). It's a good idea to pack the bulk of your things in one large bag and put everything you need for overnight, or for two or three nights, in another, to obviate packing and repacking.

If you wear glasses, take along the prescription. There is no difficulty about getting medicines, but if you have to take some particular preparation, better bring a supply.

TRAVEL DOCUMENTS. British citizens do not need travel or identity documents when traveling to Ireland. There is an informal identity check between Ireland and Great Britain, but passport control at the port of entry of either country is sufficient for both. Disembarkation cards are handed around to be filled out on board ship or aircraft before landing. **United States** and **Canadian** citizens need only a passport, no visa.

Generally there is a delay in getting a passport so apply several months in advance of your expected departure date. **US residents** must apply in person to the US Passport Agency in New York, Boston, Philadelphia, Washington DC, Miami, Chicago, New Orleans, Seattle, San Francisco, Los Angeles or Honolulu, or to their local county courthouse. In some areas selected post offices are also equipped to handle passport applications. If you still have your passport issued within the past eight years you may use this to apply by mail. Otherwise, take with you: (1) a birth certificate or certified copy thereof, or other proof of citizenship; (2) two identical photographs 2½ inches square, full face, black and white or color and taken within the past six months; (3) $13 ($10 if you apply by mail); (4) proof of identity such as a driver's licence, previous passport, any governmental ID card. Social Security and credit cards are not acceptable. US passports are valid for five years. If you are a non-citizen, you must have a Treasury Sailing Permit, Form 1040D, certifying that all Federal taxes have been paid; apply well in advance to your District Director of Internal Revenue for this. To return to the United States, you need a re-entry permit, if you intend to stay away for longer than 1 year. Apply for it at least six weeks before departure in person at the nearest office of the Immigration and Naturalisation Service, or by mail to the Immigration and Naturalisation Service, Washington DC.

Canadian citizens entering *Ireland* must have a valid passport, application forms for which may be obtained at any Post Office and then sent to the

FACTS AT YOUR FINGERTIPS

Canadian Passport Office at 40 Bank Street, Ottawa, together with a remittance of $10.

Health Certificates. Not required for entry into Ireland. Although the United States and Canada do not now require a certificate of vaccination prior to re-entry, because of frequent changes in law, we suggest you be vaccinated anyway, before you leave.

How to Reach Ireland

FROM NORTH AMERICA

BY AIR. *Aer Lingus-Irish International Airlines* link New York, Chicago, Boston and Montreal with Shannon and Dublin on a frequent daily schedule. Other carriers operating a high frequency service on the transatlantic route to Ireland are *TWA, KLM,* and (from Montreal) *Air Canada*. *Aer Lingus* and *British Airways* operate New York-Belfast. Scheduled airlines (other than Aer Lingus and TWA) on the transatlantic routes call only at Shannon, but there is a feeder service connecting flights to Dublin. Check with your travel agent for the latest position.

Transatlantic air fares are constantly under review and there are likely to be some good buys if you can book well in advance, say three months. Your travel agent will have the latest information, but an example of a round trip off-season New York-Dublin rate is approximately $380 dollars for a 22/45 day excursion.

There are a number of fare concessions that can substantially cut travel costs. Airlines offer special low rates to parties of 15 or more on the North Atlantic route, and charter flights have increased considerably. Charter and advance booking regulations are being updated so contact your travel agent for the latest and best possibilities.

Bonus Stopovers to Ireland. If you're bound for Ireland, you can include this country at no extra fare on almost all trips to the United Kingdom or continental Europe. Shannon and Dublin are stopover points for aircraft flying between New York and such destinations as London, Manchester, Glasgow, Paris, Amsterdam, Copenhagen and Warsaw. Many tourists bound for these points do in fact specify that they wish to stop in Dublin or Shannon either on the outward or inbound portion of the trip.

Most stopovers are made on the homeward leg to take advantage of two Irish attractions: Shannon's low-priced bargains at the airport duty free store, and inexpensive stopover programs with short duration tours which often contrast sharply with higher prices charged elsewhere in Europe.

FACTS AT YOUR FINGERTIPS

You can enter Ireland at Dublin and later fly to Shannon before boarding another aircraft to the USA. Many prefer, however, to travel overland from Dublin to Shannon.

BY SEA. Transatlantic services direct to Ireland (Cobh) are infrequent, but check with the Baltic Line for their schedule. Another route is to take the ship direct to Southampton and then use a ferry from the west coast of England (see "From Britain by Sea").

FROM GREAT BRITAIN

BY AIR. *Aer Lingus* provides frequent services to Dublin from all major centers in Britain: London, Birmingham, Bradford, Bristol, Cardiff, Edinburgh, Glasgow, Leeds, Liverpool, Manchester. Services also operate to Cork from most of these centers and the average flying time from anywhere in Britain to Ireland is 50 minutes. *British Airways* shares traffic on several routes and also operates services from London to Belfast. *British United Island Airways, Northeast Airlines* and *Cambrian Airways* also operate routes into Ireland.

Sample fare; London-Dublin round trip about £40. Both *Aer Lingus* and *British Airways* offer Flyaway and Freeway packages in the off-season. Sample: London-Dublin return trip including car hire and seven nights' bed, breakfast and private bath in any one of 20 top-class hotels for about £75.

Using the *Aer Lingus* "Aer Coach" service (coach from an English provincial center to Liverpool and on to Dublin by air) you can cut the cost by £8 to £10 on the return trip. Check with your travel agent. Youth fares (if you're under 21) mean a cut of about 25% in the air fares between Britain and Ireland.

British Airways also run family fare concessions which are worth asking about to check current situation.

BY SEA. There are several sea routes between Britain and Ireland, some with drive on/off car facilities (indicated below by asterisks) but all carrying cars—and passengers, of course. However, on the Holyhead-Dun Laoghaire route, non-car passengers may only travel if accommodation is available on the day of sailing: you cannot book in advance. Below we give approximate rates for cars up to 14 feet, together with passenger fares, both single trip, between ports. Return fares are double single rates.

From Wales: Fastest route is Holyhead-Dun Laoghaire* (7 miles from Dublin). 3¼ hours. Motorail service links London with Holyhead. Daily services in high season. Cars £23.35; passengers £8.35. A new Sealink ferry (9,000 tons, the biggest on the Irish Sea) becomes operational this year (1977).

FACTS AT YOUR FINGERTIPS

Fishguard-Rosslare*: Day and night services in summer. Motorail link from London. Cars £24, passengers £9.60.

Swansea-Cork*: Overnight, with linking motorail service from London. Cars £26.50; passengers £7.60.

From England: The Liverpool-Dublin* ferry is an overnight service, as is the Liverpool-Belfast* ferry. Cars £26.50; passengers £7.60. Both routes have passenger train connections from London.

From Scotland: Stranraer-Larne*, shortest route (2½ hours), twice daily crossings in summer. Cars £23.35; passengers £3.50. Cairnryan-Larne* is high frequency (four times daily) service. Rates around the same. There are additional charges on ferries for berths (about £1.15) or cabins (£1.85) on night services.

There are bargain rates for mid-week travel and at some weekends. Check with British Rail's Sealink operations and B & I Line services.

TAKING YOUR CAR. It's necessary to book well in advance for peak period travel between Britain and Ireland, particularly with a car. The formalities are simple, but motoring organizations can be helpful in booking tickets, reserving car space and looking after your documentation. Your own organization will help you on the way and in Ireland the corresponding groups will be equally helpful. They are:

Automobile Association (counterpart of the AAA in America), 23 Suffolk St., Dublin 2; 5 Oxford St., Belfast 1; 5 South Mall, Cork.

Royal Automobile Club, 65 Chichester Street, Belfast 1; *Royal Irish Automobile Club,* 34 Dawson Street, Dublin 2, and 35 St. Patrick's Quay, Cork.

You don't need a triptyque. Check at the customs at the Republic of Ireland port of entry or frontier post. Keep your registration or log book with the car. A British car must have a GB plate on the back. Car insurance policies issued in EEC countries now cover the vehicle for use in the whole EEC area and regulations (1975) provide for abolition of insurance checks on vehicles moving between member states of the EEC. Check with your insurance company that your certificate conforms. You may use your current British driving licence (but not a provisional licence) or an International Driving Permit during a visit to Ireland.

Temporary Importation Permits cover not only private cars, but also station wagons, Land Rover or Jeep-type vehicles, motor cycles or scooters, light commercial vehicles (light means less than 25 cwts. empty), caravans, luggage trailers, boat trailers and horse boxes.

Customs facilities for the clearance of vehicles under these arrangements are available at the principal ports and air ports without previous notice. They are also available at the land frontier posts between the Republic of Ireland and Northern Ireland. (See: *Driving in Ireland.*)

FACTS AT YOUR FINGERTIPS

The passenger baggage allowance on the car ferries is 150 lb. free of charge.

If you are traveling from and to Britain in the peak season it's likely that you may need a *sailing ticket* in addition to your rail/sea ticket; this costs about 30p and this ensures you a place on the ferry service specified. Get it from your travel agent or British Rail offices.

Express through motor coach services operate daily between Glasgow and Dublin, using the Northern ferry service. Roundtrip fare is about £17. Another through motor coach operates between Glasgow and Londonderry via the Stranraer-Larne ferry, with a roundtrip fare of about £15.

FROM THE CONTINENT

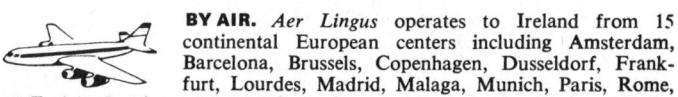

BY AIR. *Aer Lingus* operates to Ireland from 15 continental European centers including Amsterdam, Barcelona, Brussels, Copenhagen, Dusseldorf, Frankfurt, Lourdes, Madrid, Malaga, Munich, Paris, Rome, and Zurich. *Lufthansa* operate from Germany to Ireland, and from Spain, *Iberia Airlines* share the traffic. *Alitalia* operates from Milan to Dublin.

Sample air fares: Paris-Dublin £99.50; Munich-Dublin £164 both roundtrip. Inquire about excursion rates which are considerably cheaper, but vary with the season.

BY SEA. A car ferry between continental Europe (Le Havre) and Rosslare operates three days a week in each direction (*Irish Continental Line*). Sample rate (single journey), £27.50 per car, £20 per passenger including berth. Low season offers include free passage for the car if four passengers travel together, half-fare if two or three travel. A new (1977) car ferry service between Roscoff (Brittany, France) and Rosslare will operate (twice weekly) in summer. Passage will take 13/14 hours (*Brittany Ferries/Irish Continental Line*).

Arriving in Ireland

CUSTOMS. No written declaration is required for any baggage accompanied by the traveler entering the Republic of Ireland. He is expected to make a truthful declaration of what the baggage contains and whether he is bringing in any gifts for friends or relations. If you are sending any baggage by a different route to that which you take yourself, then a

FACTS AT YOUR FINGERTIPS

declaration form to cover it is needed (Form C. & E. No. 104A), and the carrier will make the necessary arrangements about it.

Personal effects are duty free, and if you are renting a furnished house, you may bring in household linen, blankets and cutlery. You can also import a boat and its equipment free of duty if it is only being brought in for the duration of your visit; if the boat comes with you, it will be cleared by the customs officers without any documentary formality.

Visitors from non-EEC countries are allowed up to 1,000 cigarettes or 200 cigars, or tobacco up to 2¼ lb. weight (or a mixture of all three); two normal-sized bottles of spirits, two normal-sized bottles of wine and a pint of toilet water or perfumes. These allowances apply to adults only. In addition, you can bring in without payment of duty gifts of dutiable goods (except tobacco, liquor, toilet water or perfume) up to £10 each, (£4 for children). If you are traveling further (or returning home), dutiable souvenirs up to a total value of £200 may be imported in baggage provided they are in transit only.

Visitors from EEC countries have a duty-free concession of up to 14 ounces of tobacco (including cigarettes and cigars); two bottles of spirits or four bottles of other distilled beverages plus four bottles of wine; plus three fluid ounces of perfume, two-thirds of a pint of toilet water and other goods of a value up to £52 (children £12).

There is no restriction on the importation of *currency* and there are no restrictions on the export of money (except gold coins) to the UK. If you are traveling further, you may take up to IR£25 plus foreign currency, including travelers' checks up to £300.

If you have paid a deposit of *duty* on any goods on your arrival in the Irish Republic, you should produce the items and the deposit receipt to the customs officer at the point of departure so that arrangements can be made to refund your money.

IMPORTATION OF PETS. Quarantine laws are strict and long: 6 months in Britain, 6 months in Ireland. This is for dogs, cats and some other animals coming from abroad. Best make arrangements at home for their care.

The current rabies control imposes *extremely serious penalties,* fines or imprisonment, on anyone trying to import animals illegally into Britain and Ireland. Be wise, don't risk it.

MONEY. In the Republic of Ireland, the currency has the same denominations as in Britain, but different designs. The currencies of both the Republic and Britain circulate in both sections of Ireland. Shops in Britain don't accept Irish currency, so it is best to change it into English currency

FACTS AT YOUR FINGERTIPS

before leaving the Republic. The currency is based on the pound sterling, divided into 100 pence ("p"). Banknotes are in values of £20, £10, £5 and £1. The designs and values of the coins are: 50 pence (50p)—a woodcock; 10 pence (10p)—a salmon; 5 pence (5p)—a bull; 2 pence (2p), 1 penny and ½ penny (stylized Irish designs). The 50p, 10p and 5p are silver; the others are copper. The 50-pence piece is seven-sided. The common obverse of all coins is the Irish harp.

Old coins retained, because they have the same value and size as the new (1971) currency are: the 2 and 1 shilling coins.

As exchange rates are liable to considerable fluctuations these days, we urge you to check on the current rates both before traveling and en route.

Banking Hours. All banks are shut on Saturdays. Open Monday through Friday, 10 a.m.—12:30 p.m. and 1:30 p.m.—3 p.m., 5 p.m. on Thursdays. Longer and 7-day service at airports.

Principal banks are *Bank of Ireland Group* (incorporating *Bank of Ireland, National Bank of Ireland* and *Hibernian Bank*, correspondents for Bank of England, Coutts & Company, National Provincial Bank); *Allied Irish Banks* (incorporating the *Munster & Leinster Bank, Provincial Bank of Ireland, Royal Bank of Ireland*, also agents for National Provincial Bank, correspondents for Barclay's Bank); *Northern Bank* (correspondents for Barclay's Bank); and *Ulster Bank* (affiliated to Westminster Bank).

Irish banks are widely represented throughout the towns of the provinces. Hotels and major stores all accept travelers' checks.

Travelers' checks are the best way to safeguard travel funds. They are sold by various banks and companies in terms of American and Canadian dollars and pounds sterling. Most universally accepted are those of *American Express* and *Thomas Cook*, while those issued by *First National Bank of New York, Bank of America*, and the biggest British banks—*Barclay's, Lloyds, Midland and National Westminster*, are also widely used.

It is also possible for British travelers to cash checks in Ireland for up to £30 each transaction on production of a Barclaycard or one of many bank check cards participating in the scheme; it is also cheaper than exchanging travelers' checks. Enquire at your bank.

FACTS AT YOUR FINGERTIPS

TIPPING. The customary tip in Ireland is 12%. Many hotels and restaurants add this in the form of a service charge; if so, it is indicated or stated on the menu or check. Special services usually get an added tip, particularly in the plushier establishments. It's not customary to tip in bars or pubs, although if you have table service, a small tip, usually 2p or 5p, is given. Porters rate a special tip of about 10p, depending on the amount of baggage; give car park attendants 5p and taxi drivers the same for a short journey and correspondingly more for longer journeys. Men's hairdressers get 10p, women's, about 20p.

Staying in Ireland

HOTELS. At the peak of the season, between June and September, pressure on accommodation is heavy, so book well ahead. A computer reservations service operates through *International Reservations Service, 70-48 Austin St., Forest Hills, Long Island, N.Y.*; your local travel agent will have the address in other areas and can get a confirmed booking for you.

If you arrive in Ireland without having booked your accommodation, contact the *Tourist Information Office* at the port of entry or, in the country, look for a similar office, indicated by the letter "I", in all the tourist centers. These offices have records of vacancies or will phone around until they locate a spot for you. The service is free, but you are usually asked to pay for the phone calls. The Central Reservations Office of Bord Fáilte (Irish Tourist Board) in Dublin does not handle reservations for individuals (only requests from travel agents), but it will channel requests to the areas in which you are interested.

Some major hotel groups will make forward reservations in other hotels for guests. There is an advance booking link between the seven *Great Southern Hotels*, the *Jury's*, and *Trust House Forte*. The *Ryans* chain of motels (Holbrook House, Holles St., Dublin), *Inter Hotels*, a family-owned chain linked to Inter Hotels in Britain (headquarters, 11 Herbert Street, Dublin) and the *Irish Welcome Hotels* (28 Herbert Place), cover main centers and resorts throughout the country.

There is an official hotel grading system, checked every year. All hotels and guesthouses must be registered with Bord Fáilte (Irish Tourist Board), which carries out an inspection system and issues the appropriate grading. The board publishes a complete list, *Official Guide to Hotels and Guesthouses*, every year, giving the current rating, details of the accommodation, and maximum prices which hotels may charge for rooms and meals. The

FACTS AT YOUR FINGERTIPS

board also has lists of hotels and guesthouses which have groundfloor accommodation for people who prefer it, of hotels with special facilities for children and of hotels with chalets. These lists can be obtained free from the Irish Tourist Board or local information offices.

Our rating of hotels follows these guidelines and uses (L) to indicate luxury grade, charging between £11 and £15 per night; (1) for first-class superior, £6.50 to £11.50; (2) for first-class reasonable, £3.50 to £7.50; (3) for moderate, £3.25 to £5; and (4) for inexpensive, £3.75. Hotel prices vary considerably, even in those of the same grading, usually because of region, and off-peak rates are 25% to 30% lower than high season.

Meal times in Irish hotels are usually breakfast, 7:30 to 10 a.m.; lunch, 12:30 to 3 p.m.; high tea (which can range from a boiled egg to a mixed grill or steak), served in places where there is no *table d'hôte* dinner, from 6 to 8 p.m.; dinner, from 6:30 p.m. on. Closing time of hotel restaurants varies but most shut by 11 p.m. There are some late spots which offer grills or snacks until around 2 a.m. Breakfast in Irish hotels, unless it is specified otherwise, is the English type, with a cereal, bacon and egg, toast and marmalade, rolls, tea or coffee. The Irish like their tea strong, so if you have a preference for a lighter brew, it is better to specify.

FARMHOUSE LIVING. The get-away-from-it-all feeling can best be realized in Ireland in a low-cost farmhouse holiday. The Irish Tourist Board has issued a special publication, *Town & Country Homes* and *Farmhouses*, listing the names of farmhouses and other accommodation that meets the board's high standards, and the rates the owners charge. Some farmhouses are converted Georgian-type mansions, and all have a warm and homely atmosphere. Many of the housewives who do the cooking and run the establishments have received special training to ensure that there is a varied and interesting menu based on an abundance of fresh country produce. But apart from sampling farm life, there's an opportunity to meet the people of the villages and the countryside in their own surroundings and homes; conversations often go far into the night around well-stacked hearth fires.

Cork and Kerry are the best represented counties in the farmhouse list, but there are farms who welcome guests in nearly every county. Prices range from £2.50 to £3 for bed and breakfast; a sample of the weekly partial board (demi-pension, or 2 meals a day) rate is £24 to £28; full board, around £30 per week, but not available everywhere. Reductions for children range from 10% to 50% and the majority provide babysitter service.

Among some of the many tours offered by American tour operators, try *Eire Tours'* (2053 Flatbush Ave., Brooklyn, NY 11234) two-week "Irish People" tour; *Lynott Tours* (350 Fifth Ave., NY 10001) or *Shannon Castle Tours* (New York).

This year there will be more charter flights to Ireland by both Irish and American carriers so you should shop around for special arrangements

FACTS AT YOUR FINGERTIPS

flying TWA (charters and scheduled services), *Pan American* (charters), and *Aer Lingus* (charters and scheduled services) in addition to leading supplemental carriers.

COTTAGE LIVING. Near Shannon Airport at Ballyvaughan and Corofin, etc., some 100 thatched cottages are available for rent; traditional in style, they are fully equipped with kitchenette, bathroom, toilet and heating. Basic rental for cottage with a large living room and three double bedrooms is around £80 a week in peak season, less than half in off-peak months. Apply to *Rent-an-Irish-Cottage Ltd.*, at Shannon Airport or the *Shannon Free Airport Travel Office* at 590 Fifth Avenue, New York. Early booking is essential. Up in the northwest, in Donegal a similar group of 20 cottages has been built in Glencolmcille: apply to the *Carrigart Hotel*, Carrigart, Co. Donegal.

ACCOMMODATING THE ANGLERS. In the centers where coarse fishing is popular (most of these areas have few hotels), the Irish Tourist Board has inspected a number of private houses open to guests to ensure the meeting of a minimum standard. Peak season (July-August) rates for bed and breakfast are from £1.75 to £3, with a week's full board from £16 to £20. Don't expect luxury, but you'll get comfort and a welcome. A few even have a bar.

YOUTH HOSTELING. Members of youth hostel associations can use the overnight facilities at any of the 59 hostels in Ireland. (47 belong to *An Oige* while the remainder belong to the *Youth Hostel Association of Northern Ireland*.) The hostels vary from castles to coastguard stations, from shooting lodges to cottages, from schoolhouses to military barracks. All belong to the self-catering category and there are ample cooking facilities available. There are city hostels in Dublin and Cork and the others are all located in scenic and historic areas. Advance bookings should be made as early as possible; write directly to the Resident Wardens enclosing booking fees and self-addressed and stamped envelope. Overnight charges are about 50p in July and August, less for under-21s and in other months.

Headquarters of *An Oige* (Irish Youth Hostel Association) is at 39 Mountjoy Square, Dublin 1; the *Youth Hostel Association of Northern Ireland* is based at 28 Bedford Square, Belfast 2. Youth hostels are what the name implies, simple accommodation and do-it-yourself service. To use Irish hostels North American visitors must hold an International Youth Hostel Card issued by *American Youth Hostels, Inc.*, 132 Spring St., New York, N.Y., 10012, or *Canadian Youth Hostel Association*, 333 River Road, Vanier City, Ottawa, Ontario, Canada.

FACTS AT YOUR FINGERTIPS

Traveling in Ireland

BY TRAIN. Because distances in Ireland are not great, there is no elaborate railway system and no need for sleeping cars. Once the network was extensive, but this has been scaled down to mainline operations and some commuter services for the suburbs of Belfast, Cork and Dublin. These are supplemented by a network of bus services in both city and rural areas. Dublin to Cork is a 3-hour journey; Dublin to Belfast 2 hours 10 mins.; Dublin—Killarney, 4½ hours; Dublin—Galway, 3½ hours. Catering services, including bars, are operated on the main line services.

Córas Iompair Eireann (National Transport Company of Ireland) operates train and bus services in the Republic. All CIE trains are hauled by diesel locomotives. There are two classes of rail travel on mainline services, standard and super-standard. Only one class (standard) tickets are issued but for £1 extra per single journey you can enjoy the super-standard luxury. The average rail cost per mile is about 5p for standard class. Seats can be booked three months in advance at a charge of 20p a seat. There is a limit on luggage accompanied by passenger of 60 lb. for standard class. Excess baggage is charged for at 85p per 28 lb. up to 100 miles and at £1.30 for 28 lb. for journeys of over 100 miles.

A 15-day Rail Rambler ticket enables you to travel where and when you like and costs around £18. A Rail/Road Rambler ticket gives the added facility of using buses where trains don't fit your schedule and are about £23. Seats can be reserved on trains at a charge of 20p. Bookings of rail tickets and seats can be made up to three months in advance of traveling.

For young people—the under 23s—Interrail Cards are a good buy if you plan to visit several countries and stay a month in Europe. They can be bought at around £65 in CIE's city office, Middle Abbey St., Dublin, and entitle the holder to half-fare travel on the system which issues it and free travel on 20 other European rail networks. Ireland and Britain are counted as a single network for the purpose of this Card.

Trains in Dublin operate out of two main stations: Connolly (in Amiens Street) for the coast north of Dublin, Belfast and also the south-east, Heuston (Kingsbridge) for the west, south and southwest.

CIE organizes a number of excursion trains, known as "Getaway Trips", at weekends and on special occasions. These are promoted seasonally and to get a list for the time of your trip, contact CIE at 35 Lower Abbey Street, Dublin 1.

FACTS AT YOUR FINGERTIPS

BY BUS. *Local (city) bus services* are an inexpensive way of sightseeing and conductors are helpful about letting you know when you've reached your destination. Minimum fare is 8p.

See "Rail" for combined rail-bus services of CIE in the republic.

Express coaches operate between a number of major points not directly linked by rail; these are convenient and cheap. They pass through some very attractive country and stop at a number of interesting towns—a bargain way to take a look at country which is not on the main tourist track. The services are operated by CIE.

From *Dublin,* bus services to provincial centers leave from Busarus (Central Bus Station) beside the Custom House; it's also the point of departure for coaches for Dublin Airport. A direct bus links Dublin Airport with Heuston Station for main rail departures. Dublin *city bus* services operate through the main thoroughfares and most have terminals near O'Connell Bridge; in *Cork* the bus terminus for services into the country and distant areas is at Parnell Place.

BY AIR. Apart from the train link, there is air service between Belfast and Shannon by *Aer Lingus*.

Air Touring. Apart from the major airports at Belfast, Dublin, Cork and Shannon, where regular customs facilities are available, there are a number of landing strips which have limited customs facilities available (for outward passengers only). The following are the main strips available (and people to contact on usage):

Ballyfree, County Wicklow: T. Philips, Ballyfree Farms, Glenealy, tel. Wicklow 5607; *Castlebar,* County Mayo: P. J. Ryan, Castlebar, tel. Castlebar 448; *Coonagh,* County Limerick: Shannon Flying Services, Coonagh, Limerick, tel. Limerick 47577; *Farranfore,* Co. Kerry: Kerry County Airport Co. Ltd., Tralee, tel. Farranfore 57; *Headfort,* County Meath: Headfort Aviation Ltd., tel. Kells 111 or 21; *Inishmore,* Aran Islands: United Development, Galway, tel. Galway 65110; *Kilkenny,* County Kilkenny: P. Nolan, College Rd., tel. Kilkenny 21427; *Oranmore,* County Galway: Galway Airways, Galway, tel. Oranmore 84105; *Weston,* County Kildare: Weston Ltd., Leixlip, tel. Celbridge 280435. Airstrips should also be operational by this year at Waterville, Co. Kerry, and Ballinrobe, County Mayo. Check with Aer Arann, Dominick Street, Galway, tel. 5119.

If you are interested in flying your own aircraft or meeting up with private fliers, contact the *Irish Aero Club,* Iona National Airways Hangar, Cloghran, County Dublin, tel. Dublin 378323.

Taxi and private charter aircraft are available from Dublin, Galway and Castlebar: contact Ireland West Airways, Castlebar Airport, County Mayo,

FACTS AT YOUR FINGERTIPS

or Dublin Airport; Aer Arann, Oranmore, Galway; Executive Air Services, 70 Northumberland Rd., Dublin 4. A helicopter service is available from Irish Helicopters Ltd., 3a Clyde Road, Dublin 4.

BY CAR. The first thing to remember when you get to Ireland is that you must drive on the left of the road, just as in Britain. Ireland has 5,152 miles of main roads and another 57,773 of secondary routes; all are well-surfaced and while the mileage of high-speed motorways is comparatively small, the standards of road building are good and sign-posting is excellent.

In Ireland, first-class roads are designated with the letter N. The road signs are usually in both English and Irish. Warning signs are all of the international pattern.

Although the roads are the least crowded in Europe—Ireland has 18.4 miles of road per head of the population compared with 3.95 in Britain and 9.4 miles in France—parking is a problem in the cities. Signs with the letter *P* indicate parking areas, but if the letter has a stroke through it, keep away or you'll likely collect an unwanted ticket for a £5 fine. Some Dublin city hotels and one in Cork have private parks for guests. Most car parks have attendants, to whom it is customary to give a tip on leaving. Meter parking in Dublin costs 5p for one hour.

Irish traffic signs are of three kinds: *direction* indicators, which are self-explanatory; the *cautionary* signs, which warn of hazards (these are diamond-shaped with a yellow background); and the *regulatory,* which warn of a rule which must be obeyed. Examples of the latter: an inverted, red-bordered triangle indicates a major road ahead on which traffic has the right of way; or an octagonal, red sign which reads "Stop" and means what it says, indicating a halt before moving out onto a main road. The other regulatory signs are round and bordered in red with the regulation (such as a speed limit) in black in the center. There is a general speed limit of 60 m.p.h., and 30 m.p.h. through towns and villages; some built-up areas have a 40 m.p.h. limit and other main roads in danger areas a limit of 30 m.p.h. If there is a yellow box marking (crossed lines painted on road) at an intersection, don't drive in unless your way is clear to drive out. Roadway markings are of the standard type—a continuous white line along the center of the road means stay on your own side as it's dangerous (and an offence) to cross it. At a junction of two roads of equal importance, it is the driver to the right of you who has the right of way. A zebra crossing (barred markings on the road and a yellow flashing beacon) gives right of way to a pedestrian who's on it. Yellow lines by the roadside mean you can't park; double yellow lines mean you can't even stop.

FACTS AT YOUR FINGERTIPS

Drinking and Driving. Ireland has breathalizer tests, as in Britain, which are liable to be requested by any police officer (*garda*) who suspects erratic driving. The limit of blood/alcohol in the Republic is 125 mill. per 100 mill., in Northern Ireland, 80 mill. To refuse the test means the driver is likely to be prosecuted.

In the cities, the Civic Guards (Garda Síochána) on traffic duty use white batons to emphasize their signals; they also use radar speed checks. Traffic wardens who hand out tickets for parking offences wear brown uniforms and hats with yellow bands—and are referred to as "yellow bands".

Cyclists, children and cattle are the three main *hazards* on Irish roads; cyclists are supposed to carry front and rear lights and reflectors, but they don't always obey the regulation. Cattle on the road at night are supposed to be led by a man with a lamp and followed by another; this is another rule that isn't kept strictly, so take it easy and use your headlights. Children are a hazard in both town and country. If you see a yellow-and-white bus bearing the words *Bus Scoile* and a symbol of children running, take care. It's a school bus.

If you're unlucky enough to have an *accident* it must be reported to the police immediately and you are required to keep your car at the scene of the accident until the police arrive. Automobile Association patrols (driving small yellow vans) cover all main roads and have a number of phone call boxes which will bring trained assistance if you have a breakdown.

If you've brought your own car, you'll know the *documents* you need. If you plan to hire one, don't forget to bring your domestic driving licence or an International Driving Permit. If you are hiring a car in the republic and want to cross the border into Northern Ireland during your tour, the staff of the rental company will provide the appropriate customs documents; the charge is usually about £1.25.

Car Hire. Many Irish car rental agencies also have U.S. representatives, so you may book here as well. Following are the U.S. and Irish addresses of some of these and we suggest that you should write directly for current figures. (1) Dan Ryan Car Rental, 575 Fifth Avenue, New York, N.Y. 10017; Punch's Cross, Limerick (Shannon). (2) Tom Maloney, 1113 Broadway, New York, N.Y., 10010; 6/7 St. Patrick's Quay, Cork, Ireland. (3) Titley Rent-a-Car, Ltd., 7 West 57 Street, New York, N.Y.; Shannon Free Airport, Ireland. (4) Economy Car Hire, c/o Brendan's Tours, 650 S. Grand Avenue, Los Angeles, California 90017; 24 Lower Abbey Street, Dublin 1.

Among the many other good car hire firms in Ireland are: *Cahill's,* 35 Annesley Place; *Kenning Car Hire,* 42 Westland Row; *Johnson & Perrott*

FACTS AT YOUR FINGERTIPS

have bases at Emmet Place, Cork, Dublin and Shannon; *Irish Multiwheel Ltd.*, 1-4 Lower Erne St., tel. 774771. The Automobile Association (which has links with the AAA in the U.S.) operates a car hire arrangement which enables members to rent self-drive from the *Hertz* and *Godfrey Davis* organization at a discount of 10%. Several of the major hirers have a pool office at Dublin, Shannon, Cork and Belfast airports.

Petrol. Middle grade gas (petrol to the Irish, as well as the English) costs 80p in the Republic. A gallon in Ireland (the same in Britain) is equal to 1.2 U.S. gallons. Familiar brands are *Shell, Esso, Caltex* (*Texaco*), *B.P.*, all of which are refined in Ireland, and *Jet,* which is imported and a few pence cheaper.

If you're accustomed to American *service* with oil, water and tyres checked automatically at a service station and the windows cleaned, you will rarely find the same service in Ireland; some are highly geared for service, but others don't bother; if you want the service, you are welcome to ask for it and they'll do what you ask willingly. It's customary to tip 10p for service other than just gas.

Maps. There is a good range of detailed *maps* issued for motoring tourists—if you want a map specially designed for the visitor to Ireland, Bord Fáilte (Irish Tourist Board) issues one with a number of suggested tours and mileages (free) but if you want something more detailed, there are Ordnance Survey maps which can be bought at tourist offices; the ¼" to 1 miles series is first class, and five of them cover the whole of Ireland, the cost being 30p each.

Convenient Conveniences. Outside the main centers there are very few public toilets, but most big gas stations have toilets, or you can always use facilities in hotels.

Frontier Posts. Although we are not including Northern Ireland in this edition, you may find yourself in the border region—or, indeed, be crossing over. So here are a few facts on the border posts.

There are 20 approved routes for *crossing the frontier* between the Republic of Ireland and Northern Ireland. If you are going to cross the border in a self-drive car, be sure to mention this to the rental company to make certain they give you the papers.

Frontier posts are on the following roads (the Northern Ireland town is given first):

Newry-Greenore; *Newry-Dundalk (via Killeen),
Armagh to Dundalk (via Newtown Hamilton),

FACTS AT YOUR FINGERTIPS

Crossmaglen-Carrickmacross,
Armagh to Castleblayney, *Armagh to Monaghan,
Roslea to Monaghan,
Enniskillen to Clones, Derrylin to Belturbet, Enniskillen to Swanlinbar, Enniskillen to Manorhamilton, Enniskillen to Ballyshannon via Belleek, Kesh to Pettigo,
Castlederg-Castlefin, *Strabane-Lifford,
Derry to St. Johnston,
Derry to Bridgend, Derry-Muff, Derry-Newtown Hamilton

Posts are normally *open* 8 a.m. to 8 p.m.; those marked * are open until midnight. It costs about 10p to have a post opened outside the normal hours (the request should be made in advance).

There are *check points* on both sides of the frontier, on the northern side by the British Customs (Northern Ireland is in fiscal union with Britain) and on the south by the Republic of Ireland Customs. On both sides the formalities are quick and friendly. Don't drive on roads near the border marked Unapproved Road, or you're likely to be in trouble with the customs.

BY CARAVAN. An informal way of seeing Ireland and meeting the people is to take a caravan on tour, or settle on a caravan site for a short time. Sites are registered with the Irish Tourist Board which ensures that they meet minimum standards. The sites are widely separated and provide good coverage of Ireland. You can either tow the caravan with your own car (or a hired one) or arrange with a towing service to move it if you wish, although this makes the trip a little expensive. About half of the sites have caravans to let on the site and camping is also allowed at most of them. Charges vary, but a nightly rate of about £1.50 or £6 a week is average. Touring caravanners are not confined to the regular sites, as overnight stopping places can be arranged along the road with the permission of local landowners or farmers. The roads are uncrowded and everywhere the caravanner meets people with time to chat and make him welcome.

There are about 20 caravan hirers in Ireland, among them: *Kenneally's Caravans,* Bishopstown, Cork; *Webb Caravan Services Ltd.,* Innishannon, Co. Cork; *Campbell Caravans,* Dublin 14; *Carefree Caravans,* Dublin 3; *Collinstown Caravans,* Cloghran, Co. Dublin; *Sprite Ltd.,* Sherrington Park, Shankill, Co. Dublin; *Young Caravans Ltd,* Dublin 14.

For an even more leisurely holiday, there's fun to be enjoyed with a horse-drawn caravan designed in the traditional round-topped Romany style but comfortably lined and fitted for camping convenience. The horses know the roads around County Cork and County Kerry, where most of them are based, and the rates are rock bottom, about £30 at season's peak for a 4/5-berth fully equipped caravan with a butane gas cooker and all you'll need except groceries and towels for a week.

FACTS AT YOUR FINGERTIPS

Horse-drawn caravans are available from *Connemara Horse Caravans,* Westport House, Westport, County Mayo; *Blarney Romany Co. Ltd.,* Lancaster House, Western Road, Cork; *West Cork Caravan Co. Ltd.,* Clonakilty, West Cork; *Dieter Clissmann Caravans,* Glenealy, Co. Wicklow; *Shannon Horse Caravans,* Adare, Co. Limerick. You don't have to be farm-reared to handle a horse with one of these caravans.

POSSIBLE ITINERARIES. It is possible to plan endless routes around Ireland, all of which would take in scenery, towns and rivers, in kaleidoscopic variety. Here are just a few possible routes. The mileage is in brackets.

A 10-day tour of over 1,000 miles, with Dublin as the starting point. Day 1. Dublin—Tramore (118). 2. Tramore—Cork (73). 3. Cork—Killarney (94). 4. Killarney. 5. Killarney—Galway (156). 6. Galway—Westport (86). 7. Westport—Bundoran (96). 8. Bundoran—Dunfanaghy (120). 9. Dunfanaghy—Carrick-on-Shannon (110). 10. Carrick-on-Shannon—Dublin (150).

A two-day tour of the quiet Lakeland heart of the country starts from Athlone. Day 1. Athlone—Mullingar, taking in Roscommon, Longford, Castlepollard and Fore (84). 2. Mullingar—Athlone, visiting Ballymore, Lissoy, Glasson (65).

The Ring of Kerry tour (see the chapter of the same name) takes one day, about 220 miles.

A four-day West Coast tour starts again in Athlone. Day 1. Athlone—Limerick (94). 2. Limerick—Galway (144). 3. Galway—Westport (122). 4. Westport—Athlone (163).

Several *car rental companies* operate chauffeur-driven tours which are a good buy for small groups. A four-day tour covering Dublin to Shannon and taking in a sightseeing tour of Dublin, Cork, Killarney, the Ring of Kerry and the medieval Bunratty Castle for four persons by sedan costs around £150, including chauffeur's expenses. A 7-day tour covering nearly 1,000 miles and taking in Belfast, Sligo and the Yeats Country, Connemara, Killarney, Ring of Kerry and Blarney Castle would cost about £250 by chauffeur-driven limousine for six travelers. Chauffeurs are well-informed guides and helpful in making arrangements for hotels and other requirements. Tours can start at Dublin or Shannon. It's also possible to hire a *minibus* on the same basis, with itineraries planned to suit the group, for about £70 per person when chartered by a group of six; charges are based on an average of about 100 miles a day and the tours can start at Dublin, Cork or Shannon.

Based holidays with a *self-drive car* are also offered on a reasonable basis. These are at a weekly rate of about £30 and up per person for a

FACTS AT YOUR FINGERTIPS

group of four staying in an hotel; charge is about £3 lower for each of the party if accommodation is in a guest house. Charges include self-drive mini car for unlimited mileage, accommodation and bed and breakfast at hotel or guest house, and all gratuities. You can have a similar deal, staying at a farmhouse for seven nights at around £22 per person.

If you're interested in through-route driving to a destination the following is a *distance guide:*

Dublin-Cork, 160 miles; Dublin-Shannon Airport, 137 miles; Dublin-Galway, 135 miles; Dublin-Sligo, 135 miles; Dublin-Derry, 148 miles; Dublin-Belfast, 103 miles; Dublin-Killarney, 191 miles.

BY INLAND WATERWAY. The River Shannon is the longest river in Ireland or Britain, and with the Grand Canal and the River Barrow, provides hundreds of miles of inland waterways for quiet cruising, pleasant meetings and parties in waterside hotels and bars. The Irish Tourist Board has spent a lot of money in improving marine and other facilities along the banks. The Shannon and its lakes, including Lough Derg and Lough Ree, is navigable for 130 miles; there are 80 miles of the Grand Canal between Dublin and Shannon Harbour; and 65 miles of the River Barrow and its connecting spur of the Grand Canal. Lough Ree, just above Athlone, and Lough Derg cover almost a hundred square miles.

Main bases for Shannon cruising are at Killaloe, County Clare; Athlone and Carrick-on-Shannon. In the north, the River Erne and Lough Erne provide additional facilities of about 300 square miles of cruising water in a beautiful lakeland, based on Castle Archdale in County Fermanagh.

All types of boats are available from sailing dinghies to 7-berth cruisers; high standards of equipment are insisted on by the boat operators' associations. Hiring a fully-equipped 4-berth cruiser on the Shannon at the peak of the season is around £145 per week, or in early May and late September about £90. There are eleven firms offering cruisers for hire, most of them designed for Irish waterways and fitted to a high standard. All are inspected and approved by the Irish Tourist Board. Among the hirers are *Emerald Star Line,* St. James's Gate, Dublin; *Athlone Cruisers Ltd.,* Athlone, Co. Westmeath. *Mitchell Marine Ltd.,* Carrick-on-Shannon. *The Shannon Guide* (£1.75) is a useful publication containing charts and information on the wild-life, fishing and sights of interest along the Shannon. If you've inland cruising in mind, and don't want a self-drive cruiser, there are cruisers carrying passengers for a week or a two-week trip along the waterways. Cost varies from £40 to £50 a week and the boats vary from barges converted as small floating hotels to cruisers with room for only six passengers. *Weaver Boats Ltd.,* Carrick-on-Shannon, are people to contact for this type of cruising; they will fix you up with shore excursions as well.

FACTS AT YOUR FINGERTIPS

SPORTS. We have dealt fairly fully with sports in Ireland in our chapter *The Sportsman's Paradise.* Here are a few useful pointers on each of the sports that might interest you.

Angling. The Irish Tourist Board publishes excellent brochures on each of the main types of fishing in the country, brown trout, coarse, sea, etc. These are full of detailed maps, advice on bait and licenses, even record catches so that you can measure up against the best.

Salmon fishing opens on rivers like the Liffey on January 1st and there's salmon to be had somewhere until the last of the western rivers closes on October 12th. Hotels own some of the fishing rights for their visitors, angling clubs control others, and there is free fishing—it's easy to find out what's available locally. A license fee varies from £3 for seven days to £4 for a full season for all fishery districts. The salmon rod license covers sea trout fishing which is available in the small lakes and lesser rivers; some is preserved and the rights let by the month—in other places, hotels have fishing for their guests and it is free in a number of lakes.

Brown Trout are the favourite fish for the Irish angler—they range in weight from 2 lb. to 8 lb. and over; mid-May to early-June is the mayfly season, and there is wet-fly fishing in March, April, early May and September. No license is needed and fishing is free on a number of big lakes. The *Inland Fisheries Trust* controls many of the lakes and rivers and these can be fished for 50p a year with an additional charge of £2 a year for some very special fisheries. Other trout waters are in the care of angling associations with subscriptions in the 50p to £2 range.

Coarse Fishing requires no license and is free in most areas. 20 lb. pike are common, rudd are usually around 2 lb., bream of over 7 lb. are common; roach and dace are found in the south (Munster Blackwater), tench are plentiful and there is an increasing number of carp. Four people can enjoy 8 days of coarse fishing, including hire of a self-drive car, hotel accommodation and all meals for about £75.

Golf is the top participant game with about 100 courses welcoming visitors at a low cost. At most courses, £3 to £4 will cover your expenses for a day including green fees, caddy, lunch and tea. Professional fees range from £2 upwards a round. A circular coastal tour of Ireland gives a choice of about 20 championship courses, one every 50 miles. Even in Killarney, where scenery is the great attraction, there are two courses beside the lakes. To keep the off-the-course golfer in form there are two golf ranges on the perimeter of Dublin, within five miles of the city center. Except on a few Dublin courses, where Saturday play is restricted because of men's competitions, women may play on the courses any day of the week. The Irish Tourist Board has an excellent Guide to Irish Golf Courses, which gives details of more than 150 courses.

FACTS AT YOUR FINGERTIPS

Shooting. Considerable progress has been made in the preservation of native game birds for shooting in various parts of the country. There is plentiful shooting for migratory wildfowl, including snipe, woodcock, duck, geese and plover. Shooting rights are privately held by landowners, some are free, and others are held by hotels for the enjoyment of their guests. The *Irish Land Commission,* 24 Upper Merrion Street, Dublin 2, has a substantial area of shooting available, rented by the season or leased for a period of years. A firearms certificate is essential for any visitor who is going shooting; this must be obtained in advance from the *Forest and Wildlife Service,* Dept. of Lands, 22 Upper Merrion St., Dublin 2. Fees are £5 for a shotgun or rifle and 75 pence for each additional shotgun. The *Irish Tourist Board* has a list of shoots and hotels in a position to make special shooting arrangements for visitors.

Horseracing. Horseracing may be "the sport of kings", but in Ireland it is the sport of every man and most women. The interest is not only in the speed and grace of the horses but in the quality and value of the bloodstock. Some of the world's finest bloodstock is to be seen at the *Royal Dublin Society's Horse Show* in the first week of August at Ballsbridge Showgrounds, Dublin. The bloodstock industry is worth about £10,000,000 a year in exports. Horsebreeding is not confined to the major studs but is also a remunerative interest for a number of farmers; if you've a special interest, contact the *Racing Board,* 9 Merrion Square, Dublin 2, or the *Irish Export Board* at 33 East 50th Street, New York. There are about 30 race tracks and about 230 meetings at which prize money totals over £1,700,000 a year. A check on entries for the five Irish Classic races in a recent year showed that 62% of the entries were bred in Ireland, 21% in England, 15% in France and 1% each in America and Italy. Admission to horse racing tracks ranges from 20p to a top of £1.50, the admission charge for a woman to the grand stand or members' enclosure always being half that for a man.

Car parking is free at the tracks and race cards cost 10 pence. Totalisator units are sold at all courses. If your interest is in riding horses rather than watching them, there are a number of centers offering riding and ponytrekking holidays in the scenic areas of Wicklow, Cork, Kerry and Tipperary.

Playing the Horses. The Irish dearly love a gamble and there are about 900 "betting shops", usually marked "Turf Accountant", throughout the country; they're generally small and frequently part of a chain operated by a big bookmaker. All bookies (there are around 570) must be licensed by the government; it is estimated that the Irish wager around £34 million ($81,600,000) a year. The Racing Board imposes a levy of 5% on bookmakers at race tracks and also on the Totalisator ($12\frac{1}{2}$%) for the benefit of racing.

FACTS AT YOUR FINGERTIPS

Horse riding Holidays are popular for novices and veterans. Lessons cost about £2 an hour, hacking about £1.50. A full day's trek is about £4.

Sailing. With its long coastline and inland waterways, Ireland has a strong attraction for yachtsmen. Principal centers on the coast are at *Dun Laoghaire*, County Dublin; *Crosshaven* and *Kinsale*, County Cork; on the Shannon at *Killaloe*, County Clare; *Nenagh*, County Tipperary and *Athlone*, County Westmeath; and on *Blessington Lakes*, County Wicklow. There are water skiing and skin diving centers at Dublin, Killaloe, Valentia, Co. Kerry, Killkee, Co. Clare, and best for skin diving, Killybegs, Co. Donegal. The Irish Water Ski Association at 20 Upper Merrion St., Dublin 2, is glad to help visiting enthusiasts.

Sailing cruisers can be hired on a charter basis from *White Rose Yachts Ltd.*, Crosshaven, County Cork. Sailing dinghies are available from the *Angling Center* and the *Skillet Sailing School, Kinsale*, County Cork, at around £4 per day; there is a six-day sailing course at the latter for about £20. The *Glénans Irish Sailing Centre* is linked to the French Glénans organization and is based in Baltimore, County Cork; a two-week course costs about £46 for those under 25, £70 for older members. Prices are about the same at the *Irish Yachting Association Sailing School* and the *Sail Training Centre* both at Dun Laoghaire.

MAIL. All first-class mail going from the Republic of Ireland to Great Britain and continental Europe is sent by air, so don't mark it with airmail labels. Sea service is used to supplement the airmail services for these areas when required. The charge for letters posted to addresses in Ireland or Great Britain is 9p for the first 60 grams; postcards 5p. For letters to European destinations 11p for the first 20 grm. Airmail rates to the U.S. and countries outside Europe, 15p for the first 15 grm; airletters 9p, postcards 9p.

The Irish Department of Posts and Telegraphs issues a number of special issue stamps of interest to collectors. Commemorative stamps are normally on sale at all post offices for about three months but are available from the Philatelic Section, General Post Office, Dublin 1, for a period of up to 6 months from the date of issue. Non-commemorative stamps which have been withdrawn can be obtained from the same source for up to three months after the withdrawal.

Letters for travelers to a town may be addressed in care of the Post Office marked "To be called for" or "Poste Restante" at any Post Office town; to ensure delivery to the proper person of Poste Restante letters, callers must produce evidence of their identity.

There is no delivery of letters on Saturdays in Dublin or Dun Laoghaire, but most big hotels collect their mail on that day.

FACTS AT YOUR FINGERTIPS

TELEGRAMS. Within Ireland the charge is 70p for the first 12 words and 6p for each additional word; for addresses in Northern Ireland or Great Britain 75p for first 12 words and 7p for each additional word. The "immediate" rate to the US and Canada is 15p per word, and for an overnight messages a minimum of £1.05 for 7 words. There's an extra charge of 15p for messages on Sundays or holidays. Telex services are available. Most rural post offices open for telegrams between 9 a.m. and 10.30 a.m. on Sundays, but you can send a telegram by phone at any time.

TELEPHONES. Public telephone kiosks are located in nearly every town and village. A local call costs 4p. The call may be cut off after three minutes unless you put another 4p in the box. Internal trunk calls between 8 a.m. and 6 p.m. cost from 13p to 39p for three minutes, depending on distance; cheaper after 6 p.m. and at weekends. Specimen transatlantic rates: Ireland-New York, £2.25 for three-minute non-personal calls plus 75p for each extra minute on full rate and personal calls. First three minutes on person-to-person calls costs £4. Rates drop after 10 p.m. On Sunday a non-personal three-minute call costs £1.68. Most hotels put a service charge on phone calls.

The Bell System's Teleplan enables US visitors with Collect or Credit charge facilities to phone home, paying only a 50p service charge to the hotel in Ireland; the cost of the call is added to your home number's bill.

For a recorded telephone Weather Service, dial 1199 in the Dublin area; outside Dublin, ask the operator for "Weather Service"

TIME. Time in Ireland is the same as in Great Britain (Greenwich Mean Time plus one hour, or British Standard Time).

CLOSING TIMES. Shops. Most shops open at 9 a.m. and close at 5:30 or 6 p.m., and in the cities have a half-day closing (usually close at 1 p.m.) on Wednesdays or Saturdays. Half-days vary in other parts of Ireland, and it is best to check. **Banks.** Open weekdays 10 a.m. to 12:30 p.m. and 1:30 to 3 p.m. (5 p.m. on Thursdays), but they are closed on Saturdays. **Post Offices** Open 9 a.m. to 6 p.m. weekdays, and until 6:30 in provincial towns. There is a 24-hour service at Shannon Airport. **Pubs.** Open weekdays 10:30 a.m. to 11:30 p.m. (closed from 2:30 to 3:30 p.m. in the Dublin area), open Sundays from 12:30 to 2 and from 4 to 10 p.m. From October to May, pubs close at 11 p.m. Mondays to Saturdays.

Public Holidays are on January 1, March 17 (St. Patrick's Day), Good Friday, Easter Monday, first Monday in June, first Monday in August, Christmas Day and St. Stephen's Day (December 26, also known as Boxing Day). Big stores, banks and offices are closed on these days.

FACTS AT YOUR FINGERTIPS

ELECTRICITY. The standard current is 220 volts, 50 cycles. Hotels usually have dual 220/110 voltage plugs, suitable for razors only.

TAXIS. Taxis don't cruise in Irish cities; they must remain on ranks at fixed points, usually near major hotels and rail or bus terminals. Fares are about a minimum of 35p, 15p a mile or time not exceeding 12 minutes; 5p for each additional ¼ mile or 3 minutes and 4p for each passenger over one. Baggage is charged at 4p per piece. These fares operate within a radius of 10 miles of city center. Outside this area, negotiate.

MEDICAL SERVICES. There is no shortage of doctors in Ireland. Your hotel certainly will have one on call. The Irish medical schools of Trinity College, Dublin, the National University of Ireland, and the Royal College of Surgeons of Ireland are world famous. So are Irish nursing standards. If you have any problem—and it's unlikely that you will have—contact the *Irish Medical Association* at 10 Fitzwilliam Place, Dublin 2. Doctors' charges are around £4 for a house (or hotel) call, about half that if you see him at his office (usually miscalled a "surgery" in Ireland). Unless it's an emergency it's courteous to phone the doctor to arrange an appointment: it saves his time, and yours. The same applies for dentists.

The major hospitals maintain emergency services, with at least two hospitals in Dublin on duty through the night.

Prescriptions are dispensed at chemists' shops (drugstores) and always by a qualified pharmacist. In country areas the pharmacist's establishment may bear the designation "Medical Hall"; it's a traditional name and you'll get the same ready and qualified assistance. The initials MPSI indicate a chemist who is a Member of the Pharmaceutical Society of Ireland.

For names of recommended medical practitioners, contact IAMAT (International Association for Medical Assistance to Travelers, Inc.), 745 Fifth Ave., New York 10022, or 1268 St. Clair Ave., West, Toronto; or Intermedic, Inc., 777 Third Ave., New York 10017.

Europ Assistance, 269/273 High Street, Croydon, England, has an excellent medical insurance plan—£1.50 per person for 28 days, 50p per additional week—which covers almost all eventualities.

ANCESTOR HUNTING. Ancestor tracing is a special interest, and one for which there are plenty of facilities. Irish surnames, such as Murphy and Kelly, are borne by a very large number of people, with the result that identification is difficult unless you have some details such as the memories of elderly relatives, the location from which your ancestors emigrated or

FACTS AT YOUR FINGERTIPS

other facts to help the search. The name of the county doesn't do much to narrow down the hunt, but the local place name does. The *Genealogical Office* at Dublin Castle is particularly helpful and provides general information about surnames and armorial bearings without charge. If special searches are required these cost about £8 for four hours' work. The *Office of the Registrar General* in the Custom House, Dublin, has registers of births, deaths and marriages from 1864, and some marriages back to 1845.

The *Public Record Office* at the Four Courts and the *Registry of Deeds* in Henrietta Street, Dublin, are two other potential sources for information; the last-named has records from 1708 to the present day relating to transactions in property. Searches may be made by the visitor for a small fee. The *National Library*, Kildare Street, Dublin, is yet another storehouse for information for the genealogist.

If you know the location of an ancestor's birthplace or marriage, the *parochial registers* in the charge of parish priests and other clergy may provide the clue—many of them cover more than 200 years. If the information you have shows that your ancestor was a Presbyterian, then the *Presbyterian Historical Society* at Church House, Fisherwick Place, Belfast, may be able to help, and for people of Quaker forebears, the *Society of Friends*, 6 Eustace Street, Dublin 2, is a likely source of information.

STATELY HOMES AND GARDENS. Ireland is rich in an extraordinary range of country houses, medieval castles and mini-palaces, often with superb gardens attached. You are welcome to wander their wide walks and enjoy the beauty of their interiors. Admission ranges from 20p to 60p for adults, children are usually half price. Several of the ones listed here (and it represents only a selection of what is available) have refreshment facilities.

Abbey Leix House (Laois). A collection of rare plants and shrubs, an oak wood, the last of Ireland's primeval forests. Easter-Sept. 30: Daily 2:30-6:30.

Adare Manor (Adare, Limerick). Neo-Gothic mansion; only Great Hall, Picture Gallery and some reception rooms on view. Staircase and fireplaces by Pugin. May 1-Sept. 30: Mon.-Fri. and Sun. afternoons.

Bantry House (Bantry, Cork). Overlooking Bantry Bay; famous for its furniture and objets d'art—especially the French tapestries. April-mid Oct.: Mon.-Fri. 10-12:30, 2-6; Sun. 2:30-6.

Bermingham House (Tuam, Galway). Georgian mansion (1770). Lovely plasterwork and antique furniture. Afternoons daily, except Suns. and Mons.

FACTS AT YOUR FINGERTIPS

Blarney Castle (Blarney, Cork). Built 1446. Famous for the Blarney Stone in the battlements which gives eloquence to those who kiss it. Summer: 9 a.m.-8 p.m. Winter: 9 a.m.-dusk.

Bunratty Castle and Folk Park (Bunratty, Clare). Built 1450-67; carefully restored; excellent collection of 14th-17th-century furniture. Folk Park an open air museum of typical farmhouses and craftshops. Medieval banquets nightly. Daily 9:30-5.

Cahir Castle (Cahir, Tipperary). 15th-century fortified castle, restored. Center for the Archaeological Heritage exhibitions. Oct.-mid-June, Wed., Thurs., Fri. 10-6; Tues., Sat., Sun. 2-4. Closed Mon. Mid-June-end Sept., 10-7 daily.

Castletown (Celbridge, Kildare). Masterpiece of Irish Palladian. April 1-Sept. 30: daily (except Tues.) 2-6. Oct.-March Sundays only 2-5.

Clonalis House (Castlerea, Roscommon). Outstanding collection of ancient Irish manuscripts and books. Woodland garden and walks. May 1-July 1: Sat., Sun. and Mon., 2-6. July 1-Aug. 31: daily (except Tues. and Wed.) 2-6.

Dublin Castle. State Apartments—magnificently restored; formerly the location of the Viceregal Court. Mon.-Fri., mornings and afternoons. Sat. and Sun. 2-5.

Garnish Island (Glengarriff, Cork) in Bantry Bay; famous for flowering shrubs. March-Oct. 10-5:30. Bank Holidays 10-6.

Howth Castle Gardens (Howth, Dublin). Famous rhododendron walks. Daily 8 a.m.-sunset.

Johnstown Castle (Wexford). Victorian gothic with excellent gardens. Grounds only, daily 9-5.

Knappogue Castle (Quin, Clare). 1497. Restored to former state . . . orchards, gardens, workshops included. Medieval banquets twice nightly in summer. Castle open 10-5.

Longfield House (Goolds Cross, nr. Cashel, Tipperary). 1760. Home of Bianconi (transport pioneer). Sundays, 2-5:30.

Muckross House and Gardens (Killarney, Kerry). Folk Life Center in heart of Killarney. Crafts at work; sub-tropical gardens; nature trails.

Powerscourt Estate and Gardens (Enniskerry, Wicklow). 40 acres of terraces, statuary, Italian and Japanese gardens, waterfall etc. Daily, Easter to Oct. 10:30-5:30.

FACTS AT YOUR FINGERTIPS

Rothe House (Kilkenny). 1594 merchant's family house, remarkably preserved. May-Sept.: weekday mornings and afternoons. Oct.-April: Tues., Fri., Sat. 3-5.

Tullynally Castle (Castlepollard, Westmeath). Largest Irish castle. June-Sept.: Sat., Sun. and Bank Holidays, 2:30-6.

Westport House (Westport, Mayo). Georgian house, with zoo. April-Oct.: daily 2-6. May-Sept.: 10:30-6:30.

MEET THE IRISH. You can arrange in advance with any branch of the Irish Tourist Office in America or Britain to meet congenial Irish folk of similar profession, hobbies and age as your own. But if you arrive in Ireland without this previous arrangement, contact *Noragh Owens* at Bord Fáilte Eireann, Baggot Street Bridge, Dublin 2. She has a list of individuals and families who are in the scheme. Hospitality is left to the discretion of the Irish host; the scheme is voluntary, the aim good friendship.

TOURIST INFORMATION OFFICES. In Ireland there are information centers in every major town and in villages in areas heavily visited by tourists. These offices can provide specific local information and general information on other areas and will help in getting accommodation.

Headquarters of the *Irish Tourist Board* (Bord Fáilte Eireann) are at Baggot Street Bridge, Dublin 2 (tel. 765871); and the main regional offices are:

Dublin City: 14 Upper O'Connell Street and 51 Dawson Street (tel. 747733); *Eastern Region* (counties Dublin, Kildare, Louth, Meath and Wicklow): Moran Park, Dun Laoghaire, County Dublin (tel. 806984): *Midlands* (counties Cavan, Laois, Longford, Offaly, Monaghan, Roscommon and Westmeath): Castle Street, Mullingar (tel. 044-8650); *Shannon* (counties Clare, Limerick and North Tipperary): 62 O'Connell Street, Limerick (tel. 061-47522); *Northwest* (counties Donegal, Sligo and Leitrim): Stephen Street, Sligo (tel. 071-2436); *Southern* (Cork and Kerry): Grand Parade, Cork (tel. 021-23251); *Southeast* (counties Carlow, Kilkenny, South Tipperary, Waterford and Wexford): 41 The Quay, Waterford (tel. 051-5788); *Western* (Galway and Mayo): Arus Fáilte, Galway (tel. 091-63081).

Most of the offices are open from 9 or 10 a.m. until 9 p.m. in the summer months and until 6 p.m. at other times of the year. Sunday service is provided at the main centers usually between 10 a.m. and noon and again between 5 p.m. and 7 p.m. in the peak travel months.

Leaving Ireland

CUSTOMS ON RETURNING HOME. Before you leave for abroad, register any foreign-made articles you may be taking with you such as cameras, binoculars, expensive timepieces, and the like. Failing this you may be called upon to prove, on your return, that you bought these items at home. If you can't, you may be charged duty on them.

Americans who are out of the United States at least 48 hours and have claimed no exemption during the previous 30 days are entitled to bring in duty-free up to $100 worth of articles for bona fide gifts or for their own personal use. The value of each item is determined by the price actually paid (so save your receipts). Every member of a family is entitled to this same exemption, and the allowance can be pooled.

Purchases intended for your duty-free quota can no longer be sent home separately—they must accompany your personal baggage.

Not more than 100 cigars may be imported duty-free per person, not more than a quart of wine or liquor (none at all if your passport indicates you are from a "dry" state, or are under 21 years of age). Only one bottle of perfume that is trademarked in the United States may be brought in, plus a reasonable quantity of other brands.

Small gifts may be mailed to friends, but not more than one package to any one address and none to your own home. Notation on the package should be "Unsolicited Gift—Value Under $10". Tobacco, liquor and perfume may not be mailed.

Antiques are defined for customs purposes as articles manufactured more than 100 years ago, and are admitted duty-free. If there's any question of age, you may be asked to supply documentary proof from the seller.

A foreign-made automobile that was ordered before your departure is subject to duty (3%) even though delivered abroad. This same rule applies to any purchase initiated in advance of your trip. In addition, foreign-made cars must conform to US safety and pollution emission standards, as established by the Department of Transportation and the Environmental Protection Agency respectively.

If your purchases exceed your exemption, list the items that are subject to the highest rates of duty under your exemption and pay duty on the items with the lowest rates.

FACTS AT YOUR FINGERTIPS

For residents of **Canada** two sets of conditions apply. After 48 hours away they may bring back, duty-free, articles (except alcohol and tobacco) worth $10 for each trip out with only a verbal declaration; and with a written declaration may claim an exemption of $50 once each calendar quarter. After 7 days out of Canada they may, upon written declaration, claim one exemption of $150 for each calendar year, and an allowance of up to 40 ounces of alcohol, 50 cigars, 200 cigarettes and 2 lbs. of manufactured tobacco. For personal gifts, the rules are the same as the US ones: "Unsolicited gift, value under $10". For details ask for Canada Customs' brochure, "I Declare".

Do not bring home foreign meats, fruits, plants, soil, or other agricultural items when you return to the United States (so don't bring Shamrock roots from Ireland). It is illegal to bring in foreign agricultural items without permission, because they can spread destructive plant or animal pests and diseases. Limitations on foods vary greatly according to the product, origin, and degree of processing involved. Ask for US Dept. of Agriculture pamphlet No. 1082, "Traveler's Tips on Bringing Food, Plant and Animal Products into the United States", for details, Quarantines, Department of Agriculture, Federal Center Building, Hyattsville, Md. 20782.

British subjects, except those under the age of 17 years, may import duty-free from any country the following: 200 cigarettes or 100 cigarillos or 50 cigars or 250 grams of tobacco; 1 litre of spirits or 2 litres of wine in excess of 38.8% proof, and 2 litres of still table wine. Also 50 grams of perfume, ¼ litre of toilet water and £10 worth of other normally dutiable goods.

Returning from Ireland (or any other EEC country), you may, *instead* of the above exemptions, bring in the following, provided you can prove they were not bought in a duty-free shop: 300 cigarettes or 150 cigarillos or 75 cigars or 400 grams of tobacco; 1½ litres of strong spirits or 3 litres of other spirits or fortified wines plus 3 litres of still table wine; 75 grams of perfume and three-eighths litre of toilet water and £50 worth of other normally dutiable goods. If you have nothing to declare you may use the Green Lane on arrival at a British Airport, but checks may be made by the Customs Officers.

Customs regulations everywhere are generally strictly enforced so it's advisable to check what your allowances are and make sure you have kept receipts for whatever purchases you made abroad.

Check-in-Times. Passengers using the airport coach service from Dublin's Busaras (Central Bus Station) should take a coach not later than 80 minutes before aircraft departure time if flying on the transatlantic route; 60 minutes for European services; coach fare costs 50p. Check-in formalities are not carried out at the bus station, only at the airport. Airport check-in times are 45 minutes before departure for transatlantic service and for groups;

FACTS AT YOUR FINGERTIPS

FACTS AT YOUR FINGERTIPS

30 minutes before departure on European services and flights to Britain. At Shannon transatlantic passengers should check in 45 minutes before departure; other passengers 20/30 minutes ahead of schedule. A coach service at 55p connects Limerick with Shannon but its departure times (from Limerick rail station and main hotels) are not related to aircraft schedules.

**IRELAND
TOWN
BY
TOWN**

IRELAND—TOWN BY TOWN

A Guide to Hotels, Restaurants and other Practical Information

> The entries in this section are by the name of the town, alphabetically listed. Cork and Dublin have longer listings and are divided from the rest of the entries by clear horizontal lines.
> Hotel entries are preceded by the letter "H", Restaurants by "R", Entertainment by "A", Youth Hostels by "YH". For an explanation of our grading system for Hotels (L), (1), (2), (3), (4) see pages 242-43. We grade Restaurants, especially in the cities, (E) for Expensive, (M) for Moderate, (I) for Inexpensive.
> Other points of interest (places to see, car rental, etc.) follow the main hotel and restaurant listings.

ACHILL ISLAND (Mayo) is reached by a bridge. H: *Ostan Gob A'Choire* (2), 38 rooms with bath. *Achill Head*, Keel, has 30 rooms; *Slievemore*, 18 rooms; and *Wave Crest*, Dooagh, 14 rooms; all are (3). There are a number of inexpensive and pleasant hotels: among them *Amethyst*, Keel; *Atlantic*, Dooagh; *McDowell's* and *Strand* at Dugort; and *Sweeney's*, Achill Sound.

ADARE (Limerick). H: On the fringe of the southwest, the *Dunraven Arms* (2), in hunting country; fine old-world character and comfort, with excellent food, and 23 rooms, 16 with bath.
Adare Manor, a neo-gothic mansion, is open to view daily (except Sat.), May-Sept.

ARAN ISLANDS (Galway). H: There is little accommodation for visitors but on Inishmore, there is one guesthouse, Johnston Hernon's *Kilmurvey House, Kilronan;* and *Day's Bofin House* on Inishere.
For the grass airstrips at Inishmore and Inishmaan, Aran Islands, contact Aer Arann, Galway (tel. 5119).

ARKLOW (Wicklow). H: *Arklow Bay* (1), 29 rooms, 19 with bath, along the coast.
A: Arklow has a big amusement center with a pool, boating lake and pitch-and-putt course.

ARRANMORE ISLAND (Donegal). H: For a fine get-away-from-it-all island holiday, *The Glen* is a modest little hotel, 10 rooms, offering a low rate, seasonal.

ASHFORD (Wicklow). H: *Bel Air* (3).
The informal botanic gardens at Mount Usher have trees and shrubs from many parts of the world. Open Suns., 10 a.m. to 6 p.m.
(For *Ashford Castle*, see Cong.)

ATHLONE (Westmeath). H: The *Prince of Wales*, 49 rooms, 6 with bath; and the *Royal*, 35 rooms, 9 with bath; both are (1). The *Hodson Bay* (2) is wonderfully sited on the banks of the Shannon, and has 28 rooms, 18 with bath.

IRELAND—TOWN BY TOWN

BALLINA (Mayo). H: *Downhill Hotel* (2) is in a pleasant spot, with heated pool and saunas, 56 rooms, 25 with bath. In a first-class fishing district.

BALLINASCARTY (Cork). H: *Ardnavaha House Hotel* (2) is an old Georgian house with an associated modern bedroom block in 40 acres; 24 rooms all with bath.

BALLINASLOE (Galway). H: *Hayden's* (2) on the Dublin-Galway road, is modern, with admirable food, 61 rooms, 22 with bath, and an attractive garden.

BALLYBOFEY (Donegal). H: *Jackson's* (2) has a good reputation with travelers; 38 rooms, 21 with bath.

BALLYBUNION (Kerry). H: *Marine* (2), 21 rooms. *Greenmount* and *West End* are both (3), latter has no liquor license.

There are a number of villas to sleep six (*Ballybunion Holiday Villas*) at a weekly rate of around £40 per villa in the high season.

BALLYCOTTON (Cork). H: *Bay View Hotel* (3) is a seaside hotel with good food and views of harbor, nearby bathing, 20 rooms, 2 with bath.

BALLYLICKEY (Cork). H: On Bantry Bay, *Ballylickey House* (2) has a long—but slightly erratic—reputation for good food, seasonal, 26 rooms all with bath. *Sea View*, small and (3).

BALLYNAHINCH (Galway). H: *Ballynahinch Castle* (1), the historic home of the Martyn family. 28 rooms, 8 with bath; the setting and the fishing are excellent.

BALLYVAUGHAN (Clare). H: *Gregan's Castle* (2) is an updated castle hotel located in the Burren country, with 14 rooms, 5 with bath. The restaurant (M) has a high reputation. (Changed ownership in 1976.)

BANDON (Cork). H: The *Munster Arms* (2) has the friendly atmosphere of an Irish inn; features local produce, particularly steaks and lobsters; 37 rooms, 21 with bath.

BANTRY (Cork). H: *West Lodge Hotel* (2), 60 rooms with bath. *Bantry Bay* and *Vickery's* are both (3). The *Bantry Motor Inn* (3) overlooks the bay; 70 rooms with bath.

A: There's a "Scoraíocht" (Irish Night) once a week during the summer in the *Boys' Club Hall*, and there are dances (not on a fixed schedule) in the same hall.

Bantry House and its gardens are open to view from Easter to mid-October, Mon. to Fri., 10-12:30, 2-6, Sun. 2:30-6.

BARLEYCOVE (Cork). H: (Near Crookhaven) *Barley Cove Motor Hotel* (1), recent, 32 rooms with bath, and several chalets on a lower level of the beach, each with bath; a get-away-from-it-all spot, but plenty of company if you want it.

IRELAND—TOWN BY TOWN

BARNA (Galway). R: The *Twelve Pins Roadhouse* (M) has a good atmosphere and reputation. Also *Tí na Mar* (House of the Sea) (E) specializes in fish dishes.

BETTYSTOWN (Meath). H: The *Village* (2), 12 rooms, 4 with bath. *Neptune* (3), 41 rooms, 23 with bath. R: Attractive 17th-century *Coastguard Inn* (M), known for its shellfish and game.

BLARNEY (Cork). H: *Hotel Blarney* (1) is in the shadow of Blarney Castle; 80 rooms with bath.
Blarney Castle, with the famous Blarney Stone, is open daily all year.

BLESSINGTON (Wicklow). H: *Downshire House* (2) is a well-converted mansion house; 32 rooms, 17 with bath.

BORRISOKANE (Tipperary). H. *Angler's Lodge* (4), 10 rooms.
R: *The Griffin Arms* (M) is first class.

BOYLE (Roscommon). H: *Forest Park* is a small (new) motor hotel, 12 rooms with bath, in an attractive area close to the upper reaches of the River Shannon.

BRAY (Wicklow). H: *Royal Starlight* (1), along the coast, 83 rooms, 54 with bath. *Strand* (3), 10 rooms.

BRIDGEND (Donegal). H: *Grianan of Aileach* (1), recent (1975), 20 rooms with bath, named for historic fort which is located three miles away.

BUNBEG (Donegal). H: *Ostan Gaoidoir* (Hotel Gweedore) (2), overlooks beach, 30 rooms with bath. *Seaview* (3), 28 rooms, 8 with bath.

BUNDORAN (Donegal). H: *Great Southern* is (1) in this, the major popular resort of the area. In Old English style, it has been updated; 104 rooms, 71 with bath, heated pool, golf course. *Central*, 29 rooms, 4 with bath; and *Hamilton*, 38 rooms, 8 with bath; both (2) and located right in the town. Top (3) are the *Holyrood*, 27 rooms, 2 with bath; and *Maghery House*, 31 rooms, 6 with bath. *Casa del Monte* and *Rossmore* are comfortable guesthouses, the latter with heated pool. Most hotels here are seasonal.
A tourist information office is at The Bridge (tel. 41350).

BUNRATTY (Clare). H: Not far from medieval Bunratty Castle is the *Shannon Shamrock Inn* (1), an attractive modern ranch-style hotel, 82 rooms with bath. Owned by the Fitzpatrick organization which operates *Fitzpatrick's Castle* at Killiney. Near but not too near Shannon Airport.
A: Dine in ancient splendor at two castles in the area, but book in advance: Bunratty Castle is around £15 off-season, £17 high-season, including two sightseeing tours, banquet, two other meals and overnight in a first-class hotel. (Year-round.) Knappogue Castle is at Quin, about eight miles northwest of Bunratty, and a banquet there

IRELAND—TOWN BY TOWN

is about £5. (May through September.) The banquets are twice nightly, at 6 p.m. and 9 p.m.

CAHERDANIEL (Kerry). H: *Derrynane* (2), is a recent motel, 62 rooms with bath, located in a suntrap situation beside the sea.

CAHIR (Tipperary). H: *Kilcoran Lodge* (2), just outside the town on the southern slopes of the Galtee Mountains, in a beautiful setting. A one-time mansion, it has been extended and furnished with fine antiques. 23 rooms, 8 with bath, well-located for hunting, shooting in the Glen of Aherlow and fishing.
Cahir House, right in the town, was once the home of the Earls of Glengall; a fine example of Georgian architecture well converted for comfort. 23 rooms. *Galtee Hotel*, 30 rooms, 1 with bath, on main road. Both (3).
R: *Earl of Glengall* (M) in the square, has both an attractive decor and excellent food.
Cahir Castle is nearby, and worth a visit; permission can be obtained from the office in the grounds.

CARAGH LAKE (Kerry). H: *Caragh Lodge*, 9 rooms, 5 with bath, comfortable, good restaurant; *Ard na Sidhe*; both (2).

CARLOW (Carlow). H: *Royal*, 40 rooms, 10 with bath; *Oakland*, 24 rooms, 4 with bath; both (2).

CARRAROE (Galway). H: *Ostan Cheathru Rua* (Hotel Carraroe) (2), in the heart of Gaelic-speaking district, has 24 rooms, 16 with bath.

CARRICKMACROSS (Monaghan). H: *Nuremore* (1), 37 rooms, 33 with bath.
This is where the Carrickmacross Lace comes from, made in the local convent.

CARRICK-ON-SHANNON (Leitrim). H: The *Bush* (1), 30 rooms, 17 with bath, is the center of activity associated with cruising on the Shannon and fishing in the area. The *County* (2), 25 rooms, 2 with shower.

CARRICK-ON-SUIR (Tipperary), H: *Tinvane* (3), 10 rooms.
Good center for mountain climbing.

CARRIGART (Donegal). H: Remote, but charmingly situated on Mulroy Bay in the north of Donegal, the *Carrigart*, top (3), 56 rooms, most with bath, a family hotel with tradition.

CASHEL (Tipperary). H: *Cashel Palace Hotel* (1) is literally what the name implies—a former archbishop's palace, just off the main street and in its own grounds, converted to a small hotel, attractively and comfortably furnished, 20 rooms with bath. Has a collection of pictures of famous racehorses of the past. *Longfield House* (2), an 18th-century Georgian residence, is an attractive guesthouse in a 60-acre estate with fishing in the lovely River Suir. The former home of Charles Bianconi, founder of the 19th-century coaching service.
R: There's an outstanding restaurant, *Chez Hans*, in a former church hall dating back to 1852, at the foot

IRELAND—TOWN BY TOWN

of the Rock of Cashel. (Closed Mondays and through January).

Guided tours of the ruins on top of the Rock of Cashel are available daily from 11 a.m. in summer.

CASHEL BAY (Galway). H: *Cashel House* (1), 18 rooms, 12 with bath, secluded and quiet. Overlooks bay and has a "Secret Garden" of shrubs and trees from Tibet. The restaurant (M) is famous for its country food.

CASTLEBAR (Mayo). H: *Breaffy House* (1), a converted mansion of character just outside the town; it has 43 rooms with bath.

There is an airstrip 610 metres long at Castlebar; contact: P. J. Ryan, Castlebar (tel. 488).

CASTLEDERMOT (Kildare). H: *Kilkea Castle* (2) is modernized and has a fully-equipped health center, while retaining the character of the old castle; 55 rooms with bath.

CELBRIDGE (Kildare). A: If there's a Georgian Caper advertised for *Castletown House* (M), go along for a lively banquet in the 18th-century style.

The house, incidentally, is the headquarters of the Irish Georgian Society, and is open to view daily in the summer, except Tuesdays, 2-6 p.m.; it is an architectural gem and well worth a visit.

CLIFDEN (Galway). H: Tops in the capital of ancient Connemara is *Alcock and Brown* (1), 20 rooms with bath, named for the first men to fly the Atlantic who landed here in 1919. The *Celtic*, 20 rooms with bath; and *Clifden*, 45 rooms, 25 with bath, are both (2). The *Connemara Inn* on the Galway Road is a motel, 10 rooms, half with bath.

R: The tiny *Lobster Pot* (M), on the island of Inishbofin, can be reached by ferry from Clifden. The unconventional sea-food dishes make the foray worth while.

There is a tourist information office on Market Street (tel. 103).

CLONMEL (Tipperary). H: *Clonmel Arms* (1) is the most recent, with 41 rooms, 20 with bath. *Hearn's* (2) is the historic base of Bianconi's coaches, 33 rooms, 14 with bath. *Minella* (1), a pleasant former mansion well updated is on the outskirts of town; 40 rooms, 37 with bath.

COBH (Cork). H: *Commodore* (3), 50 rooms, 30 with bath. The *European* and *Rinn Ronain* are smaller and (4).

CONG (Mayo). H: *Ashford Castle* (L) is on the edge of Lough Corrib where County Galway meets County Mayo, 77 rooms all with bath; based on a former castle. There is an excellent restaurant (E) and a 9-hole golf course in the grounds. Owned by the John A. Mulcahy Group, proprietors of the Waterville Lake Hotel in Kerry. *Ryan's* (3), 17 rooms.

IRELAND—TOWN BY TOWN

CORK

HOTELS. Cork is both a major industrial and commercial center and a base point from which to explore the south. There is a good range of hotels in all categories, but accommodation becomes scarce at height of the summer. The Tourist Information Office in Patrick Street or the Tourist Information Offices in the Arrivals Building at Cork Airport will help to solve any on-the-spot accommodation problems, but to get the best choice of hotels or guesthouses, make arrangements in advance. A number of the resort hotels are seasonal (usually April-October).

In the (1) category are: *Imperial*, 83 rooms with bath. It has a tradition which dates back to the coaching days of the last century; there is an 1808 mosaic rescued from a previous building on the site. *Jury's*, 96 rooms with bath, modern, has a riverside setting on Western Road. *Metropole*, MacCurtain Street, is one of the city's older hotels, considerably extended and modernized, 134 rooms, 70 with bath, special arrangements for guests' parking. *Silver Springs* at Tivoli, at the entrance to the city from main Dublin Road, 72 rooms with bath or shower, close to ferry terminal.

All (2) are: *Vienna Woods*, 16 rooms half with bath, located in old mansion in pleasant estate at the "gateway" to the city. The *Victoria*, Patrick Street, in the heart of the city, 77 rooms, 14 with bath, maintains traditional hospitality. *Arbutus Lodge*, 30 rooms, 12 with bath, has a top reputation for food (M). *Country Club*, 26 rooms, 4 with bath. *Ashbourne House*, 24 rooms, 17 with bath, heated pool.

Corrigan's, *Glengarriffe*, and *Moore's* are all (3) with comfortable accommodation.

There are two motor hotels, *Cork Airport*, 20 rooms with bath, Kinsale Road; and *Sunset Ridge*, 10 rooms with bath, Killeens, just outside the city.

Good guesthouses with low rates include *Glenvera*, Wellington Road; *Yorkville*, Summerhill; *Ashford* and *Askive House* on Donovan's Road; *Killarney* and *St. Kilda*, Western Road.

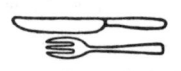

RESTAURANTS. *Blackrock Castle* (M), a 17-cent. fort, is a first-class eating spot. *Tivoli* (I), Patrick Street, has a quiet atmosphere and first-class cuisine; if you are just looking for a snack, the first floor (second floor in America) restaurant is pleasant. *Arbutus Lodge* (M) (see hotel listing). South on the Crosshaven road, at Carrigaline, is *Chez Idawalt* (M), which is worth a visit; phone ahead.

IRELAND—TOWN BY TOWN

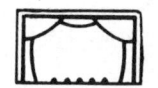

ENTERTAINMENT. *Cork Opera House* offers a wider range of entertainment than its name suggests, embracing drama and musicals. *Group Theatre,* 49 Main Street, Cork, is a little theater with a high standard of presentation; shows are also staged at Father Mathew Hall. Some hotels offer occasional "Irish Night" entertainment and informal ballad sessions in bars, so check with your hotel porter on this. Both the *Imperial* and the *Metropole* hotels have dance halls; there are a number of other dance halls in the city, which usually operate at weekends and sometimes on other nights of the week.

There is a strong musical life in the city and occasional concerts are presented in the City Hall and the auditorium of the Municipal School of Music on Union Quay. The new (1973) Irish Ballet Company, a State-aided group, has its headquarters in this lively city.

HOW TO GET ABOUT. Watch out for the one-way streets in Cork City—they seem more complicated than most and it is wise to check a street map before driving around. There are *taxi* stands at the rail terminus and in Patrick Street, and of course your hotel porter will always call one. Car Hire: *Avis,* 42 Grand Parade, also Cork Airport; *Hertz,* Patrick's Bridge, also Cork Airport; *Kenning Car Hire,* Island Service Station, Jury's Hotel, Western Road.

SHOPPING. If you are in a hurry, you will find the souvenir shops in the *Imperial, Metropole* and *Silver Springs* hotels most helpful. Shopping hours in Cork, 9 a.m.—6 p.m., Monday through Saturday. On Patrick Street there are several first-class department stores. The *Munster Arcade, Cash's* and *Roche's* have nearly everything you might want. For Irish linens, there is *Shannon's,* Prince's Street. For quality, *Egan's* on Patrick Street is a famous jewelers' and silversmiths showing some exquisite craftsmanship. Look around for Glengarriff lace in the stores, traditional in West Cork and highly prized as a souvenir of beauty. *Feehan's* in Bridge Street is an interesting antique shop. *Mercier Press* in the same street publishes an interesting range of books on Ireland and by Irish authors, and discs of Irish ballads. Locally produced statues and plaques (reproductions of Celtic masterpieces of the past) are good. Pottery from Shanagarry, Carrigaline and Youghal. The *Antique Shop* in Academy Street is worth taking time to visit. Believe it or not, Turkish Delight (Rahat Lakoum) is a delicacy made in Cork and worth sampling.

MUSEUMS. Cork's *Municipal Museum* in Fitzgerald Park has a collection representative of the region from the days of pre-history, open weekdays, 11 a.m.—1 p.m., 2:15—5 p.m. Saturdays, 11:30 a.m.—1 p.m. Look for

IRELAND—TOWN BY TOWN

such items as the Gold Bird from Garryduff. The *Cork Art Gallery* (statuary and paintings) is in the Municipal School of Art, Emmet Place, open weekdays, 10 a.m.—5:30 p.m.

PARKS AND GARDENS. *Fitzgerald's Park* has some pleasant walks and flower beds, and the *Mardyke* is a popular promenading place for Cork people.

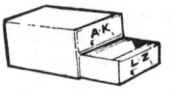

USEFUL ADDRESSES. Cork City: *General Post Office*, Oliver Plunkett Street, open weekdays 8 a.m. to 6:30 p.m. *Aer Lingus-Irish International Airlines*, 38 Patrick Street; *British Rail*, 98 Patrick Street; *British and Irish Steam Packet Company*, 8 Bridge Street. *Banks:* Bank of Ireland, Allied Irish Banks and First National City Bank are all on South Mall; Ulster Bank is on Patrick Street.

TOURIST INFORMATION OFFICES. *Cork City*, 109 Patrick Street (Cork 23251); *Cork Airport*, Arrivals Building.

COURTOWN HARBOUR (Wexford). H: a resort very popular with Irish families, it has four small pleasant hotels, *Courtown, Middletown House, Oulart*, all (2); *Ounavarra* (4).

CROSSHAVEN (Cork). H: *Grand* (2), 25 rooms with bath. *Compass Rose* and *Helm* are two smaller hotels in the resort, favored by Cork city people; both (3).
R: *The Cobbles* (I) converted farm-house with simple, good food and served in the garden in summer.

DALKEY (Dublin) is a smallish seaside spot linked to the long sweep of Killiney Bay to the south. H: *Cliff Castle* (2), 11 rooms. *Colamore* (3), 15 rooms, 5 with bath.

DELGANY (Wicklow). H: *Delgany Inn* (2), 11 rooms, 6 with bath.

DINGLE (Kerry). H: The *Sceilig* (1), 80 rooms with bath, spectacular location. *Dun an Oir Hotel*, 20 rooms, 8 with bath, has 10 cottages, each with accommodation for 6 to 8. A great place to hear folklore of Kerry.
R: *Doyle's Seafood Bar* (M) has excellent seafood.

DONEGAL (Donegal). H: *Central* (1), 44 rooms, half with bath. *National*, 16 rooms, 2 with bath; and *Abbey*, 19 rooms, 5 with bath, are both (2). All are well located for exploring the Donegal Highlands.
YH: *Ball Hill*, Donegal Town (32 men, 28 women) is located in a

274

IRELAND—TOWN BY TOWN

former coastguard station near the point of a headland between Donegal town and Mountcharles.

DOWNINGS (Donegal). H: Another away-from-it-all spot where the *Beach,* 24 rooms, 4 with bath, is (2) and well situated. Seasonal.

YH: *Tra na Rosann,* 18 men, 16 women, is the most northerly hostel in Ireland and in the Irish-speaking district of Ulster. The house was designed for its former owner by Sir Edward Lutyens.

DROGHEDA (Louth). H: *Boyne Valley, White Horse* and nearby *Rossnaree* all have about 20 rooms and are (2).

R: Cellar Grill (I), Laurence Street, is what the name implies.

DROMINEER (Tipperary). H: *Sail Inn* (3), 12 rooms, 3 with bath, small but wonderfully located on Lough Derg for fishing and sailing on the Shannon.

DRUMCONRATH (Meath). H: *Aclare House* (2) is in hunting country; 16 rooms, 5 with bath.

DUBLIN

HOTELS There has been a sharp increase in hotel accommodation but like most capitals, Dublin is short of middle-grade rooms at the height of the season. *Bord Fáilte Eireann* (Irish Tourist Board), **Baggot** Street Bridge, has a central reservations system for advance group bookings and the *Dublin Regional Tourism Organisation* office, 14 Upper O'Connell Street, can help late arrivals; it also has an office in the arrivals building at Dublin Airport, but early reservations are advisable when the travel schedule is set. A 12% service charge is put on the bill in the top grade hotels but in a number of others, it is best to check. If there is no service charge, a tip of 10% to 15% spread over the service staff is usual.

All in the (L) range are: **Jury's** in Ballsbridge, ten minutes from the city center, 314 rooms with bath, ballroom, restaurant, bar and rooftop *Martello Room,* which provides excellent food and breathtaking views; coffee shop has good menu.

Shelbourne, St. Stephen's Green, 166 rooms with bath; has a quiet dignity that is very much in accord with its century-old position in the top flight of Irish hotels. Two separate dining rooms and a grill bar well deserve their reputation for excellent food and fine service. There's a new Shelbourne Bar opening directly on the street which features snacks at lunch time.

Gresham, O'Connell Street, right at the hub of the city, 180 rooms, most with bath. The *Gandon Restaurant* and *Hunting Lodge Grill* are smart and first class. Downstairs bar, *The Malt*—colloquial name for Irish whiskey—is a public meeting place for Dubliners.

Royal Hibernian, Dawson Street, 93 rooms with bath, puts the stress on elegance; fine dining room and basement grill.

Those which are (**1**): *Burlington,* 435 rooms with bath, penthouse nightclub, sauna, heated pool.

Royal Dublin, O'Connell Street, 110 rooms with bath, popular grill room.

International Airport, Dublin Airport, 150 rooms with bath; a Trust House/Forte group hotel, conveniently located, with an atmosphere that's relaxed and comfortable.

Rated (**2**) are: *Clarence,* Wellington Quay, 70 rooms, 32 with bath, overlooking River Liffey, modern and comfortable.

Ashling, Parkgate Street, near rail termini for south and west, 50 rooms, half with bath, attractive restaurant, family-run with all the warmth that implies.

Buswell's, Molesworth Street, is good value, 64 rooms, 45 with bath. Located just across the street from Leinster House, seat of the Irish Republic's Oireachtas (parliament). Charges slightly above (**2**) rates.

Wynns' is one of Dublin's older hotels, 64 rooms, 16 with bath, located in Abbey Street, near the Abbey Theatre. It's been updated and has new restaurant.

Powers Royal, Kildare Street, small, centrally-located spot, 30 rooms, 17 with bath. Attractive bars and restaurant.

Wicklow, just off main shopping center, 40 rooms, 17 with bath.

Central, Exchequer Street, recently modernized, 50 rooms with bath.

Broc House, Nutley Lane, 30 rooms with bath, for students in winter but open to the public July-Oct.

Marine, 29 rooms, 13 with bath, pleasant edge-of-town location, good spot for golfers, heated pool. *Sutton House,* 20 rooms with bath, is in a converted mansion; maintains good reputation for food. Both in Sutton.

Skylon, Upper Drumcondra Road, ten minutes from city center on road to Dublin Airport, 88 rooms with bath.

Crofton Airport, Whitehall, 96 rooms with bath. On north side of the city, handy for Dublin Airport; rooftop restaurant.

Green Isle, Clondalkin, 56 rooms with bath, on southwestern side of city, just off main road to the south.

On the Stillorgan (or Bray) road, southeast edge of the city, the *Montrose,* 190 rooms, most with

IRELAND—TOWN BY TOWN

bath, located opposite the new campus of University College, Dublin, and near the studios of Radio Telefís Eireann, the Irish TV/radio service, is good for the visitor who does not want a city center location.

Also on the south side, on the road to Dun Laoghaire, *Tara Tower,* 84 rooms with bath.

Among the many hotels in the (3) range, many owned by families, are: *Mont Clare,* Clare Street, 30 rooms. *The Lansdowne,* Pembroke Road, not far from US Embassy, 30 rooms, 18 with bath. *The Embassy* on the same street is small but comfortable, 10 rooms. *Kenmore,* 120 Pembroke Rd., is another near the US Embassy, 10 rooms.

All (4) are: The *Lenehan,* Harcourt Street, 23 rooms. The *Pelletier,* on the same street, 33 rooms, 5 with bath; and yet another in this same area is the *Holyrood,* 29 rooms, 9 with bath. *North Star,* Amiens Street, 35 rooms, 8 with bath, convenient to Connolly Station, rail terminus for the north. *Ormond,* Upper Ormond Quay, 80 rooms, 32 with bath, is close to city center. *Montclare,* on Clare Street, at the corner of Merrion Square, has 30 rooms, 4 with shower; and a little further out from the center, the *Old Shieling,* Raheny, has 17 rooms, 12 with bath.

Dublin has a number of modestly priced **guesthouses** checked by the Irish Tourist Board and given graded listing. The majority are around the inside perimeter of the city. Few offer the facility of rooms with bath, but the *Mount Herbert,* Herbert Road, Ballsbridge (in the American Embassy district), has 88 rooms, 77 with bath. This is the largest, most having 5-12 rooms.

HOWTH on the north arm of Dublin Bay, has two hotels in the (2) caegory. The *Claremont,* 26 rooms, is close to the beach, and the *St. Lawrence,* 24 rooms, 2 with bath, overlooks the harbor.

The *Deer Park,* 25 rooms with bath, is an attractive estate; has a 9-hole golf course.

RESTAURANTS. As in most places in Ireland, the top hotels have excellent dining rooms that rate high in cuisine, wine cellars, decor and service. A few bars around the center provide light meals, mostly of the cold meat and salad variety, with a soup as a starter. *Neary's* in Chatham Street and *Mooney's* in Lower Abbey Street are both good spots. So is upstairs in *Lloyds,* North Earl Street. A little bit off the mainstream, *Searson's* in Upper Baggot Street, offers a good menu in pleasant surroundings. Other spots include *Slattery's,* Suffolk Street, and *Tobin's,* Duke Street. Remember that all bars shut down for an hour from 2:30 p.m. on weekdays. On Sundays, there is a two-hour closure from 2 p.m.

There are a number of coffee bars which can also offer light meals. In the

IRELAND—TOWN BY TOWN

Grafton Street shopping area there are several in the side streets but on the main line there is *Jonathan's*, near the top of the street, *Bewley's* lower down on the opposite side, another Bewley's in Westmoreland Street (near O'Connell Bridge) and a third in George's Street. The *Indian Tea Centre* in Suffolk Street is a favorite for those who enjoy a choice of blends of the beverage in pleasant surroundings. Some places put a 12% service charge on the bill; where they don't, a 10% tip is in order.

Wine lists in Dublin restaurants range from the elaborate to the unpretentious. Carafe wines are offered in most spots at reasonable rates and are usually easy on the palate, just right for the non-expert.

A sample listing of some of Dublin's restaurants is given below (most close early—those open late are so indicated).

Arnott's (I) in Henry Street, is a department store restaurant which presents a pleasant, reasonably priced lunch. Self-service, which is good if you're in a hurry.

The *Bailey* (E), in Duke Street, just off Grafton Street, has an attractive restaurant for relaxed dining with service that takes genuine interest in the patrons.

The *Bay Leaf* (M) in Pleasant Street has a high reputation; open late.

Bernardo's (E), Lincoln Place, is smallish but has a truly Italian cuisine, with Bernardo on hand to discuss preferences and make suggestions. Quiet, attractive; advisable to ring for a reservation. A place for an after-theater meal.

Berni Inn (I), Nassau Street, with four dining rooms and five bars, is associated with the English group. Good standard.

Captain America's Cookhouse (I) in Grafton Street, provides pleasant light meals in a fashionable shopping area.

Celtic Mews Restaurant (E), Lr. Baggot Street, another one of the good spots.

Charcoal Grill (I), Upper O'Connell Street, is just what its name suggests, but also offers a good range of other dishes. It's the sort of place where the waitress asks if the patron has enjoyed the meal and means what she says.

For Chinese dishes, *Chopstick* (M), in Dame Street, near the Olympia Theatre.

Dobbin's in Mount Street Mews (E) has a French character and invariably an interesting menu.

The *Europa* (M), Lr. Baggot Street, a comparatively new restaurant, open late.

The Golden Orient (E), 27 Lower Leeson Street, and *Tandoori Rooms* (E), at the same address, are right for oriental dishes, and particularly curries. Open late.

Gresham Hotel on O'Connell Street has a smart Georgian-style restaurant, the *Gandon Room* (E),

IRELAND—TOWN BY TOWN

with top cuisine and service; also *The Tain* (I), a smart, quick grill bar.

By Christchurch Cathedral, the *Lord Edward* (E), is a specialty seafood spot.

Good for Chinese food is the *Luna* (M), 11 Upper O'Connell Street, over shops near the Gresham Hotel.

Maxim's (M), in Clare Street, is a small restaurant which stays open late and has a good reputation.

There's an excellent restaurant with an attractive atmosphere in the *National Gallery* (M), on Merrion Square, closes at 6 p.m. most days, 9 p.m. Thursdays. Once a month, usually the third Thursday, there's a Painting of the Month Dinner which features a painting and an entertaining short talk by the gallery's articulate Director, James White.

In the heart of the old city, *Old Dublin* (E), at 91 Francis Street, is excellent for lunch or dinner, but phone for reservation.

Royal Hibernian Hotel (E), has gourmet-standard restaurants plus a rôtisserie and the *Bianconi Grill Bar* (I) in the basement.

Sach's (E), Morehampton Road, Donnybrook, for excellent food in this top-rated Regency restaurant; lunches served in the bar downstairs.

Shelbourne Hotel Restaurant (E), St. Stephen's Green. Famed for fine food in a delightful setting. Admirable wine cellar. Or try the *Saddle Room* (M) for roast beef and steak (also seafood); the *Grill Bar* (I) has inexpensive quick service meals.

The *Skandia* (M), Upper Baggot Street, is a recent late-night restaurant and also serves lunches.

Snaffles (E), Leeson St., is another small spot with outstanding food.

In Lincoln Place there's *The Squirrel's Nest* (M) which is a pleasant spot in the evening; it's near the back entrance to Trinity College.

Abbey Tavern (M), authentic tavern for admirable food plus bright ballad-singing. The *King Sitric* (M) is small but good for friendly service and seafood. Book early for either; both at Howth, on the north side of Dublin Bay.

The Leopardstown Inn's *Brewery Grill* (M), is nowhere near a brewery (that's disappeared long ago) but is close to Leopardstown racecourse, at Stillorgan, 5 miles from center. Good à la carte menu as well as grills. Also at Stillorgan is the *Beaufield Mews* (M), primarily an antique dealer's establishment, but also a pleasant place for dinner.

The *Goat Grill* (M), Goatstown, is an updated inn with busy bars and a pleasant restaurant.

The Lamb Doyle's (M), at Sandyford is half-way up one of the Dublin mountains but easily reached from O'Connell Street in about 15 minutes. Not only provides good food in comfortable surroundings but a wonderful panoramic view of Dublin and the coastline. For a window seat, early reservation is recommended.

IRELAND—TOWN BY TOWN

Oyster Grill (M), Ranelagh, about 10 minutes from city center, is excellent for steaks and top grade cooking. Best to book.

Overlooking Dublin Bay from the north, *Sutton House Hotel* (E), has a first class cuisine in elegant surroundings.

BEST BARS. *Palace Bar,* Fleet Street, is a meeting place for thirsty journalists and literati. *Davy Byrne's,* Duke Street, popular with students. *The Bailey,* Duke Street, is on a site which has been a hostelry since the seventeenth century. James Joyce mentions it in *Ulysses,* but under its original name of *Burton's* which was a billiards room and hotel. A popular meeting place for university students, literati and businessmen.

The *Horseshoe Bar* in the Shelbourne Hotel is a meeting place for VIPs of commercial, industrial and government circles, with a strong sporting element at the weekend. The *Gresham Hotel* bar is another meeting place for the top status people and the *Dubliner Bar* at Jury's is a good visitors' spot.

Sinnott's in South King Street is a likely place to meet up with actors, or they may be around the corner in *Neary's* of Chatham Street. There is another meeting place for theater folk in *The Plough,* in Abbey Street, not far from the Abbey Theatre. *Bowe's* in Fleet Street is a favorite spot for newsmen. The *College Mooney's* is a popular spot with students from Dublin University just across the road. The *Long Hall,* South Great George's Street, has a room on the left with a 19th-century atmosphere and some fine plates worth seeing; the *Brazen Head* in Bridge Street is reputedly the city's oldest bar, dating from 1666.

International Bar, Wicklow Street, catches the businessmen of Dublin. *Mooney's,* Abbey Street. *The Buttery* in the *Royal Hibernian Hotel* is a fashionable meeting place. *Madigan's* in North Earl Street is the place where you'll find a true cross-section of Dubliners. *Patrick Conway's,* opposite the Rotunda Hospital, is another pub with real Dublin character. It's also the nearest bar to the Gate Theatre which hasn't a bar!

There are some bars in the neighborhood of the docks and markets which have a special permit to open at 5 a.m. for the benefit of those "with business in the neighborhood".

"Singing Pubs" provide some good evening entertainment around the city. Some places have a cover charge, but the majority do not. Ballads are main attraction, although some offer vaudeville show. Around the city center, *Slattery's,* in Capel Street; *O'Mara's* at Aston's Quay, beside O'Connell Bridge; *McGovern's,* Wexford Street and the *Limelight Bar,* Thomas Street are representative. A bit out of town, *The Embankment,* Saggart; *The Chariot,* Ranelagh, and *Clontarf Castle,* Clontarf, are high on the popularity list. As some of them don't present shows every night it is worth checking the notices in the evening newspapers, or asking the hotel porter.

IRELAND—TOWN BY TOWN

NIGHTLIFE. *Jury's* at Ballsbridge offers nightly Irish cabaret. *Clarence Hotel,* Wellington Quay also presents regular Irish cabaret shows. There are no nightclubs in the international sophisticated sense of the word.

Weekends there is the Gaelic equivalent of square dancing, a *Ceilidh* (pronounced "kay-lee"). Your partner will show you the steps.

Fashions in discothèques vary, but the *Zhivago* in Baggot Street, and *Sloopy's,* Fleet Street, are among the most popular. *Good Time Charley's* on O'Connell Street is a good spot for the young; or try *Barbarella* at 76 Fitzwilliam Lane.

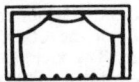

THEATERS. The famous *Abbey Theatre* has an impressive modern building on Marlborough Street. Company performs mainly Irish plays (in English); including those by W. B. Yeats, J. M. Synge, Seán O'Casey as well as new writers. If you take time out to look at the portraits of players of the past in the foyer, you'll recognize some famous figures who moved on to make movies in Hollywood; from Sara Allgood and Barry Fitzgerald to Siobhán McKenna and Cyril Cusack. *Peacock Theatre* in same building is used for experimental plays, sometimes of considerable interest; there is occasional lunch-time theater in the Peacock which offers drama in lively form. *Gaiety,* South King Street, grand opera, musical comedy, drama. *Gate Theatre,* Parnell Square, for modern drama and Irish plays (in English). *Olympia,* Dame Street, for modern drama and vaudeville.

Dublin is inclined to erupt in little theater groups: there's a pocket theater, the *Eblana,* in the basement of Busaras (the bus station); the *Project Theatre,* East Essex Street, is a spot where you'll often catch something interesting in the way of a new play. *Dublin University Players* have a tiny theater inside Trinity College at College Green where some outstanding work is to be seen. Bills in hotels and at the front gate of the college announce when the company is playing. *The Lambert Puppet Theatre* at Clifton Lane, Monkstown, about 4 miles out of town (south side) is also worth a visit.

Theater prices in Dublin are low by most big city standards. The *Dublin International Theatre Festival* (October) is the occasion for a concentration of new plays by Irish and foreign writers.

MUSIC. There are many musical groups in Dublin: the Trinity College Choral Society and the Palestrina Choir of the Pro-Cathedral, and other groups present concerts along with soloists, orchestras, and opera groups that come in to Dublin for special programs in winter. The symphony orchestra of Radio Telefís Eireann also presents regular public concerts. Recitals are given by visiting and Irish artists occasionally in

Trinity College Examination Hall and on Monday afternoons and evenings through the winter in the Royal Dublin Society's Concert Hall at Ballsbridge.

Inquire about recitals at St. Catherine's Church (no longer used as a church), Thomas Street; they're occasional but invariably worthwhile. The Abbey sometimes has Sunday night concerts and recitals. Connolly Auditorium in Liberty Hall is another spot for music and song, mostly ballads.

HOW TO GET ABOUT. It's very easy to get around Dublin by bus; many of the buses start out from the center of the city in O'Connell Street, northbound on one side of the street, southbound on the other, near the General Post Office building. Buses marked *An Lár* (The Center) have their terminus here, but many routes go right across town. Other bus termini are on quays adjoining O'Connell Bridge or D'Olier Street, College Street, Lower Abbey Street, and Parnell Square.

If you are good at walking there is a "Tourist Trail" sign posted through Dublin. It takes around three hours and the Dublin Tourism people have a booklet of supplementary information about the sights published at 10p.

The C.I.E. organization runs rail and bus tours in and around Dublin, at reasonable prices, from Central Bus Station, Store Street; among them, to (1) Liffey Valley and Blessington Lakes (all day). (2) Glendalough and Avoca (all day). (3) Glendalough (half-day). (4) Afternoon scenic drive around Dublin. (5) Sightseeing tour of city. For more particulars apply to C.I.E., 59 Upper O'Connell Street.

They offer many tours during the summer: By rail and road (from Connolly Station). (1) Inishowen Peninsula. (2) Hills of Donegal. (3) Donegal Bay and Southwest Highlands. (4) Glens of Antrim. (5) Mountains of Mourne. (6) Armagh (ecclesiastical capital). (7) Carlingford Peninsula. (8) Ards Peninsula. Train tours operate from Heuston Station to the south. Pearse Station is terminus for southeast and west.

Taxis: Taxis don't cruise on the streets but are confined to stands. These are located near main hotels and other strategic points. (Tel. 766666, 772222, 761111).

Car Hire: *Dan Ryan,* 42 Parkgate St.; *Avis,* 1 Hanover St. E.; *Budget Rent a Car,* Swords Rd.; *Ryans (Hertz),* 20 Pearse St.; *Kenning Car Hire,* 42 Westland Row.

IRELAND—TOWN BY TOWN

GUIDES. A tourist guide service is available in Dublin through the *Dublin Regional Tourist Organization,* 14 Upper O'Connell Street, Dublin 1, tel. 44718. Guides have been trained, and although the tourist organization will make the booking for individuals, tour operators or groups, payment is made direct to the guide. Rates per assignment (irrespective of numbers) are: up to half-day, £8; a full day, about £12. Bilingual guides (French, German, Spanish, Italian) and specialist guides (history, literature, architecture, shopping) are also available. Rates don't include transport, meals or entrance fees to entertainments.

SHOPPING. For *haute couture* you'll find international names. There's *Sybil Connolly* and *Raymond Kenna* on Merrion Square; *Ib Jorgensen,* 24 Fitzwilliam Square, and *Mary O'Donnell,* 43 Dawson Street. Best department stores for women are *Switzer's,* and *Brown Thomas's,* both on Grafton Street, and *Arnott's* on Henry Street (there's a smaller branch on Grafton Street), the area where you'll find many boutiques. For tweeds try *O'Beirne & Fitzgibbon,* Upper O'Connell Street, the *Weavers' Shed* in Duke Lane, off Grafton Street, or *Irish Cottage Industries* at 18 Dawson Street.

For best buys in Aran knitwear try the well-stocked *Creation Boutique* in Creation Arcade, Duke Street. For men's wear *F. X. Kelly* on Grafton Street. For souvenirs look in *Fergus O'Farrell's place,* Duke Street. For antiques there's *Fine Art Showrooms* in South Anne Street and *Danker's* just across the street, and *Louis Wine* around the corner on Grafton Street. *Gerald Kenyon,* South William Street, and *J. W. Weldon,* Anne Street, are other good antique shops in this area. There are more antique and furniture shops, such as the *Butler Sisters,* on the north quays from O'Connell Bridge towards the Four Courts, and if you chance on an auction at *Adam's,* St. Stephen's Green, you'll enjoy the excitement and maybe find a bargain.

Market Ireland, Grafton Street, have first-class handmade souvenirs and *Rionore of Kilkenny* have modern Irish silver jewelry at 38 Molesworth Street. *Royal Irish Silver* at 7 Prices Lane specialize in fine reproductions of the older designs of Irish silver. *Glencolumbkille Co-Operatives* at 17 Trinity Street feature much of the craft work done by the cottagers of Donegal in jewelry, knitwear, pottery, leather, suede, glass, embroidery and woodwork. For blackthorn sticks the place is *Johnston's* at 11 Wicklow Street.

The duty-free shop at Dublin Airport is available for transatlantic passengers flying via Shannon, and passengers on continental routes from Dublin, and prices are well below those at most European airports.

IRELAND—TOWN BY TOWN

MUSEUMS. *The National Museum of Irish Antiquities,* Art and Industrial and Natural History Divisions. Between Kildare and Merrion Street. Open 10 a.m. to 5 p.m. weekdays except Mondays, 2 to 5 p.m. Sunday. See the torques from Tara, the Tara brooch, the famed Ardagh chalice, and the Cross of Cong.

National Gallery, Merrion Square, 10 a.m. to 5 p.m. Monday to Friday, 10 a.m. to 1 p.m. on Saturday and 2 to 5 p.m. on Sunday; open for late viewing until 9 p.m. on Thursdays.

Trinity College Library has the famous *Book of Kells,* the richly ornamented book of the Gospels, considered the world's most beautifully illuminated manuscript. Open on weekdays 10 a.m. to 4 p.m. February-October; 10 a.m. to 3 p.m. November-January; Saturdays, 10 a.m. to 1 p.m. mid-July to mid-September. Porters at main gate (on College Green) will act as guides. Trinity College also has a museum of Biblical antiquities which may be visited by the public: contact J. Weingreen, M.A., Ph.D., Director, School of Hebrew and Oriental Languages, Trinity College, Dublin 2.

Chester Beatty Library, Shrewsbury Road, has a fine collection of Oriental and medieval manuscripts, including the oldest manuscript of the New Testament. Open Tuesday-Friday, 10 to 1, 2:30 to 5:30. Monday, 2 to 5:30.

Kilmainham Jail, Kilmainham, has a museum associated with the Irish fight for independence. Open on Sundays, 2 to 6 p.m.

Marsh's Library (near St. Patrick's Cathedral), founded in 1707, has an important collection of old books of theology and medicine, with Hebrew, Syriac, Greek and Latin literature. Open Mondays, Wednesdays, Thursdays and Fridays from 2 p.m. to 4 p.m. and on Saturday from 10:30 a.m. to 12:30 p.m.

The *Brewery Museum* at Guinness's Brewery is an industrial museum with a good section relating to the ancient craft of coopering (making wooden barrels); regular tours on weekdays.

Heraldic Museum, Dublin Castle, is part of the Genealogical Office, where family histories can be traced. It was from this building that the Irish Crown Jewels were stolen, just before a royal visit in 1907. Open weekdays 9:30 a.m. to 1 p.m. and 2:15 to 4:30 p.m.; Saturdays, 10 a.m. to 12:30 p.m.

Joyce Museum, Sandycove, has a collection of material associated with writer James Joyce, who once lived in this old Martello Tower. Open daily in summer from 11 a.m. to 4 p.m.

Hugh Lane Gallery of Modern Art, Parnell Square, weekdays (except Monday), 10 a.m. to 6 p.m. and Sunday from 11 a.m. to 2 p.m.

IRELAND—TOWN BY TOWN

Royal Irish Academy Library, open from 9:30 to 5:30 p.m. on weekdays and from 9:30 to 1 p.m. on Saturdays (closed last three weeks in August).

National Library of Ireland, Kildare Street, open weekdays from 10 a.m. to 10 p.m. and 10 a.m. to 1 p.m. on Saturday; closes for three weeks late July/August.

The fine *Civic Museum,* South William Street, full of interesting sidelights on old Dublin, is open at the same times as the Gallery of Modern Art.

There is an *Aviation Museum* at Dublin Airport. Check with the Information Officer (tel. 370011) on times of opening.

At Donard, Co. Wicklow (just outside Dublin), is a Transport Museum with interesting old vehicles.

PARKS AND GARDENS. *Phoenix Park,* main gate at end of Parkgate Street. *Zoological Gardens,* on right through main road of Phoenix Park, is the third-oldest zoo in the world, famed for breeding lions, some of which it exports. Many of its animals are in open range pens. *Botanic Gardens,* north side of city near Glasnevin Cemetery. *St. Stephen's Green,* at top of Grafton Street. *Herbert Park,* near Ballsbridge.

BANKS. Open weekdays 10 a.m. to 12:30 p.m. and 1:30 to 3 p.m. (5 p.m. on Thursdays), but they are closed on Saturdays. Bank of Ireland Group, Allied Irish Banks, Northern Banking Company, Ulster Bank, all have a number of offices in the city.

Bank of America, 27 Grafton St.; *First National Bank of Chicago,* St. Stephen's Green; *Chase and Bank of Ireland (International),* 10 College Green; *First National City Bank,* 71 St. Stephen's Green; *Bank of Nova Scotia,* St. Stephen's Green.

POST OFFICES. The General Post Office, O'Connell Street, is open to sell stamps, handle telegrams, registered and express mail on weekdays, 8 a.m. to 11 p.m.; other business, 8 a.m. to 8 p.m.; Sundays and holidays, 9 a.m. to 10:30 a.m. and 5 p.m. to 7 p.m. Branch post offices in the city are usually open from 9 a.m. to 6 p.m. on weekdays; some of the smaller offices close at 1 p.m. on Saturday. There is no delivery of letters on Saturdays in Dublin or Dun Laoghaire, but most big hotels collect their mail on that day. Post boxes may be green or orange in color.

IRELAND—TOWN BY TOWN

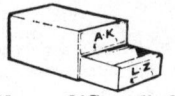

USEFUL ADDRESSES. *American Express*, 116 Grafton St. *Thomas Cook*, 118 Grafton St. *United States Embassy*, 42 Elgin Road, Ballsbridge. *British Embassy*, Merrion Rd. *C.I.E.*, 35 Lower Abbey St. *Aer Lingus*, Upper O'Connell St. *T.W.A.*, 44 Upper O'Connell St. *British Airways*, 112 Grafton St., opposite Trinity College, near American Express and Cooks. *Air Canada*, 4 Westmoreland St. *Automobile Association*, 23 Suffolk St. *City Air Terminus*, Busaras (the bus station), Store St.

The representation of all foreign countries in Dublin will be found in the telephone directory listed alphabetically under the heading "Diplomatic and Consular Missions". A similar heading in Part Two of the directory lists the addresses of foreign consular offices in Bantry, Clonmel, Cork, Cobh, Galway, Limerick, Sligo and Waterford.

TOURIST INFORMATION OFFICE. *Bord Fáilte Eireann* (Irish Tourist Board), Baggot Street Bridge (tel. 65871), *Irish Tourist Office*, 14 Upper O'Connell St. (tel. 44718) and at 51 Dawson St. (tel. 47733).

DUNDALK (Louth). H: *Ballymascanlon House*, 44 rooms, 24 with bath, is a converted mansion of character set in a pleasant garden overlooking Dundalk Bay, high, well-deserved ranking; the *Imperial*, 50 rooms with bath, in town and operated by the same family. Both are (1). *Derryhale*, on the landward side of the town, 21 rooms, 13 with bath or shower, is another of the converted mansion hotels. *Fairways*, south of the town, is on the main road to Dublin, 53 rooms, 30 with bath. Both (2).
R: *Angela's* (M), comfortable renovated hackney pub.
The modern (1971) Church of the Redeemer has sculptures by Oisin Kelly, Imogen Stuart and Michael Biggs, stained glass and mosaics from French artist Gabriel Loire.

DUNFANAGHY (Donegal). H: Another of Donegal's pleasant but remote places, has the excellent *Arnold's* (3), 40 rooms, 10 with bath; and *Carrig Rua*, 18 rooms.

DUNGLOE (Donegal). H: *Ostan na Rosan* (Hotel of the Rosses), 50 rooms with bath, is (2); indoor heated swimming pool.

DUN LAOGHAIRE (Dublin). H: *Royal Marine* (1) overlooks the harbor, 115 rooms, 90 with bath, it is an attractive hotel, modernized without destroying its character. *Ross's*, 42 rooms, 8 with bath, has a dining-room view of the sea; the *Avenue* (in the town), 27 rooms; and the *Pierre*, 32 rooms, 26 with

IRELAND—TOWN BY TOWN

bath; all three are (2). *Elphin* and *Victor* are (3). The range of guesthouses is long. Hotels and guesthouses here handle a lot of traffic for the car ferry to Britain.

R: *Realt na Mara* (M), on the south side of Dublin Bay, is in the top bracket for fish. (Closed Sun. and Mon.). *Hatters* (M), for excellent vegetables and seafood.

A tourist information office is on Marine Road.

DUNMORE EAST (Waterford). H: *The Haven*, 20 rooms, 3 with bath, and *Candlelight Inn*, 11 rooms, 7 with bath, are (2) and comfortable; latter has heated pool.

ENNIS (Clare). H: *Old Ground* (1) attracts many of Shannon's arrivals. An old building, carefully updated and extended, retaining plenty of character; 63 rooms with bath. *Auburn Lodge* (2), 20 rooms, 16 with bath, is on Galway Road, and the restaurant (M) is known for its beef stroganoff and scallops mornay. *Queen's* (3), 27 rooms. *West County Inn* is a motel, 50 rooms, most with bath.

ENNISCRONE (Sligo). H: *Benbulben House*, *Killala Bay* and *Atlantic* are small and inexpensive resort hotels.

ENNISTYMON (Clare). H: A convenient spot 32 miles from the airport, well located for golfers planning to play at Lahinch: the *Falls* (3), 39 rooms, 16 with bath.

FEAKLE (Clare). H: *Smyth's Village* (2), is a recent (1975) hotel built in old style with modern conveniences. Attractive atmosphere and setting. 12 rooms with bath.

GALWAY (Galway). H: *Great Southern* (L) overlooks the John F Kennedy Memorial Park, 128 rooms with bath, rooftop pool, several good dining rooms, friendly service, Irish Night entertainments through the season. *Ardilaun House*, on Taylor's Hill, 68 rooms, most with bath; and *Corrib Great Southern*, just outside the city, 117 rooms with bath; both are (1).

All in the (2) grade and around Kennedy Sq. are the *Imperial*, 72 rooms, 36 with bath; *Odeon*, 60 rooms, 31 with bath; and *Skeffington Arms*, 21 rooms, 5 with bath. Also (2) are the *Anno Santo* and *Sacre Coeur*. The *Galway Ryan*, 100 rooms with bath, is a motel on the Dublin side of the city; *Flannery's Motel*, nearby, 72 rooms with bath; both are (2).

There are many modestly priced guest-houses in the neighborhood including *Ardeen* at Rockbarton; *Capri*, Oaklands; *Gentian Hill House*, Knocknacarra; *Muskerry House*, Gentian Hill, *St. Anne's*, Woodquay.

R: The *Great Southern Hotel* (E) has a character dining room on the ground floor, the *Seomra Cois Farraige* (M) ("Coast Room") on the lower floor for Irish specialties and light meals and a sophisticated rooftop-room, the *Claddagh Grill* (E), where you can see the sun go down on Galway Bay. The *Old Galway Grill* (M) in Shop Street has a medieval atmosphere. *Lydon's*

IRELAND—TOWN BY TOWN

(I), also in Shop Street, is good for a quick grill or snack. *Ty Ar Mor* (M), excellent luncheon crepes and good dinner service.

A: *Taibhdhearc na Gaillimhe*, Galway's Gaelic Theatre, presents plays in Gaelic and has contributed some outstanding artists to the Irish stage, including Siobhan McKenna. *Seoda* is a well-staged traditional entertainment. Salthill Pavilion and Seapoint Ballroom are the spots for dancing in the Galway area. Westport House has a zoo park.

There is a tourist information office at Arus Failte (tel. 091-3081).

Salthill is a lively seaside resort adjacent to Galway. Hotels which are in the (2) grade are: *Banba, Beach, Galway Bay, Oslo, Rockland,* and *Warwick*. The Warwick is the largest with 70 rooms, 30 with bath, and the center of much of the convivial life of the resort.

Modestly priced guesthouses are: *Fermoyle House, Osterley Lodge* and *Lochlurgain* (Upper Salt Hill).

A: There is a large entertainment center in the resort.

There is an *airstrip* of 640 metres at Oranmore, near Galway; contact: Galway Airways, Galway (tel. 84105). Oranmore has a service to the Aran Islands.

Car hire: *Avis*, 6 Francis St.; *Hertz*, 5 William St.; *Dan Ryan Rent-A-Car — Godfrey Davis*, Higgins Garage Ltd., Headford Rd.

GARRETTSTOWN (Cork). H: *Coakley's Atlantic* (2), 40 rooms, 24 with bath, has a splendid setting overlooking the Atlantic and an attractive beach.

GLENBEIGH (Kerry). A quiet seaside spot with more than a fair share of scenic beauty. H: The *Towers*, 21 rooms, 4 with bath, has bar collection of antiques, paintings and cartoons, outstanding for food; also, *Glenbeigh*, 21 rooms, 4 with bath; both are (1) and run by the same family. *Falcon Inn* (3), 15 rooms, has a grill (I).

GLENCOLUMBKILLE (Donegal). H: On the Rosguil Peninsula, *Glenbay* (2), 20 rooms, has a traditional Irish family hotel atmosphere and own boat to visit Rathlin O'Beirne Island and the deep-sea fishing grounds in "The Sound".

GLENDALOUGH (Wicklow). H: *Royal* (2), 34 rooms, 10 with bath, located right in the historic valley.
R: *Armstrong's Barn* (M), closed Sun. and Mon. *Laragh Inn* (M), for good service and food.

GLENGARRIFF (Cork). Traditional tourist center of West Cork. H: *Casey's* (1), 22 rooms, 5 with bath. *Eccles*, 65 rooms, 16 with bath, pool; *Golf Links*, 21 rooms; also, *Blue Pool;* all are (2).

One-half mile off shore and reached by boat from Glengarriff, is *Ilnacullin*, sometimes called Garnish Island or Bryce's Island after the owners who made the gardens, now one of the great showpieces of Ireland. The island exhibits a remarkable collection of exotic plants and trees gathered from many parts of the world, all thriving in this pleasant climate; also incorporates a delightful Italian garden. Open weekdays, 10 a.m. to 5:30 p.m.; Sundays and Holy Days, 1 to 6 p.m.; landing charge is 50p.

IRELAND—TOWN BY TOWN

GLEN-OF-THE-DOWNS (Wicklow). H: *Glenview* (1), 23 rooms with bath, with a cuisine worth traveling far to enjoy.

GLENTIES (Donegal). H: The *Highlands* (3), as the name suggests, is close to the mountains at the meeting of two glens, 22 rooms.

GORTAHORK (Donegal). H: *McFadden's* (2) is one of the best-known hotels in the northwest; 35 rooms, 5 with bath.

GREYSTONES (Wicklow). H: *La Touche* (1), 55 rooms, 18 with bath. The pleasantly located *Woodlands* (2), 16 rooms, 7 with bath, has a deserved reputation for its food.
R: The *Copper Kettle* (M) is first class.

HOWTH (see DUBLIN).

JENKINSTOWN (Kilkenny). YH: *Foulksrath Castle* (16th-century), 30 men, 16 women.

KANTURK (Cork). H: *Assolas* (1), is a 16th-cent. country house with a friendly atmosphere and award-winning cuisine. *Isle of Skye* (2), 16 rooms, half with bath. Attractive spot for exploring West Cork and Kerry.

KELLS (Meath). H: *Headfort Arms*, top (3), 22 rooms, 3 with bath. Situated in the town but convenient for hunting.
The Monastery of Kells is here.

KENMARE (Kerry). H: *Great Southern* (1), 60 rooms, over half with bath, a one-time bishop's palace carefully converted and standing on its own grounds. *Kenmare Bay*, 50 rooms with bath; and *Riversdale House*, 40 rooms, most with bath; both (2).
R: *The Purple Heather Bistro* (M).

KILCULLEN (Kildare). R: *The Hide-Out* (I), a good place to stop off for a grill.

KILKEE (Clare). H: Popular coastal resort with the *Royal Marine* (3), 43 rooms, 7 with bath. *Thomond*, 26 rooms, 5 with bath; and *Esplanade*, 15 rooms, are both (4).

KILKENNY (Kilkenny). H: *Newpark*, (1), modern, 46 rooms, 33 with bath, attractive setting, bar and dining room. *Rose Hill House*, 13 rooms, 3 with shower, period house well converted; *Club House*, 39 rooms, 8 with bath, fine collection of old *Spy* cartoons. Both are (2).
R: For a meal in a colorful setting, *Kyteler's Inn*.
The Kilkenny Archaeological Society has a museum in Parliament Street, open weekdays, May-Sept., Tues., Thurs. and Sat., 3-5, Oct.-April, and Sun. all year, 3-5.
There is a private airfield (grass runway) 1½ miles west of Kilkenny —longest runway is 595 yards; P. Nolan. Limited customs facilities on 48 hrs. notice.

KILLALOE (Clare). Lovely lakeside spot on shore of the Shannon. H: Appropriately named *Lakeside* (2),

28 rooms, 16 with bath. *Ballyvalley* (3), 15 rooms with bath, also overlooks the lake from the Ennis-Killaloe road. Good center for water-skiing and sailing.

KILLARNEY (Kerry). H: *Great Southern* is another excellent establishment in the chain run by a subsidiary of C.I.E. (national transport co.), 165 rooms with bath, very pleasantly located; *Dunloe Castle*, 140 rooms with bath; and *Europe*, 168 rooms with bath, bowling alley, indoor pool; all are (1), only Europe operates year round.

Those in the (1) class are: *Aghadoe Heights*, recent, 46 rooms with bath, overlooks Lower Lake, attractive restaurant and bar; *Castlerosse* with 49 rooms all with bath; *Cahernane*, 40 rooms, half with bath; *International* (in town), 128 rooms, 77 with bath; *Three Lakes*, 76 rooms, 70 with bath; *Lake*, 79 rooms, 44 with bath; and *Torc Great Southern*, 96 rooms with bath.

The *Gleneagle*, 56 rooms, 34 with bath; and the motels, *Whitegates Inn* and *Killarney Ryan* are (2).

There is plenty of accommodation in the (3) grade: *Arbutus*, 40 rooms, half with bath; *Dromhall*, 57 rooms; *Glen Eagle*, 63 rooms, half with bath; *Grand* on Main Street, 30 rooms; *Castle Heights*, 30 rooms; *Ross*, 40 rooms half with bath.

Top of a long list of guest houses are *Pine Grove*, College Street, *Castle Lodge*, and *Cooldruma*, Muckross Road. *Linden House*, New Road, is another excellent guesthouse and a top place for food.

R: *Aghadoe Heights Grill Bar* (M) overlooking the Middle Lake and the *Linden* (M) on New Road is excellent (wine license only): booking for dinner advised. If you want to picnic, *Shepherd's Inn* near Moll's Gap on the Killarney-Kenmare road, supplies packed lunches.

A: During the season there are "Irish Nights" at the leading hotels. Irish traditional dancing and entertainment is staged six nights a week in the Old Town Hall. A repertory company stages Irish plays (in English) in the Town Hall and Aras Phádraig; the Kerry Drama Festival in the spring attracts a strong display of amateur talent. If you see *Siamsa* billed anywhere in Kerry, go and see it: an excellent (if romanticized) view of rural life.

There is a tourist information office in the town hall (tel. 064-31633).

Car Hire: *Murrays-Pal Rent a Car*, Culloty's Garage, Market Place.

KILLINEY (Dublin). H: *Fitzpatrick's Castle* (1), 48 rooms with bath, indoor pool and saunas. The *Court* (2) is closer to the beach.

R: *Rollard* (E), view across Dublin Bay from this French restaurant.

KILLORGLIN (Kerry). H: *Bianconi Inn*, 20 rooms, has a restaurant, *The Stables* (I) with a high reputation; *Castle*, 7 rooms; and *Goat Inn*, 6 rooms. All are (3).

IRELAND—TOWN BY TOWN

Puck Fair is staged here in mid-August.

KILLYBEGS (Donegal). H: In summer, the hotel school becomes *Killybegs Hotel*, 34 rooms, 18 with bath. Located in major angling and scuba-diving center.

KINGSCOURT (Cavan). H: *Cabra Castle* (2), 24 rooms with bath, offers gracious living in a castle on a golf course.

KINSALE (Cork). H: *Acton's* (owned by Trust Houses), 68 rooms, 32 with bath, overlooks the harbor, heated pool; *Trident*, modern and built around boat quays, 40 rooms with bath, restaurant and bar. Both built out over the sea and are open to non-residents; both hotels are (1).

R: Three top restaurants, *Gino's* (M) in the Market Square; *Man Friday* (M) and *The Spinnaker* (M) both at Scilly.

Most unusual museum of the region is in the 16th-century courthouse. Centerpiece is a scale model of the *Kinsale*, one of the ships built in the Kinsale dockyard in 1700; the model was made from the original drawings. Harpoons recall the town's association with whaling, while other weapons and models made by French prisoners during the Napoleonic Wars recall Kinsale's storied past. This is one for the "must" list. Open weekdays 4 to 6 p.m.; Saturdays, 11 a.m. to 1 p.m.

KINVARA (Galway). YH: *Doorus House*, 16 men, 17 women—this house has a special interest because it was here that the first discussion took place between W. B. Yeats, Lady Gregory and Edward Martyn, leading to the founding of the Abbey Theatre.

A: *Dun Guaire Castle:* dining and top entertainment is offered for about £5. Banquets are twice nightly at 6 p.m. and 9 p.m., May through September.

KNOCKFERRY (Galway). H: *Knockferry Lodge* (3), 10 rooms, 2 with bath. This remote guesthouse has become known for its simple and comfortable atmosphere, and for its home-made food.

KYLEMORE (Galway). H: *Kylemore Pass*, 11 rooms, half with bath, in a great away-from-it-all location for a touring base.

LAHINCH (Clare). H: *Aberdeen Arms* (2), 55 rooms, most with bath. *Claremont*, 40 rooms, 2 with bath; and *Atlantic*, 21 rooms; both (3). Golf center and seaside resort.

LEENANE (Galway). H: Overlooking the deep Atlantic inlet of Killary Harbour is the *Leenane* (2), 42 rooms, 14 with bath, seasonal.

LETTERKENNY (Donegal). H: The *Ballyraine* (1), 56 rooms with bath. *Gallagher's* (2), 19 rooms, 2 with bath. Good touring area.

LIMERICK (Limerick). H: *Jury's* 96 rooms with bath; and the recent *Limerick Inn*, 120 rooms with bath, are both (1). In the (2) category are: *Cruise's Royal*, 80 rooms, 55 with bath, on O'Connell St. *Hanratty's*, 43 rooms, 28 with bath, and the *Limerick Ryan*, a motel with 208 rooms, most with bath, are especially pleasant. *Parkway Hotel* is on the edge of the city on the Dublin road, 100 rooms with bath. There are several inexpensive guesthouses including *Alexandra House*, 5/6 Alexandra Terrace; *Ballineen* and *Ennismore*, both on the Ennis Road, and *Springmount* on Shelbourne Road.

R: *Brazen Head Grill*, *Ted's* and *Merryman* are good spots and all (M).

There is a tourist information office on 62 O'Connell Street (tel. 061-47522).

For taxis, railway station (8 a.m.- 11 p.m.) tel. 46825. Thomas Street (9 a.m.-midnight), tel. 45550 and 46230. For car hire, Dan Ryan, 27 O'Connell St., tel. 45566.

There is an *airstrip* at Coonagh, 2 miles northwest of Limerick, longest runway (grass and consolidated surface) 518 meters. Limited customs facilities for outbound passengers only; operated by *Shannon Flying Services, Ltd.*, Coonagh.

LISCANNOR (Clare). H: The *Liscannor* (1), 36 rooms with bath, close to spectacular Cliffs of Moher.

LISDOONVARNA (Clare). Still famous for its spa and a very lively spot in the fall. H: *Imperial* (1), 53 rooms. *Keane's*, 16 rooms, most with bath; *Carrigan*, 12 rooms, most with bath; and *Lynch's*, 23 rooms, are all (2). *Spa View*, 19 rooms, is (3).

LISMORE (Waterford). On the River Blackwater, good for anglers. H: *Ballyrafter House* (3), 14 rooms, 4 with bath.

The gardens of Lismore Castle are open Tues.-Fri., 2-5 p.m., from mid-May to Sept.

LISTOWEL (Kerry). H: *Listowel Arms* (2), 37 rooms, most with bath. A literary center and a popular race course.

LOUISBURGH (Mayo). H: Up near the sea-angling grounds of Clew Bay is the *Old Head* (2), 22 rooms, 8 with bath. *McDermott's Tourist* and *Clew Bay* are (4). All are seasonal.

MALAHIDE (Dublin). H: The *Grand* (2), located beside the sea, has elegance without being oppressive, 59 rooms, 23 with bath. Has Ireland's largest indoor riding school.

R: *Johnny's* (M) is first-rate.

The grounds of Malahide Castle are open to visitors on Wednesdays and Fridays during the summer.

MALLOW (Cork). H: *Longueville House* (1) is a peaceful mansion on Killarney road; the restaurant is good value.

Mallow Castle Museum (open weekdays, May-Sept.) has relics of three centuries including those of an ancestor who was on H.M. Stanley's African expeditions.

IRELAND—TOWN BY TOWN

MONAGHAN (Monaghan). H: *Four Seasons*, 24 rooms with bath; *Hillgrove*, 28 rooms, 21 with bath; both (1). *Westenra Arms* (2), 24 rooms, 4 with bath.

MOSNEY (Meath). Butlin's only Irish *holiday camp* is on the coast, 1,555 rooms, 489 with bath. All the entertainments associated with a holiday center open from May until late September. Some self-catering accommodation is available.

MOYARD (Galway). H: *Crocnaraw*, is a first-class guesthouse, with a restaurant (M) which specializes in fish dishes.

MULLAGHMORE (Sligo). H: The *Beach* (2), 22 rooms, 9 with bath, pool.
Near Classiebawn Castle.

MULLINGAR (Westmeath) is in hunting country. H: The *Greville Arms* (1), 27 rooms, 11 with bath, well organized for golfers and fishermen.

MULRANY (Mayo). H: *Great Southern Hotel* (1), 71 rooms, 46 with bath, is in a beautiful country setting, heated pool, seasonal, pony trekking in the neighborhood. There are several guesthouses in this lovely district, among them *Avondale House*, *Moynish*, and *Aisling House*.

NENAGH (Tipperary). H: *O'Meara's*, 42 rooms, 20 with bath; and *Ormond*, 20 rooms, 13 with bath or showers, are (2). Same family owns the *Nenagh Motor Inn* on the Dublin Road, 20 rooms with bath. Puckane, a village of 100 inhabitants, six miles from Nenagh, has several centrally-heated, fully-furnished thatched cottages for renting on a self-catering basis; home help is available. Contact Rent-an-Irish Cottage at Shannon Airport.

NEWBRIDGE (Kildare). H: *Keadeen* (1), 20 rooms with bath, a converted mansion outside Newbridge, on the edge of the Curragh, headquarters of Irish racing.
R: *Jockey Hall* (E), a Georgian house near the racecourse, good food. *The Red House Inn* (E), just off the main road between Naas and Newbridge (advisable to book).

NEWMARKET-ON-FERGUS (Clare). H: *Dromoland Castle* (L), expensive, 67 rooms with bath. The present castle was built around 1825 and transformed a few years ago into a luxury hotel in a baronial setting (350 acres) with excellent sports facilities. *Clare Inn* (1), 121 rooms with bath, located on same estate with same sports facilities, magnificent view.

NEWPORT (Mayo). H: *Newport House* (1), 30 rooms, most with bath, seasonal. Area known for the fresh-water angling.

NEW ROSS (Wexford). H: An old mansion, overlooking the River Barrow, has been modernized to become the pleasant *Five Counties Hotel* (1), 35 rooms, 27 with bath.
R: *Galley Cruising Restaurant*

IRELAND—TOWN BY TOWN

for a tour on the rivers Barrow and Suir; operates daily April through October. Dinner or lunch about £3.50 and £2.50 respectively.

J. F. Kennedy Park is just south of New Ross at Slieve Coillte; the forest garden there is open daily, 10 a.m. to 6 p.m.

OUGHTERARD (Galway). Angling is the main activity in this area. H: *Oughterard House* (1), 33 rooms, 20 with bath. *Egan's Lake* (2), 24 rooms, 16 with bath. *Connemara Gateway Motor Hotel*, 48 rooms with bath, seasonal. A guesthouse, *Currarevagh*, is in a peaceful setting and noted for its service and food; also seasonal.

PARKNASILLA (Kerry). H: The *Great Southern* (L) sits in a subtropical garden setting beside the sea, 75 rooms, 58 with bath, indoor heated pool, quiet comfort and good food.

PONTOON (Mayo). H: *Pontoon Bridge* (2), 24 rooms, 10 with bath. Another favorite angling resort of the west.

PORT-NA-BLAGH (Donegal). H: The *Port-na-Blagh* (2), 60 rooms, 23 with bath, has a high reputation. *Shandon*, (2), 63 rooms, half with bath. Both are seasonal.

PORTNOO (Donegal). H: *Lake House*, 12 rooms, 8 with bath; *Portnoo*, 20 rooms; both (3) and in a great exploration district. Seasonal.

PORTSALON (Donegal). H: A north spot worth visiting. The *Portsalon*, 30 rooms, all with bath, has a high reputation. Seasonal.

RATHKEALE (Limerick). A: *Castle Matrix*, about £5 for a banquet and top entertainment, twice nightly at 6 p.m. and 9 p.m., May through Sept. (tel. Rathkeale 139 to book).

RATHMULLEN (Donegal). Another good spot on the Rosguil Peninsula. H: *Rathmullan House* (1), 41 rooms, 29 with bath, has chalets and good restaurant. *Port Royal* (2), 28 rooms, 9 with bath. Both seasonal.

RATHNEW (Wicklow). H: *Hunter's* (2), 17 rooms, 5 with bath.

RATHVILLY (Carlow). H: *Lisnavagh House*, built in 1848 in Victorian Gothic; modernized: offers old world comfort and 1,100 acres of space, (2).

RENVYLE (Galway). *Renvyle House* (1), once the home of Oliver St. John Gogarty; 70 rooms, most with bath. In top bracket for cuisine, particularly for seafood straight from the nearby Atlantic. Seasonal.

ROBERTSTOWN (Kildare). A: From May through September there are candlelight banquets in a one-time canal hotel. Charge is around £5 and includes canal barge trip, museum visit and entertainment. Check time with Tourist Office.

ROCHESTOWN (Cork). H: *Norwood*

IRELAND—TOWN BY TOWN

Court Hotel (2), 12 rooms with bath, has links with William Penn (who stayed here before setting out for Pennsylvania) and with novelist Charles Dickens; the incident which gave him the story for "Great Expectations" is said to have taken place in the old house.

ROSAPENNA (Donegal). H: *Rosapenna* (1), modern, is close to one of the finest golf courses in the country, 40 rooms with bath. Seasonal.

ROSCOMMON (Roscommon). H: The *Abbey* and *Royal* are small, comfortable, and (4).

ROSSES POINT (Sligo). H: *Yeats Country Ryan* (2), motel beside the international championship golf course and looking towards the sea and the mountains, has 79 rooms with bath.

ROSSLARE (Wexford). H: *Rosslare Great Southern* (1), modern, 100 rooms with bath, heated pool, sauna, overlooks the harbor; *Strand Hotel*, 95 rooms, 73 with bath, right on beach, heated pool, a hotel with a strong family tradition, and tops for food; both (1). *Golf Hotel* (2), 25 rooms, 13 with bath, pleasant and popular with visitors using the neighboring championship golf course.

ROSSNOWLAGH (Donegal). H: *Sand House* (1). 45 rooms, 15 with bath, another of County Donegal's best-known resort hotels; seasonal. A great spot for surfing.

ROUNDWOOD (Wicklow). R: *Roundwood Inn* (M), outstanding for character, comfort and cuisine.

SCHULL (Cork). H: *East End*, 17 rooms with bath.
R: Fresh crab soup and freshly-caught turbot are specialties at *O'Keffe's* (M); closed Sept. to Easter.

SHANAGARRY (Cork). R: The Yeats Rooms at *Ballymaloe House* (E) is where Cork people take their distinguished visitors for dinner (lunch isn't served). Phone Midleton 62531 in advance before making the trip (about 16 miles).

SHANNON AIRPORT (Clare). H: *Shannon International* (1), owned by Dromoland Castle's Bernard McDonough, is right at the airport, 126 rooms, all with bath; perfectly sited for a quick trip.

R: The cuisine of *Shannon Airport's* restaurant (E) is better than that of most airports.

There is a tourist information office in the main concourse of the airport (tel. 061-61664).

Passengers outward bound through Shannon Airport can stock up at the *Duty Free Store,* Europe's largest duty-free shopping which offers a large range of perfumes, cigarettes, cameras, watches, suits, dresses and fabrics. The store also operates a *Mail Order Service* through which goods can be ordered personally or by post for mailing to any part of the world. Passengers traveling to the US and Canada from

IRELAND—TOWN BY TOWN

Ireland can give their orders for duty-free liquor and cigarettes at Dublin Airport before boarding the aircraft for Shannon. When the plane touches down at Shannon the order is ready to be put on board, leaving more free time for browsing around the store to check up on the many other bargains . . . and having another Irish Coffee just so that you keep the taste fresh in your memory when you get home. Incidentally, you can buy Irish Coffee glasses, and a towel with details of the recipe and technique.

Car Hire: *Avis, Budget, Flannery's, Hertz, InterRent, Murrays-Pal, Kenning Car Hire, Dan Ryan.*

SKERRIES (Dublin). H. *Holmpatrick House* (2), 39 rooms, 11 with bath. Pleasant base for touring and for golfers.

SKIBBEREEN (Cork). On an inlet of Baltimore Bay. H: *Eldon,* 26 rooms, 7 with bath; and *West Cork,* 41 rooms, half with bath; are (2).

SLANE (Meath). H: The *Conyngham Arms* (3), 14 rooms, 11 with bath. This is hunting country.

SLIGO (Sligo). H: *Jury's,* 60 rooms with bath; *Great Southern,* 58 rooms. 28 with bath; and *Ballincar House,* 18 rooms, 14 with bath; are all (1). The *Silver Swan,* 24 rooms, half with bath; and *Clarence,* 20 rooms, 2 with bath; are both (2). *Kelly's* (3).
R: *Nine Bean Rows* (E) at Knocknahur, near Sligo, specializes in Mexican food.
A: The Sligo Feis Ceoil and the Feis Shligigh, held at Easter, are major competitive music festivals, the latter concentrating on Irish music, singing and dancing.

There is a tourist information office on Stephen Street (tel. 2436).

SNEEM (Kerry). H: *Cantharella Motel,* 16 rooms with bath.

THURLES (Tipperary). H: *Hayes's Hotel* has 44 rooms, 16 with bath; *Anner* has 15 rooms, 3 with bath; both (3).

TIPPERARY (Tipperary). Tipperary isn't the principal town in the county (Clonmel is), but it has one (2) hotel: *Royal,* 20 rooms, 2 with bath.

TRALEE (Kerry). H: *Mount Brandon,* 164 rooms with bath, has a big ballroom with entertainment; *Ballyseede Castle* (15th-cent.), well updated, 13 rooms, most with bath; *Earl of Desmond,* 52 rooms with bath. All three are (1).

Benners, 56 rooms, 17 with bath, long established and particularly known to anglers, is welcoming; and *Manhattan,* 21 rooms, 2 with bath, are both (2). *Horan's Motel,* 12 rooms with bath, is pleasant. Guesthouses at attractive rates are *Kinard House,* Oakpark, and *Oakley House,* Ballymullen, small but comfortable.

R: The *Old Brogue Inn* has a good antique bar with the atmosphere of the time when the Rose of Tralee lived hereabouts. Oak settles, old lamps, open fire, copper

IRELAND—TOWN BY TOWN

utensils, all recall the days when shoemaking (brogue=shoes) was a great craft in the neighborhood.

TRAMORE (Waterford). Tramore, 8 miles south of Waterford city, is very busy in the summer season. H: *Majestic* (1), 91 rooms, 58 with bath, indoor heated pool. *Grand* (2), 50 rooms with bath. (3) are: *Sea View, Atlantic, Shalloe's Cliff* and *Tramore.*

The number of guesthouses is substantial, with *Ocean View* on the Esplanade (18 rooms) at the top of the list and modestly priced. Smaller and with low prices are *Central, Clarence,* and *Crobally House,* Riverstown.

VALENTIA ISLAND (Kerry). Connected to the mainland by a road bridge. H: The *Royal* (2), 48 rooms, 20 with bath, is a good base for island exploration, fishing, shooting and skin-diving. There are two inexpensive guesthouses on the island, *Ring Lyne* and *Valentia Heights.* The latter has a restaurant (M) with a high reputation.

VIRGINIA (Cavan). H: *Park Hotel* (1), 34 rooms, 17 with bath, in a fine old stone house in the middle of a golf course sloping down towards Lough Ramor; good fishing, which, like the golf, is free. Park has a dozen courtyard cottages for rent on weekly basis, with tenants using hotel facilities at will. *Virginia Lake,* (2), 19 rooms, 8 with bath, is, as the name suggests, also handy for local fishing.

WATERFORD (Waterford). H: *Ardree,* 100 rooms with bath, on height overlooking River Suir and the port; *Tower,* 100 rooms with bath or shower; both modern and (1). *Dooley's,* 26 rooms, 4 with bath; *Metropole,* 21 rooms, 2 with bath; *Maryland House,* 28 rooms, 8 with bath or shower; all are (2). Guesthouses include *Diamond Hill, Mandalay House* and *Portree,* all (4).

The gardens at the estate of Mount Congreve can be seen by appointment; famous for an 18th-century conservatory.

The Waterford Glass Works is worth seeing (check times for free tours).

There is a tourist information office at 41 The Quay (tel. 051-5788).

Car Hire: *Murrays-Pal Rent a Car,* Sheridan's Garage, The Mall.

WATERVILLE (Kerry). Once upon a time only the anglers knew about Waterville, but the news has spread to discriminating travelers who've never cast a line.

H: Delightfully located *Waterville Lake* (L), 102 rooms with bath, near championship golf course. *Butler Arms* (1) has a long and well-maintained reputation, 45 rooms, 10 with bath. There are some fine paintings in the sun porch. Good base for pony-trekking and sand-yachting holidays.

Also (1) are: *Ostlann Rinn Rua,* 45 rooms with bath; and *Bay View,* 29 rooms, 8 with bath, which has what its name promises, and the management is helpful about special interests around, and has a booklet of archeological notes and map. The *Jolly Swagman* is a well-run motel, 20 rooms with bath, in a pleasant out-of-town location.

IRELAND—TOWN BY TOWN

WESTPORT (Mayo). H: *Jury's* (1), 58 rooms with bath, is operated by the same company as in Dublin, Cork and Limerick. (2) are: *Clew Bay*, 35 rooms; *Cavanaugh's*, 18 rooms, some with bath; and *Westport*, 49 rooms all with bath. Guesthouses include *Riverbank House*, *Rosbeg House* and *Angler's Rest*.

WEXFORD (Wexford). H: *White's*, 100 rooms, 60 with bath, modern but linked with an historic coaching inn and run by same family for three generations, particularly popular during Wexford Festival; *Talbot*, 116 rooms, 90 with bath, plenty of lounge space and scores high on service; both are (1) and have top restaurants. *Bargy Castle* (2), 18 rooms, some with four-poster beds, 10 with bath, built in the 12th century and modernized; shooting, fishing, riding.

A: The famous *Opera Festival* takes place here every October at the Theatre Royal. *Mumming*, a traditional entertainment in southeast Wexford, is worth inquiring about. It is not presented on an organized scale, but the tourist offices will know when the Mummers are likely to be seen—and where.

There is a tourist information office on the Crescent Quay (tel. 053-23111), and there is also a voluntary corps of guides; members call to hotels in the evening to assist visitors who want information.

Car Hire: *Murrays-Pal Rent a Car*, Meyler's Garage, Redmond Place.

WICKLOW (Wicklow). H: The *Grand* (4) 18 rooms, 2 with bath.
R: *Knockrobin House* (M), is peaceful and provides wholesome food with a German touch.

YOUGHAL (Cork). Seaside resort popular with city folk. H: *Hilltop*, 50 rooms with bath, attractive view; and *Monatrea House and Country Club*, 19 rooms with bath; both are (2). *Walter Raleigh* and *Harbour View* are (3). Several pleasant guesthouses, among them *Avondhu* and *Darwin*.

ENGLISH-IRISH
VOCABULARY

ENGLISH-IRISH VOCABULARY

Although nearly everyone in Ireland speaks English, you may wish to try your hand at the Irish language (often referred to as "Gaelic"), especially when you are out in the western parts of the country. Please note that the pronunciations given below are only approximate, and are designed for ease of understanding rather than for accuracy as such!

Useful Phrases

ENGLISH	IRISH	PRONUNCIATION
Welcome	Fáilte	*faw*ltye
Thank you	Go raibh maith agat (*singular*)	Gura *moh*aguth
	Go raibh maith agaibh (*plural*)	Gura *moh*agwiv
Good day, evening	Dia dhuit (*sing.*) Dia dhíbh (*pl.*)	Deeagwich, Deeayeev
—*reply*	Dia's Muire dhuit (*sing.*)	Deeas*mwir*agwich
	Dia's Muire dhíbh (*pl.*)	Deeas*mwir*ayeev
Good night	Oíche mhaith	*Ee*ha woh
How are you?	Conas tá tú? (*sing.*)	*Kun*as *thaw* thoo
	Conas tá sibh? (*plural*)	*Kun*as *thaw* shiv
	or	
	Cén chaoi a bhfuil tú (sibh)?	*Kaykh*wee will thoo (shiv)
	or	
	Goidé mar tá tú (sibh)?	Gwid*jay* mar *tha* thoo (shiv)
Well, thank you	Go maith, slán a bhéas tú (sibh).	Gu *mah*, slawn a *vayse* thoo (shiv)
Fine	Go breá	Gu *braw*
Tired	Tuirseach	*Thir*shock
A fine day	Lá breá	Law braw
A wet day	Lá fliuch	Law flukh
A "soft" day	Lá bog	Law bug
It is cold	Tá sé fuar	Thaw shay *fooar*
It is hot	Tá sé te	Thaw shay *teh*
Good-bye	Slán	slawn
	Beannacht	Ban-okhth

ENGLISH-IRISH VOCABULARY

ENGLISH	IRISH	PRONUNCIATION
Please	Más é do thoil é *or* Led' thoil	Mawshay dhu hell ay Leh-*dhell*
Excuse me	Gabh mo leithscéal	Gow mu *lehshkhayl*
Forgive me	Maith dhom é	*Moh* gum ay
What time is it?	Cén t-am é?	Kane *thow*may
Are you ready?	'bhFuil tú ullamh?	Will thoo *u*lav
Wait a moment	Fan nóimeat	Fohn *no*math
Where is . . .?	Cá bhfuil . . .?	Kaw will . . .
Here is . . .	Seo . . .	Shuh . . .
That is it	Sin é	*Shin* ay
I understand	Tuigim	*Thig*im
I do not understand	Ní thuigim	Knee *hig*im
Do you understand?	An dtuigeann tú? (*sing.*)	A *dhig*an thoo
	An dtuigeann sibh? (*pl.*)	A *dhig*an shiv
Irishman	Eireannach	*Ayra*nokh
Irish language	Gaeilge	*Gway*lig
English language	Béarla	Barela

Hotels, Restaurants, Bars

Hotel	Tigh ósta	Tea *ohs*tha
Restaurant	Bialann	*Bea*lan
Bar, tavern	Tigh tabhairne	Tea *thawr*nyeh
Food	Bia	*Be*-ah
Drink	Ol, deoch	Ole, dyukh
Room	Seomra	*Show*mrah
Bed	Leaba	*Lab*ah
Breakfast	Bricfeásta	Brick*faws*tha
Luncheon	Lón	Lone
Tea	Tae	Tay
Dinner	Dinnéir	Din*air*
Supper	Suipéir	Sup*air*
Meat	Feol	Fyole
Fish	Iasc	Ee-ask
Menu	Carta	*Kawr*-tha
Soup	Anra	*On*-ra
Egg	Ubh	Uv
Cheese	Cáis	Kawsh
Beef	Mairtfheol	*Mart*yole
Mutton	Caorfheol	*Queery*ole
Bacon	Bagún	Bawgoon
Ham	Liamhás	Leevaws
Sausage	Ispín	Eeshpeen

302

ENGLISH-IRISH VOCABULARY

ENGLISH	IRISH	PRONUNCIATION
Sandwich	Ceapaire	Kapareh
Cup	Cupán	Kupawn
Plate	Pláta	*Plawthah*
Knife	Scian	*Shkee*an
Fork	Forc	Furk
Spoon	Spiúnóg	Spyoonoge
Napkin	Naipcín	Napkeen
Glass	Gloine	Glinye
Bottle	Buidéal	Budyale
Salt	Salann	Sohlan
Pepper	Piobar	Pyubar
Mustard	Mustárd	Musthawrd
Sauce	Anlann	Onlan
Wine	Fíon	Feen
Whiskey	Uisce beatha	*Ish*ke *ba*ha
Ale	Lionn	Lyun
Stout	Lionn, dubh, pórtar	Lyun dhuv, porther
Pint	Pionta, piúnt	*Pyunth*ah, pyoonth
Half-Pint	Leathphionta, leath-phiúnt	Lah*fyun*tah, lah-*fyoonth*
Half-glass	Leathghloine	*Lath*glineh
Lemon	Liomóid	Li*moh*dj
Orange	Oráiste	U*rawsh*teh
Fruit	Toradh	Thorough
Vegetable	Glasra	Glossrah
Jam	Subh	Suv
Ice cream	Uachtar oidhre	Ookthar ireh
Water	Uisce	Ishke
Ice	Oidhir	Ire
Raw	Amh	Of
Cooked	Bruite	Britje
Hard	Cruadh	*Kroo*-ah
Soft	Bog	Bug
Hot	Te	Teh
Cold	Fuar	Fooar
Early	Moch	Mukh
Late	Mall	Moll
Call	Glaoch	Glayukh
Service	Freastal	*Frass*thal
Lounge	Tolglann	*Thula*glan
Sitting-room	Seomra suí	*Showm*rah *see*
Radio	Raidió	Radio
Television	Teilifís	Tellafeesh
Newspaper	Nuachtán	Nookh*thawn*
Magazine	Iris	Irrish
Book	Leabhar	Lyowr
Telephone	Teileafón	Telephone

ENGLISH-IRISH VOCABULARY

ENGLISH	IRISH	PRONUNCIATION
How much?	Cé mhéid?	Kay vaidj
Change	Briseadh	*Brish*ah
Bill	Bille	*Bill*eh
Waiter	Freastalaí	*F*rasthalee

Shops and Shopping

Draper	Eadaitheoir	*A*ydhehor
Shirt	Léine	*Lay*neh
Handkerchief	Ciarsúir	Keer*shure*
Tobacconist	Tobacadóir	Tha*back*adhore
Cigarette	Toitín	Thityeen
Tobacco	Tobac	Tha*bock*
Cigar	Todóg	Thad*hoge*
Grocer	Grósaera	Grow-sarah
Tin	Canna	*Konn*ah
Bread	Arán	Arawn
Butter	Im	Eem
Biscuits	Brioscai	Briskee
Chemist	Potaicéara	Puthakareh
Toothbrush	Scuab fiacal	Skoob feekal
Toothpaste	Taos fiacal	Thays feekal
Razor	Rásúr	Rawsoor
Blades	Lanna	Lonnah
Powder	Púdar	Poodhar

Other Useful Words and Phrases

Post Office	Oifig an Phoist	Effig a *Fwisht*
Church	Eaglais, séipéal	*Og*lish, shaypale
Catholic	Caitliceach	*Kath*lickokh
Protestant	Protastúnach	Prutha*sthoona*kh
Garage	Garáiste	Ga*rawsht*eh
Car	Carr, gluaisteán	Kawr, glue-shtyawn
To hire a car	Carr a fhostú	Kawr a *ust*hoo
Station	Stáisiún	Sthawshoon
Train	Traen	Thrayn
Timetable	Amchlár	*Omkh*lawr
Picture	Pictiúir	Picktyoor
Postcard	Carta poist	Kawrtha *pwisht*
Airport	Aerphort	*Air*furth
Airplane	Eiteallán	Ettyalawn
To book, reserve	Airithint	Awrahint

ENGLISH-IRISH VOCABULARY

ENGLISH	IRISH	PRONUNCIATION
Cheap	Saor	Sare
Dear	Daor	Dhare
Shilling	Scilling	Shkilling
Sixpence	Réal	Rale
Penny	Pingin	Pingin, peen
Pound	Punt	Poonth
Today	Inniu	An*you*
Yesterday	Inné	An*yay*
Tomorrow	Amárach	Am*aw*rakh
I am going away	Táim ag imeacht	*Thaw*im a gimokhth
I am going out	Táim ag dul amach	*Thaim* a dhull amokh
Key	Eochair	Ukhir
Stamp	Stampa	Sthampa
Dictionary	Foclóir	Fuclore
Map	Léarscáil	Layrskawl
Bank	Banc	Bonk
Money	Airgead	*Arri*gadh
Check	Seic	Sheck
To cash a check	Seic a bhriseadh	Sheck a *vrish*eh
Travelers' check	Seic thaistealaí	Sheck hashthalee

INDEX

INDEX

In this Index we use the following symbols: "A" for Entertainment; "H" for Hotels; "R" for Restaurants; "S" for Sports; "Sh" for Shopping; "YH" for Youth Hostels.

Abbeyleix, 122
Achill, 72
Achill Island, 210; H267
Adare, 185, 251, 258; H267
Aghada, 160
Aghadoe, 176
Aghamore, 213
Aghla Mountain, 221
Aherlow Glen, 148
Annagh, 181
Antrim Glens of, 282
Anure Lough, 220
Aran Islands, 82-4, 86-7, 183, 196, 198-9, 202-4, 246; H267
Ardfert, 55, 182
Ardmore, 55, 162-3
Ardnacrusha, 192
Ards Peninsula, 282
Arklow, 112, 124; HA 267
Armagh, 228, 249-50, 282
Arranmore Island, 212, 220; H267
Arrow Lough, 67
Ashford, 124; H267
Ashford Castle—see also Cong—H207
Athea, 189
Athlone, 56, 150-2, 251-2; S230, 255; H267
Athy, 122
Aughavanagh, 125
Avoca River, 124, 282

Balbriggan, 114
Ballina (Co. Mayo), 69; HS268
Ballina (Co. Tipperary), 150
Ballinahinch Lough, 205

Ballinascarthy, H268
Ballinasloe, H268
Ballinrobe, 206-7, 246
Ballinskelligs Bay, 179
Ballintober Abbey, 209-10
Ballybofey, 217; H268
Ballybunion, 184-5; H268
Ballycotton Bay, 72, 161; H268
Ballydehob, 168
Ballyferriter, 184
Ballyfree, 246
Ballyhack, 136
Ballyhoura Mountains, 148
Ballylickey, 168; H268
Ballymacward Castle, 216
Ballymahon, 119
Ballymascanlon, 118
Ballymore, 251
Ballymote, 215
Ballynagaul, 162
Ballynahinch, H268
Ballyporeen, 148
Ballysampson, 132
Ballyshannon, 54, 56, 119, 216, 250
Ballyvaughan, 196, H244, 268
Ballyvourney, 170
Baltimore, S78, 168-9, 255
Baltray, S77
Banagh, 219
Banagher, 153
Bandon, H268
Bandon River, 166
Banna Strand, 182
Bansha, 149
Bantry, 167-8, 258; HA268

Bantry Bay, 168, 172, 258-9
Barleycove, H268
Barna, 204; H269
Barnesmore Gap, 217
Barrow Navigation, 135
Barrow River, 69, 122, 131, 133, 135-6, 192, 252
Beara Peninsula, 171
Belleek, 216, 250
Belturbet, 250
Bennettsbridge, 131
Bertraghboy Bay, 204
Bettystown, 114-15; HR269
Birr, 122-3
Blackrock, 144
Blackstairs Mountains, 139
Black Valley (Cummeenduff Glen) 175
Blackwater River/Valley (Munster Blackwater), 154-5, 161, 163-4
Blackwater River (Co. Meath), 161
Blackwater River (Co. Wexford), 161
Blarney, 166, 234; H269
Blarney Castle/Stone, 165-6, 228, 251, 259, 269
Blasket Islands, 54, 171, 179, 184
Blessington Lakes, 78, 126, 282; S255
Blessington Village, 126; H269
Blue Stack Mountains, 217
Boliska Lough, 69

309

INDEX

Borrisokane, HR269
Boyle, 209; H269
Boyne River/Valley, 68 112, 115-17, 233; S115
Brandon Bay, 183
Brandon Mount, 171, 183
Bray, 92, 112, 124, 126; H269
Bridgend, 250; H269
Bulloch, 124
Bunbeg, H269
Buncrana, 218
Bundoran, 215-16; HS 216, 230, 251, H269
Bundrowes River, 68
Bunratty Castle—*see also* Old Bunratty — 187, 234, 251, 259; HA269
Bunratty Folk Village, 27, 229, 259
Burren, 196
Burtonport, 220

Caha Mountains, 171, 180
Cahercivcen, 178, 184
Caherdaniel, 180; H270
Cahir, 145-6, 148, 259; HR270
Callan, 130
Camp, 182-4
Campile, 135-6
Cappoquin, S78; 163-4
Caragh Lough, 69, 178; H270
Carlingford/Lough 117-18, 282
Carlow, S78; 127, 131; H270
Carna, 204
Carndonagh, 218
Carra Lough, 67
Carrantuohill, Mount, 175, 177-8
Carraroe, 204; H270
Carrick-on-Shannon, S78; 215, 230, 251-2; HS270

Carrick-on-Suir, 146-8; H270
Carrickart (Carrigart), 218-19, 244, H270
Carrickmacross, 250; H270
Carrigaline, 166
Carrigamore Lough, 205
Carrigart—*see* Carrickart
Carrowmore, 215
Cashel, 55, 143-5, 259; H145, 270; R270-1; S270
Cashel Bay, H271
Cashel Rock, 144-5, 149, 271
Cashelmore, 219
Castle Archdale, 252
Castlebar, 209, 246; H271
Castleblayney, 250
Castlecove, 179
Castledermot, H271
Castlefin, 250
Castlegregory, 183
Castlepollard, 119, 251, 260
Castlerea, 259
Cavan, 119
Cavan County, 67, 73, 113, 118-19
Celbridge, 120, 259; A271
Cheekpoint, 136, 139
Clare County, 67, 77, 174, 185-7, 189, 202, 234
Clarinbridge, 60, 208
Classiebawn Castle, 216
Clear Island, 168-9
Clew Bay, 210; S292
Clifden, 205, 230; S204-5; HR271
Clogheen, 148, 163-4
Clogherhead, 117
Cloghran, 246, 250
Clonakilty, 251
Clonbur, 206
Clones, 250

Clonfert, 183
Clonmacnois, 151-2
Clonmel, S77; 146-7, 160; H271
Clontarf, 40, 93, 98-9, 144; A280
Clounanna, S77
Cloyne, 161
Cobh, 159-60; RS160; 237; H271—*see also* Cork
Coleraine, S78
Collon, 117
Comeragh Mountains, 139, 148
Cong, 55, 206-8; HS271
Conn Lough, 66-7, 69
Connacht Harbour, S150
Connemara, 68-9, 85, 198-9, 204-6, 229, 233-4, 251
Convoy, 217
Coonagh, 246, 292
Cooley Peninsula, 117-18
Cork, 21, 40, 54, 61, 63; S77-8; Sh81, 273; 155-9, 165, 169, 228-9, 234, 237-8, 245-52, 260; A230, 273; H272; R61, 272; YH244
  arts, 156, 158, 274
  churches, 156, 158-9, 161
  museums, 273-4
  University College, 156—*see also* Cobh
Cork County 22, 67, 69, 72, 144, 148, 154ff, 167ff, 171, 177, 228, 243, 251, 254
Cork Harbour, 159
Corofin, 194-5; H244
Corrib Lough 66-9, 199, 204-6
Corrib River 200, 205
Courtmacsherry, 167
Courtown Harbour, H274

INDEX

Craggaunowen Castle, 190
Creeragh, 206
Creeslough, 219
Creevykeel, 215
Crew Lough, 55
Croaghan Hill, 218
Croaghnamaddy, 219
Croagh Patrick Mountain, 230
Crolly, 220
Crosshaven, HR274; S255
Cuildrevne, 214
Culdaff, 218
Cullin Lough, 69
Cummeenduff Glen
—see Black Valley
Curragh race track, 73-4, 121, 230
Currane Lough, 69

Dalkey, H274
Dalkey Island, 124
Deenish Island, 180
Delgany, H274
Derg Lough, 66-7, 78, 141, 150, 153, 193, 216-17, 252
Derravaragh Lough, 67
Derry, 217, 252
Derrynane, 179-80
Derrynasaggart Mountains, 170
Derryveagh Mountains, 220
Devil's Bit Mountains 142, 144
Dingle, 183; HR274
Dingle Bay, 175, 178, 184
Dingle Peninsula 72, 171, 181-3
Doe Castle, 219
Donegal, 217; H274; YH274-5
Donegal County, 68-9, 82, 86, 119, 212, 215, 218-22
Donegal Highlands, 212, 216, 229, 282
Donnybrook—see under Dublin
Dooagh (Achill Island), H267
Dooney, 213
Downies
—see Downings
Downings (Downies), 219; H275; YH275
Dowth, 55, 116
Dripsey, 169
Drogheda, 63, S78; 114-15; HR275; churches 115
Dromineer, 150; HS275
Drumcliff, 212-14, 216
Drumconrath, HS275
Dublin, 21-2, 25-9; A32, 52-3, 98-9 108, 229, 231, 280-2; 40-2, 46-8, 52-3, 56-9, 61-3; S66, 73-80, 101, 111, 229-31, 253-5; Sh81, 86, 106, 283; 91-126, 135, 192, 227-30, 232-7, 239, 242, 245-52, 255-8, 260, 275-86; H275-7; R61, 63, 277-80; YH244
arts, 52-3, 59, 92-4, 98-9, 101-4, 106-7, 110
Ballsbridge, 75, 111, S204, 254; 230, 285; H277; A281
churches, 94, 99-101, 103, 105-6, 108-11, 137
Croke Park, 79, 229; Custom House, 94-5, 100; Donnybrook, 105; R279; English Pale, 42, 112-13, 131; Howth, 113, 259; H277; R64; S277; Merrion Square, 94, 103-4, 284
museums, 106-9, 111, 208, 284-5
O'Connell Bridge, 94-5, 101, 282-3; Parnell Square, 98-9, 282; Phoenix Park, 74, 91, 94-5, 100-1, 285; Ranelagh, A280; Saggart, A280; St. Stephen's Green/Square, 92, 94, 105-6, 145; Sh283; 285, Sandyford, R279; Stillorgan, R279
Trinity College, 21, 51, 91, 101-3, 107, 110, 117, 123, 207, 257, 284; University College, 21, 35, 105, 277

Dublin Airport, 246-7, 249, 285
Dublin Bay, 23, 60, 64, 95, 113, 290
Dublin Castle, 92, 108, 258-9, 284
Dublin County, 22, 77, 113-14
Dublin Mountains, 92
Dun Aengus, 203
Dundalk, 63, 112, 117, 230, 249, 286; HR286
Dun Conor, 203
Dun Eochla, 203
Dunfanaghy, 219, 251; H286
Dunganstown, 135
Dungarvan, 130, 162
Dungloe, 220; H286
Dun Guaire/Castle, 187, 190, 196, 208, 229, 234
Dun Laoghaire, S78, 255; 80, 123-4, 237, 255, 260; H286-7; R287
Dunlewy, 220
Dunloe Castle/Gap
—see Killarney

311

INDEX

Dunmanway, 167
Dunmore East, 139; H287
Dunquin, 184
Dysert O'Dea 194

Ea Lough, 221
Edgeworthstown (Mostrim), 119
Egish Lough, 118
Emly, 149
Ennel Lough, 67
Ennis, 194; H234, 287
Enniscorthy, 131-2
Enniscrone, H287
Enniskerry, 259
Ennistymon, H287
Erne Lough/River, 119, 229, 252
Erriff River, 206
Errigal Mountain, 220

Fahan, 218
Fairyhouse, S74; 229
Falcarragh, 220
Fanad, 218
Farranfore, 246
Feakle, H287
Fenit, 182
Fergus River, 186, 194
Fermoy, 165
Fern Lough, 69
Ferrycarrig, 132
Finn Lough, 221
Finn River, 217
Fore, 251
Forty Foot Island, S80
Foyle Lough, 212
Friar's Island, 193

Galty (Galtee) Mountains, 141, 148-9, 164, 177
Galtymore, 148
Galway, 68; S74; 79; 86, 183, 197-200, 202, 204-6, 208-9, 229-30, 245-6, 251-2, 260 H199, 287; R287-8; A200.. 288
  churches, 200, 202, 229
  Salthill, S79, 202; 123, 202, 204; HA 288; Oranmore, 202, 246-7, 288
  University College, 21, 202
Galway Bay, 60, 187, 196, 200, 202, 204, 208; S230
Galway County, 67, 69, 75, 79, 183, 196-8, 204
Gara Lough, 209
Garavogue River, 213
Garnish Island (Ilnacullin), 168-9, 259, 288
Garrettstown, H288
Garrykennedy Quay (Lough Derg), 150
Gartan Lough, 69
Gaugin Mountain, 221
Giant's Causeway, 72
Gill Lough, 213
Glanaskagheen, 181-2
Glanmire, 165
Glashaboy River, 165
Glaslough, 118-19
Glasnevin, 99
Glasson, 251
Glenbeigh, 178; H288
Glencan Lough, 214
Glencolmcille, H244, 288; R288
Glencolumbkille, 221
Glendalough, 55, 112, 125-6, 228, 282
Glenealy, 251
Glengarriff, 167, 169, 172, 180, 259; H288; Ilnacullin, 288
Glen-of-the-Downs, H289
Glenties, 221; H289
Goold's Cross, 146, 259
Goramullin, 180

Gorey, 131
Gort, 198, 208
Gortahork, 220; H289
Gougane Barra Lake, 168
Gowlane, 196
Gowran Park, S74, 229
Grand Canal, 121-2, 135, 153, 252
Grange, 216
Greenore, 249
Greystones, 124; HR289
Gur Lough, 193-4
Grianan of Alleach, 217
Gweebarra Bay, 212, 220
Gweebarra Lough, 69
Gweebarra River, 212, 220
Gweedore, 220

Haulbowline Island, 160
Hayes' Island, S150
Headford, 208
Headfort, 246
Holmpatrick, 113
Holy Island (Inis Cealtra), 193
Horn Head, 219
Howth—see under Dublin
Howth Head, 92, 113

Inacullin—
  see Garnish Island
  and Glengarriff
Inchagoill, 205
Inchigeelagh Lakes, 167
Inis Cealtra—
  see Holy Island
Inishbofin, 205-6
Inishark, 205
Inisheer (Aran), 196, 202; H267
Inishmaan (Aran), 196, 202, 267
Inishmore (Aran), 202, 246, 267; H267

312

INDEX

Inishmurray Island, 216
Inishowen Peninsula, 217, 282
Inishturk, 205
Inniscarra, 169
Innishannon, 250
Inniskeen, 118
Inny River, 119
Islandbridge, 78, 92

Jenkinstown, YH289

Kanturk, H289
Keel (Achill Island), H267
Keem Bay, 210
Keimaneigh Pass, 167-8
Kells, 103, 116-17; H289
Kenmare, 180-1, 290; HR289
Kenmare Peninsula, 171
Kenmare River, 180
Kerry, Ring of, 171-2, 177-8, 180, 228, 251
Kerry County, 67-9, 169, 171ff, 228, 243, 254, 290
Kerry Head, 171, 185
Kesh, 215
Key Lough, 209, 215
Kilcar, 222
Kilconry, 186
Kilcullen, 121; R289
Kildare, 121
Kildare, Curragh race track—*see* Curragh

Kildare County, 75, 113
Kildowner Castle, 210
Kilfenora, 195-6
Kilkee, H289
Kilkenny City/County, 63, 87, 128-31, 136, 229-30, 246, 260; HR289
Kilkieran Bay, 204
Killaloe, S78, 150, 192-3, 230, 252, 255; H289-90, 290

Killarney, S66-7, 77, 253; 69, 169-70, 172, 174-6, 180-1, 228, 233-4, 245, 251-2, 259; HR290; A290
  Dinis Island, 174-6; Dunloe Castle, 175; Dunloe Gap, 175-6; Innisfallen Island, 176-7; Long Range, 175; Lower Lake (L. Leane), 172, 175-6, 290
  Mangerton Mountain, 175-7; Meeting of the Waters, 175-7; Middle Lake, 175-6, 290; Muckross Abbey/Estate, 172, 174-5, 259
  Torc Mountain/Waterfall, 175, 177; Upper Lake, 175
Killary, 206
Killeany, 203
Killeen, 249
Killibegs, 219, 221-2; H291
Killimer, 174, 185
Killiney/Hill, 124; HR290
Kilkee, S255
Killorglin, 177-8, 230; H290, A291
Kilmacduagh, 209
Kilmacow, 136
Kilmore, 135
Kilworth Mountains 164-5
Kimego West, 178-9
Kincora, 193
Kingscourt, H291
Kinsale, 72, 160, 166-7, 291; HR291; S255
Kinvara, HA291
Kinvara Castle—*see* Dun Guaire

Knappogue Castle, 189-90, 229, 234, 259; A269-70
Knockalla Mountain, 218
Knockcosgrey Hill, 123
Knockeen, 140
Knockferry, H291
Knockmealdown Mountains, 141, 148, 163
Knocknarea Mountain, 215
Knowth, 55
Kylemore, H291
Kylemore Abbey, 206
Kylemore Lough, 206

Lady's Island, 134
Lahinch, S77, 195, 291; 195; H291
Lambay, 39, 114
Laois/County, 122, 258
Laracor, 117
Laragh, 125
Larne, 238-9
Laune River, 175, 178
Leane Lough—
  see Killarney (Lower Lake)
Lee River/Valley, 154-6, 160-1, 167-9
Leenane, H291
Leenaun, 206
Leighlinbridge, 131
Leitrim County, 197, 212
Leixlip, 119
Lemaneagh Castle, 195
Leopardstown, S73-4, 229, 231; R279
Letterkenny, 217-18; H291
Liffey River/Valley, 68, 78, 91-3, 95, 100-1, 109, 282; S231, 253
Lifford, 250
Limerick, 40, 44; R61, 292; S74, 78-9, 231; 190, 192-3; Sh192;

313

INDEX

229, 248, 251, 260, 263; H291-2
National Institute of Higher Education, 21
Limerick County, 75, 77, 149, 177, 184-5, 189
Liscannor, S77; 195, H292
Lisdoonvarna, 196; H292
Lismore, 148, 161, 164; H292
Lissoy, 55, 251
Listowel, 184; HS292
Little Island, S77
Londonderry, 239
Longford, 119, 251
Longford County, 73, 119
Loughrea, 209
Louisburgh, HS292
Louth County, 113, 117
Lucan, 119

Maam Cross, 205
Macgillycuddy's Reeks, 175, 178
Macroom, 167, 169
McSwyne's Bay, 221
Mahon Lough, 160
Malahide/Castle, 114; HR292
Malin, 218
Malin Head, 212, 218
Mallow, S74, 174; H292
Manorhamilton, 214, 250
Marble Hill, 219
Mask Lough, 66-7, 206
Matrix Castle, 190
Maumturk Mountains, 205-6
Maynooth, 21, 23, 120; St. Patrick's College, 21, 23
Mayo County, 69, 87, 197, 209

Meath County, 22, 55-6, 74, 103, 112-13, 116
Melleray Mount, 163
Mellifont, 55; Abbey, 117
Melvin Lough, 216
Middle Lake—
see Killarney
Midleton, 163
Milford, 218
Miltown-Malbay, 195
Mitchelstown, 148, 163-4
Mizen Head, 168
Moher Cliffs, 234, 292
Monaghan, 118-19, 250; H293
Monaghan County, 73, 118
Monasterboice, 117
Monasterevin, 121-2
Monkstown, 113, 123-4
Moone, 122
Mosney, H293
Mostrim—
see Edgeworthstown
Mourne Mountains, 112, 118, 125, 228, 282
Moy River, 69, 230
Moyard, H293
Muckish Mountain, 219-20
Muckross—
see Killarney
Muff, 218, 250
Mullaghmore, 216; H293
Mullarany, 210
Mullingar, S74, 293; 112, 119, 251, 260; H293
Mulrany, H293
Mulroy Bay, 218
Munster Harbour, S150
Myrath, 220

Naas, S74, 229; 120
Nafooey Lough, 206

Navan, S74
Neagh Lough, 66
Nenagh, 149-50; S255; H293
Newbridge, 120-1; HR293
Newcastle West, 185
Newgrange, 112, 116, 228
New Grange, 55
Newmarket-on-Fergus, H293
Newport, 143; HS293
New Ross, 133, 135-6; H293; R293-4
Newtowncunningham, 217
Newtown Hamilton, 249
Nore River, 68-9, 131, 136

Offaly, 67, 103, 122
Oghill, 203
Old Bunratty, 189
Old Ross, 135
Oranmore—
see Galway
Oughter Lough, 119
Oughterard, 204-5; S230, 294; H294
Owel Lough, 67
Owenea River, 221

Parknasilla, 180; H294
Partry Mountains, 206
Passage East, 136, 139
Pettigo, 250
Pollnagollum, 196
Pontoon, HS294
Portlaoise, 122
Porkmarnock, S77; 113-14
Port-na-Blagh, 219; H294
Portnoo, H294
Portrush, S77-8
Portsalon, 218; H294

314

INDEX

Portumna, 150
Poulaphuca Lake—
see Blessington
Punchestown, S74-6, 229

Quin, 189, 259; A269-70

Ramor Lough, 119
Rathfarnan, 113, 125
Rathkeale, 190; HA294
Rathmullan, 218; H294
Rathnew, H294
Rathvilly, H294
Recess, 205
Ree Lough, 151, 153, 209, 252
Renvyle, H294
Rineanna, 186
Ring of Kerry—
see Kerry
Riverstown, 165; A294
Rochestown, H294-5
Rosapena, 219; HS295
Roscommon, 51, 208, 251; H295
Roscommon County, 197, 209
Roscrea, 142, 144
Rosguil Peninsula, 219
Rosmuc, 204
Ross Castle, 172, 175-6
Rosses, The, 86, 220
Rosses Point, S77, 295; H295
Rosslare, S77, 295; 127, 134, 238-9; H295
Rossnowlagh, HS295
Roundstone, 205
Roundwood, H295
Royal Meath—
see Meath County

St. Johnston, 250

St. MacDara's Island, 204
Sallybrook, 165
Saltee Islands, 127, 135
Salthill—
see Galway
Sandycove, S80
Sandyford—
see Dublin
Scariff Island, 180
Schull, HR295
Shanagarry, RA295
Shangarry, 161
Shankill, 250
Shannon, 22, 185-96, 249, 251; Upper 73
Shannon Airport, 22-3, 27, 30; Sh81, 234, 236, 283, 295-6; 171, 186-7, 189-90, 202, 227, 229, 234, 236-7, 244, 246, 248-9, 252, 256, 263; HR295
Shannon—the Burren, 187, 195-6
Shannon Harbour, 122, 153, 252
Shannon River, 63, 78, 122, 135, 141, 150-3; S151, 230, 255; 171-2, 185, 192, 209, 228, 252, 270
Shannonbridge, 152-3
Shantonagh, 118
Sheelin Lough, 67
Sheep Haven, 212
Sherkin Island, 169
Silvermine Mountains, 142, 149
Skellig Rocks, 179
Skerries, H296
Skibbereen, H296
Slane/Hill of, 55; HS296
Slaney River, 68, 132
Slieve Beagh Mountains, 118
Slieve Coillte, 135, 294

Slievemore, 211
Slievenamon/Valley, 146-7
Slieve Felim Mountains, 143
Slieve League, 221
Slieve Mish Mountains, 182
Slieve Miskish Mountains, 171
Slieve Snaght, 217
Sligo, 212-16, 229, 251-2, 260; HRA296
churches, 213; museums, 213
Sligo Bay, 212-13
Sligo County, 22, 67, 197, 212
Sneem, 180; H296
Spiddal, 204
Staigue Fort, 179-80
Station Island, 216-17
Stillorgan—
see Dublin
Stracashel River, 221
Stradbally, 122
Straffan, 122
Stranorlar, 217
Suir River, 68, 136, 139, 143-4, 146-7
Sullane River, 170
Summer Cove, 166
Swanlinbar, 250
Swilly Lough, 212, 217-18
Swords, 114

Tacumshane, 136
Tara, 55, 85, 93, 115, 228
Tarbert, 185
Templemore, 144
Terrybawn, 87
Thomastown, 130-1
Thoor Ballylee, 208
Thurles, 142-3; S229; H296
Tipperary, 148-9; H296

315

INDEX

Tipperary County 22, 141-53, 163-4, 177, 254
Tory Island, 212
Tralee, 181-2, 230; H296; R296-7
Tramore, S77; 139, 154, 251
Tramore Bay, 139-40
Trawbreaga Bay, 218
Trim, 117
Tuam, 208, 258
Tullamore, 122-3
Tyrone, 86

Ulster, 19, 43, 46-7, 231
Urnagh, Hill, 123
Ushnagh Hill, 55

Valentia, 179; S255; H297
Vee Gap, 148, 163-4
Virginia, 119; HS297

Waterford City, 40, 63; S78; 86; Sh86, 297; 136-9, 192; A230; 260; H297
Waterford County, 86, 136-40, 148, 154ff
Watergrasshill, 165
Waterville, 179-80, 184, 246; H297
Weston, 246
Westport, 72, 210; S230; 251, 260; H298
Westport House, 210, 260; A288
Wexford, 40, 87, 132-4; A133, 231, 298; 259; H298
Wexford County, 72, 127, 131-6
Whiddy Island, 168-9
Wicklow 87, 112, 124; HR298
Wicklow County, 22, 87, 112, 124-7, 254
Wicklow Hills/Mountains, 92, 95, 108, 125, 233

Yeats's Country, 212-13, 251
Youghal, 158, 161-3; H298

MAP
OF
IRELAND

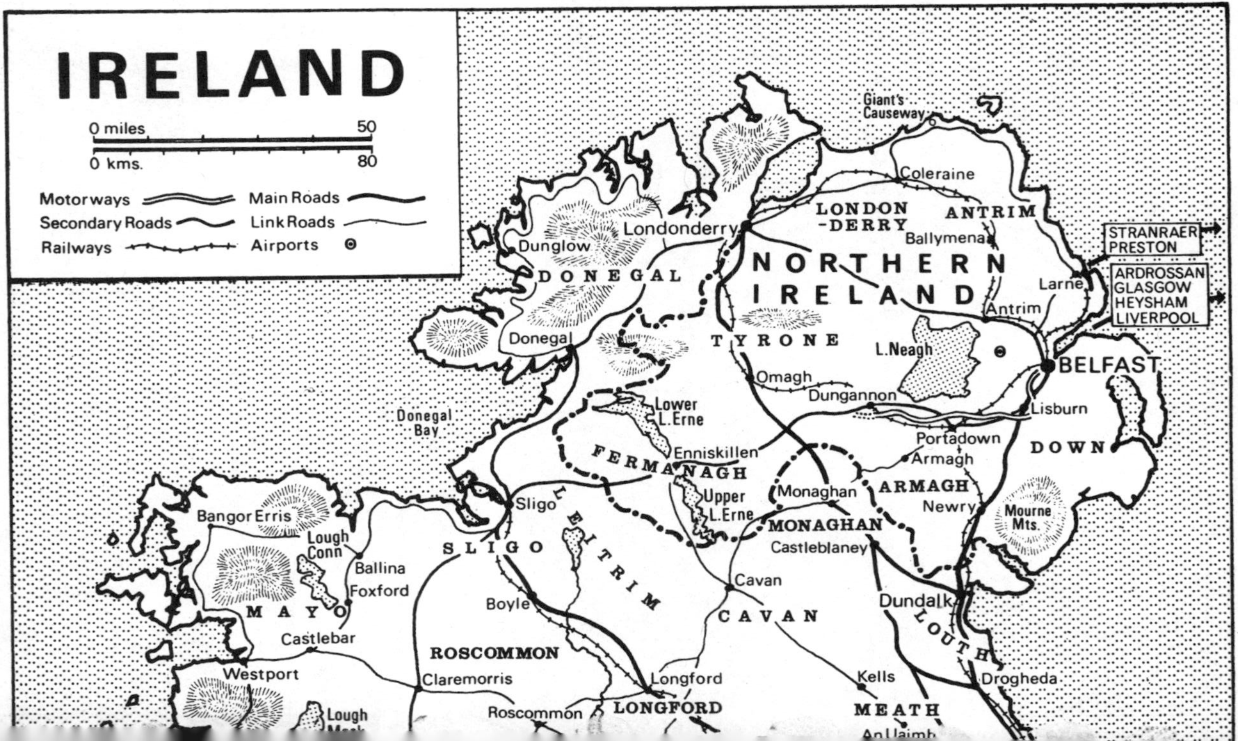
IRELAND
0 miles 50
0 kms. 80
Motorways
Main Roads
Secondary Roads
Link Roads
Railways
Airports
STRANRAER
PRESTON
ARDROSSAN
GLASGOW
HEYSHAM
LIVERPOOL
Giant's Causeway
Coleraine
LONDON -DERRY
ANTRIM
Ballymena
Londonderry
Dunglow
DONEGAL
NORTHERN IRELAND
Larne
Antrim
Donegal
TYRONE
L.Neagh
BELFAST
Omagh
Dungannon
Lisburn
Donegal Bay
Lower L.Erne
Portadown
DOWN
Enniskillen
Armagh
FERMANAGH
Monaghan
ARMAGH
Sligo
Upper L.Erne
Newry
Mourne Mts.
Bangor Erris
LEITRIM
MONAGHAN
Lough Conn
Castleblaney
SLIGO
Ballina
Cavan
Foxford
Boyle
Dundalk
MAYO
CAVAN
LOUTH
Castlebar
ROSCOMMON
Westport
Claremorris
Longford
Kells
Drogheda
Roscommon
LONGFORD
MEATH
Lough

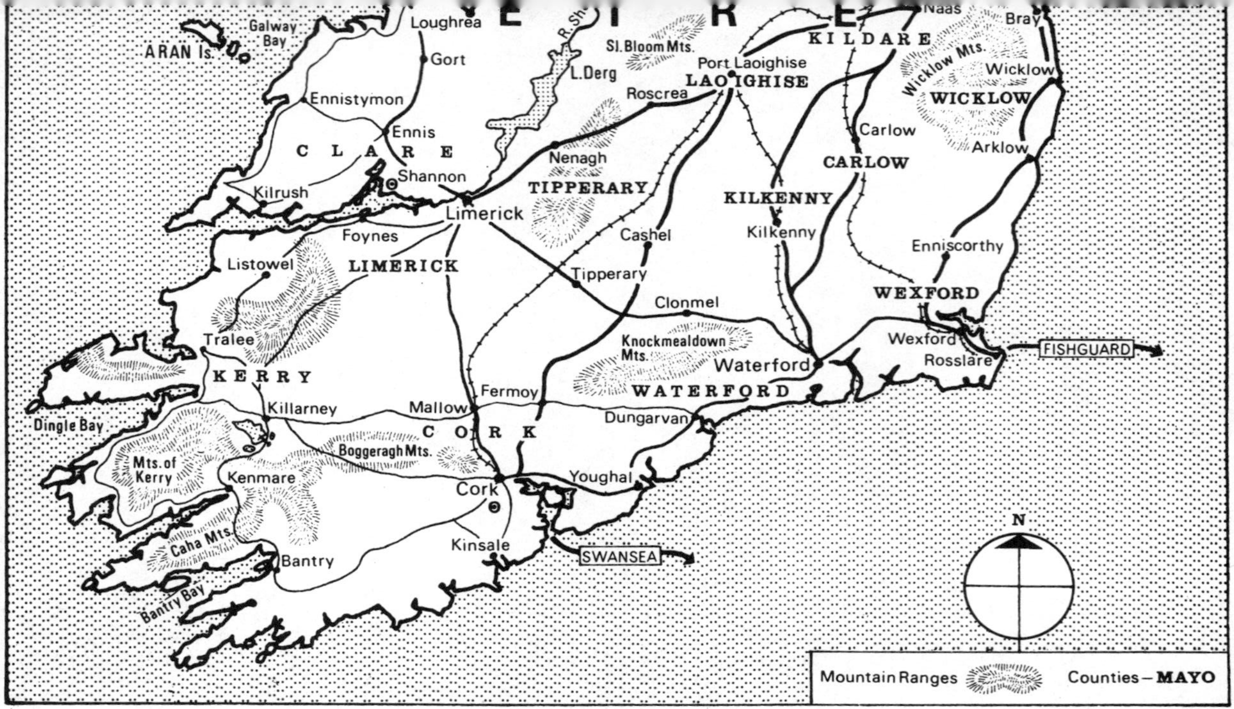

ARAN Is.
Galway Bay
Loughrea
Gort
Ennistymon
Ennis
CLARE
Shannon
Kilrush
R. Sh
L. Derg
Sl. Bloom Mts.
Port Laoighise
LAOIGHISE
Roscrea
Nenagh
TIPPERARY
Limerick
Foynes
LIMERICK
Listowel
Tralee
KERRY
Dingle Bay
Mts. of Kerry
Killarney
Kenmare
Caha Mts.
Bantry
Bantry Bay
Boggeragh Mts.
Mallow
Fermoy
CORK
Cork
Kinsale
SWANSEA
Youghal
Dungarvan
Cashel
Tipperary
Clonmel
Knockmealdown Mts.
WATERFORD
Waterford
KILKENNY
Kilkenny
KILDARE
Naas
CARLOW
Carlow
Wicklow Mts.
WICKLOW
Wicklow
Bray
Arklow
Enniscorthy
WEXFORD
Wexford
Rosslare
FISHGUARD
N
Mountain Ranges
Counties—MAYO